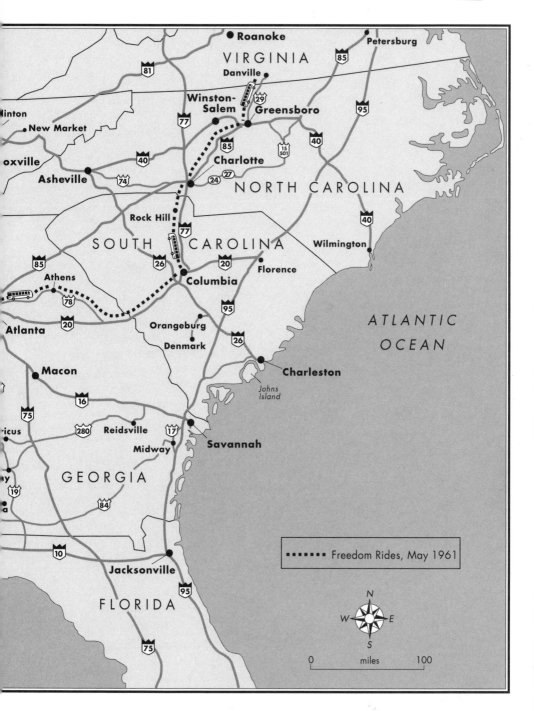

Weary Feet, Rested Souls

W. W. Norton & Company

New York * London

Weary Feet, Rested Souls

A Guided History of the

Civil Rights Movement

Townsend Davis

Copyright © 1998 by Townsend Davis
Maps © 1997 by Mark Stein Studios

For information about permission to reproduce selections from this book, write to Permissions, W. W. Norton & Company, Inc., 500 Fifth Avenue, New York, NY 10110.

The text of this book is composed in Meridien with the display set in Trixie.
Manufacturing by The Courier Companies, Inc.
Book design by Chris Welch

Library of Congress Cataloging-in-Publication Data
Davis, Townsend.
    Weary feet, rested souls : a guided history of the Civil Rights Movement / by Townsend Davis.
    p. cm.
Includes bibliographical references (p.) and index.
ISBN 0-393-04592-7
1. Afro-Americans—Civil rights—History—20th century. 2. Civil rights movements—Southern States—History—20th century. 3. Southern States—History—1951– I. Title.
E185.61.D36 1998
973'.0496073—dc21   97-6749
        CIP

W. W. Norton & Company, Inc., 500 Fifth Avenue, New York, N.Y. 10110
http://www.wwnorton.com

W. W. Norton & Company Ltd., 10 Coptic Street, London WC1A 1PU
1 2 3 4 5 6 7 8 9 0

For Wallace Fowlie

Contents

Alabama

Arkansas

Georgia

Mississippi

North Carolina

South Carolina

Tennessee

ACMHR—Alabama Christian Movement for Human Rights. Founded in 1956 in Birmingham under the leadership of Rev. Fred Shuttlesworth after the Alabama attorney general shut down the NAACP in Alabama.

AME Church—African Methodist Episcopal Church. Founded in Philadelphia, Pennsylvania, in the late eighteenth century in response to segregation in the ritual of communion in the majority white Methodist Church. Opposed slavery and, along with a separate AME Zion denomination, founded black colleges throughout the South during Reconstruction.

COFO—Council of Federated Organizations. Mississippi umbrella group created in 1962 after the Freedom Rides to coordinate the activities of the NAACP, SNCC, and CORE.

CORE—Congress of Racial Equality. Northern peace group founded in Chicago in 1942 that initiated the Freedom Rides and conducted voting drives in Mississippi and Louisiana.

DOJ—U.S. Department of Justice, Civil Rights Division. Division of the federal government responsible for enforcing voting laws.

FBI—Federal Bureau of Investigation. Agency responsible for investigating federal crimes, including civil rights violations.

FOR—Fellowship of Reconciliation. Founded during World War I and supportive of integration since the 1920s. Led by Movement pioneers of nonviolence, such as Glenn Smiley and James Lawson.

ICC—Interstate Commerce Commission. Federal agency that issued an order in 1961 desegregating all interstate bus stations after the Freedom Rides.

KKK—Ku Klux Klan. Founded in Pulaski, Tennessee, in 1866 and organized into local and regional groups called klaverns. Terrorized people active in the Movement through bombings, night patrols, and propaganda. Joined in its attack on integration by the Citizens' Council, a group that specialized in economic retaliation, and the National States Rights Party, a white supremacy group that monitored Movement activity.

MFDP—Mississippi Freedom Democratic Party. Founded in 1964 as an alternative to the all-white leadership of the state Democratic Party. Sent a delegation to the Democratic National Convention in Atlantic City in 1964 and supported several candidates for state and local office in the late 1960s.

MIA—Montgomery Improvement Association. Founded in 1955 to coordinate the bus boycott. The first of several local and regional Movement groups.

NAACP—National Association for the Advancement of Colored People. The oldest civil rights organization, founded in 1909, with state, local, and youth chapters.

SCLC—Southern Christian Leadership Conference. Founded in New Orleans in 1957 by young black preachers concerned with civil rights. Dr. King led the group from its founding until his death in 1968.

SNCC—Student Nonviolent Coordinating Committee (pronounced Snick). Student-led civil rights group founded in Raleigh in 1960 after the sit-ins in Greensboro, North Carolina, that served as a vanguard of Movement activity throughout the 1960s.

Introduction

For this book to make sense you have to imagine the world before air conditioning. Imagine having finished a full day's work and approaching a wood-frame church by a dirt road at night. The church is lit like a lantern against an inky sky, with the shadows of a few people hunched and sitting on the inside window ledges. As you approach, you can see it is packed with people. A slow and fervent humming already has begun. Perhaps you packed some food and have a bag of it hitched under one arm. If the church is big enough, bare lightbulbs are blazing in the kitchen out back.

Once inside and blinking from the light, you take your seat on a scuffed pew. If it is any time other than the dead of winter, it is hot. The air is alive not just with hymns and prayers but with the continuous swish of fans, stiff paper squares on sticks provided by the local funeral home that bear the face of a bearded white Jesus. You join in the slow, measured singing of melodies well known and get ready for a night of testimonials, prayers, incessant appeals for money, and, most of all, talk about freedom.

People take turns telling their stories while the fanning continues. One old black man has gone to the courthouse and patiently withstood a maze of questions from a white registrar of voters. A sheriff's deputy has roughed up a neighbor. The white city commissioners, just awakening to the possibility of black voting power, are acting jittery. You hear tales of courage and of how just talking about civil rights, better known simply as "that mess," is turning the town upside down.

A preacher tells of big plans, and you join the roar of approval from the congregants. Your children will be in that brick school one day, will be voting soon. A college student explains how voting works now and refers to the Justice Department in Washington as if it were just down the road. Terms of jail and bail are explained. You are asked to alter your routine: Don't buy downtown; don't ride the buses; do wear your old clothes at Easter. You stand and volunteer for something, to carry someone to a rally or house a student visiting from the North. You walk down and drop some coins in a hat or basket on the table in front of the altar. A church choir belts out a few hymns, altering the words of some old standards to fit the new crusade. The meeting ends with a prayer for a better day.

Everywhere in the South in the 1950s and 1960s, gatherings of this sort, called mass meetings, laid the groundwork for the American Civil Rights Movement. They took place in the largest place in the community where black people were allowed to congregate undisturbed, a church. Often it was a Baptist church, although Methodists, Catholics, and other denominations also opened their doors. At first it was not the silk stocking churches but usually smaller, rural churches that allowed the meetings. In the most affluent urban congregations black professionals and schoolteachers had limited influence within the sphere of segregation and were threatened most directly by the activists' grand designs. Once a Movement campaign got going, however, nearly every black church got involved in some way.

The church was more than a meetinghouse; it was a political arena. Emancipation Day services on January 1 were a tradition in the black church, and the Movement gave new purpose to the liberating aspects of the Gospel. The Gospel not only described a resplendent hereafter but also spoke directly to unjust conditions of the day. It gave the Movement familiar ways to gather and multiply its strength.

Other vital gathering places in the black community became sites from which to launch attacks on segregation. Meeting halls and offices of black fraternal organizations, such as the Masons, Elks, and unions, were pressed into service. Black businesses and properties that were relatively immune from white retaliation were critical. Black farmers who owned their own land were called upon to house activists, students, and marchers for months at a time. Not surprisingly, the black barbers, funeral directors, insurance agents, and restaurant owners often took the lead and provided refuge for the Movement. If they were lucky, they could continue to count on the patronage of their black customers. To a lesser extent, blacks in academia and the federal government had some measure of protection against dismissal, blacklisting, and boycotts. Decades of segregation had forced the black economy to exist apart from the white economy, and the resulting enclaves gave black people some protection as they laid their plans.

The Movement, and its opposition, transformed neighborhoods. A quiet middle-class residential area in Birmingham called Smithfield was renamed Dynamite Hill after a rash of racial bombings beginning as early as 1949. Later, churches were swept up in the tide of racial hatred. Confrontations took place everywhere from a courthouse lawn to a deserted highway. It was a struggle played out in everyday byways—homes, shops, schools, meeting halls, and churches—rather than on designated fields of battle.

These places deserve their rightful place in history. In the thirty-five years since they served as staging grounds for the Movement, many have been razed or left to decay. Integration, urban "renewal," white flight, interstate highways, and emigration have had profound effects on many communities that were once thriving black centers of commerce, worship, and entertainment. Some communities have not recognized the historical importance of their own structures. Others have erected historical markers and made an effort to inform citizens and visitors of the sites' role in history. My hope is that preservation and recognition will outlast the wrecking ball. But the fact that there are only three Movement sites in the South designated by the federal government as National Historic Landmarks—the Dexter Avenue Baptist Church in Montgomery, Rev. Martin Luther King, Jr.'s home and church in Atlanta, and Central High School in Little Rock—suggests that this effort is just beginning.

How have these sites been selected? As many have pointed out, the Movement came in some form to every community large enough to have a post office and left no home, office, or graveyard undisturbed. Out of necessity I have limited myself in this book to the modern protest Movement for the civic equality of black Americans. I have concentrated on campaigns that involved whole communities more so than on legal cases, although they often were intertwined. Exactly when the Movement started is unanswerable, although scholars traditionally point to a cluster of events in

1954–55: the issuance of the U.S. Supreme Court's *Brown v. Board of Education* decision outlawing segregation in public schools, the murder of Emmett Till in Money, Mississippi, and the bus boycott in Montgomery, Alabama. When it ended is even more difficult to say. The signing of the Civil Rights Acts of 1964 and 1965 were legislative milestones, and the assassination of King in 1968 marked the demise of mass nonviolent protests for racial reforms at the national level. Somewhat arbitrarily, then, the events of 1954–68 will get the most mention here. I also have limited myself to the South, although there are many northern sites of importance.

The book is organized alphabetically by state, and within each state a roughly chronological order of events is maintained where possible. A strict chronology is impossible because each locality played an important role in the national Movement at different times (see "Chronology"). A geographical focus helps explain Movement events and the particular challenges faced in each community. From this angle the contributions of local people who organized, preached, petitioned, supplied, drove, and registered to vote in their communities become immediately apparent. These communities each went through their own racial transformations that did not necessarily coincide with national events. The unique racial history of each place reaches back as far as Reconstruction and as far forward as the present. I have tried to sketch these local histories and added a few observations about conditions as I found them during my travels in 1994–96.

Context is all-important when one thinks about these places. Times have changed. Today it requires imagination to see the world according to segregation, a landscape of unequal pairs. When people drove the length of Mississippi, there often were no rest rooms for blacks to use along the way. Passengers had to pack a meal in ice and sometimes sleep in the car, choosing between a swarm of insects and near asphyxiation. In a 1952 travel guide for blacks called *Vacation and Recreation without Humiliation,* even large cities sometimes listed only the NAACP or the YMCA as places to find decent lodging. A black lawyer appearing in an unfamiliar county might carry two pieces of equipment not needed by his white colleagues at the bar: proof of his license to practice and a revolver.

Recall also that in many black communities cars and phones were far from universal. Street marches, today a staple of political protest, were used for ceremonial parades. They were not used to voice every grievance from the plight of marsupials to the price of movie tickets. Most people viewed protest marches as provocation and considered sit-ins, kneel-ins, and other elbow-rubbing varieties of -ins as virtual revolt, even when exercised entirely within a code of nonviolence.

Arrests were no joking matter either. Not only did they carry the weight of heavy fines equal to several months' salary and the prospect of hard labor in a tough jail but also the stigma of breaking the law. As Rev. Ralph Abernathy noted in recalling his first of many arrests in service of the Movement, "I had been taught that the law was next to God in its claim on my conscience, and that there was almost nothing worse than a jailbird." For women the venture into the Movement carried additional burdens. One woman who housed the Freedom Riders remembered that even as all Montgomery was in the grip of martial law in May 1961, the female Freedom Riders still found time to iron the shirts of their male cohorts before heading on to Jackson under armed guard.

Perhaps most important to keep in mind, the marches and speeches that made the newspapers were only a small fraction of Movement activity. As one Montgomery woman active in the bus boycott of 1955–56 remembers: "There were so many things. We paid rent. We paid gas bills. We paid water bills. We bought food. We paid people's doctor's bills. We even buried somebody . . . bought washing machines. We did everything trying to get along with the people."[1]

A few more words about the method of the book. In the text, the capitalized *Movement* refers to both the national civil rights struggle and its local counterparts. At various times during the historical period covered here, *colored, Negro,* and *black* were acceptable terms. I have used the term *black* to denote race because that is what most of my sources did. Other people may have perfectly good reasons for using other terms.

In surveying the sites, I have relied not only on the vast literature on the Movement but also on my interviews (more than one hundred of them) with people familiar with the neighborhoods from that time and on collections of papers, photographs, and recordings. Also indispensable have been countless roadside conversations and visits to gas stations, restaurants, and public libraries. I tried wherever possible to rely on contemporaneous material to resolve conflicting accounts. My list of historical Movement sites obviously is selective and illustrative. I wish I had been able to include the sites of many other important Movement campaigns, such as those in

Natchez, Canton, Danville, Tuskegee, and St. Augustine. Any suggestions about listed sites, or ones that should have been included, are welcome, care of the publisher.

The title is taken from a well-worn Movement story about an old woman named Mother Pollard. She was walking down a road during the Montgomery bus boycott in 1955 and was offered a ride by a passing car. She declined and, when asked why, replied, "My feet are weary, but my soul is rested." The reply made the rounds of mass meetings in Montgomery and became a staple in King's speeches.

Acknowledgments

This book was possible only through the generosity and insight of my sources, who are listed elsewhere. In my research and travel, I was amazed at the willingness of these people to recall— sometimes for the first time, sometimes for the hundredth—their involvement in the Movement. Listening to them was both sobering and inspiring.

I also would like to thank my editor, Ed Barber, at Norton and his able assistants, Omar Divina and Sean Desmond. I am indebted to my agent, Kim Witherspoon, and am grateful for the support of Maria Massie and John Hoberg of her agency. I want to thank Rex Miller and Curt Middleton for their work on the book proposal. Thanks to Mark Stein for his extraordinary maps, Jessica Allan for her photographs (and patience), Wendy Gordon for her beautiful black-and-white prints, Lizzie Berne for dogged fact checking and correspondence, and Marc Regelski for his indispensable word processing, quote checking, and database work. Thanks also to my brother, Henry P. Davis, for wise counsel, my parents for their support, and Judge Phyllis Kravitch, who started me down this road.

Thanks to the people who reviewed the manuscript (and its bulky predecessors), especially my sister, Ruth G. Davis, Richard Blow, and Peter Johnson, who read and commented on the entire book. Other people gave indispensable comments on particular sections: Jim Baggett, Harry Bowie, Edgar Bridges, Owen Brooks,

Crumpler, Fred Davis, John Dittmer, Alston Fitts, Lillie Gillard, Ethel Grimball, Evans Harrington, Lola Hendricks, Jan Hillegas, Endesha Ida Mae Holland, Jacqueline Jefferson, Bill Jenkins, David Jordon, Clennon King, Ed King, Bernard Lafayette, W. W. Law, Florence Mars, Liz Massie, Ellen Mertins, Sheila O'Flaherty, Charles Payne, Bill Saunders, Cleveland Sellers, Jim Sessions, Charles Sherrod, Marvin Whiting, and Florence Wilson-Davis. Numerous other people reviewed shorter sections about the churches and other historical sites with which they were familiar, and I am equally indebted to them.

Dozens of people provided leads, encouragement, assistance, and advice when I most needed it. In this group I especially want to thank Amy Adler, James Armstrong, William Barbour, Jack Bass, Joanne Bland, Ruby Bradley, Georgia Calhoun, Guy and Candie Carawan, Selwyn Carter, J. L. Chestnut, Jr., Lucinda Childs, Judge Charles Clark, Major Cox, Vernon Dahmer, Jr., Beth Dalik, Tracy Day, Robin Desser, Charles Eagles, William Ferris, Cheryl Finley, Joel Fleishman, Lilibet Foster, Marie Foster, Lisa Freed, David Garrow, Deric Gilliard, Natalie Goldstein, Keba Makele Gordon, Fred Gray, Edah Grover, Rev. Christopher Hamlin, Lola Hendricks, Charles and Carol Horowitz, Frank Hudson, John Hulett, Philip and Deanna Kaminsky, Steve Kasher, Christina Baker Kline, Patricia LaPointe, Steve Lehman, John Lewis, James Loewen, William Love, Bill Lynch, Jean Martin, Spider Martin, Nikki Davis Maute, Lauren McCollester, James Meredith, Jerry Mitchell, Wendy McDaris, Louise McKigney, Charles McLaurin, Lillie McLaurin, Neil McMillen, Jerry Mitchell, Ramyar Moghadassi, Charles Moore, Juanita Moore, Nettie Ann Moore, Claudette Murphree, Mary Ann Neeley, Nancy Nethery, J. T. Noblin, James Orange, Ophelia Paine, Bruce Payne, Judy Peiser, Burke Pickett, Nancy Rousseau, Dean Rowley, Constance Slaughter-Harvey, Nancy Smith, Joe Sullivan, Carrie Teegardin, Judge Myron Thompson, Charles Tisdale, Ramsey Walker, Wyatt Tee Walker, Hollis Watkins, Percy Watson, Jennifer White, Marjorie White, Randall Williams, Arance Williamson, Louretta Wimberly, Katherine Winningham, and Jim Yardley.

Also important were the many libraries and archives where firsthand sources are deposited. In particular, I am grateful to Marvin Whiting and Don Veasey of the Birmingham Public Library; Cynthia Lewis, formerly of the Martin Luther King, Jr., Center for Nonviolent Social Change; Paul de Leon and Juanita Householder of the Highlander Research and Education Center; Clarence Hunter at Tougaloo College; the staff of the New York Public Library, particu-

Acknowledgments

larly those at the Schomburg Center for the Study of Black Culture; and the Mississippi Department of Archives and History. The staff at AP/Wide World Photos, the *Birmingham News*, Black Star, Corbis-Bettmann, Magnum, and Time-Life, as well as G. Rollie Adams, Frederick Baldwin, Ida Berman, Sheila Bowen, Bob Fletcher, Matt Herron, Claude Jones, Andy Kraushaar, Dean Livingston, Strawberry Lock, Spider Martin, Jack Moebes, Charmian Reading, Jack Ryan, Flip Schulke, Tom Stanford, Tamio Wakayama, and Sandra Weiner, were helpful in locating the historical photographs. Matt Herron, who took the jacket photo and several others in the book, was especially helpful in locating rare images.

Finally, I thank the people who put me up during my travels, particularly Paula Allan, Dick Doidge, Frankie Fisher, Jim and Mary Hendrick, Mary and Marc Holladay, Byrd and Lanelle Looper, John and Sylvie Robinson, and the good people at the Highlander Center.

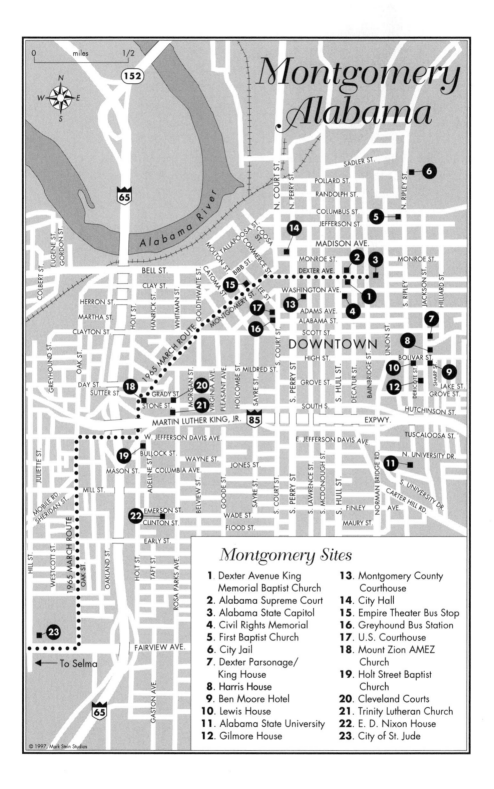

Montgomery
Alabama

152

65

Alabama River

SADLER ST.
POLLARD ST.
RANDOLPH ST.
COLUMBUS ST.
JEFFERSON ST.
MADISON AVE.

N. COURT ST.
N. PERRY ST.
N. RIPLEY ST.

BELL ST.
CLAY ST.
HERRON ST.
MARTHA ST.
CLAYTON ST.

MONROE ST.
DEXTER AVE.
WASHINGTON AVE.
ADAMS AVE.
ALABAMA ST.
SCOTT ST.

MONROE ST.

EUGENE ST.
GORDON ST.
COLBERT ST.

HOLT ST.
HANRICK ST.
WHITMAN ST.
GOLDTHWAITE ST.
CATOMA ST.
MONTGOMERY ST.
BIBB ST.
COMMERCE ST.
COOSA ST.
TALLAPOOSA ST.
MOTON ST.
LEE ST.

S. RIPLEY
JACKSON ST.
HILLIARD ST.

DOWNTOWN

HIGH ST.

BOLIVAR ST.

GREYHOUND ST.
OAK ST.
DAY ST.
SUTTER ST.
GRADY ST.
STONE ST.

MORGAN ST.
VIRGINIA AVE.
PLEASANT AVE.
HOLCOMBE ST.
MILDRED ST.
SAYRE ST.
S. COURT ST.
S. PERRY ST.
GROVE ST.
S. HULL ST.
DECATUR ST.
BAINBRIDGE ST.
UNION ST.

DERICOTE ST.
SHARP ST.
LAKE ST.
GROVE ST.
HUTCHINSON ST.

1965 MARCH ROUTE

MARTIN LUTHER KING, JR. **85**
SOUTH S.
EXPWY.

W. JEFFERSON DAVIS AVE.
E. JEFFERSON DAVIS AVE.
TUSCALOOSA ST.

BULLOCK ST.
WAYNE ST.
MASON ST.
COLUMBIA AVE.
JONES ST.

JULIETTE ST.
ADELINE ST.
BELVIEW ST.
GOODE ST.
SAYRE ST.
S. COURT ST.
S. PERRY ST.
LAWRENCE ST.
McDONOUGH ST.
S. HULL ST.
NORMAN BRIDGE RD.
CARTER HILL RD.
N. UNIVERSITY DR.
S. UNIVERSITY DR.
AVE.

MILL ST.
MOBILE RD.
SHERIDAN ST.
EMERSON ST.
CLINTON ST.
WADE ST.
FLOOD ST.

EARLY ST.

HILL ST.
WESTCOTT ST.
OAKLAND ST.
HOLT ST.
TAFT ST.
OAK ST.
ROSA PARKS BLVD.

1965 MARCH ROUTE

FAIRVIEW AVE.

← To Selma

FINLEY
MAURY ST.

GASTON AVE.

65

© 1997, Mark Stein Studios

Montgomery Sites

1. Dexter Avenue King Memorial Baptist Church
2. Alabama Supreme Court
3. Alabama State Capitol
4. Civil Rights Memorial
5. First Baptist Church
6. City Jail
7. Dexter Parsonage/ King House
8. Harris House
9. Ben Moore Hotel
10. Lewis House
11. Alabama State University
12. Gilmore House
13. Montgomery County Courthouse
14. City Hall
15. Empire Theater Bus Stop
16. Greyhound Bus Station
17. U.S. Courthouse
18. Mount Zion AMEZ Church
19. Holt Street Baptist Church
20. Cleveland Courts
21. Trinity Lutheran Church
22. E. D. Nixon House
23. City of St. Jude

Alabama

Montgomery, Alabama

The Bus Boycott and
Rev. Martin Luther King, Jr.

On a warm and muggy Thursday morning, March 25, 1965, thousands of civil rights marchers gathered on the outskirts of Montgomery to walk to the Alabama state Capitol. They had set out from Selma four days earlier and were poised to complete the last leg of a march that had capped a triumphant but traumatic voting rights campaign there. In downtown Montgomery hundreds of national guardsmen, carbines slung over their shoulders, patrolled the broad expanse of Dexter Avenue, which sloped up to the Capitol steps. Green-helmeted MPs ringed the styrofoam-white Capitol building. Governor George Wallace ordered the special precaution of covering the bronze star on the portico with plywood; both he and Jefferson Davis had been sworn into office on that spot. Wallace had given all female employees the day off, and government operations were at a standstill. Fluttering from the white Capitol dome were the Alabama flag and the Confederate battle flag.

When the marchers finally arrived, they filled the entire Capitol plaza to hear one of Rev. Martin Luther King, Jr.'s greatest speeches, delivered within shouting distance of Wallace's office. By that time, King felt secure in telling the throng that his vision of an integrated society would be realized, using the refrain "How long? Not long."

Much had changed since 1954, when the Movement was just beginning and Montgomery was the frontier of nonviolent protest. In those days it was a quiet city of 120,000 residents, about one third of whom were black. Few blacks were registered to vote, and none held political office except a handful of black policemen hired that year. The capital city of Alabama was segregated from the cradles of the city hospitals to the headstones in separate graveyards. The only exceptions were nearby Maxwell and Gunter Air Force bases, which were subject to President Truman's order to desegregate the military. A separate "colored" edition of the daily newspaper, with stars on the front, was delivered to the front yards of black homes. The combination of a highly organized, educated black population and the glacial pace of change made Montgomery an ideal setting for what was to become the Movement's first citywide protest, the Montgomery bus boycott.

Most blacks did not own a car and used the city bus lines seven days a week. Sixty-two yellow buses traversed the city along fourteen routes, carrying thirty thousand to forty thousand black passengers each day and as many whites. Usually blacks paid the fare at the front of the bus and walked back outside to the rear entrance to get on. When the back of the bus was filled, blacks were forced to stand over empty white-only seats. In May 1954 Jo Ann Robinson, an English professor at Alabama State College (now University) and the president of a black activist group called the Women's Political Council, had written the mayor to complain. In March 1955 and again in October black women were arrested for failing to comply with separate seating on a city bus. Neither incident sparked widespread protest.

By contrast the arrest of Rosa Parks—a Tuskegee native, high school graduate, and youth leader of the local NAACP—on December 1, 1955, instantly mobilized Montgomery's black community. "She was too sweet to even say 'damn' in anger," as one resident put it. Three people, all longtime activists, came to retrieve her from police custody: black leader E. D. Nixon, white patrician lawyer Clifford Durr, and his wife, Virginia. After the three had escorted Mrs. Parks home and they discussed the incident over coffee, she agreed to let her arrest be the basis for a legal test case. A heavy leafleting campaign and stories in the Montgomery newspapers over the weekend spread the word of a bus boycott, and on Monday the buses swung through their usual routes virtually empty of black passengers. A twenty-six-year-old black Baptist preacher named Martin Luther King, Jr., who had assumed the helm of Montgomery's elite Dexter Avenue Baptist Church fifteen months earlier, was designated the Movement spokesman.

To replace the bus rides, blacks constructed their own community car pool. They formed the Montgomery Improvement Association (MIA) to take three mild demands to the city: (1) more driver courtesy toward black passengers, (2) first-come, first-served seating, from front to back for whites and back to front for blacks, and (3) black drivers for routes going to black areas. None of these demands called for an end to segregation, but they were quickly rejected. Ultimately the intransigence of the bus company and the city commissioners escalated the conflict and led black leaders to call for more sweeping changes. The boycott took its steady toll, depriving the bus company of three thousand dollars in fares per day. Negotiations

A deputy sheriff fingerprints Rosa Parks after her arrest on antiboycotting charges in February 1956. Her arrest and conviction for violating segregated bus seating the previous December prompted the bus boycott. (AP/Wide World Photos)

continued through February 1956 until boycott leaders filed a lawsuit aimed at reversing the state's segregation law as applied to the city buses.

Still, white leaders held on. While white housewives smuggled their maids to work, the Montgomery police went on a traffic ticket binge against black drivers. Two human figures were hung in effigy in Court Square: One was labeled "NAACP," the other "I talked integration."

The Montgomery boycott continued for a year until the U.S. Supreme Court affirmed the decision of a lower court that the segregation law was unconstitutional. On December 20, 1956, the boycott ended. The MIA issued guidelines for riding the buses in the new era, warning blacks not to boast, to remain calm at all times, and to exercise nonviolence. When blacks began riding again after 381 days, their absence had been so long that most were unaware that the fare had been raised from ten to fifteen cents, and some forgot to pay at all.

Change took longer to sink into the rest of Montgomery. On New Year's Day 1959 city officials closed the thirteen public parks rather than obey a federal order to integrate them. Upon his departure for Atlanta in January 1960, King noted that WHITE and COLORED signs were still up, the schools were not integrated, and no black bus drivers or policemen had been hired. When a group of activists known as the Freedom Riders arrived in the Deep South in May 1961 to desegregate interstate transportation facilities, they met their first violent resistance in northern Alabama and were savagely beaten at

The Car Pool: Montgomery's Web of Volunteers

During the bus boycott blacks constructed a complete system of transportation centered on work routines. At first people volunteered their cars, including the occasional Cadillac of a preacher's wife or a gift from an out-of-town supporter. By March 1956 the MIA had bought fifteen new station wagons for the car pool, each with the name of its sponsoring church emblazoned on the side. These "rolling churches" in red, green, and blue crisscrossed the entire city. Insurance companies pulled coverage from the cars, and the Movement managed to get Lloyd's of London to back them for a year.

Transfer stations were set up downtown, including the E. L. Posey parking lot on the southwest corner of Monroe and McDonough streets (now a city park). The lot was owned by an association of black farmers, and it had been the traditional congregating point for farmers' Saturday journey to town. In the 1950s Eddie Posey had leased it and turned it into a commercial parking lot holding fifty to sixty cars, nearly all owned by white customers. The MIA rented it for thirty dollars a month during the boycott. It was the heart from which all the arteries of the car pool flowed in and out.

During the boycott Posey's lot handled two thousand black workers a day. Rev. J. H. Cherry served as a no-nonsense dispatcher while police motorcycles cruised by looking for minor traffic infractions or recording license plate numbers. Citations for carrying more than three persons in the front seat, stopping too near to the curb or a pedestrian walk, and unloading in an unauthorized zone all carried a stiff penalty. As a result, loading and unloading took less than a minute.

The car pool system, devised with the aid of two postal workers, worked remarkably smoothly. Fifteen dispatchers, twenty full-time drivers, and seventy-four part-time drivers served without pay. Black service stations furnished supplies and made repairs at a cut rate. At one point the MIA even sought the permission of the city commission to charter its own transportation service called the Montgomery Transit Lines, but the request was rejected. On November 1, 1956, the city finally moved to stop the car pool, filing a lawsuit against fifteen churches and the MIA leadership. Boycotters patched together rides for the next month until segregation on the city buses was struck down, and bus service resumed.

the Montgomery Greyhound Bus Station. When riders finally pulled out of the station on May 24 to continue the trip, they drove through a protective corridor of National Guard bayonets.

By 1962 the city had decided to allow the public library and art museum to be integrated, and two blacks were hired to drive city buses. A biracial city commission, which was established in early

Rev. Martin Luther King, Jr., his wife, Coretta, and daughter Yolanda on the steps of the Dexter Avenue Baptist Church, with the Alabama Capitol behind them, in 1956. (Dan Weiner/Courtesy Sandra Weiner)

1964, oversaw a relatively smooth implementation of the Civil Rights Act of 1964. By February 1965 the city parks had been reopened. In 1970 Fred Gray and Thomas Reed, both from Macon County, became the first black Alabama legislators since Reconstruction. Fred Gray had been a lawyer for King in Montgomery and had represented the black residents of Tuskegee in a landmark gerrymandering case. Thomas Reed had run on the ticket of the National Democratic Party of Alabama, the independent party that had grown out of voting drives in neighboring Lowndes County.

Today, with segregation long gone, Montgomery is a modern southern capital. An integrated public work force is housed in gleaming government buildings, and downtown is filled with the clamor of new construction. The city has added the intersection of Interstates 85 and 65 just below a bend in the Alabama River. Churches still outnumber malls by a large margin. And one of the declared goals of the Montgomery Area Chamber of Commerce is to work with the remnant of the MIA to commemorate civil rights history.

Empire Theater Bus Stop
Montgomery Street between Lee and Molton Streets

Rosa McCauley Parks worked in men's alterations at Montgomery Fair, a large department store on Dexter Avenue. After work on December 1, 1955, she went to the drugstore across the street and walked to her usual bus stop at Court Square (at the intersection of Commerce and Montgomery streets) to await a Cleveland Avenue bus back to her home in west Montgomery. In those days the rearmost ten seats were for blacks, the front ten were for whites, and the middle sixteen were a floating zone that could be for black or white, as the bus driver wished. Mrs. Parks paid her fare and sat in a middle row at that time designated for blacks. By the time the bus went two blocks to the Empire Theater stop, the white section in front was full, and the bus driver ordered the row in which Mrs. Parks was sitting vacated to make room for white passengers.

Three people got up and moved back, as had Mrs. Parks on other occasions. This time she refused to move, even after the driver said to her and other black passengers, "You'd better make it light on yourselves and let me have those seats." The driver got off the bus and summoned the police, who questioned Mrs. Parks briefly and then took her down to City Hall to be photographed and finger-printed. She was arrested for disorderly conduct and tried the following Monday. For the next year blacks stayed off the buses until the U.S. Supreme Court struck down the segregated system as unconstitutional.

Today a historic marker stands on the spot where she was arrested.

What Was on the Mind of Rosa Parks?

In March 1956, at an executive committee meeting of the Highlander Folk School, then in Monteagle, Tennessee, Rosa Parks and others gathered to discuss the Montgomery bus boycott that was then three months old. Myles Horton, head of the center, asked Rosa Parks what she was thinking about the day of her arrest:

"Well, in the first place I had been working all day on the job, not feeling too well after spending a hard day working. The job required that I handle and work on clothing that white people would wear, and that accidentally came into my mind. This was what I wanted to know: when, how, would we ever determine our rights as human beings. . . . Just having paid for a seat and riding for only a couple of blocks and then having to stand was too much. These other persons had got on the bus after I did. It meant that I didn't have a right to do anything but get on the bus, give them my fare, and then be pushed wherever they wanted me."[3]

Cleveland Courts

1026 Rosa Parks Avenue

Rosa Parks lived here with her husband, Raymond, a barber, and her mother, Leona Edwards McCauley. It was one of Montgomery's first housing projects, built in 1941, and the family lived in apartment 634 from 1951 to 1957. Mrs. Parks moved to Detroit, where her brother lived, in 1957, and she still lives there. The street, formerly Cleveland Avenue, was renamed Rosa Parks Avenue in 1986.

Dexter Avenue King Memorial Baptist Church

454 Dexter Avenue

In the late 1940s the small black letters on the signboard of this church announced to Montgomery the blunt, bold sermon titles of its pastor, Vernon Johns: "It's Safe to Murder Negroes," "Segregation after Death," and "When the Rapist Is White." About fifty yards from the steps of the Capitol, these challenges to the white community, and the Dexter congregation itself, captured the pent-up frustration with Jim Crow and voiced the Movement's most potent claims of racial injustice. Johns's successor at the pulpit, Martin Luther King, Jr., later became its most eloquent spokesman.

Dexter was an unlikely home for racial prophecy. It had always been an example of black achievement, a conservative society church that boasted the most educated blacks in Alabama and a model of what could be accomplished within the system of segrega-

Dexter Avenue King Memorial Baptist Church in 1993. (Townsend Davis)

tion. Ever since historically black Alabama State College was moved from Perry County to Montgomery in 1887, Dexter had harbored its faculty and students. Sermons were typically laced with classical and literary references, which made even established churches in the city appear to be "shouting" churches by comparison.

Founded in 1877 in a former slave holding pen, the church broke away from the First Baptist Church and purchased the property on Dexter Avenue, the main street of Montgomery, for $250. Work began on the building in 1883 under builder William Watkins, who used discarded bricks from the paving of the street. By 1895 the building already had its distinctive double staircase leading to a raised entrance (to compensate for a steep hill), checkered stained glass, and pointed bell tower.

After World War II Pastor Johns rocked its congregation every week with provocative proclamations. He periodically took up the cause of a black person caught in the wheels of the justice system and upbraided his own congregation for showiness. He celebrated the land, preaching "Mud Is Basic," and distressed some members of the congregation by selling onions, potatoes, and watermelons outside the church. He also was an itinerant preacher who took long trips in his green Buick. His constant theme was that Negro prosperity for the few was chimerical without total economic independence from whites. When the strain of Johns's iconoclasm became too great for the Dexter deacons, he was asked to step down in 1952. After a long search the deacons settled on Martin Luther King, Jr., who became the highest-paid minister in Montgomery in September 1954. He came armed with thirty-four proposals to reinvigorate the church.

On Friday, December 2, 1955, as word spread that Rosa Parks had been arrested and released, King called a meeting here in the basement at which Mrs. Parks told about fifty people her story. After heated discussion a boycott was endorsed. More copies of the boycott announcement were made in the Dexter basement and distributed at Montgomery's black churches that Sunday.

In addition to civil rights work and his dissertation, King attended to the usual duties of the pastor during his time at Dexter: presiding over weddings and funerals, attending the sick, and devoting about fifteen hours to each of his Sunday sermons. He stepped down on February 1, 1960, to move to Atlanta.

King preached his last sermon at Dexter, "The Meaning of Hope," on December 10, 1967, four months before his assassination. The church was renamed in his honor in 1978 and today is the only Movement church to be designated a National Historic Landmark. A mural in the basement by painter and Dexter member John W. Feagin portrays the life of King and other leading figures of black history.

Dexter Avenue Baptist Church Parsonage/ King House
309 South Jackson Street

Before King came to Montgomery in September 1954, he wrote the Dexter deacons to say he required a furnished home for himself and his wife. The church had used this house as a parsonage since 1919. Rev. Vernon Johns had cultivated his vegetable garden in back of it and had stayed here long after his dismissal from Dexter, keeping up his scholarly pursuits by candlelight after the power and water were disconnected. King requested that the house be restored to working order, and he lived here from 1954 to 1960.

On January 30, 1956, in the first months of the bus boycott, someone threw a bomb onto the front porch that shattered the front

The porch of the Dexter Avenue Baptist Church Parsonage, where the Kings lived from 1954 to 1960. A plaque on the floor marks the spot of a bomb blast. (Jessica Allan)

windows. King's wife, Coretta, their two-month-old daughter, Yolanda, and Mary Lucy Williams, a friend, were in the house at the time, but they were unhurt. King hurried back from a mass meeting and found the house crowded with police, fire officials, and Mayor William ("Tacky") Gayle. Of greater concern was an angry crowd gathered outside, and King successfully pleaded for calm from the wreckage of the porch. Thereafter the church installed spotlights on the roof, and watchmen rotated in three four-hour shifts. Two days later, when his creed of nonviolence was still in its infancy, King went to the sheriff's office to request a pistol permit, but it was denied.

The King home continued to be a target after the boycott was over, and the Kings frequently stayed with friends elsewhere in Montgomery. Today the house is very much the same, maintained by Dexter but no longer a pastor's residence. A gash on the front porch where the bomb exploded remains and is marked with a plaque; the original diamond-paned north front windows contrast with the plain replacements on the south side.

Ben Moore Hotel
902 High Street

When it opened in 1951 in the heart of the former black business district, this four-story brick building was the only hotel in Montgomery for blacks. It had a large ballroom and a roof garden restaurant, where black organizers met with political candidates for the city commission in 1955. The hotel is inactive today but still standing.

Alabama State University
Carter Hill Road and Norman Bridge Road

Founded as a private school for ex-slaves in 1866, this historically black college educated and led black communities for decades and was nicknamed Little Morehouse after its Atlanta counterpart. For years the students and faculty of the school (formerly Alabama State College) were the backbone of racial change in Montgomery and risked periodic wrath from their benefactor, the state legislature.

Somewhere in the Alabama State duplicating room, there was a mimeograph machine that should have been bronzed. In the early-morning hours of December 2, 1955, teacher Jo Ann Robinson composed the leaflet proposing a bus boycott in response to the arrest of Rosa Parks the previous afternoon. She and two students spent all night reproducing it, three messages to a page, thirty-five reams in all: a total of 17,500 pages. They were cut, bundled, and distributed the next day as black citizens began to hear the news about Mrs. Parks. That weekend, once the boycott was agreed upon, the group ran off several thousand more and distributed them at beauty parlors, bars, factories, and barbershops.

Four years later the student sit-ins in North Carolina inspired Alabama State students to mount the state's first sit-in. On February 25, 1960, Bernard Lee and thirty-five other students walked into the snack bar in the basement of the Montgomery County Courthouse and requested service. The students were not arrested, but the snack bar instantly closed. Governor John Patterson then demanded that the Alabama students who had gone to the snack bar be suspended and the out-of-state students be expelled. On March 2 the Board of Education complied, expelling nine students. Later it fired a number of faculty members, including Lawrence Reddick, a historian and early biographer of King, and Jo Ann Robinson for their support of the sit-in.

The Alabama State sit-in brought mass protest and counterprotest into the streets of Montgomery for the first time. At the baseball stadium two days later Klansmen held a rally, followed by a bat-wielding racist romp through downtown. Six hundred Alabama State students marched in a silent double file to the Capitol on March 1. On March 6 about seven hundred blacks gathered at Dexter Avenue Baptist Church and began a short walk to the Capitol, only to be forced back by thousands of hostile whites and a buffer of about four hundred policemen. And on March 8, thirty-five students and a faculty member were arrested on campus for failing to obey police orders to disband.

Today the Joe L. Reed Acadome, named for a former Alabama State student arrested for integrating the courthouse snack bar, hosts regional college athletics. Reed later became a force in Alabama politics as chairman of the Alabama State Teachers Association and the statewide Alabama Democratic Conference.

Richard Harris House

333 South Jackson Street

When a black *New York Post* reporter wanted leads on the bus boycott in 1956, he didn't wait for the local paper to come out. He went down to the only modern black drugstore in the city, Dean's Drug Store on the corner of Monroe and Lawrence streets (now a park). People met over a burger at this boycott command center on

The Essential Role of Women in Montgomery

Black women did not shy away from political activism and played crucial roles during the bus boycott of 1955 and before. When the League of Women Voters refused to integrate, Mary Fair Burks, an English professor at Alabama State College, formed the Women's Political Council in 1946. Her colleague Jo Ann Robinson pledged to redouble efforts to improve conditions for blacks on the city buses after she had been rudely ejected from the front section of a nearly empty city bus in 1949.

By 1954 Robinson was president of the council and had already alerted city officials to dissatisfaction with the bus system. Two women were arrested for failing to comply with the segregated seating system before the famous Rosa Parks arrest.

Once the boycott started, women were vital to maintaining it. Robinson served on the MIA board and joined negotiations with the city and Governor Jim Folsom. Many other women served as accountants, secretaries, drivers, cooks, messengers, and fund-raisers, complementing the leadership role of the black preachers and car pool dispatchers.

In the months that followed, four female plaintiffs bravely testified about abuse on the buses in the federal lawsuit that ultimately undercut the segregated bus system. In 1967 Johnnie Carr, whose son Arlam was the lead plaintiff in the suit to desegregate Montgomery's public schools, became the fifth president of the MIA.

the same block as the E. L. Posey parking lot to get rides, listen to the radio, and exchange messages. Dean's was run by pharmacist Richard Harris, who sometimes spoke in minstrel dialect to confuse the police he was sure were listening in on his phone conversations.

In this house Harris lived with his wife, Vera, two houses down from the Kings, and provided a haven during the Movement. Here the Freedom Riders decided to push on to Jackson, Mississippi, after the melee at the Montgomery Greyhound Bus Station on May 20, 1961. Before departing on May 24, the riders gathered and prayed in the hallway in a scene that reminded Mrs. Harris of "Crusaders going to the lions." Alabama national guardsmen then escorted them to the Trailways Bus Station, where they got some snacks and coffee at the counter and, along with sixteen reporters, boarded the bus for Jackson. Mrs. Harris next heard from several of the riders in letters written from the Hinds County jail in Jackson, where many of the Freedom Riders were held.

Rufus Lewis House

801 Bolivar Street

Before they were moved to the basement of First Baptist Church for fear of midnight raids, the records of the MIA were kept in the Citizen's Club, a wood-paneled nightclub that announced its membership policy by the blue neon sign at the entrance that read EVERY MEMBER A REGISTERED VOTER. The club (now gone) was one of many groups headed by Rufus Lewis, a leading spokesman for educated blacks, member of Dexter Avenue Baptist Church, coach of the Alabama State football team, and administrator of a veterans' training program. He was often paired with the roughhewn E. D. Nixon. A common observation was "Mr. Nixon had the masses, and Coach Lewis had the classes."

In 1951 Lewis led the boycott of a grocery store whose white owner was accused of raping a black baby-sitter while driving her home. The campaign closed the store and prodded authorities to bring the owner to trial, a remarkable achievement in those days despite the predictable acquittal. In 1955, Lewis helped organize the car pool system. He also was one of the pioneers in voter registration in Montgomery County and the surrounding Black Belt, leading World War II veterans through the process in the 1940s and 1950s

Boycotters awaiting rides from the carpool at the E. L. Posey parking lot in 1956.
(Dan Weiner/Courtesy Sandra Weiner)

and mentoring the SNCC workers who came later. Coach Lewis later served as a state representative, the chairman of the powerful Alabama Democratic Conference, and a U.S. marshal, the first black to gain that post in Alabama.

E. D. Nixon House
647 Clinton Avenue

As a Pullman car porter, Edward Daniel Nixon traveled the length of the East Coast in a uniform. He still managed to push relentlessly for civil rights in Montgomery and was instrumental in the bus boycott. At the first meeting of the MIA, when some preachers advocated a traditional behind-the-scenes approach, Nixon seized the moment and urged the leaders to embrace the protest openly.

A protégé of A. Philip Randolph, president of the Brotherhood of Sleeping Car Porters, Nixon was the man to see about anything in black Montgomery. He was president of his union local, head of the state and local NAACP in the 1940s, founding member of the Montgomery Progressive Democratic Club, and treasurer of the MIA. On June 13, 1944, about 750 black men followed him to the county courthouse in a courageous attempt to register.

E. D. Nixon was the first person to be arrested under the sweeping antiboycott indictment of 1956. When he found out he had been indicted, he walked to the county courthouse and said to the sheriff, "Are you looking for me? Well, here I am." Many others later followed his example, shedding the dread commonly associated with an encounter with the judicial system. Two nights after the King house was bombed in January 1956, a bomb was thrown from a passing car near Nixon's house, but no one was injured. Nixon was on a train from Chicago to Birmingham at the time. Still, he and his wife resolved to stay put.

In his later years E. D. Nixon resented the inordinate amount of credit given to King for the Montgomery bus boycott and did not campaign for civil rights in other cities. Nixon disapproved of the Selma to Montgomery March in 1965 and endorsed Governor George Wallace. In the 1970s Nixon was instrumental in creating low-income housing and in establishing programs for the handicapped and the elderly. He died and was memorialized in 1987 after more than sixty years of civic effort. He is buried in Eastwood Memorial Gardens (7500 Wares Ferry Road).

Georgia Gilmore House

453 Dericote Street

Georgia Gilmore was a midwife with six children and an exceptional baker who lived near the King family. Her Club from Nowhere raised a hundred dollars a week for the MIA from the sale of her cakes and sweet potato pies. She testified in the antiboycott case and uttered King's favorite line of the trial about the bus system: "When they count the money, they do not know Negro money from white money." Her son Mark was arrested in 1958 for walking through Oak Park (between Hall Street and Forest Avenue), and the arrest generated the lawsuit that desegregated the public parks. He is currently a member of the City Council, which deliberates in the Montgomery City Hall, the same chamber where he was tried as a youngster. Mrs. Gilmore died in 1990.

Old Mount Zion AME Zion Church

657 South Holt Street

On December 5, 1955, after buses had rumbled through Montgomery nearly empty, black leaders met here to form a new organization to continue the campaign and appeal to the city for change. In suggesting the name the Montgomery Improvement Association, Rev. Ralph Abernathy wanted to avoid the word *council* to distance the group from the White Citizens' Council. Rufus ("Coach") Lewis nominated twenty-six-year-old Martin Luther King, Jr., to head it. His status as a polished newcomer made him an ideal alternative to the more established leaders Nixon and Lewis. Rev. L. Roy Bennett, the pastor here, was chosen vice-president, and E. D. Nixon treasurer. The MIA oversaw all aspects of the boycott, from negotiations to the purchase of vehicles, and attempted to broaden its mission once it was over.

The church now is housed in a new building on West Jeff Davis Avenue.

Holt Street Baptist Church

903 South Holt Street

Some of the most inspiring moments of the entire Movement came when this church was packed, its balcony overflowing. Pastor A. W. Wilson, who led the church for more than fifty years, opened the doors of his church to the Movement from its beginning.

On the evening of December 5, 1955, after the trial of Rosa Parks and the first day of the boycott, King gave his first Movement speech here. That day the church started filling up at 3:00 P.M., and by

"If We Are Wrong . . ."

After a meeting at the Mount Zion AME Zion Church on December 5, 1955, King went home, skipped dinner, and after about twenty minutes drove to the Holt Street Baptist Church. There he delivered his first speech as the just-appointed president of the MIA. This speech contained bedrock themes that he returned to over and over in hundreds of speeches during the next twelve years.

"We are here because of our love for democracy, because of our deep-seated belief that democracy transformed from thin paper to thick action is the greatest form of government on earth. . . . And you know, my friends, there comes a time when people get tired of being trampled over by the iron feet of oppression. There comes a time, my friends, when people get tired of being flung across the abyss of humiliation where they experience the bleakness of nagging despair. There comes a time when people get tired of being pushed out of the glittering sunlight of life's July and left standing amidst the piercing chill of an alpine November. . . . [W]e are not wrong in what we are doing. If we are wrong, then the Supreme Court of this nation is wrong. If we are wrong, the Constitution of the United States is wrong. If we are wrong, God Almighty is wrong. If we are wrong, Jesus of Nazareth was merely a utopian dreamer and never came down to earth. If we are wrong, justice is a lie. And we are determined here in Montgomery to work and fight until justice runs down like water, and righteousness like a mighty stream. . . ."[4]

King addresses a mass meeting at First Baptist Church in Montgomery. (Dan Weiner/ Courtesy Sandra Weiner)

6:00 P.M., still an hour before the official starting time, there wasn't a parking space within three blocks. Loudspeakers were set up to reach the crowd outside. When the boycott leaders finally emerged from the pastor's study, the crowd clapped and shouted "amen." King's inspiring talk drew thunderous applause, and foot stomping shook the church. Even the dignified deacons nodded and waved in assent. The congregation endorsed continuing the boycott until its demands were met. The first collection for the MIA brought $500, beginning a process that was to bring $250,000 in local donations to the organization in the coming months.

In August 1957 an emerging group of black activist preachers adopted the name the Southern Christian Leadership Conference (SCLC) at this church after preliminary meetings in Atlanta and New Orleans.

First Baptist Church ("Brick-a-Day")

347 North Ripley Street

First Baptist was a Movement fortress, at times bombed, pelted with debris, and ringed by national guardsmen. From 1952 to 1961 it was led by Rev. Ralph David Abernathy, a mirthful Movement prince and King's closest friend. When Abernathy first arrived from the farms of Marengo County in the Black Belt by way of Alabama State College and Selma University, the church seemed to him as vast as the Hollywood Bowl.

This church, founded in 1867, was the first black Baptist church in Montgomery. It was the founding place of the Alabama Colored Baptist Convention in 1868 and the organization that became the National Baptist Convention in 1880, the national umbrella for all black Baptist churches. The original wood church (called Columbus Street Baptist) burned down, and in the services that followed in borrowed churches and the open air, Pastor Andrew Stokes exhorted his flock to bring one brick each day for the new building, which gave it the nickname Brick-a-Day.

Abernathy was the first person E. D. Nixon called about the arrest of Rosa Parks, and Abernathy spread the word among the city's ministers. From that point on he was an energetic boycott strategist, a gripping and saucy speaker, and King's successor as head of the MIA. First Baptist served as a frequent meeting church and was the location for the first of the regular Monday night mass meetings on January 30, 1956, also the night King's home was bombed. The church itself was bombed on January 10, 1957, along with Abernathy's home and three other churches.

Three years later the church came under siege during a harrowing standoff. On May 21, 1961, the night after the Greyhound Bus Station attack on the Freedom Riders, King addressed a mass meeting here. First Baptist had become a headquarters of sorts for the riders, and they were sprinkled through the congregation to prevent an easy roundup by lawmen. Meanwhile a crowd of white teenagers gathered in a public park across Ripley Street near Oakwood Cemetery, and a line of U.S. marshals sent by President Kennedy held them at bay. When the crowd started to throw bricks and rocks toward the church, the marshals responded with tear gas, and cars were overturned. As wisps of tear gas drifted in through the church windows, King urged calm from the pulpit while breaking away to call Attorney General Robert Kennedy on the phone from the church basement.

By midnight Governor John Patterson had declared martial law and sent national guardsmen to disperse the mob outside. About a thousand weary people who had come for the rally rested on the wooden pews until shortly before dawn. Martial law continued throughout the tense city until May 29, 1961.

Abernathy fulfilled King's pledge to mount a Poor People's March to Washington in 1968 and vowed to carry on his spirit. Abernathy died on April 17, 1990, and is buried in Atlanta.

Montgomery's Night of Terror: January 10, 1957

Montgomery was rocked by six explosions in the early-morning hours of January 10, 1957. At the time King and Abernathy were in Atlanta spreading the lessons of the boycott to the first organized conference on nonviolent integration. Although there had been scattered violent incidents on the buses, this was an organized attack on the MIA's strongholds that caused seventy thousand dollars in damage after the boycott was over. Miraculously no one was hurt.

First hit were the homes of Abernathy, whose wife and child were home, and Rev. Robert Graetz. Then four churches were hit: First Baptist, Bell Street Baptist, Hutchinson Street Baptist, and Mount Olive Baptist. Upon arriving back at First Baptist, Abernathy found a CONDEMNED sign on it and the structure listing like a sinking ship. Later a plot to bomb King's Dexter Avenue Baptist Church was discovered, and explosives found on the porch of the Dexter parsonage were dismantled gingerly by the state's bomb squad. The bombing suspects were freed after charges were dropped or they were acquitted.

Trinity Lutheran Church

1104 Rosa Parks Avenue

Early in the Movement white citizens who sympathized with black efforts at integration were singled out for special scorn. Rev. Robert Graetz, the white pastor of this predominantly black Lutheran church at the time of the boycott, was one of them. "If I had a nickel for every time I've been called a nigger-loving SOB," he once said, "I'd be independently wealthy."

Even before the boycott Graetz and his blue Chevy were known in Montgomery because he tried to avoid using white-only facilities. As a result, when he went to the Carver Theater, used by blacks, the attendant would whisk him in for free rather than risk causing a scene. When the bus boycott was announced, he immediately supported it.

From the beginning Graetz drove people to work from 6:00 to 9:00 A.M. each day. This activity led whites at first to suspect him of masterminding the entire boycott. He was arrested by Sheriff Mac Butler for operating an illegal taxi, and one day he found sugar in his gas tank and his tires slashed. The church parsonage (at 1110 Rosa Parks Avenue) was bombed twice, once in 1956 and again in 1957. In 1958 he moved to Columbus, Ohio, where he had gone to seminary school.

The Graetz Family Receives a Crank Call

More than thirty crank calls came to Rev. Robert Graetz's home in the days following his profile in the local newspaper. He also received piles of hate mail, some of it addressed simply to "Lutheran Minister, Montgomery, Alabama." The Graetzes got in the habit of logging the calls and even kept a reel-to-reel tape recorder hidden in a baby buggy to monitor hostile statements. Here is one of the more civil calls they got, as recorded in Graetz's log:

"**J**an. 10. 2:15 A.M. White man who seemed to be drunk. Demanded that I come and give him taxi service like what has been furnished to the dark-complected people. Suggested that we set up car pool for white people so [he] can save the ten-cent fare. Refused to give name but he called himself Roger."[5]

Montgomery City Jail

934 North Ripley Street

When King was arrested for the first time on January 26, 1956, he was brought here. He was driving home from Dexter in his '54 Pontiac and had stopped to pick up people at a boycott car pool station when he was pulled over and taken into custody. When a crowd of blacks came to the jail to see what had happened, he was quickly released. That night an unprecedented seven mass meetings were held in Montgomery. Today the building, bearing

"1941" over the entrance, is used by the City Maintenance Department and can be approached only with the permission of a guard at the entrance to the parking lot.

Montgomery City Hall
103 North Perry Street

The Montgomery City Council now meets in the chamber of the former Recorder's Court, where Rosa Parks was tried on December 5, 1955, for failing to comply with segregated seating on the city buses. In a short trial in the segregated chamber her lawyer, Fred Gray, raised a number of unsuccessful constitutional arguments. She was fined ten dollars plus four dollars in court costs. In keeping with the boycott, about five hundred blacks who had come to attend the trial walked home or to the first mass meeting at the Holt Street Baptist Church that night. The crowd gathered on the courthouse steps signaled a new boldness and solidarity.

This building was also the site of King's first photographed arrest. On September 3, 1958, he was in court to attend a hearing on the case of an assailant of Rev. Ralph Abernathy when police charged him with loitering. The police walked King to the police station, bending his right arm behind him, leaned him over the desk, and threw him into a cell in his suit. After he had been tried and found guilty, King decided to serve his time in jail to magnify injustice. Plans made for a vigil outside the city jail were defused when Clyde Sellers, the police commissioner, paid the fourteen-dollar fine to get King out of his hair.

Montgomery County Courthouse
142 Washington Avenue

The county jail became a focal point on February 21, 1956, after the indictment of nearly every black leader in Montgomery, eighty-nine in all, for violating a state antiboycott statute. The law, drafted in 1921 after a violent mining strike in Birmingham, was put to new use against the organizers of the bus boycott. But by indicting so many people, the authorities unwittingly triggered a prototype of the Movement: the arrest as a badge of leadership. Several people volunteered to be arrested, and soon the sheriff was complaining that the booking process had become a "vaudeville show." King was the last of the twenty-four ministers booked and released on bond.

In the end only King was tried here for leading an illegal boycott. He was defended vigorously (his lawyers moved to integrate the courtroom itself), and black spectators at the trial wore crosses on their lapels reading, "Father, Forgive Them." He was found guilty in

March 1956 and fined five hundred dollars. The charges against the other boycotters were later dropped in a joint deal that also resulted in the dropping of charges against five men suspected of bombing black homes and churches in January 1957. King also was tried on tax evasion charges here in 1960 and was acquitted.

Years later, in 1965, SNCC conducted a short-lived voter registration campaign here that prompted the worst street violence in Montgomery since the Freedom Rides. SNCC had organized a series of marches in Montgomery, and on March 16, 1965, marchers, including a group of sweater-toting white college students, marched toward the Capitol. They got only as far as the intersection of Decatur Street and Washington Avenue, up the hill from the Dexter Avenue Baptist Church, and were told by the sheriff that they could go no farther without a parade permit.

After a brief standoff mounted possemen hit, chased, and beat the protesters with canes and nightsticks while white residents watched from their porches. The marchers retreated to the Jackson Street Baptist Church (430 South Jackson Street). Eight of the demonstrators, some of whom displayed their wounds for news photographers, were hospitalized. The next day King led three thousand people to the courthouse, forcing a negotiation session in the sheriff's office that stretched until midnight. Sheriff Mac Butler apologized for the violence, and the protesters worked out future ground rules for demonstrations.

Greyhound Bus Station
210 South Court Street

By mid-May 1961 the original Freedom Riders from CORE had given up their attempts to desegregate public bus terminals in major cities in the Deep South. They had been beaten in Birmingham and been burned out of a bus in nearby Anniston. Twenty college students from Nashville decided to continue the journey into equally hostile territory, and they cruised down to Montgomery in a bus loaded with guardsmen and the Greyhound supervisor, whom the driver insisted come along.

When the bus pulled into this station on May 20, 1961, a few reporters and cabdrivers were visible. The students hadn't even intended to test the waiting rooms, preferring to do that on the way out. The driver announced over the loudspeaker, "Here comes the Freedom Riders to tame the South." John Lewis, then in seminary in Nashville, stepped first onto the landing, and a mob of whites surged out of hiding with pipes and bats. They indiscriminately beat the reporters, smashing their cameras and bags, and then turned on the passengers, setting their luggage afire with cigarettes. Some of the students ended up jumping or being pushed over a railing into the parking lot of the federal courthouse next door.

In the frenzy an old man's cane and white women's pocketbooks were added to the makeshift arsenal of farm implements and construction tools used against the marchers. John Lewis was knocked over the head with a wooden Coca-Cola crate. William Barbee and Jim Zwerg were beaten badly and, while bandaged and dazed in their hospital beds, pledged to continue the Freedom Rides. Barbee was saved by Floyd Mann of the Alabama Highway Patrol, who had to draw a gun to get the assailants to back off. The rest either escaped in taxis or fled on foot.

John Seigenthaler, an aide to Attorney General Robert Kennedy, tried to rescue a woman who had been knocked across the hood of his car, but he was clubbed unconscious with a pipe. Up above from a window in the federal courthouse, DOJ's lead civil rights lawyer, John Doar, relayed the scene by phone to Washington while watching in helpless agony. Sometime later police and sheriff's deputies arrived and read the injured Freedom Riders a circuit court order

Freedom Riders are escorted by national guardsmen as their bus leaves Montgomery for Jackson, May 24, 1961. (Bruce Davidson/Magnum Photos)

forbidding the ride that had just ended so brutally. The marchers repaired to First Baptist Church or the home of Rev. Solomon Seay.

Four days later the same group went to the Trailways Bus Station (formerly at 221 Lee Street), ate at the white lunch counter, and departed for Jackson under heavy guard. That same day northern priests, professors, and activists copied the students by arriving on another bus and submitting to arrest. These incidents, combined with the hair-raising siege of First Baptist Church, prompted the federal Interstate Commerce Commission to order on September 22, 1961, that all interstate bus facilities be desegregated. By late 1964 the "colored" waiting room had been replaced by lockers, and the remaining waiting room was integrated.

U.S. Courthouse
(Frank M. Johnson, Jr., Federal Building)
14 Lee Street

With political weight working against the Movement at every turn, there was one official building where civil rights claims stood a chance: the federal courthouse. Formerly also the U.S. post office, this building served as a refuge when the Freedom Riders were beaten and scattered at the Greyhound Station next door. For twenty-three years both Alabama's highest officials and the Movement's legal firefighters labored in the Middle District of Alabama under the steady gaze and deliberative opinions of Judge Frank Minis Johnson, Jr., in the second-floor courtroom.

Judge Johnson's independence was characteristic of his native Winston County in the Alabama hill country, which contributed more Union than Confederate soldiers to the Civil War. In January 1956, at age thirty-seven, Johnson was confirmed as the youngest federal judge in the nation. Three days later lawyer Fred Gray filed *Browder v. Gayle,* the case that challenged the system of segregation as enforced on the city buses and defined Judge Johnson's career forever. Sitting on a three-judge panel consisting of Appellate Judge Richard Rives and Judge Seybourn Lynne of Birmingham, Johnson voted with Rives to extend desegregation from the schools to the buses. The result was widely hailed by blacks as a godsend and was upheld by the U.S. Supreme Court. It also began a lifelong series of personal threats against Judge Johnson that culminated in a burning cross near his home in December 1956 and a bomb in the yard of his mother's house in April 1967, after school desegregation was required statewide.

During the Movement Johnson's nemesis was the voluble George Wallace, a friend from law school at the University of Alabama. Their first clash occurred over a federal investigation into racially skewed voting in 1958 in Barbour and Bullock counties, where Wallace was a circuit judge. In a visit to Judge Johnson's house, Wallace asked the judge to hold him in contempt for failing to turn over voting records to the U.S. Civil Rights Commission and to jail him for a short while; the contempt citation would have helped him politically. Johnson refused to make such a deal. Ultimately Wallace turned the records over, initiating a pattern that later served him well as governor in his ongoing tug-of-war with the federal government: Breathe defiance, but ultimately comply. In his race for governor in 1962 Wallace repeatedly used one of the most memorable vituperations in American politics by referring to Judge Johnson as an "integrating, scalawagging, carpetbagging liar."

In 1979 Judge Johnson was elevated to the Fifth Circuit Court of Appeals, which during the 1950s and 1960s was known for issuing desegregation orders despite massive resistance. On the appeals court through the eighties and nineties Judge Johnson continued to rule on many important cases involving civil liberties and criminal law. Judge Myron Thompson, a black lawyer and Yale Law School graduate from Tuskegee, took his place in the district court and has taken care to preserve the courtroom's historical character. On May 22, 1992, the building was renamed for Judge Johnson.

Alabama State Capitol
Bainbridge Street and Dexter Avenue

From his first-floor office in the corner of the Capitol, Governor George Wallace could see clear down Dexter Avenue. When he looked out on the afternoon of March 25, 1965, he saw one of the largest marches of the entire Movement stretching back to the statue of Hebe, Goddess of Youth, atop the Court Square fountain.

Montgomery was the first capital of the Confederacy—for about three months. On February 18, 1861, Jefferson Davis was inaugurated as its provisional president and took up residence at the first Confederate White House (644 Washington Avenue), which still stands to the south of the Capitol. A century later George Wallace began working to resurrect the Confederate identity.

In 1958 Wallace lost the governorship to John Patterson during the first full-throated racial election in modern Alabama after *Brown* and its tempestuous aftermath. Four years later Wallace carried fifty-

Marchers arriving at the state Capitol in Montgomery from Selma on March 25, 1965: (left to right) Rosa Parks, Rev. Ralph and Juanita Abernathy, Ralph Bunche, King, Jean Young, and Coretta King. (Bruce Davidson/Magnum Photos)

six of Alabama's sixty-seven counties by energetically embracing segregation and flogging the federal government. His quintessential act of defiance occurred on June 11, 1963, when he stood in the entranceway of Foster Auditorium at the University of Alabama in Tuscaloosa, physically barring the admittance of two black students. He relented when a federalized National Guard showed up.

To circumvent an Alabama law preventing consecutive terms, Wallace thrust his wife Lurleen into the campaign of 1966. Lurleen Wallace, who openly promised to "let George do it," won the election but died in office and was the first person to lie in state in the Capitol rotunda since Jefferson Davis.

Plotting a comeback in 1970, this time with three hundred thousand black voters on the rolls, George Wallace roared back with a racial display considered the dirtiest campaign in Alabama history and won. He won again in 1974, after being shot and paralyzed in the heat of his 1972 presidential campaign. After appointing blacks to government offices and finally dropping his bitter defense of segregation, he got 25 percent of the black vote in a landslide. Fob

On a chilly January 14, 1963, George Wallace gave a ringing defense of segregation in his inaugural address, which was followed by a six-hour spectacle of bands and floats:

"**T**oday I have stood where Jefferson Davis stood and took an oath to my people. It is very appropriate then that from this Cradle of the Confederacy, this very heart of the great Anglo-Saxon Southland, that today we sound the drum for freedom. . . . Let us rise to the call of freedom-loving blood that is in us and send our answer to the tyranny that clanks its chains upon the South. In the name of the greatest people that ever trod this earth, I draw a line in the dust and toss the gauntlet before the feet of tyranny, and I say: segregation now, segregation tomorrow, segregation forever."[6]

James took over from Wallace from 1979 to 1983, and Wallace then served a final term, departing in 1987.

In recent years Wallace has been outwardly remorseful, convincing some and leaving others skeptical. In 1979 he appeared at Dexter Avenue Baptist Church seeking reconciliation, and in 1982 he issued an apology for his past racism to SCLC. In a 1995 scene reminiscent of his famous stand at the schoolhouse door, he was hoisted,

"How Long? . . . Not Long"

Two years later, on March 25, 1965, King answered Wallace in front of the Alabama state Capitol in one of his greatest speeches:

"**I** stand before you this afternoon with the conviction that segregation is on its death bed in Alabama, and the only thing uncertain about it is how costly the segregationists and Wallace will make the funeral. . . . I come to say to you this afternoon, however difficult the moment, however frustrating the hour, it will not be long because truth crushed to earth will rise again. How long? Not long, because no lie can live forever. How long? Not long, because you shall reap what you sow. How long? Not long. Truth forever on the scaffold, wrong forever on the throne. Yet that scaffold sways the future. And behind the dim unknown standeth God within the shadow, keeping watch above his own. How long? Not long because the arc of the moral universe is long, but it bends toward justice."[7]

Flying the Confederate Battle Flag

In 1961, for the first time since the Civil War, Alabama Governor John Patterson raised the Confederate battle flag at the Capitol as a centennial tribute to the Confederacy. It was not the flag of the Confederacy itself, which had three thick horizontal stripes and a circle of stars (the Stars and Bars), but rather the diagonally striped battle flag favored by the Ku Klux Klan. On April 25, 1963, Governor Wallace ordered it raised again, this time to rankle Attorney General Robert Kennedy, who had traveled to Montgomery to discuss the admission of the first blacks to the University of Alabama. Throughout his governorship Wallace left it flying. A master of symbolism, he considered replacing it during the march from Selma in 1965 with a black flag of mourning.

Once in office, black legislators introduced several bills to have the battle flag taken down. All failed. In 1988, when the Capitol was ringed with a chain-link fence during renovations, members of the NAACP were arrested for trespassing after going to the fence and vowing to bring the flag down. Even in the 1990s the Capitol flew the U.S. flag at the top, the Alabama State flag (red diagonal stripes on white background), and the Confederate battle flag below the other two.

Alvin Holmes, a black legislator, first filed a lawsuit in 1975 to have the battle flag removed, and finally, in 1993, a state court ordered it taken down on the basis of an obscure state law that required only the official state flag to be flown from the Capitol.

frail and ailing in his wheelchair, onto the steps of the school at the City of St. Jude to greet marchers commemorating the Selma to Montgomery March. He had refused to meet the first march as governor in 1965, but this time he clasped hands with the marchers and whispered, "I love you all."

Alabama Supreme Court

455 Dexter Avenue

The highest court in Alabama was housed here beginning in 1940. Some of the Movement's most famous cases were argued here at the top tier of the state justice system.

In this building the Movement faced several temporary legal defeats, including King's conviction for leading the Montgomery bus boycott, the outlawing of the Alabama NAACP, and the libel suit of Montgomery Police Chief L. B. Sullivan. With the exception of a few sit-in cases, the court interpreted the law to maintain segregation until it was finally reversed by the U.S. Supreme Court.

The lawsuit by Attorney General John Patterson against the state NAACP was one of the most effective legal roadblocks the Movement ever faced. On June 1, 1956, Patterson secured an order banning all fund raising and solicitation of new members and demanded a membership list. The NAACP in Alabama was forced to disband until, after four trips to the U.S. Supreme Court and eight years of litigation, Patterson's order was found to violate the NAACP's constitutional right to associate for the advocacy of ideas. Meanwhile local groups like the MIA, SCLC, and the Alabama Christian Movement for Human Rights (ACMHR) in Birmingham had grown to fill the organizational vacuum.

This court also affirmed a five-hundred-thousand-dollar libel judgment against the *New York Times* that became the foundation of modern First Amendment law. At issue was an advertisement in the *Times* entitled "Heed Their Rising Voices" designed to raise money for the legal defense of King in his tax case. The ad purported to describe the expulsion of Alabama State students for the sit-in at the county courthouse, but its drafters in New York got a few things wrong. They exaggerated the law enforcement response, placed the students at the state Capitol, incorrectly stated that the Alabama State cafeteria had been padlocked, and said Reverend King had been arrested seven times instead of four. In a landmark ruling the U.S. Supreme Court overturned the verdict and ruled that unless a press account is deliberately false or is based on shoddy reporting, public figures are obligated to endure harsh and sometimes inaccurate press coverage in order to ensure that "debate on public issues should be uninhibited, robust, and wide-open."

The building currently is vacant. Today the Alabama Supreme Court is housed in the State Judicial Building at 300 Dexter Avenue.

Civil Rights Memorial

404 Washington Avenue (in front of the Southern Poverty Law Center)

A black granite echo of her massive Vietnam Veterans Memorial in Washington, D.C., designer Maya Lin's memorial to those slain in the Movement was dedicated in 1989. Water flows from its conical fountain, on which are inscribed the names and dates of forty people, black and white, who were killed from 1955 to 1968 in the South. Behind the fountain is a granite wall also sheathed in running water and engraved with one of Reverend King's favorite exhortations from the Bible, Amos 5:24: "Until justice rolls down like waters, and righteousness like a mighty stream."

The Southern Poverty Law Center, which sponsored the memorial

Civil Rights Memorial in front of the Southern Poverty Law Center, 1993.
(Townsend Davis)

and is housed securely behind it, continues to fight discrimination as a not-for-profit foundation. Founded in 1971 by lawyer Morris Dees, the center successfully sued to integrate the Alabama state troopers and is credited with bankrupting the largest Klan organization and other white supremacy groups nationwide through litigation and education.

City of St. Jude

2048 West Fairview Avenue (I-80 extension)

A celebration during the last overnight stop of the Selma to Montgomery March in 1965 took place at this Catholic complex. It was muddy and crowded; official estimates ranged from ten thousand to thirty thousand people. One activist, who was both thrilled and galled by the extravagant outdoor night concert on March 24, 1965, characterized it as a circus.

With its well-kept lawns and serene Madonna statues, the unincorporated City of St. Jude was an unlikely setting for the Movement's Woodstock. It was the only place that could hold a large black audience, and once Father Paul Mullaney granted permission to use St. Jude as a staging ground, the nuns and staff worked with the SNCC radicals to make it happen.

Montgomery

Sammy Davis, Jr., who had closed his Broadway show *Golden Boy* for one night to attend, sang the national anthem, prompting two army officers standing on a truck bed to salute. People flocked to the athletic fields to hear Joan Baez and Harry Belafonte perform and to hear James Baldwin speak. Seven spectators were overcome by the heat, and one was hospitalized. Gusty winds blew down a tent, and marchers slept behind the school under the stars before regrouping the next morning to march to the Capitol.

For decades St. Jude had filled a huge gap caused by segregation. Its founder, Father Harold Purcell, envisioned nothing less than a city within a city, a place for housing, medical care, and training in black west Montgomery where none existed. An Irish Catholic priest from Union City, New Jersey, Father Purcell planned a social complex with a tall Catholic church in the middle. "I'll build a church with a roof so blue that it will just shout out the thought of the Blessed Virgin Mary!" he supposedly exclaimed.

He erected the first building on a tract of land in what was then called Washington Terrace, once part of a large plantation. Starting in 1938 with the church, built by black workers and fitted with a crucifix of Carrara marble from Italy, St. Jude grew to include a social center, an educational institute, and a full-service hospital. It offered night classes for black World War II veterans. St. Jude also tended to the battered Freedom Riders Jim Zwerg and William Barbee in May 1961. The first two of the King children were born here, as were the Abernathys' three children.

Today St. Jude still serves thousands of people in need. Contained in its nine buildings are two parochial schools (one elementary, one high school), a Head Start program for preschoolers, an adult literacy center, a nursing facility for children, two convents, and ninety-six units of low-income housing for the elderly.

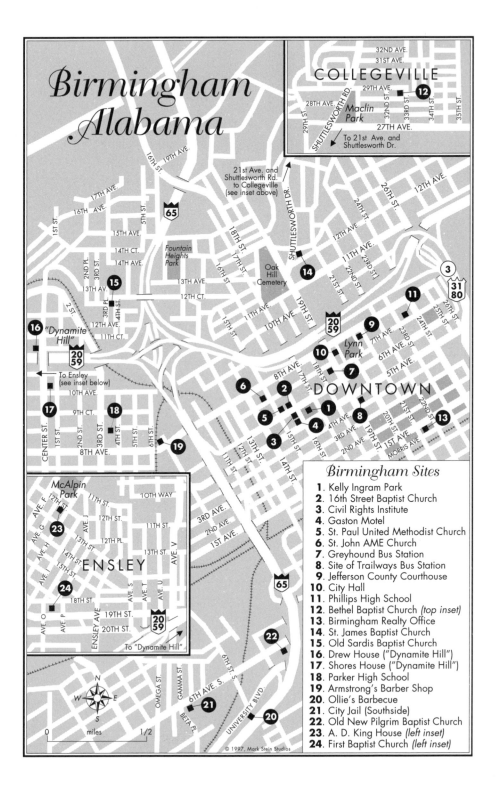

Birmingham Alabama

32ND AVE.
31ST AVE.
29TH AVE.
28TH AVE.
27TH AVE.

Maclin Park

To 21st Ave. and Shuttlesworth Dr.

21st Ave. and Shuttlesworth Rd. to Collegeville (see inset above)

Fountain Heights Park

Oak Hill Cemetery

"Dynamite Hill"

To Ensley (see inset below)

DOWNTOWN

Lynn Park

McAlpin Park

ENSLEY

To "Dynamite Hill"

Birmingham Sites

1. Kelly Ingram Park
2. 16th Street Baptist Church
3. Civil Rights Institute
4. Gaston Motel
5. St. Paul United Methodist Church
6. St. John AME Church
7. Greyhound Bus Station
8. Site of Trailways Bus Station
9. Jefferson County Courthouse
10. City Hall
11. Phillips High School
12. Bethel Baptist Church *(top inset)*
13. Birmingham Realty Office
14. St. James Baptist Church
15. Old Sardis Baptist Church
16. Drew House ("Dynamite Hill")
17. Shores House ("Dynamite Hill")
18. Parker High School
19. Armstrong's Barber Shop
20. Ollie's Barbecue
21. City Jail (Southside)
22. Old New Pilgrim Baptist Church
23. A. D. King House *(left inset)*
24. First Baptist Church *(left inset)*

© 1997, Mark Stein Studios

Birmingham, Alabama

From "Bombingham" to Project C

From the outside Birmingham in the 1950s was a kind of Oz, a gleaming city with its secrets hidden behind perpetual white smoke. Ash poured from the Sloss Furnaces and from houses that still burned coal. One businessman remembers having to scrape emissions off the windshield of his car every morning. Birmingham was divided by a hill of the ore-reddened soil used for manufacturing iron. Atop it stood a fifty-six-foot-high cast-iron statue of Vulcan, the god of fire and forge. In his hand a torch glowed green most nights but shone red if there had been a traffic fatality in the city within the preceding twenty-four hours. Vulcan overlooked the largest city in Alabama.

The city nearly doubled in size between 1940 and 1960, and its miraculous growth gave it the name the Magic City. Fully half of all its jobs were in some way related to the steel industry, and many blacks, who constituted 40 percent of the population, provided the necessary labor to man the city's huge ironworks. The median income for white families was sixty-two hundred dollars; for blacks it was three thousand dollars.

Segregation was in place everywhere. Blacks were permitted to shop downtown as long as they used separate parking lots, elevators, water fountains, and fitting rooms. By law blacks and whites could eat under the same roof only if they used different entrances and were separated by a seven-foot partition. Strict racial separation contrasted with the perky civic boosterism displayed on signs that said IT'S NICE TO HAVE YOU IN BIRMINGHAM.

Five different Klan organizations roamed Birmingham along with the National States Rights Party and other white supremacy groups. Throughout the civil rights era their presence was a constant threat. The Cahaba Boys met off the Cahaba River Bridge near Highway 280, where they planned vicious night rides and low-grade bombings that were the unmistakable signature of the Klan.

The Movement in Birmingham was fueled by the banning of the NAACP in Alabama in 1956 and the leadership of a preacher born in Mount Meigs, Alabama, named Fred Shuttlesworth. Shuttlesworth was president of the local NAACP chapter, which was dominated by

The Birmingham City Code on Gaming

Segregation was explicitly woven into the city code governing every walk of life: buses, taxis, rest rooms, restaurants, theaters, pool halls, ball parks, and outdoor exhibition spaces. Violation of the code was punishable by a one-hundred-dollar fine or six months in jail or both. Here is one such provision:

"**SEC. 597. NEGROES AND WHITE PERSONS NOT TO PLAY TOGETHER.** It shall be unlawful for a negro and a white person to play together or in company with each other in any game of cards or dice, dominoes or checkers."[8]

local black businessmen who ran their own fiefdoms within the system of segregation. Shuttlesworth had attended the founding of the MIA in 1955 and had seen how the Montgomery bus boycott had corralled segregation. Only days after the Alabama NAACP had been shut down by court order on June 1, 1956, he helped found a new organization led by a younger group of preachers eager to push for change.

On June 5, 1956, at Sardis Baptist Church a crowd ushered the Alabama Christian Movement for Human Rights (ACMHR) to the forefront of racial struggle. The name signified a new approach: explicitly Christian, recognizing the emerging doctrine of nonvio-

The ACMHR's Original Declaration of Principles

Five preachers called the first meeting of the ACMHR: Fred Shuttlesworth, N. H. Smith, T. L. Lane, R. L. Alford, and G. E. Pruitt. Once they resolved to form a new organization, they drafted a statement for the founding meeting at Sardis Baptist Church on June 5, 1956:

"**W**e are not echoing the will or sentiments of outsiders; but our own convictions and will to be free, so help us God. We will not become Rabblerousers; but will be sober, firm, peaceful, and resolute, within the Framework of Goodwill. . . .

"[V]acillation, procrastination, or evasion and the hastily enacted laws and enflamed statements of public Officials do not lead us to embrace 'Gradualism.' We want a beginning now! We have already waited 100 years."[9]

lence, and a Movement, not a mere council that could be shuttered as the NAACP chapter had been. The ACMHR sought to challenge segregation by forcing its way into white-only domains and creating legal test cases. Still, many thought the ACMHR preachers should stick to the Bible rather than use the pulpit for social reform.

The ACMHR requested black police officers and bus drivers and desegregated seating on the city buses. By 1953 black police officers were working in eighty cities in the South, including Nashville and Atlanta but not Birmingham. The request for black officers was supported by a petition of 4,500 people, including 119 whites, but the city commission, a triumvirate that dictated virtually all city policies, would not budge. Given that Birmingham was nearly three times larger than Montgomery and more sprawling, the fledgling ACMHR did not have the leverage to back up its demands with a boycott.

After the U.S. Supreme Court ruled in December 1956 that segregated bus seating was illegal, the ACMHR instructed its members how to "ride integrated." The day after Christmas Shuttlesworth, who had just walked away unharmed from the dynamiting of his home during the night, led a line of fifty blacks through the downtown business district, where they boarded buses at Second and Third avenues North at Nineteenth and Twentieth streets. The move caught the police by surprise and sent reporters scurrying to the

Rev. Edward Gardner, who led numerous mass meetings in Birmingham, at home in 1996. (Jessica Allan)

phones. By the end of the day police had tracked down and arrested twenty-one riders and arrested Shuttlesworth for driving without a license and having an improper tag on his car. On March 21, 1957, after the city commission reaffirmed that bus segregation was "necessary for the avoidance of friction, violence and enmity between the races," the twenty-one riders were convicted and fined fifty dollars each.

For the next six years the ACMHR and Shuttlesworth kept up the pressure. On March 6, 1957, Shuttlesworth tried to use the front door of the train station. His attempt to register two of his children at Phillips High School in fall 1957 drew a crudely armed mob from which he barely escaped. The mere announcement of his intention to send his children to integrate the schools had in September 1957 triggered a grisly Klan initiation ritual in which four white men abducted a black man named Judge Aaron from a street corner in Tarrant north of the city, castrated him, and poured turpentine on his wound. Integration of the schools, more so than lunch counters or government offices, continued to be the flint that caused the Klan to explode in years to come. The following fall the Klan burned eighteen crosses in Jefferson County, an act that was repeated several times each fall.

In 1957 a series of bombings gave the city the nickname Bombingham and gave urgency to a previous ACMHR request to limit the sale of explosives. Bombs had been planted in a synagogue, Shuttlesworth's church, and a number of houses bought by blacks in formerly all-white neighborhoods. Between 1957 and 1962 seventeen black churches and homes were bombed, and no one was charged, a fact not lost on wary preachers in town and elsewhere in the state. By 1963 the number of unsolved bombings had grown to twenty-eight.

By 1960 Shuttlesworth had grown frustrated with delays and the cost of legal challenges. In its first four years the ACMHR had paid forty thousand dollars in bonds and legal fees, yet Birmingham was as segregated as ever. Shuttlesworth's cynicism could only have been reinforced when Birmingham police impounded and sold his car to satisfy the libel judgment against the *New York Times* and other Movement preachers. The city commissioner in charge of police then was Theophilus Eugene ("Bull") Connor, who had acquired his nickname from his uninhibited cornpone style of announcing baseball games on the radio. Connor had been in local politics since 1937.

Freedom Riders arrived in Birmingham from Atlanta on Mother's Day, May 14, 1961, and they caught the brunt of local tensions that had been simmering for several years. They arrived at the Trailways Station (formerly at Nineteenth Street and Fourth Avenue North, now a parking lot with a historical marker), three blocks from police headquarters. A white mob converged on the interracial group of passengers with pipes and sticks for ten to fifteen minutes before the police arrived. After stalling in Birmingham for four days and embroiling the Kennedy administration in a test of wills with state authorities, the Freedom Rides continued on to Montgomery.

In November 1961 Arthur Hanes was sworn in as new mayor, and he shut down the city's recreational facilities rather than submit to a federal court order requiring desegregation. This meant that thirty-eight playgrounds, six swimming pools, and four golf courses were closed, an action that some whites as well as blacks opposed. Birmingham sacrificed its baseball team, theater bookings, and annual visits from the Metropolitan Opera company on the altar of segregation.

Meanwhile, change was brewing. Students from traditionally black Miles College (5500 Myron Massey Boulevard, Fairfield) held a vigil in Kelly Ingram Park in 1960, conducted a voter registration drive in the summer of 1961, and issued a declaration on December 29, 1961, signed by seven hundred students denouncing segregation as both "unChristian and undemocratic." In 1962 the students announced a "selective buying" campaign, which was a boycott in all but name, and listed demands that SCLC would take up a year later. During the Easter shopping season students promoted the slogan "Wear Your Old Clothes for Freedom," cutting black purchases by about 80 percent.

Shortly thereafter SCLC began planning its best-organized campaign: Project C (for confrontation). In January 1963, reviewing the lessons of an exhausted effort in Albany, Georgia, SCLC targeted Birmingham with the intent of securing commitments from the federal government. The method would be a simultaneous campaign of sit-ins and boycotts of downtown stores coinciding with Easter sales. Nothing was left to chance. Bond funds for expected mass jailings were raised, and Rev. Wyatt Tee Walker figured out how long it would take to walk from the Sixteenth Street Baptist Church to downtown. Stores were selected for sit-ins, and the number of stools, tables, and chairs was considered. SCLC was conscious of its role as an outsider and involved local preachers in the campaign.

The Freedom Rides Hit a Wall in Alabama

In 1961 a group of northern pacifists from the Congress of Racial Equality (CORE) decided to use federal authority over interstate bus terminals as the basis for the first interracial demonstrations in the Deep South. They envisioned a tour from Washington, D.C., to New Orleans with brief stops to challenge segregated waiting rooms and lunch counters, which were still common even if illegal. As predicted, violence erupted in and around Birmingham. The riders eventually made it on the ground only as far as Jackson, Mississippi, and then only under heavy guard.

The Greyhound bus that carried the Freedom Riders burns outside Anniston, May 14, 1961. (Archives Collection, Birmingham Public Library/Courtesy *Birmingham News*)

In those days Greyhound and Trailways each maintained separate bus fleets that crisscrossed the country. Towns of significant size usually had one station for each, equipped with separate waiting rooms and lunch counters for black and white. Segregated facilities cost up to 50 percent more in construction but were considered a necessity.

After the Supreme Court outlawed segregated seating in interstate travel in 1946, CORE tested its enforcement in the border states of Maryland, Virginia, North Carolina, and West Virginia. CORE called it the Journey of Reconciliation. After its members were arrested at the Trailways Station in Asheville, they were sentenced to thirty days on a North Carolina chain gang.

In 1960 the Supreme Court ruled that not only buses but also the attendant facilities serving interstate travelers had to be desegregated. Many southern terminals had adopted a semantical dodge by posting signs for WHITE INTRASTATE PASSENGERS, attempting to maintain segregation for in-state trips. In reality most bus stations in the Deep South were segregated for all passengers regardless of their destination.

CORE decided to test the law again, this time venturing into the Deep South states formerly considered too dangerous. The group was made up of six whites and seven blacks, including CORE's president, James Farmer. Their goal was to reach New Orleans by May 17, 1961, in time to celebrate the seventh anniversary of the *Brown* decision. The Freedom Riders, as they became known, set out on one Greyhound and one Trailways bus from Washington on May 4.

After minor incidents at stations in North Carolina, South Carolina, and Georgia, the buses approached Anniston, Alabama. The Greyhound bus was set upon by a mob of whites toting chains, sticks, and iron rods. They dented the bus, knocked out the windows, slashed the tires, and almost boarded the bus before Alabama patrolmen blocked their way. After about fifteen minutes police cleared a path for the bus to escape. It got about two miles out of town on Route 202 (near Hunter Street) before the tires gave out. The mob had followed in cars and descended on the bus in a frenzy of wild yells. They tossed a smoke bomb into the bus, and the passengers emerged gasping and sprawling onto the grass by the roadside. Many were beaten and hospitalized before highway patrolmen came to clear the area. A charred skeleton of the bus remained.

Meanwhile the Trailways bus driver, after hearing the sirens surrounding the Greyhound bus in the distance, stopped briefly in Anniston and then drove on to Birmingham. At the Trailways Station in Birmingham that same day a mob attacked the passengers as they exited the bus. James Peck required fifty-three stitches to close the wounds in his head from a beating with a iron pipe. Commissioner Bull Connor explained that the slow police response was a result of officers' celebrating Mother's Day. A group of riders appeared at the Greyhound Station, but no driver was willing to transport them. They went to the airport to take a twin-engine flight to New Orleans. Bomb threats delayed their departure. Finally, at 11:00 P.M., they took off.

After they heard of the original Freedom Riders' decision to complete their trip by air, a group of students from the Nashville Movement arrived, vowing to complete the journey on the ground. Two groups of ten students left final exams behind and traveled to Birmingham by car. When they showed up at the Greyhound Station, where no driver had yet materialized, they were taken to jail. Before dawn Bull Connor drove some of the Nashville students 120 miles to the state line, bantering all the way. Then he left them by the side of the road. They were back in Birmingham by nightfall and staged an all-night vigil at the Greyhound Station. After frantic negotiations among Kennedy officials, Alabama Governor John Patterson, and the bus company, the Nashville group left Birmingham by bus under state protection the next day.

At the city limits of Montgomery the Greyhound's escort of sixteen highway patrol cars and a plane melted away. By the time the bus arrived at the station

(continued on next page)

adjacent to the federal courthouse, the streets were eerily quiet. When the passengers got out, they and several bystanders were savagely beaten. Tension in Montgomery mounted until martial law was declared, and national guardsmen and U.S. marshals were sent in to restore calm. Four days later the Trailways bus headed for Jackson, proceeding past rows of national guardsmen with fixed bayonets. It bypassed Selma, where another hostile crowd reportedly was waiting. At the Mississippi border a change of the guard took place as Mississippi troopers took over for those from Alabama. After a nerve-bending 260 miles the bus arrived in Jackson, where some students were immediately arrested for crossing over into the white section of the station. They were the first of more than three hundred people to be arrested for testing transportation hubs in Jackson that summer. Although the mission was only partially fulfilled, it minted a new kind of Movement soldier.

Each day they hunkered down in room 30 of the Gaston Motel to talk strategy.

Simultaneously the city government was changed from a city commission, whose three members had stood firm as a post against integration, to a separate city council and mayor. A new nine-member council was elected on April 2, 1963, along with a new mayor, Albert Boutwell, who had defeated Bull Connor with the aid of black votes. But the old government refused to leave, and until a court decision ratified the reorganization, Birmingham was run by two parallel governments that took turns in the chairs of City Hall while SCLC's street demonstrations were going on. Bull Connor remained in control of the police department. In the extraordinary weeks that followed, a popular joke was that Birmingham was the only city with two mayors, a King, and a parade every day.

Mayor Boutwell had been in office only one day when the joint Movement forces launched Project C on April 3, 1963. Their demands were the desegregation of downtown lunch counters, rest rooms, and drinking fountains, the employment of black clerks in stores and city government, the reopening of the parks, and the establishment of a permanent biracial committee to deal with future problems. On that Wednesday morning, twenty-four Miles College students sat in at four local lunch counters—Kress, Woolworth's, Pizitz, and Loveman's—each of which responded by closing down.

Flashes of things to come appeared on Palm Sunday, April 7, when the Reverends A. D. King, N. H. Smith, and John Porter led

Children singing and marching in Birmingham, May 1963. (Charles Moore/Black Star)

about twenty-four protesters toward City Hall and were arrested. The following week black preachers appeared in their pulpits in blue jeans to emphasize the need to forgo new Easter clothes and to boycott downtown stores. SCLC still had trouble finding volunteers to march. As expected, the city got an order forbidding M. L. King, Jr., or Abernathy from leading demonstrations. King announced a Good Friday march and decided to violate the order to revive a lackluster campaign.

When King and Abernathy, dressed in new jeans, led a march on Good Friday, April 12, only fifty people followed them. At a police roadblock on Fifth Avenue North, Bull Connor arrested them. The arrest and jailing had the desired effect: a call from President Kennedy, renewed press interest, relief funds, and federal mediators. While in jail, King penned a sixty-five-hundred-word letter, a passionate, learned tour de force that months later became known as the "Letter from a Birmingham Jail." Eight days in jail had failed to coax marchers downtown, and once released on bond, King agreed to a risky strategy change: sending forth marching children.

Recruiting schoolchildren to face lines of armed police without protection was untested, and many people in the community were against it. Some whites complained that SCLC was brainwashing

The Letter from a Birmingham Jail

This wide-ranging and oft-studied polemic was written on a tear and under the pressure of solitary confinement. It is not only a potent argument for direct confrontation of segregation but also a glimpse down the well of King's psyche during a crisis. Here is one passage in which he rebuts the opinion of white moderates that direct action had come at the wrong time:

"Frankly, I have yet to engage in a direct-action campaign that was 'well timed' in the view of those who have not suffered unduly from the disease of segregation. For years now I have heard the word 'Wait!' It rings in the ear of every Negro with piercing familiarity. This 'Wait' has almost always meant 'Never.' We must come to see, with one of our distinguished jurists, that 'justice too long delayed is justice denied.'

"We have waited for more than 340 years for our constitutional and God-given rights. The nations of Asia and Africa are moving with jetlike speed toward gaining political independence, but we still creep at horse-and-buggy pace toward gaining a cup of coffee at a lunch counter. Perhaps it is easy for those who have never felt the stinging darts of segregation to say, 'Wait.' But when you have seen vicious mobs lynch your mothers and fathers at will and drown your sisters and brothers at whim; when you have seen hate-filled policemen curse, kick and even kill your black brothers and sisters; when you see the vast majority of your twenty million Negro brothers smothering in an airtight cage of poverty in the midst of an affluent society; when you suddenly find your tongue twisted and your speech stammering as you seek to explain to your six-year-old daughter why she can't go to the public amusement park that has just been advertised on television, and see tears welling up in her eyes when she is told that Funtown is closed to colored children, and see ominous clouds of inferiority beginning to form in her little mental sky, and see her beginning to distort her personality by developing an unconscious bitterness toward white people; when you have to concoct an answer for a five-year-old son who is asking: 'Daddy, why do white people treat colored people so mean?' . . .

"[W]hen you are harried by day and haunted by night by the fact that you are a Negro, living constantly at tiptoe stance, never quite knowing what to expect next, and are plagued with inner fears and outer resentments; when you are forever fighting a degenerating sense of 'nobodiness' then you will understand why we find it difficult to wait."[10]

"our Negro children," while many blacks thought luring them away from school was irresponsible. Nonetheless, hundreds of school children appeared at the Sixteenth Street Baptist Church on Thursday, May 2, 1963. Before King had a chance to see them off, they filed out into the sunshine and down the street, singing and clapping. While adults circled around with walkie-talkies, five hundred young marchers were arrested, necessitating the use of school buses when police vans became overloaded. Parker High School reported that up to 40 percent of the student body was absent that day.

The scene was repeated the next day; this time Bull Connor attempted to seal off the downtown business district with firemen and police officers holding leashed German shepherds. Black bystanders tossed bricks and bottles at the police and lobbed debris from nearby rooftops while four hundred whites lined the sidewalks to cheer the police on. By using water hoses and dogs to clear the streets surrounding Kelly Ingram Park of young demonstrators in full view of the cameras, Bull Connor in a few hours unwittingly branded Birmingham for life as an epitome of racial repression. Firefighters' tripod monitors channeled water from two hoses, which knocked the bark off trees a hundred feet away. The sight of jets of water pushing the children around like rag dolls as they huddled in storefronts, balled up on the sidewalk, or hid behind trees shocked the world.

On May 7 waves of students reached Twentieth Street in the middle of the business district, and some entered one store and sang freedom songs while sitting on the floor. Some students danced and

Firefighters hosing down student protesters, May 1963. (Charles Moore)

Police Monitors: Nothing but the Facts

Mass meetings, including outbreaks of ecstasy, were dutifully recorded by police monitors, who went in pairs to the meetings and transmitted the proceedings via shortwave radio to a patrol car to be condensed into written reports. Once the Movement lost a legal case to exclude the police from the meetings, the officers became useful props as a source of jokes and as examples of the enemy that the Movement faithful were supposed to love under the creed of nonviolence. Here is part of one police report of a meeting at the Sixth Avenue Baptist Church on May 2, 1963. That day hundreds of children had marched and been arrested for the first time:

"We arrived at approximately 6:00 p.m., and the main floor of the church was already full. Reverend Gardner was the first speaker. 'This has been a great day in Birmingham. We are going to change the name of the "tragic city" to the "magic city." ' . . . At this time they started taking up the offering. 'If you are dead broke, see me after the meeting.' . . . Fred Shuttlesworth came on. 'All we want to do is just walk, but everywhere we went the police blocked our way. They sure were tired. One policeman said to me, "Hey, Fred, how many more have you got," and I said at least 1,000 more; and the policeman said, "God Almighty."' . . . At this time Reverend King came back and said that James Bevel's wife is in jail in Atlanta for freedom and that Bernard Lee has been working with James Bevel stirring up the students. He said that Dick Gregory, the Negro comedian, is coming to Birmingham Sunday and will stay as long as he is needed. . . . [Bevel] led the church in singing, and the Negroes got all worked up while singing, stomping their feet and waving their arms and screaming. There were about 300 people standing and marching. The entire attendance was between 1,800 and 2,000. . . . They had another singing and that was the end."[11]

got soaked by the water again, quickly drying in the eighty-seven-degree heat and vowing to come back the next day with soap. The "freedom dash" downtown lacked the orderly formation of the previous marches and surprised white shoppers. Later that day Bull Connor brought out the high-powered hoses one more time. When he heard that Shuttlesworth had been injured by a water blast and taken to a hospital in an ambulance, Connor said, "I wish they'd carried him away in a hearse." The jails were jammed, as were the jails of neighboring towns, and the state fairgrounds were pressed into service to handle the overflow of prisoners.

At this point white negotiators, who had witnessed the protests firsthand during a lunch break, began to soften. That night they met with Movement negotiators at the downtown office of an insurance brokerage firm. Both the merchants, who felt the boycott immediately, and the executives in national companies, concerned about Birmingham's image elsewhere, had reasons to extend an offer. Movement negotiators agreed to their terms, and after some initial objections by Shuttlesworth, the leaders announced the settlement in the courtyard of the Gaston Motel on May 10, 1963.

The agreement to phase in integration was a victory for SCLC but hardly resolved racial tensions. On May 11 the Klan held a meeting of twelve hundred under two twenty-five-foot burning crosses in Moose Park in nearby Bessemer. That night a bomb exploded at the Gaston Motel, and another one went off at the home of Rev. A. D. King, Martin Luther King, Jr.'s brother, in Ensley. An angry crowd of blacks near the motel reacted violently to the dispatch of white state troopers, resulting in a fiery riot that destroyed stores and houses. A white armored police vehicle patrolled downtown. The next day federal troops were stationed in a twenty-eight-block area around the motel while M. L. King, Jr., made one of his periodic pool hall pilgrimages to plead for nonviolence. Fortunately the desegregation agreement—its reforms nearly a decade in the making—held.

The summer was calm, but the beginning of the school year revived racial violence. On Sunday morning, September 15, 1963, a blast was heard clear across the city. Dynamite left at the Sixteenth Street Baptist Church during the night exploded and killed four black girls, the oldest of whom was fourteen. Ambulances and police cars swarmed to the area, and some of the other parishioners who had arrived early for the Sunday service staggered away or drove off in whatever was left of their cars. In the disorder that followed, two other black children were shot and killed in other parts of Birmingham. The bombing crystallized for many people the sickening depths of racial hatred and contributed to the passage of the Civil Rights Act of 1964.

By late 1965 public life had been largely integrated, and the telltale WHITE and COLORED signs were gone. The city council had abolished the city's segregation ordinances. Thousands of new black voters had registered under the new Civil Rights Act. Blacks and whites lined up together for buses, attended integrated football games, and shopped at the downtown stores, which had hired about a dozen blacks. Still, no black police officers or firefighters had been hired, and the public school system was only beginning to integrate.

A sea change came in 1975, when black votes provided the mar-

The Postman's March

A quixotic white postal worker from Baltimore embarked on a fatal solo journey in northern Alabama while Birmingham was in the midst of Project C.

William Moore was born in Tennessee, served as a marine in Guam, and was committed in the 1950s to a psychiatric hospital, where he wrote a vivid account of the crude treatments he received called *The Mind in Chains*. After his release he moved back to his childhood home of Binghamton, New York, married, held a steady job as a letter carrier, and devoted all his free time to causes ranging from the fluoridation of the water supply to pacifism. He was drawn to racial injustice by the Freedom Rides and joined CORE when he moved to Baltimore in 1962.

He had tried freedom excursions before with little effect. He had walked from Baltimore to Annapolis to deliver a letter to the governor of Maryland, and on another occasion he had walked from Baltimore to Washington to deliver a letter to President Kennedy. His plan for the South was to walk three hundred miles from Chattanooga, Tennessee, across the northwest corner of Georgia into northeast Alabama and diagonally across the entire state, then another one hundred miles into the heart of Mississippi. He carried with him a letter addressed to Governor Ross Barnett that he intended to deliver at the state Capitol in Jackson. "The end of Mississippi colonialism is fast approaching," he wrote. "Be gracious."

On April 21, 1963, Moore set out from the Chattanooga bus station heading southwest on Highway 11 (now paralleled by U.S. 59), pushing a shopping cart full of leaflets and his belongings. He headed for Alabama wearing a sign that read END SEGREGATION IN AMERICA, EAT AT JOE'S BOTH BLACK AND WHITE on one side and EQUAL RIGHTS FOR ALL, MISSISSIPPI OR BUST on the other. The first day went smoothly as he crossed into Georgia. "No criticism of walk so far," he wrote in his journal. "Typical 'come back, hear' when I buy something." He got a free milk shake, lent a black boy a dime, and slept by the side of the road.

When he crossed over into De Kalb County, Alabama, he started to attract gawkers, who called him a "nigger lover," questioned his religious beliefs, or evinced plain bafflement. A motel owner in Fort Payne suggested he get a license plate for his pushcart. One bystander wondered whether he was promoting a new restaurant. By the time he crossed into Etowah County, he was walking barefoot but was still optimistic with reporters about making it the whole way. On the evening of April 23, 1963, however, Moore was found shot dead near a roadside stand near Attalla, Alabama. A grocer from Collbran who had accosted Moore twice on the road was arrested but never indicted for his death.

SNCC and CORE staffers vowed to retrace the postman's walk and continue it to Jackson. A band of ten activists, five from CORE and five from SNCC, took off from the Greyhound Station in Chattanooga with camping equipment to make the journey on May 1, 1963. Sam Shirah, a white SNCC worker, reproduced and wore a copy of Moore's original sandwich board message. On May 3 the marchers were arrested, taken to the De Kalb County jail in Fort Payne, and held for thirty-one days on charges of breaching the peace. Their convictions and two-hundred-dollar fines were reversed on appeal.

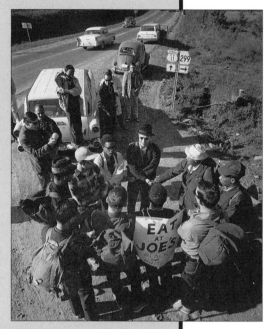

Marchers join hands during a break in their journey in memory of marcher and slain postal worker William Moore, May 1963. (Charles Moore)

gin in a close mayoral contest won by David Vann, a white liberal lawyer and negotiator during Project C. In October 1979 the city elected its first black mayor, former science teacher Richard Arrington, Jr. He had led the drive for affirmative action in the police and fire departments as a city council member in the 1970s. In office Arrington dealt with typical issues facing many southern cities in transition: reform of the police department and revitalization of downtown. After winning reelection in 1983 and 1987, Arrington supported the creation of the Civil Rights Institute and the overhaul of the area around Kelly Ingram Park, the most extensive commemorative effort of the Movement yet undertaken.

Old Sardis Baptist Church

1240 Fourth Street North (new church at 1615 Fourth Court West)

On June 5, 1956, people packed this 850-seat church, and the crowd spilled out onto the grass outside to witness the birth of a new organization in Birmingham, the ACMHR.

A thermometer near the pulpit read eighty-eight degrees, and Rev. Fred Shuttlesworth mopped his brow during his spirited address. "Our citizens are restive under the dismal yoke of segregation. Aren't you?" he said, drawing a roar of approval from the

---

A Profile of the ACMHR: More Than the "Talented Tenth"

In the spring of 1959 a graduate student from Ohio came to Birmingham and compiled a portrait of the nine hundred to twelve hundred members of the ACMHR when the Movement was in its adolescence. Although only a fraction of the black population, the ACMHR was one of the most unified and effective local groups in all of Alabama. Here is what she found:[12]

average family income	$3,715/year
women	60%
married	75%
never lived outside Alabama for a year	90%
professional	10%
semi-skilled workers (including housewife)	50%
unskilled workers	35%
practicing Baptists	90%
registered to vote, or attempted to	73%
said they attended weekly mass meetings	50%
said race relations had not improved since *Brown*	83%
favored nonviolent techniques	80%
favored mass meetings	51%
favored boycotts	32%
favored negotiation for change	22%
favored picketing	6%
considered themselves American first, then Negro	70%

Comment: "I try to think of myself first as an American, but usually not a day passes that I am not somehow reminded that I am first a Negro."

---

crowd. "Would you be willing tonight for a white man to sit down beside you?" Another roar of assent. "Then you believe in integration." A resurgent spirit continued through the usually mundane election of officers and discussion of the mechanics of expected legal challenges. During the first offering the ACMHR collected $245.

Bethel Baptist Church (Collegeville)

3233 Twenty-ninth Avenue North

In the 1950s tire tracks on a dirt road took a ninety-degree turn at this church. At 9:40 P.M. on Christmas Day 1956 six sticks of dynamite were tossed toward the parsonage next door to the church and landed near the corner of the house. Inside, Rev. Fred Shuttlesworth was sitting in his bedroom with a deacon from the church. The explosion knocked out the floor, collapsed the roof, and blew the springs of the mattress away, but somehow left Shuttlesworth unharmed. Mrs. Shuttlesworth recalled seeing the Christmas tree lights shining through the dusty wreckage. Both the fire department and a crowd of angry neighbors arrived. Shuttlesworth ducked out from under the splintered roof to calm the crowd, but not before he had put some pants on to go with his pajama top. Shuttlesworth was ever philosophical: "[T]hat bomb had my name on it, but God erased it off."

Bethel Baptist Church, formerly led by Rev. Fred Shuttlesworth, in 1996.
(Jessica Allan)

It was an anxious baptism for this residential corner of north Birmingham where the Bethel congregation teetered between inspiration and violence for the next seven years. Bethel members typically were engineers and other workers for the city's powerhouse steel, railroad, and pipe industries. Black union members guarded the church and rallied behind Shuttlesworth for the Movement cause.

Shuttlesworth had come to Bethel in March 1953 from a congregation in Selma. A slight man with ferocious personal courage, he was a driving force behind the founding of the ACMHR and frequently put himself and his family on the line to shame segregation. He was not one to delegate authority. As he said at the founding of the ACMHR, "If anybody gets arrested, it'll be me; if anybody goes to jail, it'll be me; if anybody suffers, it'll be me; if anybody gets killed, it'll be me." When Bull Connor later challenged him to take a lie detector test, he said he would, but only if Connor would as well. The idea was quickly dropped. This type of bravado won him devoted admirers, but not among the established blacks of Birmingham, some of whom considered him autocratic and impulsive.

After the first bombing Bethel built a brick parsonage across the street, and guards were posted outside. On June 29, 1958, a young girl returning home told the watchmen that something was smoking near the church. When they went and found the lit fuse of dynamite in a paint bucket, they hustled it across the street, dropped it, and ran. The blast blew out the just-replaced windows of the church and adjoining houses but did no damage to the structure. The church was bombed a third time in 1962.

In June 1961 Shuttlesworth surprised everyone by accepting the call of a church in Cincinnati, Ohio. He said he moved to the new church, which tripled his salary, to finance the college education of his children, but some people saw the move as a betrayal of his absolutist rhetoric. By that time his tangles with segregation had placed him in fourteen different lawsuits, landed him in police custody eleven times, and resulted in two bombings of his church. Still, he stayed involved and encouraged SCLC to make Birmingham the target of Project C in 1963.

After Shuttlesworth's departure the new pastor made it a policy that civil rights meetings would be held elsewhere. J. B. Stoner, a rabid white segregationist whom the watchmen here had identified as the man who frequently surveilled the church in a yellow cab, was convicted of the 1958 bombing in 1980.

Phillips High School

2316 Seventh Avenue North

On September 9, 1957, Shuttlesworth approached this block-long structure in his car with the intention of visiting the registration office. With him were his wife, fellow preacher Rev. J. S. Phifer, and four black teenage children, two of whom were his own. As Shuttlesworth got out of the car, groups of white men approached from either side of the block and across the street, while a single patrolman radioed for help. A group grabbed Shuttlesworth and subdued him with brass knuckles and chains. When the police finally arrived to break up the melee, Shuttlesworth escaped to his car, but not before the gang had smashed the windows, grabbed at the passengers, and stabbed Mrs. Shuttlesworth in the hip. Birmingham police arrested three of the assailants, but a grand jury later dropped the charges.

Greyhound Bus Station

Seventh Avenue North and Nineteenth Street

Despite Bull Connor's attempts to deport them, the Nashville Freedom Riders stayed at this station until they could get a ride to Montgomery in May 1961. At this point in the trip the Freedom Rides were transformed from a barely noticed pilgrimage to a hot-button issue for the Kennedy White House and the military. Today the depot still operates as a bus station.

Kelly Ingram Park

Sixteenth and Seventeenth Streets, Fifth and Sixth Avenues North

Nothing in the civil rights landscape has changed as much as this public park, named for a Birmingham firefighter who was the first sailor in the U.S. Navy killed in World War I. It is best known today as the battlefield where lines of children faced Bull Connor's forces in 1963.

The park in those days bordered a black business district built around Fourth Avenue. People filled the streets, lined with beauty shops, barbershops, shoe repair shops, and cleaners, and ate hot dogs or drank milk shakes at the drugstore. In the Masonic Temple (1630 Fourth Avenue North) were the law offices of Peter Hall, Arthur Shores, and Orzell Billingsley. The office of Oscar Adams, Jr., later the first black to hold a statewide judgeship, and the *Birmingham World*, a leading black newspaper, were nearby.

At the northwest corner of the park stood the Sixteenth Street

A statue in Kelly Ingram Park depicting a demonstrator in the grip of a police officer . . . (Jessica Allan)

. . . and the photograph on which it was based. (AP/Wide World Photos)

Baptist Church, the origin of many marches during Project C. When black children emerged in droves from the church on May 2, 1963, and came into the park to face police dogs and fire hoses, Bull Connor said, "Let 'em have it." Their singing was silenced by rushing water from the fire hoses, which sent many children fleeing back into the church.

More dangerous by far were the early-morning hours of May 12, 1963, when the fragile desegregation agreement was jeopardized by a bombing at the Gaston Motel and a riotous aftermath in and around the park. Patrons of the nearby local bars and pool halls reacted to the explosion with anger and rock throwing, and cars were overturned and burned. In the end, six businesses and an apartment complex were burned, and seventy people were hospitalized. President Kennedy had to call in army troops to restore calm.

Today the park is serene, handsomely paved with multicolored brick. Landscape designers have renovated it under the dual banner of revolution and reconciliation. Water slips quietly over four quadrants of granite, balanced by sculptures of snarling dogs in mid-leap and a black demonstrator in the grip of a police officer (based on a famous newsphoto from the Project C demonstrations). Three preachers who preceded King's trip to jail are rendered in white stone kneeling before their arrest in the eastern corner of the park.

Birmingham Civil Rights Institute

520 Sixteenth Street North

Opened in 1992, the Civil Rights Institute was the centerpiece of a fifteen-million-dollar renovation that encompassed Kelly Ingram Park and the Sixteenth Street Baptist Church. A stately brick building with a white dome, it educates visitors about the Movement in innovative ways. The journey from the ticket window into the courtyard is meant to evoke a minimarch. The rotunda is designed for eighty people, the equivalent of two busloads of arrested children. After a visual presentation, a screen rises to reveal a single water fountain, marked COLORED.

In the extensive installations that follow, the institute succeeds where simple memorials fall short. A burned and bashed Greyhound bus—which was found in Maine, treated in Nashville, and hoisted onto the second floor during construction of the building—simulates the Freedom Riders' bus that was burned by a mob in Anniston. The actual bars of King's cell from the City Jail (Southside) have been reinstalled in another exhibit. Out front a bronze Rev. Fred Shuttlesworth looks out over the park with his trademark furrowed brow.

A. G. Gaston Gardens (formerly the Gaston Motel)

1501 Fifth Avenue North

"Cool, Comfortable, Air Conditioned" was how the Gaston Motel was described in a motor touring guide for blacks in the early 1960s. The only first-class accommodation for blacks in the Magic City, it was a Movement headquarters. King and Abernathy both were registered to double room 30 during Project C, although one of them sometimes slept in room 29 under an assumed name. Today the motel is a home for the elderly.

The motel was just one piece of a downtown empire created by black entrepreneur Arthur George Gaston. He got into business by selling burial insurance, then steadily acquired a funeral home, a bottling company, an insurance company, a savings and loan, a boys' club, a drugstore, a home for the elderly, and a radio station. The Gaston Motel opened in 1954, and its restaurant quickly became a popular place for family dinners. By the time SCLC arrived in 1963, downtown black Birmingham was a virtual Gastonopoly. Gaston also provided bail money and arranged special classes for black men to study for the police examination. A. G. Gaston died in 1996 at the age of one hundred and four.

Room 30 was the scene of numerous strategy meetings, including Rev. King's momentous decision to defy a court order banning marches and to go to jail after leading a demonstration on Good Friday in 1963. Less than a month later, on May 10, Shuttlesworth, King, and Abernathy announced the desegregation agreement that concluded Project C to a crowd of reporters in the motel courtyard and balcony.

King, Rev. Wyatt Tee Walker (standing), and Rev. Ralph Abernathy during a press conference in the courtyard of the Gaston Motel, 1963. (Ernst Haas/Magnum Photos)

Peace did not last long. A bomb pitched into a parking lot next door to the motel the next night ripped through the reception area, apparently intended for room 30 above. SCLC's Rev. Joseph Lowery had been scheduled to stay there that night, but he had boarded the night train home to Nashville; King had returned to Atlanta for Sunday services. The blast knocked a hole in the Fifth Avenue side of the building, and four blacks were taken away in ambulances. The Gaston Motel then became the epicenter of rioting that seized downtown until dawn.

Birmingham Realty Office

2118 First Avenue North

The 1963 Birmingham campaign was one of the few that ended with a negotiated settlement rather than a court order or legislation. Although the long-standing animosity between Shuttlesworth and the old city commission made meaningful discussion impossible, the combined force of a new city government and SCLC's 1963 campaign paved the way for a new pragmatism. Mediators included scholar Vincent Harding and Kennedy official Burke Marshall. Much of the negotiating was done by local people either at downtown spots such as this office or at churches and private homes. Businessman Sidney Smyer, lawyer David Vann, and Billy Hamilton, aide to Mayor Boutwell, represented the white business community and the government. The Movement demands came from negotiators Shuttlesworth, attorney Arthur Shores, Andrew Young, A. G. Gaston, John and Addine Drew, Mrs. Tyree Barefield-Pendleton, Dr. Lucius Pitts of Miles College, and the Reverends Harold Long, Nelson H. Smith, John T. Porter, and Abraham L. Woods, Jr. This office is also where the campaign to institute the mayor-council form of government was planned.

City Jail (Southside)

417 Sixth Avenue South

After his arrest on Good Friday in 1963 King was held here for eight days along with Rev. Ralph Abernathy. King's initial hours in solitary confinement with no mattress were "the longest, most frustrating and bewildering hours I have lived," he wrote later that year. He called his wife, Coretta, and found out that President Kennedy had called her to express sympathy, a call similar to one he had made before his election in 1960, when King was held in a Georgia jail.

After reading that eight white ministers had issued a joint statement decrying the street marches of Project C, King sat down and wrote his "Letter from a Birmingham Jail" in the margins of the newspaper where the ministers' criticism had appeared. The letter reached the outside world in pieces through people who came to visit him and was typed by Rev. Wyatt Tee Walker and his staff back at the Gaston Motel. After the Birmingham campaign was over, the letter became a classic document of American history.

All in all, about twenty-five hundred people were arrested during the Birmingham campaign of April and May 1963. When the city jail was full, they were taken to one of the two county jails or a state campground. At mass meetings the prisoners frequently were called upon to recount their jail experiences, and one group reported that the Southside jail had been renamed Connor's Chapel Church for Freedom. Today it is a three-story tan administrative building used by the Birmingham Police Department, and King's cell has been reconstructed with the original bars in the Birmingham Civil Rights Institute.

Old New Pilgrim Baptist Church
903 Sixth Avenue South
(new church at 708 Goldwire Place Southwest)

The first regular Monday night mass meeting was held here on June 11, 1956. With the ACMHR less than a week old, the goals of desegregating the city buses and cracking the civil service exam were announced. Rev. R. L. Alford, an ACMHR founder, said, "The South is dealing with a new Negro. It's too free for some, not free enough for others."

Phone Call From a Birmingham Jail

King called his wife from a pay phone at the City Jail during his confinement, although he suspected correctly that he was being bugged. Here is an excerpt:

Coretta: Hello, dear.

Martin: Hi, darling.

Coretta: How are you?

Martin: Pretty good, how are you making it?

Coretta: We're doing pretty good, wanting to hear from you.

Martin: I just read your lovely letter.

Coretta: You just got it?

Martin: Yes.

[Reverend King speaks with two of his children, and Coretta informs him that President Kennedy has called.]

Martin: Who did you say called you?

Coretta: Kennedy, the President.

Martin: Did he call you direct?

Coretta: Yes, and he told me you were going to call in a few minutes. It was about thirty minutes ago. He called from Palm Beach. I tried to phone him yesterday.

Martin: Is that known?

Coretta: It's known here, I just got it.

Martin: Let Wyatt know.

Coretta: The Executive in Birmingham?

Martin: Yes, do that right now. How's the baby, how's Bernice?

Coretta: Fine, growing and cute as a button.

Martin: That's wonderful. . . .

Coretta: Is your spirit all right?

Martin: Yes, I've been alone, you know.

Coretta: Yes, I know that.

[They discuss the FBI, press reaction, travel plans, and their income tax return.]

Coretta: Are you getting your vitamin pills?

Martin: Yes, everything is fine. Don't worry, and I'll see you Thursday.[13]

New Pilgrim was pastored by Rev. Nelson H. Smith, Jr., nicknamed Fireball for his rousing preaching style. He joined Shuttlesworth's first campaign to desegregate the city buses and was frequently at his side.

New Pilgrim was also the origin of a remarkable spontaneous march on May 5, 1963, at the height of the Project C street demonstrations. Rev. James Bevel, the firebrand organizer, urged a packed congregation to walk in protest up Sixth Avenue toward the City Jail (Southside) after white folksingers Guy and Candie Carawan had been arrested on the church steps. After walking several blocks to a hastily assembled police and fire roadblock, Rev. Charles Billups led the line down to its knees in prayer. Then he stood and said, "Turn on your water. Turn loose your dogs. We will stand here till we die." For some reason, mechanical or human, the firefighters did not unleash the water, and after Bull Connor granted the marchers' request to pray in the park, they simply walked past the hoses.

After the bombings of A. D. King's house and the Gaston Motel in May 1963, New Pilgrim was the site of a meeting hosting the National Council of Negro Women, one of the few contemporaneous recognitions of female contributions to the Movement. Smith is still the pastor, as he has been since 1953, now in a new church. The old one is a day-care facility.

The Vital Energy of Mass Meetings in Birmingham

The art of the mass meeting reached its highest form in Birmingham. Beginning in June 1956, every Monday night and then nightly for nearly two months during Project C, mass meetings were the essential ingredient of the Movement. They were held at night so that working people could attend, and they began at seven, although people often arrived hours earlier to get a seat. Speakers from the pulpit fed the audience with exhortations, satire, and information and drew strength from the responses of "well," "yes," and "all right" that rolled from the crowd along with rollicking applause and the rumble of feet drumming on wooden floorboards. Ushers sat people down or escorted them outside when they were seized with the spirit.

The meetings played both a cathartic and a solidifying role. They often lasted two to three hours, running longer during the 1963 campaign when celebrities were in town. During a crisis meetings begun in one church overflowed into a second, third, or fourth church nearby. As in Montgomery, several dozen churches took turns hosting the meetings.

Reverends Shuttlesworth, Nelson ("Fireball") Smith, and J. S. Phifer frequently rallied the crowd with inspirational speeches. "A man told me yesterday that what we were doing in Birmingham was creating nothing but chaos," Smith said at one meeting in April 1963 at the outset of the SCLC campaign. "I told him it's dark in Birmingham now and that it's going to get darker, but when it is the darkest, that's when you can see the stars of freedom."

St. James Baptist Church

1220 Twentieth Street North

Here King announced his 1963 Good Friday march. "I can't think of a better day than Good Friday for a move for Freedom," he said. The church also hosted an inspiring mass meeting on May 6, 1963, when the children's marches were bringing the Birmingham campaign to a close. The meeting overflowed to Thirgood Memorial CME Church (1027 Seventh Avenue North), to St. Luke AME Church (3937 Twelfth Avenue North), and finally to St. Paul United Methodist Church. A staggering forty thousand dollars was collected that night, as five thousand to ten thousand people filled the four churches. Originally at Sixth Avenue North, the church moved to its present site in 1968.

St. John AME Church

708 Fifteenth Street North

Once terms of the Birmingham agreement were announced, a triumphant mass meeting was held here with Abernathy stirring the crowd until it started a rhythmic "King" chant. King then announced the details of desegregation of downtown stores and noted the support the Birmingham campaign had garnered from the far corners of the world.

The service for fourteen-year-old Carole Robertson also took place here. The girl's father was a church member who declined the request of King to memorialize his daughter along with the other three bombing victims. On September 17, 1963, with about two thousand people present, Rev. John Cross led the memorial service for her. Rev. C. E. Thomas urged the congregation to "keep cool heads" in the midst of tragedy. "We cannot win freedom with violence." Afterward a silent crowd proceeded to Shadow Lawn, a segregated cemetery.

Site of Sixth Avenue Baptist Church

formerly at Sixteenth Street and Sixth Avenue South
(new church at 1101 Martin Luther King Drive Southwest)

When Rev. John Porter was installed as pastor here on December 9, 1962, King came over from Ebenezer Baptist Church in Atlanta to deliver the installation sermon. At King's first church, Dexter Avenue Baptist in Montgomery, Porter had served as King's assistant, and he hosted the SCLC campaign the following spring.

The church (now torn down) mirrored the Sixteenth Street Baptist Church, which was designed by the same architect in a similar

Rev. Fred Shuttlesworth at the Sixth Avenue Baptist Church, where three of the four girls killed in an explosion at the Sixteenth Street Baptist Church were memorialized. (Danny Lyon/Magnum Photos)

Byzantine style. It offered the largest sanctuary in the city and was a natural place for mass meetings. Porter was one of three prominent preachers who on Palm Sunday 1963 marched toward City Hall, knelt in front of a line of police, and were carted off to jail. The scene is now depicted in a white stone sculpture in Kelly Ingram Park.

Two momentous meetings were held here after Movement and white business leaders had agreed to a desegregation plan. After the rioting in and around Kelly Ingram Park on May 12, King, bolstered by the presence of baseball player Jackie Robinson and boxer Floyd Patterson, announced that the agreement would hold. Four months later on September 18, 1963, the funeral for three of the four girls killed in the Sixteenth Street Baptist Church bombing also was held here. About seven thousand people lined the streets and filled the church to hear the eulogy of Rev. John Cross and a speech by King. Today the site is part of Cooper Green Hospital.

First Baptist Church (Ensley)
Nineteenth Street and Avenue O, Ensley

This church was led by King's younger brother, Alfred Daniels Williams King, known as A.D., who made significant contributions of his own to the Movement in Birmingham and elsewhere.

In April 1963 Rev. Wyatt Tee Walker briefed about sixty-five people who had signed up to go to jail on the first day of the downtown demonstrations here, mapping maneuvers out on a blackboard. On April 7 A. D. King himself, along with Reverends Porter and Smith, led the Palm Sunday march toward City Hall and was jailed.

After being released from jail, A. D. King returned to his house (721 Twelfth Street, Ensley) from a mass meeting at First Baptist to retire for the night on Saturday, May 11, 1963. A bomb exploded in the front of the house, and he rushed to the living room to retrieve his wife, Naomi, and their five children. They escaped out the back door just before a second blast demolished the front. When an angry crowd gathered and threatened to vent its rage on white police, A. D. King performed an act similar to his brother's postbombing speech from the porch of his house in Montgomery six years before and requiring as much courage. He took a bullhorn, pleaded for nonviolence from his porch, and successfully led the crowd in a rendition of "We Shall Overcome." He calmed the crowd again when another explosion twenty minutes later rocked the Gaston Motel downtown. Even though his house had just been bombed, he urged adherence to the desegregation settlement that had been reached the previous day.

A. D. King later went on to pastor the Zion Baptist Church in Louisville, Kentucky. He died in a swimming pool accident in 1969.

Today First Baptist is pastored by a Movement activist who made his name in the Black Belt of Alabama. Rev. Thomas Gilmore was born in Eutaw, Alabama, and was recruited for the Movement by James Orange, a longtime activist who started in Birmingham. Gilmore later became the first black sheriff of Greene County in the pathbreaking elections of 1970. He stayed there for three terms, reputed to be "the sheriff without a gun," until his departure in 1983.

Sixteenth Street Baptist Church
1530 Sixth Avenue North

When architects from the U.S. government came to this church in 1993 to assess it as a historic site, they made a remarkable discovery. Since its construction in 1909–11, the building walls had shifted only a quarter of an inch, a testament to the high quality of its masonry. The church was designed by black architect Wallace Rayfield and built by black contractor Thomas Windham. It served for decades as a center of black society and worship. During the civil rights era it was adopted as the Movement's fortress, sheltered marchers, and survived a tragic bombing in fall 1963. Through it all, it had remained a rock of faith, situated on a corner across from Kelly Ingram Park.

Sixteenth Street was not initially a Movement church. Although its pastor was willing to let SCLC use the building for its preparatory conference in fall 1962, he asked that the church be reimbursed for the cost of using the lights for two night meetings. But by 1963 Pastor John Cross had allowed the Movement in for the all-important tasks of dispensing news, recruiting volunteers, and shoring up the hopes of the doubtful. The SCLC campaign moved into high gear when thousands of children appeared here on May 2, 1963, and poured out into the park and eventually to jail. When police and firefighters set up high-powered hoses at the edge of the park, they sprayed so much water toward retreating marchers that the church basement flooded and had to be pumped out.

After the desegregation settlement was announced a week later, parishioners had reason to believe that things might be calmer. On Sunday morning, September 15, 1963, the church was abuzz with preparations for Youth Day, during which children would conduct the service. After Sunday school five girls were primping in front of a mirror in the ladies' lounge in the basement. One girl was fixing another's dress sash. Several adults were attending class in the choir loft. Although dozens of people, including the church custodian, had walked up the staircase leading to the northeast entrance of the church that morning, none noticed a greenish brown paper package full of dynamite just below the stairs.

Window of the Sixteenth Street Baptist Church after the fatal explosion on September 15, 1963. (Danny Lyon/Magnum Photos)

At 10:22 A.M. a thunderous blast shook the church, followed by a torrent of glass and debris. The blast knocked out the staircase, dislodged the brick and stone outside wall, and brought it down on the girls in the basement. Out of the rubble came twelve-year-old Sarah Collins, calling the name of her sister Addie Mae. Partially blinded and riddled with twenty-one pieces of glass, she was the only one in the room who survived.

In the hours that followed, the bodies of four other children were extracted and carried off on stretchers: Denise McNair, eleven; Addie Mae Collins, fourteen; Carole Robertson, fourteen; and Cynthia Wesley, fourteen. The immediate aftermath was a whirlwind of sirens, distraught mourners, and police barricades. The pastor, John Cross, attempted to calm the crowd, even as his four-year-old daughter, Susan, was taken to the hospital.

When the smoke cleared, most of the stained glass windows were gone or damaged. One pane on the north wall across the sanctuary from the bomb blast, which depicted Jesus as described in Revelation ("Behold I stand at the door and knock"), remained intact except for an eerie pocket of air where the face had once been.

In the worldwide outpouring of sympathy that followed, no act was more fitting than that from the people of Wales: a new stained glass window in the balcony. Welsh artist John Petts created one of the first representations of Christ as a black man, a crucified figure with a left hand raised in protest and a right hand extended in reconciliation. The window was unveiled on June 6, 1965, bearing the inscription "You Do It to Me."

A renovation begun in 1991 has restored the church to its original stateliness outside and given it a plush new inside.

Shadow Lawn Cemetery
120 Summit Parkway, Homewood

Denise McNair, a victim of the Sixteenth Street church bombing, is buried here. Her headstone reads, "She loved all, but a mad bomber hated her kind."

Greenwood Cemetery
Airport Boulevard and Aviation Drive (southeast corner)

Three of the four girls who died in the Sixteenth Street bombing are buried here: Carole Robertson, Cynthia Wesley, and Addie Mae Collins.

Jefferson County Courthouse
716 Twenty-first Street North

Etched in stone over the courthouse entrance is a quote from Thomas Jefferson: "Equal and Exact Justice to All Men of Whatever State or Persuasion." Here Judge William A. Jenkins issued orders forbidding more than three people to gather and march, forcing King and his followers to conduct Project C in violation of a court order.

Fourteen years after the 1963 campaign, in room 306, Alabama closed the book on one of its bleakest chapters. The case of the Sixteenth Street Baptist Church bombing of 1963, despite a thorough FBI investigation, had never resulted in a murder indictment until state Attorney General William Baxley reactivated it in 1977.

Baxley brought to trial a man notorious for racial hostility. Robert Chambliss was a lifelong Klan member who had once pushed Rev. Fred Shuttlesworth from the entrance of a train station. Along with two associates, Chambliss had earlier been charged with transportation and possession of dynamite, a misdemeanor. In November 1977 he was tried for the murder of Denise McNair, one of the four girls who died in the bombing.

At the trial a changed Birmingham got a glimpse of the old world. Elizabeth Cobbs, a niece of Chambliss who as a little girl had worked with her mother and two aunts to sew Klan robes, testified for the prosecution after more than a decade in exile from her own family. The pastor of Sixteenth Street Baptist Church, John Cross, described how he had conducted Sunday school on the morning of the explosion. Sarah Collins Riley, now twenty-seven and having lost her right eye and her sister in the explosion, testified as the only surviving witness from the basement lounge where the explosion hit hardest. Defending Chambliss was Art Hanes, the segregationist former mayor of Birmingham, and his son, Art Hanes, Jr.

The evidence showed that on September 4, 1963, Chambliss went to Leon Negron's general store in Daisy City and bought a case of dynamite, blasting caps, and a roll of fuse. Over breakfast on Saturday, September 14, he went into a rage in front of Cobbs, his young niece. "Just wait until after Sunday morning, and they'll beg us to let them segregate," he said. "I've got enough stuff put away to flatten half of Birmingham."

This statement, combined with the recovery of a fishing bobber used to trigger the fuse and an eyewitness who placed Chambliss at the scene, was key to the jury's verdict finding Chambliss guilty as charged. After winning the convictions, Baxley ran for governor in 1978 and lost. The state's star witness, Elizabeth Cobbs, later wrote a book about the investigation and trial under her new name as a man, Petric Justice Smith.

Armstrong's Barbershop
708 Eighth Avenue North

For more than forty years former army man James Armstrong has been cutting hair here. Owning his own business gave him the independence to support the Movement from the beginning. If there were front-line duties, he was there: at the Greyhound Station attempting to integrate the waiting room, with Shuttlesworth in Gadsden to retrieve Shuttlesworth's jailed children, and in the city jail in April 1963 after the ACMHR's first effort to integrate downtown stores. Armstrong's family was one of the eight black families who sued in August 1957 to integrate the public elementary schools, and his children, Dwight and Floyd, were the first blacks to be admitted to Graymont School in 1963.

A flag bearer in his army unit, Armstrong also was designated to carry an American flag during the 1965 march from Selma to Montgomery. Since then he has carried a flag during commemorative retracings of that route. During one of the

James Armstrong, barber and Movement veteran, in his shop, 1996. (Townsend Davis)

marches, which went all the way to Washington, D.C., he wore out two pairs of size 11D shoes.

The barbershop is still in operation. The window bears the warning "If You Don't Vote, Don't Talk Politics in Here." Old magazines are stuffed in a rack, and photos of black officeholders from across the nation adorn the walls. Why doesn't he give it up, as his children have urged? "I just stay down there and enjoy the lies," he says.

Dynamite Hill

Center Street

Birmingham's zoning ordinances, enacted in 1926, dictated that blacks and whites live in separate neighborhoods. Although these laws eventually were invalidated in the courts, people clung to the old boundaries. Blacks lived on the east side of Center Street and north of Eleventh Avenue; whites lived on the west side of Center

Street. In the 1940s blacks began to buy property in formerly white or border areas, and the city commission in March 1949 made crossing by either race into the area of the other a misdemeanor. Soon thereafter explosions went off simultaneously at three houses recently purchased by blacks. In 1950, when it became apparent the city police were not investigating the prior incidents, blacks formed an armed guard. When they got word of a Klan plan to torch a house purchased by a black from a white resident, they lay in wait and engaged the Klansmen in a full-scale shoot-out. These incidents transformed the neighborhood known as Smithfield into a racial borderland called Dynamite Hill.

After the creation of the ACMHR in 1956, blacks continued to buy in formerly white neighborhoods, and the bombings resumed. The hill was full of activity during the negotiations over Project C in May 1963 and again became a bombing target with two bombings of Arthur Shores's house in fall 1963.

John Drew House

1108 Center Street North

Insurance executive John Drew and his wife, Addine, were frequent hosts to King at their house, which also became a haven for negotiators. Both Drews maintained the respect of blacks and whites and labored hard for the defeat of segregation. The original house was near the top of Dynamite Hill.

On May 6, 1963, Kennedy aide Burke Marshall held initial talks with King at the Drews' house to curtail street demonstrations while negotiations with merchants went forward. The next day, after students had swamped the downtown sidewalks and business leaders had approved direct talks, black negotiators and King gathered at the Drews' to hammer out details of an agreement.

Later, when a new freeway ran straight through the Drews' property, they rebuilt on what remained of the land, the site of the current house. Mrs. Drew still lives here.

Arthur Shores House

1021 Center Street North

The son of a Birmingham man who worked for a prominent white Alabama judge, Arthur Shores passed the Alabama bar in 1937 and became the first black trial lawyer in the state. He devoted much of his long legal career to dismantling segregation, serving as dean to a group of pioneering Alabama black lawyers.

Early on Shores became the NAACP's point man in Alabama, representing black labor leader Will Hall and pushing for equalization of black teachers' salaries and job opportunities on the railroad. He represented Mary Means Monk, a black schoolteacher who had moved into Dynamite Hill. The favorable ruling he won in 1949 was followed by a Klan bombing that destroyed her house. By the time Shores represented King in the antiboycott trial in Montgomery in 1956, he had already handled many of the formative cases in civil rights law.

His most celebrated case was his petition to get black student Autherine Lucy admitted to the University of Alabama in a graduate program in library sciences. After a three-and-a-half-year legal battle, Lucy attended her first class at Smith Hall on the Tuscaloosa campus on February 1, 1956. After she was pelted with rocks and eggs by angry white students, she fled the campus in a patrol car and was suspended by the university in the name of public safety. The school remained impervious to integration until George Wallace's notorious schoolhouse door stance in 1963 was reversed by federal force.

In August 1963, the day after a court order integrating Birmingham's high schools, Shores was sitting in his living room watching television when he heard a blast that dug a three-foot hole in his driveway. The explosion damaged two cars parked in his attached garage and destroyed a game room over it. As one jaded neighbor told reporters, "It sounded like the usual explosion we've had in this area." On September 5 a second blast ripped the house, this time blowing down the front door just before Shores reached for it to take a walk outside.

In 1968 Shores was appointed to the city council, and he was elected in 1969 and 1973, when he got more votes than any other candidate. On the basis of his work in Jefferson County, he became the first president of the Alabama Democratic Conference. He died in 1996.

Ollie's Barbecue

515 University Boulevard

This family-owned barbecue spot was one of the two facilities (the Heart of Atlanta Motel was the other) to take its constitutional challenge to the 1964 Civil Rights Act all the way to the U.S. Supreme Court. Ollie's refused to serve blacks in its dining room, although blacks were allowed to purchase takeout and constituted about two thirds of the service staff. The issue in the legal case was whether Ollie's was sufficiently engaged in interstate commerce to

Three preachers rendered in stone in Kelly Ingram Park today, based on the Palm Sunday march of April 7, 1963, with the Sixteenth Street Baptist Church in the background. (Townsend Davis)

justify a federal mandate that blacks be served on an equal basis. The Court decided that because half of Ollie's food supplies originated out of state, its business crossed state lines, enabling Congress to impose a racially neutral service policy. The restaurant, now a fourteen-sided building at a new location since the Court challenge, celebrated its seventieth year in business in 1997.

Selma, Alabama

Bloody Sunday and the March to Montgomery

When twenty-two-year-old activist Bernard Lafayette pulled into Selma in his '48 Chevy in February 1963, the city still clung to its image as a genteel cotton trading town. SNCC had assigned Lafayette to start a voting registration campaign here almost as an afterthought.

The outlook was not very promising. As of 1961, only 156 of

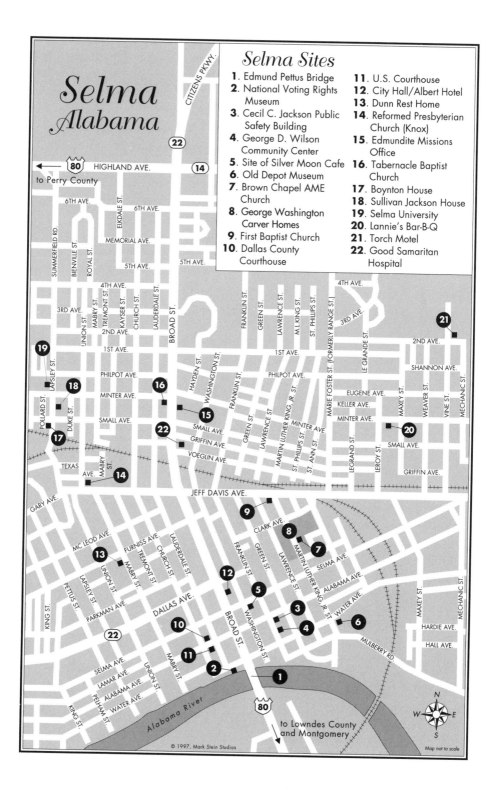

Selma
Alabama

to Perry County

Selma Sites

1. Edmund Pettus Bridge
2. National Voting Rights Museum
3. Cecil C. Jackson Public Safety Building
4. George D. Wilson Community Center
5. Site of Silver Moon Cafe
6. Old Depot Museum
7. Brown Chapel AME Church
8. George Washington Carver Homes
9. First Baptist Church
10. Dallas County Courthouse
11. U.S. Courthouse
12. City Hall/Albert Hotel
13. Dunn Rest Home
14. Reformed Presbyterian Church (Knox)
15. Edmundite Missions Office
16. Tabernacle Baptist Church
17. Boynton House
18. Sullivan Jackson House
19. Selma University
20. Lannie's Bar-B-Q
21. Torch Motel
22. Good Samaritan Hospital

© 1997, Mark Stein Studios

Map not to scale

to Lowndes County and Montgomery

15,000 eligible blacks had registered to vote in Dallas County, of which Selma was the seat. Two years of Justice Department litigation under federal voting rights laws had raised the number to only 300. After initial forays SNCC had concluded that Selma's black leaders were not interested in jeopardizing their selective influence with whites, and in the rural areas SNCC found people who didn't know what voting was. Lafayette and his new wife were the entire staff, and they had trouble finding a landlord who would rent to them. Selma had lost its major-league farm team the year before, after the Southern League had refused to integrate, and George Wallace had just been inaugurated governor of Alabama.

Situated on a bluff above the Alabama River in the heart of the Black Belt, Selma had been home to blacks who had served as congressmen, city councilmen, tax collector, and criminal court judge during Reconstruction and supported thriving black businesses. In 1867 Selma hired the first black police officer in Alabama and had blacks on the force for the next thirty years. The city boasted both

The Alabama Black Belt

The Alabama Black Belt got its name from the rich dark soil, ideal for farming, that cuts through south-central Alabama from Montgomery to Meridian, Mississippi. It covers about thirteen thousand square miles and fifteen counties. According to one resident, the thick "gumbo-type soil" is legendary. Local lore warns that a horse should tread lightly in the area when it rains for fear of sinking a foot into the mud and losing a horseshoe in trying to escape. The mud's adhesive power made for slow going during the Selma to Montgomery March of 1965. Although the Black Belt supplied more than half of Alabama's cotton crop before the Civil War, erosion and a shift to cattle and timber reduced its role as a supplier of crops.

The Black Belt also has a political meaning. The region relied heavily on slave and sharecropping labor and has a majority black population. It long attracted the interest of activists because it contained not only the harshest conditions for blacks and dismal voting registration figures but also the potential for eventual impact at the polls. Movement efforts in the mid-sixties focused on eight counties that straddled the white majority in Montgomery County, home to the state capital: Lowndes, Wilcox, Dallas, Perry, Marengo, Hale, Sumter, and Greene. The Black Belt then was alternately thought of as a bastion the Movement should take on or as a nut that was too hard in its old ways to crack. Today, after successful registration drives in these counties, blacks predominate in local offices.

Selma University, a Baptist college founded in 1878, and Payne University, founded by the AME Church in 1899. But by the early 1900s the grip of Jim Crow laws and the sharecropping system had returned blacks to a self-contained, parallel world. In the decades that followed, blacks lived primarily in east Selma, and whites in the west, each constituting about half the population. All the government officials and civic leaders were white. Almost all the roads in the black neighborhood were dirt because the city required blacks to pay for their own paving.

Through the years blacks in Selma had made periodic efforts to organize for better treatment. The Dallas County Voters League (DCVL) was founded in the 1920s and was revived by Samuel W. Boynton in 1936 with a proposal to extend a black public school up to the twelfth grade. By fall 1955 blacks in Selma had joined dozens of communities across the South in submitting a petition to the school board echoing a recent U.S. Supreme Court ruling that required the *Brown* decision to be enforced "with all deliberate speed." Boynton kept an honor roll of blacks who successfully negotiated the maze of voting registration, and in the case of a dental hygienist named Marie Foster, that took eight years. Mrs. Foster, herself a member of the DCVL, held citizenship classes starting in 1963 with a single sixty-three-year-old man at her first session, and recruited others by driving from church to church.

Still, Selma in 1963 was untested ground for direct action. With

School Petition from the Parents of Selma

Twenty-nine Selma parents signed a petition in 1955 that demanded desegregated schools, but they couched that demand in traditional politesse. The reaction of the white Citizens' Council was swift and effective. Within a month sixteen of the signers had lost their jobs, and nearly all of them withdrew their support for the statement:

"The May 31st decision of the Supreme Court, to us, means that the time for delay, evasion or procrastination is past. Whatever the difficulties in according our children their constitutional rights, it is clear that the school board must meet and seek a solution to that question in accordance with the law of the land. As we interpret the decision, you are duty bound to take immediate concrete steps leading to an early elimination of segregation in public schools. Please rest assured of our willingness to serve in any way we can to aid you in dealing with the question."[14]

the passage of the Civil Rights Act of 1964 blacks attempted to desegregate several restaurants and a movie theater, but soon the focus shifted to voting. Activists began with a quiet campaign to recruit high school students to canvass residents and to march downtown. An essential element of the plan was the temperament of Dallas County Sheriff Jim Clark, who had a martial demeanor and a habit of being rough on demonstrators. By late 1964 Clark had arrested several hundred people for lining up to register to vote outside the Dallas County Courthouse. In December 1964 SCLC and local leaders summoned Rev. Martin Luther King, Jr., to lead a full-fledged campaign.

At this point cracks in Selma's facade were beginning to show. Probate Judge Bernard Reynolds removed the COLORED and WHITE signs from the courthouse drinking fountains and furnished paper cups, although the bathrooms remained segregated. At first chairs were removed from the public library to prevent integrated seating, but eventually they were returned, and the library books were made available to all.

King led a series of marches and was jailed, along with hundreds of others. The Selma drive was overshadowed in February 1965, when state troopers went on a rampage against black marchers in nearby Marion and shot twenty-six-year-old Jimmie Lee Jackson. This brought thousands of supporters of the Movement to the region and prompted a series of three marches over the Edmund Pettus Bridge, two of which were stopped by a line of Alabama state troopers on the highway. The last of these marches, on March 21, 1965, ended at the steps of the state Capitol in Montgomery after a five-day journey, one of the Movement's unqualified triumphs.

Five months later, in August, the Voting Rights Act was law. It stripped away the barriers to voting imposed by state law and local registrars, including obscure written tests and whimsical procedural requirements. This enabled many blacks to vote for the first time and to hold office throughout the South.

Today the city that was overrun with clerics, activists, movie stars, and what the local publisher called "every screwball in the United States" retains much of its small-town rhythm. Some families are proud of having lived here since they "dug the river," a claim still leveled at anyone who arrived after they did. The downtown stores have ceded to a mall, but the streets are still stitched with seams of railroad track. The white mayor since 1964 is Joseph T. Smitherman, a master politician and former segregationist who was elected to his ninth term in 1996.

Alabama state troopers approaching marchers, led by Hosea Williams (left) and John Lewis (right), who crossed the Edmund Pettus Bridge on March 7, 1965. Troopers broke up the march seconds later. (© 1995 Spider Martin/The Spider Martin Collection)

Racial progress has been slow but steady. In 1972 five blacks were elected to the city council after the area switched from an at-large election system to one based on geographical districts. By 1988 blacks had a majority on the Dallas County Commission, and today blacks constitute a majority of registered voters. The black neighborhoods, thanks largely to federal grants, are much improved.

Edmund Pettus Bridge
Highway 80 (Broad Street) and Water Avenue

The humpbacked Edmund Pettus Bridge, named for a Confederate general and U.S. senator, arches over the murky swirls of the Alabama River. It has been Selma's gateway to the east for fifty-five years. After an attack on civil rights marchers here on March 7, 1965, speechmakers compared the site with the Revolutionary War battlefields of Lexington and Concord. What was an engineering showcase and a tribute to the Confederacy now stands as a reminder of state troopers beating marchers in a fog of tear gas.

When Jimmie Lee Jackson succumbed to gunshot wounds in a Selma hospital on February 26, 1965, the chemistry of the Selma campaign instantly became more volatile. Several ideas emerged for laying the blame for the Black Belt's first civil rights killing at the

John Lewis's View from the Bridge

John Lewis, a Baptist minister and chairman of SNCC, probably endured more routine punishment on the front lines of civil rights than anyone else. Here he describes the view from his place at the front of the line during the first march across the Edmund Pettus Bridge:

"We lined up in twos. It was a silent march. There was no talking, no singing. Hosea Williams and myself started walking. . . . I was one of those carrying a knapsack on my back. I had a toothbrush, toothpaste, an apple, an orange, one or two books, but we thought we would be arrested and placed in cells. But as we walked through the streets of Selma, and got to the top of the bridge, the apex of the bridge, we saw a sea of blue. Alabama state troopers. And we continued to walk and we came within hearing distance of the state troopers. And a man identified himself and said, 'I'm Major John Cloud of the Alabama state troopers. This is an unlawful march. It will not be allowed to continue. I give you two minutes to disperse and go back to your church.'

"Hosea and I conferred for a moment and said we would kneel and pray and pass the word back. Before we could get the word back, Major Cloud said, 'Troopers, advance.' They put on their gas masks, and came toward us, beating us with nightsticks and bull whips, trampling us with horses, and using tear gas. . . . I was hit in the head and had a concussion. I don't know from that day to this day how I made it back to the church."[15]

feet of Governor Wallace, including depositing Jackson's body on the steps of the state Capitol in Montgomery. A fifty-four-mile walk to the Capitol eventually was decided upon to express outrage over Jackson's death.

Meanwhile Governor Wallace huddled with his advisers, including Al Lingo, the state public safety director and former pilot of Wallace's 1962 campaign plane. Initially the governor considered allowing the march to go forward, reasoning that without logistical support it would not make it all the way to Montgomery and would be "the laughing stock of the nation," in the words of his press secretary. He changed his mind, though, and ordered state troopers, with the aid of Dallas County Sheriff Clark, to halt the march in the name of public safety.

The date set was Sunday, March 7. After church five hundred marchers from Selma and Marion gathered at Brown Chapel to line up double file behind John Lewis of SNCC and Hosea Williams of SCLC, standing in for King. Some in their Sunday finery were prepared only for a symbolic march, but those in the front carried knapsacks, bedrolls, and coats for either a longer march or a stint in jail. They marched south on Sylvan Street (now Martin Luther King, Jr., Street), west on Alabama Avenue, and south on Broad Street to the bridge. It was overcast, and downtown was eerily quiet.

On the other side of the bridge about fifty state troopers in blue helmets were arrayed across four lanes of Highway 80. Behind them stood several dozen members of a posse, each a volunteer recruited by Sheriff Clark whose only uniform was a sheriff's badge stuck to his headgear and work clothes. Fifteen of the possemen were on horseback. Reporters and photographers stood off to the side near a car dealership, while the Selma city police directed traffic in town.

The marchers walked over the bridge along the east sidewalk until they reached the troopers standing shoulder to shoulder and stopped in front of them. Major John Cloud of the state troopers then announced that the marchers had two minutes to turn around and return to their church. The troopers donned gas masks. About one minute into the count he ordered the troopers to advance. The troopers started pushing forward, and once they broke the formation of the marchers, they ran after them and beat them with wood billy clubs and unleashed tear gas canisters. The cries of the marchers mixed with whoops of the possemen, who pursued the marchers on foot and horseback across the bridge, through town, and all the way back to Brown Chapel, beating on the hoods of cars as they went. Within thirty minutes downtown was completely cleared of marchers, and the bridge was strewn with their abandoned belongings. By evening the two hospitals in Selma that would admit black patients had treated more than sixty-five people for injuries. It became known as Bloody Sunday.

Footage of the troopers' attack was carried on national television, made all the more poignant by the interruption of ABC's "Sunday Night Movie" about Nazi crimes, *Judgment at Nuremberg*. Expressions of outrage poured from the floors of Congress, newspapers, and homes nationwide.

King immediately returned to Selma and called for a second ministers' march over the bridge to be held two days later. A court ordered it halted until a hearing was held, prompting marathon discussions among Movement leaders about whether to march as originally announced. King had never before defied an order of a federal court, traditionally the Movement's protector.

In the end he decided to lead a march up to the site of the previous skirmish and turn around, a compromise quietly worked out with intermediaries from the White House. On Tuesday, March 9, without disclosing this plan to an eager crowd, King told supporters at Brown Chapel to "put on their walking shoes" and led about two thousand marchers over the bridge to another blockade of state troopers. The marchers knelt in prayer. Then King bent the line back and walked back across the bridge. Not to be outdone, the troopers parted and left the road open just as the marchers turned back. Afterward SNCC and their more militant recruits felt betrayed, as did several of the ministers who had come to Selma determined to go the distance. This march became known as Turnaround Tuesday.

That night James Reeb, a white minister from Boston, was clubbed unconscious by four white ruffians outside the Silver Moon Cafe. He died two days later in a Birmingham hospital. President Johnson then took the unprecedented step of directly addressing Congress to push for a hastily assembled voting rights bill and used the Movement refrain "We shall overcome" to describe the fight against racial prejudice. This part of the nationally televised speech struck blacks as astonishing and reportedly moved King to tears. Many southern whites thought it a stab in the back.

On March 17, 1965, Judge Frank Johnson issued his order restraining state officials from any further interference with the marchers, and a third march to the bridge was organized. After a service at Brown Chapel on Sunday, March 21, King led a group of three thousand marchers down Sylvan Street (now Martin Luther King, Jr., Street) to Water Street, then west along the river to the bridge once more. This time the scene was biblical, with King and his aides wreathed in flowers, walking arm in arm with other activists, nuns, and celebrities who had flown and driven to Selma from all over the country. The streets were lined with federalized Alabama national guardsmen with orders to protect the marchers, and press and army helicopters whirled overhead as the stream of people headed over the hump of the bridge and eastward for Montgomery.

Today the bridge serves as an annual staging ground for reenactments of the marches, and in 1985, 1990, and 1995 it was as the send-off point for a full march to Montgomery. The Selma Police Department, which, unlike its state and county counterparts, did not play a major role in the "Bloody Sunday" violence, escorts the marchers during these annual ceremonies. A marker of the Alabama Historical Commission stands on the Selma side of the bridge.

The Edmund Pettus Bridge, seen through a window at the National Voting Rights Museum that pays tribute to Movement figures, in 1994. (Rex Miller)

National Voting Rights Museum and Institute

1012 Water Avenue

This small museum was founded in 1992 by local organizers as a grass roots alternative to a tamer city-sponsored exhibit. Its founder, Rose Sanders, epitomizes the approach of today's leaders who took up the torch of the Movement: Honor political advances, but emphasize youth education and job programs. After district lines for the state legislature were redrawn, her husband, Hank Sanders, a native of south Alabama, was elected in 1983 as the first black legislator from the Black Belt since Reconstruction.

The museum houses a collection of messages from living Bloody Sunday marchers, whose footprints are cast in plaster. It contains a small memorial chapel, photos of current minority officeholders, and an exhibit on the golden age of Reconstruction, all supported by local funding. Most striking are the black-and-white photographs of the marchers, originally taken by the Alabama Department of Public Safety for surveillance in 1965 and subsequently donated to the museum. The museum helped found the 21st Century Youth Lead-

ership Project in which students from grade school to college interview civil rights veterans for a living history exhibit, and it coordi-
nates the commemorative Bloody Sunday bridge crossing and street
festival each March.

Cecil C. Jackson Public Safety Building

1300 Alabama Avenue

Named for a Selma native who was an aide to Governor Wallace,
this building included the jail where King was held during the voting rights campaign. During the 1960s the city hall was on the first
floor, the city jail was on the second, and the county jail was on the
third.

It became the holding pen for demonstrators who marched and
deliberately sought to fill the jail cells in January 1965. By February
the building was bursting with them, and some marchers were
trucked out to decrepit rural camps. Jailing had become so routine
that Rev. Ralph Abernathy, when asked before a march what his
message to the police was, said, "Tell them to have my supper ready."

King and Abernathy both spent five days in the city jail after
being arrested and refusing bail on February 1, 1965. Although they
were offered ham and turnip greens, they stuck to their policy of
fasting for the first two days of any jail term. While protesters continued to pour in, King issued a "Letter from a Selma, Alabama,
Jail," which emphasized the contrast between his recent acceptance
of the Nobel Peace Prize in Oslo and his current predicament. Those
who were arrested switched the WHITE and COLORED signs over the
bathrooms to confuse the officers. Many other activists also spent
time in that second-floor jail. They included John Lewis and Rev.
Louis Lloyd Anderson, who was held there five different times and
had to run in place and do push-ups to keep warm.

At the time the director of public safety was Wilson Baker, an
experienced lawman who had narrowly lost to Jim Clark in the race
for sheriff in 1958 and who taught at the University of Alabama.
When SCLC announced Selma as a target, Baker studied the way
Sheriff Laurie Pritchett had handled demonstrations and arrests in
Albany, Georgia, in 1961–62 and similarly sought to avoid direct
confrontations. He actually was aware of SCLC's blueprint from
papers in a briefcase someone stole from King in Anniston,
Alabama. Baker's general approach was to let marchers march as
long as they stayed in orderly lines on the sidewalks and obeyed
traffic signals, conditions SCLC was willing to honor. In the midst of
the marches Baker was quoted as saying: "Our demonstrators are

nonviolent. I am nonviolent. When two nonviolent forces meet, nothing can happen."

Baker's rivalry with Sheriff Clark complicated law enforcement during the voting rights campaign and continued after it. Clark had courted black votes as a protégé of Alabama's Governor Jim ("Big Jim") Folsom in the 1950s, but by the time the battle lines hardened in Selma over voting rights, he was advocating giving no quarter to the demonstrators. Both officials had responsibility for policing Selma, and the agreement was that Clark would handle the area in and around the county courthouse and Baker the rest of the city, including Brown Chapel. However, because the sheriff had the authority to roam the city and activists were constantly changing plans, the men frequently crossed paths, disagreed, and nearly came to blows.

Today this building still houses the Selma Police Department, which hired its first black officer shortly after the voting rights campaign. Blacks initially patrolled only the black neighborhoods but then were assigned to patrol the whole city. The force now is about 40 percent black.

George D. Wilson Community Center
14–16 Franklin Street

In the 1930s and long afterward Saturday was market day. On their day off from farm work, blacks came to Selma in trucks and wagons and on foot from six surrounding counties to sell produce and buy supplies. During a long day they had nowhere to rest, get medical attention, or hold meetings.

The Works Progress Administration (WPA) provided funds for this building, which contained lavatories, a doctor's clinic, an assembly hall, and offices for the county demonstrator and home economics agent. Named for a local black contractor and builder, it was the only gathering place of its size in the area, hosting up to three thousand people each Saturday. At night Duke Ellington and other big bands would play a late show here after entertaining the white servicemen at Craig Air Base.

The community center also housed two remarkable murals by a black Birmingham painter named Felix Gaines, one of hundreds of WPA murals that adorned public buildings throughout the nation. The murals depicted views of the old and new South. On one wall a cloud-borne chariot descended to carry off a black farmer, as sung about in the spiritual "Swing Low, Sweet Chariot"; on the opposite wall another black farmer carried a giant bale of cotton with smokestacks behind him. The murals are now at the Old Depot Museum.

During the civil rights period this part of Franklin Street bustled with activity near the Boynton real estate and insurance office at 21 Franklin (now gone). At one point during the voting drive Sheriff Clark learned that activists were meeting in the black Elks Lodge, also on this street, and ripped the liquor license off the wall. A more common sight was that of SCLC and SNCC workers, Movement lawyers, and white emissaries shuttling back and forth between the Boynton office and the jail across the street. Today the community center is an administrative building for public safety.

Site of the Silver Moon Cafe
34 Washington Street

James Reeb was one of the white ministers quick to answer King's call for a second march to the bridge. As a Unitarian minister from Boston he had worked to improve the ghettos and remained in Selma after marchers had been turned back from Highway 80 on Turnaround Tuesday, March 9, 1965.

That night he ate a soul food dinner at Walker's Cafe (formerly at 118 Washington Street), then walked north toward the corner with two other ministers. The Silver Moon was a tough place; no one had dared integrate it during the Movement campaign the previous summer. Someone in front of a novelty shop across the street yelled, "Hey you, niggers," and before the three could escape, someone landed a pipe or club on Reeb's head with a left-handed baseball swing. Reeb, groggy and with a bad headache, was escorted back down Washington to the SCLC setup in the Boynton office on Franklin Street.

What followed was a heartrending logistical nightmare. Reeb was first taken to the Burwell Infirmary (formerly at 508 Philpot Street) in Selma, where he was examined by a black Selma doctor and fell into a coma. The doctor decided he should go to a Birmingham hospital, but the journey was fraught with delays. Finally, four hours after the attack, Reeb was admitted to the University Hospital in Birmingham with a skull fracture and blood clot from which he died two days later.

The outpouring of sympathy that followed included a personal call from President Johnson, who sent yellow roses and flew Mrs. Reeb down to Selma on a government jet. Activists pointed out that national concern erupted only after a white man had been killed, although black man Jimmie Lee Jackson had met a similar fate two

The Last Hours of James Reeb

Orloff Miller and Clark Olsen, who had come from out of town for the ministers' march, accompanied James Reeb from Walker's Cafe on the night of March 9, 1965 and were with him during his last hours. Here are some selected entries from Miller's diary, beginning shortly after the attack on Reeb:

"**D**octor called immediately for Jim. I am given a cold towel. Jim goes incoherent. Blood pressure taken (Jim's and mine). Dr. Dinkins arrives, arranges transfer to Birmingham University Hospital. I get ice and aspirin. Meanwhile local police arrive and begin questioning. . . . We depart in doctor's car for Boynton's to pick up check [the Birmingham hospital told the doctor by phone that it required $150 up front for admittance]. . . . Ambulance (with Jim) arrives. . . . We depart with local police following a few blocks. Siren in use—we run several lights—very nearly crash into Cadillac—slow a bit—ten minutes from Selma we get right rear flat. 9:30 P.M. Turned around . . . attempted radio contact—variety of channels, 'emergency'—no response! Pulled in at local radio station . . . called second ambulance. Several cars pulled in and gave us once-over. . . . Sat and waited for Dr. Dinkins' car to arrive (and act as escort). . . . [D]river began helping (?) with siren wires; unable to repair (even after borrowing my knife). Doctor's car arrives. He drives it and we depart, Clark and I holding stretcher in place (brackets do not hold) around curves. 60–70 mph except bad curves. Get police escort for several twisting miles—to interstate highway. 80 mph. Then more twists and turns. . . . Arrive Birmingham University Hospital 11 P.M. Jim's personal effects turned over to hospital and recorded. Blue Cross card found. Tracheostomy. Evaluate brain damage. Martin Luther King gave prayer for Jim (all of us). 12:30 A.M. Wednesday. Massive skull fracture. Very large clot. 15th floor room reserved for Mrs. Reeb to stay in hospital. 7:30 A.M., cardiac arrest. Mayo surgeon in constant attention. 9:30 A.M., 'We have lost a patient.' "[16]

weeks earlier. Three men were indicted in mid-April for murder, but they were acquitted on December 7, 1965. The site of the Silver Moon is now a vacant lot.

Tabernacle Baptist Church
1431 Broad Street

When ex-slave and builder D. T. West sought to erect this columned church on Broad Street in 1922, he was told no black church would be allowed to face Selma's main street. So he simply designed it with a dome and two entrances: one on Minter Avenue and

Rev. L. L. Anderson in 1994 in the balcony of the Tabernacle Baptist Church, site of the first mass meeting in Selma. (Rex Miller)

another on Broad Street. Inside, it is clear that the builder had the last laugh: The pulpit, the stained glass transom, and the balcony all are oriented toward Broad Street. As long as current church members can recall, both entrances have been used for many decades. Rev. David V. Jemison, the pastor for forty-four years, was a tireless proselytizer, known to preach in pool rooms, who rose to the pinnacle of the organized Baptists as president of the National Baptist Convention.

When his successor, Rev. Louis Lloyd Anderson, came to Selma from Montgomery in 1955, he was already emphasizing racial disparities in his sermons. Early on he preached that blacks had felled the trees, built the bridges, carried the garbage, picked the cotton, pulled the corn, and even suckled the white babies of Selma and were entitled to a better life than they had. This scared churchgoers used to more scriptural fare. Anderson frequently accompanied blacks to criminal court and assisted in voting registration lines at the courthouse, which attracted death threats on the phone and regular parades of robed Klansmen by his church during services and choir practice.

With Anderson's permission SNCC organizer Bernard Lafayette began to hold seminars in the church basement, educating high school students about nonviolent protest. Church elders did not mind because it looked like Sunday school and kept the children occupied. But when in 1963 activists sought to use Tabernacle for the first mass meeting of the Selma campaign, the elders objected vehemently. No other church in Selma was willing to host a Movement rally, and the deacons were well aware of bombings in other parts of Alabama. The meeting went forward anyway because Anderson had given the Movement permission to announce it, and the announcement had appeared in the newspaper.

The meeting took place on May 14, 1963, shortly after Samuel Boynton, Selma's prominent black leader, died in the Burwell Infirmary, and many thought it a fitting tribute to the man who had labored for four decades to improve the lives of blacks in the area. About three hundred people poured into the church as police lights flashed outside in the night. Police officers fanned out along the back walls of the church, while others checked the license plates of arriving cars. A band of young whites showed up with unfinished table legs taken from a local furniture shop. According to Anderson, "That night the street was full and the balcony was loaded." Speeches ranged from the cautious Rev. C. C. Hunter, who preached a traditional message of restraint and self-improvement, to the fiery James Forman, then SNCC chairman, who urged blacks to descend upon the courthouse en masse.

Brown Chapel AME Church
410 Martin Luther King, Jr., Street

Founded in 1867 as the first AME church in Alabama, this barrel-vaulted church served the black community for nearly one hundred years before it became the starting point for nearly every civil rights march in Selma and the site of countless mass meetings.

It was not the first black church in Selma to host the Movement. But by the time King announced the Selma voting rights campaign to a crowd of seven hundred people on January 2, 1965, one hundred years to the day after the issuance of the Emancipation Proclamation, it had become the local headquarters. The police monitored that meeting and subsequent ones, prompting Abernathy to ridicule their conspicuous rabbit-eared recording device in a sermon as a "doohickey."

On February 4, 1965, while King and Abernathy were in jail in Selma, Malcolm X spoke here, causing anxiety among the Movement's nonviolent proponents. He claimed he was merely acting as a foil to get local whites to accept King's more moderate program. Less than three weeks later he was assassinated in Harlem, having only met King once briefly and by chance in 1964.

After the melee in Marion on February 18, 1965, black leaders tried to reinforce a pledge of nonviolence by calling for people to bring their weapons to the front table of the church, where they were taken out of circulation. The church held a memorial service for Jimmie Lee Jackson, and the front door was draped with a hand-made banner that read RACISM KILLED OUR BROTHER. After James Reeb was killed, SCLC's plans for risky night marches were reduced to night vigils outside the church, and most of the Selma police force was assigned to patrol its perimeter.

After Bloody Sunday, Brown Chapel was besieged by parading troopers, and troopers' horses mounted the steps of the church and attempted to go inside. Ambulances provided by the local funeral homes carried the wounded to the only hospitals for blacks, the Good Samaritan Hospital and the Burwell Infirmary. That night, and many others, women made sandwiches in the basement, and people slept on the floor and in the balcony. Throughout the campaign the Sunday school room downstairs was used as a strategy and meeting room.

Ceremony outside Brown Chapel during the 1994 commemoration of the Selma voting rights campaign. (Rex Miller)

In the 1970s, 1980s, and 1990s Brown Chapel continued to be a meeting place for job campaigns and other initiatives by the black community, as well as for an annual Bloody Sunday commemorative service. A plaque for the four people killed during 1965 (James Reeb, Jimmie Lee Jackson, Jonathan Daniels, and Viola Liuzzo) hangs to the left of the apse. The adjoining parsonage, which during Bloody Sunday served as a makeshift hospital, is now an exhibition space for civil rights, and a bust of King stands outside. The church is listed on the National Register of Historic Places.

George Washington Carver Homes and Civil Rights Walking Tour

Martin Luther King, Jr., Street

Surrounding Brown Chapel on all sides are the two-story George Washington Carver homes, built in 1951 as an apartment complex for blacks and named for Tuskegee's renowned scientist. Residents here typically attended Brown Chapel and housed some of the students, medics, and clerics who came to Selma in 1965. The open space between the houses was used as a training ground for nonviolent protests.

Martin Luther King, Jr., Street (formerly Sylvan Street), which runs in front of Brown Chapel, was renamed in 1976 after a protracted struggle in the city council. In March 1994 the city erected

Malcom X Issues a Warning

On February 4, 1965, after speaking to students at Tuskegee, Malcolm X made an unscheduled visit to Selma and spoke at Brown Chapel. Here is an excerpt from his statement to the press:

"I might point out that I am one hundred percent for any effort put forth by black people in this country to have access to the ballot. And I frankly believe that since the ballot is our right that we are within our rights to use whatever means is necessary to secure those rights. And I think that the people in this part of the world would do well to listen to Dr. Martin Luther King and give him what he's asking for—and give it to him fast—before some other factions come along and try to do it another way. . . . I don't believe in any kind of nonviolence. I believe that it's right to be nonviolent with people who are nonviolent. But when you're dealing with an enemy who doesn't know what nonviolence is, as far as I'm concerned, you're wasting your time."[17]

ten mounted placards of text and photographs along this street to depict the critical events leading up to the march to Montgomery. Although the placards are substantially accurate and highlight the monumental tasks faced by black organizers, they do contain a turn of historical gymnastics. The members of the white power structure of 1965, including Mayor Smitherman, the city council president, the city prosecutor, the chief of police, and the publisher of the *Selma Times-Journal*—all of whom resisted basic change—are proudly credited for their appearances as "Political Leaders in the Selma Movement."

First Baptist Church

709 Martin Luther King, Jr., Street

As is common in many southern communities, Selma has two First Baptist churches: a white one on Lauderdale Street, one of whose pastors served as a chaplain for the Confederacy and died in the Civil War, and a black one that broke away and built its own house of worship on this corner near the railroad tracks. Since then the black First Baptist has been dedicated to community efforts. Before Hudson High School was built in 1949, black schools held their graduation ceremonies in the church's sanctuary. First Baptist also helped found and nurture Selma University, a Baptist seminary that is now a four-year college. Both Ralph Abernathy and Fred Shuttlesworth attended Selma University before going on to their respective pulpits—and civil rights trials by fire—in Montgomery and Birmingham. Shuttlesworth also pastored this church from 1951 to 1953.

Led by Pastor M. C. Cleveland, First Baptist opened its doors to weekly mass meetings in 1963, after activist Bernard Lafayette had been beaten and arrested. People were taught how to register and vote in classes in the basement. It was a natural meeting place for the Dallas County Voters League. While Brown Chapel became a Movement headquarters, students from Hudson High School, Selma University, and Concordia College (1804 Green Street, then a Lutheran academy) still often gathered at First Baptist, numbering up to nine hundred at the height of the campaign.

When Sylvan Street (now Martin Luther King, Jr., Street) was filled with galloping troopers on Bloody Sunday, police fired tear gas into the church. One black teenager escaped, or was thrown, through the stained glass window to the left of the organ above the baptismal. First Baptist was the send-off point and coordinating center for the 1965 March to Montgomery, and its basement was loaded with boxes of food, tents, electric generators, shovels, camping gear, and foodstuffs. Throngs of people waited in a crowd that reached across the railroad tracks before the march got started. After the march was completed, the First Baptist basement became a warehouse for material contributions from northern supporters. A tornado in 1978 ripped the fifty-foot steeple off the church. Previously the tallest in town, it has only partially been rebuilt. The church, built by D. T. West (also the builder of Tabernacle Baptist Church, which split from First Baptist in the 1880s), is listed on the National Register of Historic Places.

Old Depot Museum (Selma—Dallas County Museum of History and Archives)
4 Martin Luther King, Jr., Street

The former L&N railroad station is now a museum with exhibits on the history of Selma and the Black Belt. Its Black History room features memorabilia from the voting rights campaign: a newspaper announcement for the first mass meeting at Tabernacle Baptist Church, a Good Samaritan Hospital patient log for Bloody Sunday, and a cardigan sweater King wore when he stayed at the Sullivan Jackson house on Lapsley Street. It also houses the WPA paintings of Felix Gaines (formerly in the George D. Wilson Community Center) and an exceptional collection of photographs of black rural life from the turn of the century.

City Hall (site of the former Hotel Albert)
Broad Street between Selma and Dallas Avenues

This was the Hotel Albert, an ornate replica of a palace in Venice, Italy, built by former slaves. When King arrived in the hotel lobby and asked for a room in January 1965, he was registered graciously. The only complication was that during the check-in he was assaulted by American Nazi leader George Lincoln Rockwell, who had come to town to harass the Movement and was promptly arrested by police. The press also stayed at the hotel during the campaign.

Since the early 1970s this brick City Hall has been the domain of Mayor Joseph T. Smitherman. The Hotel Albert was his campaign headquarters in 1964, and he has remained in office for more than thirty years except for a brief interregnum in 1979–80, during which he resigned. He was a white, skinny former appliance salesman with a crew cut when he first was elected as a relative progressive with the support of businessmen who wanted to attract new industry to Selma. As a result, the Hammermill Paper Company moved to Selma just as the voting rights campaign was heating up. This company, and others like it, pushed the city toward racial moderation as other business communities in Alabama began to pledge compliance with federal civil rights laws.

On race Mayor Smitherman initially was no more progressive than his white supporters. Selma had never been a Klan stronghold, but it was the spawning ground for the first Citizens' Council in Alabama, which sought to preserve racial dominance through social and economic pressure. A Citizens' Council advertisement in the *Selma Times-Journal* on June 9, 1963, asked citizens to ponder the question "What Have I Personally Done to Maintain Segregation?" In an apparent slip of the tongue, Smitherman once said he opposed the efforts of "Martin Luther Coon" to organize in Selma. He nonetheless appointed Wilson Baker to be Selma's first police chief, and throughout the Selma campaign Baker handled demonstrations with restraint and resisted some of the strong-arm tactics of the county sheriff.

In the years following the voting rights campaign, Smitherman has been energetic and, on racial issues, chameleonlike. In 1970 he barricaded the entrance to the federal poverty program office in Selma because he said it discriminated against whites; in 1979 he told a group of Klansmen who showed up at City Hall to get out of town. Smitherman's victories have included a sizable percentage of black votes, and on his long watch there have been tangible gains. Blacks hold a number of local offices, and themes of reconciliation and repentance have become standard in political speech. He was last reelected in 1996.

Dallas County Courthouse
105 Lauderdale Street

This courthouse, pea green in Movement days and now painted tan, is the tallest building in Selma. The front steps were the stage on which demonstrators repeatedly sparred with Sheriff Jim Clark in early 1965. Many times marchers approached the steps only to be prodded back by club-wielding police or carted off to jail.

In practice and later by formal agreement this was Jim Clark's territory. Clark was legendary for his swaggering defense of segregation. He wore a crisp military uniform with a gold-braided cap and hung a billy club and cattle prod from his belt. The prod was a metal

Attorney J. L. Chestnut, Jr., in 1994 in front of the Dallas County Courthouse, scene of several standoffs between marchers and Sheriff Jim Clark. (Rex Miller)

cylinder with a hand grip that delivered a battery-powered shock when touched to the skin. Clark prided himself on spit-polished boots ("white spit," he noted) and sported a round white button with the single word *Never* on it. His martial bearing and temper made him a target for activists attempting to bring the brutality of local lawmen out into the open.

The courthouse also housed the county office for voter registration. In the early 1960s the office was open only two days a month. The registrar required blacks to take an extensive citizenship exam and seized on uncrossed *t*'s, undotted *i*'s and poor penmanship to disqualify them. As a result, even black preachers and college graduates were turned down. One prospective registrant complained of "subterfuge" and was met by the puzzled looks of registrars who didn't know what that meant. Once blacks started giving classes on registration, white officials constantly changed the questions to keep the pass rate down. In addition, someone already on the voting rolls had to vouch for the character of a new registrant.

A local drive had succeeded in getting seventy-one new black registrants on the rolls between June 1961 and the following May. By fall 1963 SNCC activist Worth Long regularly led marches of students willing to skip school and submit to arrest. On October 7,

1963, three hundred potential registrants showed up at the court-house for a "Freedom Day." Movement leaders were arrested for contributing to the delinquency of a minor when they assisted or led students, and by July 1964 seventy people were in jail.

The consequences of showing up in a registration line were seri-ous in those days. Blacks were frequently dismissed from their jobs if they even attempted to register. In fall 1963 the proprietor of the Dunn Rest Home for the elderly went to the courthouse and found two of his employees. He later beat them when they refused to be photographed and fired them. These women, and forty other employees who quit in solidarity with them, were blacklisted by businesses in Selma.

After the enactment of the Civil Rights Act in 1964 Circuit Judge James Hare, who came from a prominent Dallas County family and believed in the anthropological inferiority of blacks, issued an order from his chambers in room 204 banning the meeting of more than three people in public. The order eventually was reversed for violat-ing the constitutional right to free association, but it effectively made every meeting and march in the county illegal for the six months preceding King's arrival.

When King arrived in January 1965, the courthouse steps became the Movement's primary target. On Monday, January 18, 1965, King and SNCC chairman John Lewis led four hundred marchers from Brown Chapel to the courthouse. Clark and his men ushered the marchers through a side entrance on Lauderdale Street and into an alley, where they stood for hours in the cold and then went home without anyone's having registered. The next day the marchers again lined up along the sidewalk in front of the court-house, and Sheriff Clark arrested Amelia Boynton, a leading figure in the black community and a registered voter. He hustled her down the street by her coat collar in front of a clutch of reporters and dozens of bystanders.

The arrest prompted a group of black teachers to march to the courthouse on January 22, 1965. The teachers' march was led by Frederick D. Reese, a preacher and president of the Dallas County Voters League. The sight of 105 teachers—who had waited until classes were over on Friday and marched double file in coats and ties or in dresses—was a breakthrough for the Movement in recruiting respectable members of the community. They were barred at the door by Clark's men and twice were pushed from the steps. Then, when it was apparent they were neither getting in the building nor heading for jail, they marched past surprised, clapping onlookers to

Brown Chapel and sang "This Little Light of Mine." After the teachers' march protests at the courthouse lost some of their stigma, and demonstrations by undertakers and other black businessmen followed.

Eventually demonstrations at the courthouse became common, and every move elicited a countermove. When the people in line were asked to take a number and respond only when their number was called, they devised a verbal relay to make sure no one was passed over. On Friday, February 12, 1965, Sheriff Clark was admitted to the hospital for exhaustion, saying, "The niggers are givin' me a heart attack." Black teenagers responded by marching to the courthouse and praying for his physical recovery and mental conversion. The following week Sheriff Clark had recovered enough to deliver a left jab to the face of SCLC's Rev. C. T. Vivian, who had led a group of marchers to the front door in the rain and had badgered Clark and likened him to Hitler. In one of his calmer moments Clark referred to the regular appearance of blacks at the courthouse steps as Disneyland.

With the passage of the Voting Rights Act, registration in the courthouse became more routine, and within six months nine thousand blacks had been added to the rolls. In 1983 Marie Foster, who

---

Definitions: The Dallas County Voting Test

In the early 1960s blacks attempting to register were asked to answer questions about the three branches of the federal government and the Constitution. In Dallas County registrants also were asked to define certain words, some of which were legal terms having nothing to do with voting. Here are some of them, along with the expected responses:

"**Secular**—Not under church control, not sacred, not belonging to a religious order. As, secular courts, education, music.

"**bona fide**—Without fraud, in good, as, a bona fide citizen or a bona fide transaction.

"**previously**—Going before, or has happened before.

"**turpitude**—Corruption, a corrupt act or practice.

"**interrogatories**—Words used in asking questions. Sentences implying questions.

"**affiliate**—To connect or associate oneself.

"**the man on the street**—The man on the street should act and live morally high."[18]

had taught some of the early voting classes, became a deputy registrar. In 1995 a street (Range Street from Jeff Davis Avenue to Highland Avenue) was named after her.

U.S. Courthouse
908 Alabama Avenue

Across the street from the Dallas County Courthouse stands the statelier federal courthouse with its arched entranceway. FBI agents and DOJ lawyers used to watch the standoffs on the county courthouse steps from their third-floor offices. J. L. Chestnut, Jr., a black Selma lawyer who has tried dozens of cases in both courthouses, imagines this building turning to its neighbor and saying, "You can't do that."

Although federal judges' chambers during the Movement were in Mobile (Southern District) or Montgomery (Middle District), federal Judge Daniel Thomas occasionally heard argument here. Often skeptical of the Movement's legal claims, Judge Thomas finally issued an order on February 4, 1965, barring state officials from using the knowledge-of-government test questions and ordering them to process at least one hundred applications each day. After the Voting Rights Act was signed in August 1965, three federal employees, including a black postal worker, set up an office on the third floor to register voters and processed eighty-five hundred new black registrants, nearly equaling the number of white voters by the time of the first primary in May 1966.

In 1966 a tooth-and-nail sheriff's race between Wilson Baker and Jim Clark ultimately was decided here. Clark took out an ad in the *Selma Times-Journal* that insisted, "We Have Not Been Overcome," and chastised Baker for treating King and the protesters with kid gloves. In the primary Clark challenged six boxes that were from black polling areas. DOJ sued, its first intervention in a local primary, and got a federal order to count votes in the boxes. Baker came out ahead and then went on to beat Clark again in the general election by five hundred votes, effectively ending Jim Clark's political career.

In the 1980s the courthouse also was the site of important second-generation voting rights cases. The federal court stepped in to redraw the city council districts in 1984 to reflect better the racial composition of the city. It also was the site of the trial of the Marion Three, in which black local officials in Perry County were charged with altering the absentee ballots of twenty-six voters in the 1984

Democratic primary. In this case DOJ switched from its usual role of guardian against white intimidation to investigator of black officials fairly new to office. Combined with the excitement generated by Jesse Jackson's presidential candidacy that year, the case became a focus for civil rights activists who objected to the policies of the Reagan administration.

After a two-month trial at which many elderly rural residents were called in from the shacks of yesteryear to testify, a jury of seven blacks and five whites acquitted the Marion Three on all counts. The federal courthouse currently houses the office of Earl Hilliard, the first black U.S. congressman from the area since Reconstruction.

Lannie's Bar-B-Q Spot

2115 Minter Avenue

For decades just about everyone in town has gone to Lannie's in east Selma for a spicy fix. The restaurant is a racial neutral zone where tangy barbecue is served on white bread and hot sauce can be bought by the half gallon. At the height of the voting rights campaign, civil rights workers came here, as did the police. The people from Lannie's took food over to Brown Chapel and the county courthouse during the marches. When Lannie's got a phone, they even got takeout orders from City Hall. In those days there was only one thing on the menu: barbecue.

Lula Hatcher, the current proprietor, was a young girl when she first watched her mother, Lannie Moore Travis, make barbecue on the stove in 1942. She later grilled it over coals in pits in the ground and moved the operation to a small storage shed on the site of its current structure. The closest thing you will find to a vegetable in here today are the pimento bits in the potato salad. Every time the owner tries to introduce something new, she is greeted with howls of protest from already satisfied customers.

Torch Motel

1802 Vine Street

Although King often sought the relatively comfortable guest room in the home of local dentist Sullivan Jackson (1416 Lapsley Street), activists had to settle for a five-dollar room or a spot on the floor here. During the height of the Selma campaign room 2 became a war room for King, SNCC activists, black reporters, and visiting doctors. The motel was managed by Annie Cooper, a nurse who was

Movement workers stayed at the Torch Motel, photographed in 1994. (Rex Miller)

one of the Dunn Rest Home employees fired for joining the voter registration line at the courthouse. Cooper's image flashed briefly on the pages of national newspapers in January 1965, when she scuffled with Sheriff Clark, grabbing his billy club before he subdued her outside the county courthouse. Visionary organizer James Bevel sometimes took reflective walks in the woods behind the Torch, far from the frantic downtown, and here he thought of the long protest walk to Montgomery.

At the time the Torch was one of only two hotels that served blacks in Selma. It was built by Charles Moss, a builder and one of five sons of a bricklayer, who opened it in 1961, after he and his wife had journeyed north for the World Series and had a hard time finding a place to stay along the way. He had already built the only swimming pool for blacks in the city; there were separate YMCAs, and the public pool had been closed rather than integrate. On the grounds he also built a picnic area that was used for dances and featured a toy train for children to ride on. Moss expanded the motel even as other hotels desegregated and siphoned off many of his customers. Today it is run-down, "a victim of the Holiday Inn," as one resident explained it. In January 1994 the street in east Selma where Annie Cooper lives was renamed Annie Cooper Avenue. It was formerly called Medley Avenue, named for a family Annie Cooper's mother once worked for as a maid.

Boynton House

1315 Lapsley Street

Amelia Boynton, part Cherokee and part African, is at eighty-five Selma's oldest living activist. Her throat is permanently damaged by the tear gas she inhaled during Bloody Sunday. She first came to Selma during the Depression to teach farming techniques to black farmers as an agent of the U.S. Department of Agriculture. She and her husband, Samuel W. Boynton, helped revive the Dallas County Voters League, which encouraged blacks to register to vote. She managed to register herself in the 1930s.

The Boyntons were civil rights stalwarts. They helped secure a WPA grant for Selma's community center in the 1930s, created Joyland, a recreational center for blacks outside Selma in the 1940s, and testified before Senate subcommittees in Montgomery in the 1950s. The paths they beat down the dirt roads all over the Black Belt were followed by SNCC workers in overalls decades later.

When SNCC came to Selma in 1963, Samuel Boynton's insurance and real estate office at 21 Franklin Street became its headquarters. The Boynton home on Lapsley Street became a safe house and civil rights hotel, drawing frequent surveillance and bomb threats. When a film crew from the University of Georgia set up in the living room, the sheriff's men ringed the house and the newspaper reported the event. The house hosted frequent visitors, including King, writer James Baldwin, comedian Dick Gregory, and dozens of politicians allied with the Movement. When Judge Hare's injunction forced all meetings underground in July 1964, this house often was the meeting place for strategy sessions.

Today the house is maintained by Bruce Carver Boynton, son of Amelia and Samuel, who made his own mark on civil rights as a law student. In December 1958, returning home from Howard University for Christmas, he sat in the white section of a Trailways lunch counter in Richmond, Virginia. He originally sat down in the black section, but it was unsanitary and had water on the floor, so he went to the cleaner white section. He ordered a sandwich and tea and promptly was arrested and fined ten dollars for trespassing. The arrest eventually was thrown out by the U.S. Supreme Court in a

1960 decision desegregating interstate travel, which was the basis for the Freedom Rides in 1961 and a forerunner of the Civil Rights Act of 1964 enacted by Congress. Amelia Boynton Robinson now lives in Tuskegee, the city of her alma mater.

Reformed Presbyterian Church (Knox)

625 Jeff Davis Avenue

Rev. Claude C. Brown was pastor here and a central figure in the black community who allowed mass meetings in the church but opposed the more provocative tactics of the Movement. Brown founded the black YMCA and gave generously to Selma University and other institutions. The church also was the site of the most visible street protest by whites during the voting rights campaign. On March 6, 1965, the day before Bloody Sunday, Rev. Joseph Ellwanger led a group of about seventy people called the Concerned White Citizens of Alabama to the county courthouse, where they were threatened by angry bystanders.

Edmundite Missions Office

1428 Broad Street

Catholic Father Maurice Ouellet allowed voting registration classes to be held in the St. Elizabeth's parish hall near here early in the SNCC campaign. He was later asked to leave Selma by church authorities because of his civil rights activities. Earlier the Edmundites had helped found the first credit union available to blacks and built the Good Samaritan Hospital.

Postscript: Whatever Happened to Jim Clark?

In the days after the Voting Rights Act went into effect on August 6, 1965, blacks once again formed long lines outside the Dallas County Courthouse in order to register to vote. Jim Clark, then still sheriff, told the newspapers: "The whole thing's so ridiculous I haven't gotten over laughing at it yet. In fact, I'm nauseated."

After a hard-fought campaign Clark was narrowly defeated in his run for sheriff in 1966 by Wilson Baker, his rival during the voting rights campaign. He later sold mobile homes and was convicted on charges of smuggling marijuana. He currently lives in Elba, Alabama.

The Selma to Montgomery March of 1965

The flat open space on the Montgomery side of the Edmund Pettus Bridge where marchers and troopers faced off in March 1965 bore the commercial signs from the pre-mall era: 15-cent burgers, gas for 31.9 cents a gallon, and the Haisten's Mattress and Awning Company ("Invest in Rest, Buy the Best"). Here marchers heading for Montgomery on March 21, 1965, got their first look at open country.

Highway 80, then known as Jefferson Davis Highway, stretched east past Craig Air Base and crossed into Lowndes County. Stores dropped away, and the road narrowed to two lanes and a three-foot shoulder. From there it undulated through pastures and under the Spanish moss of the wetland area known as Big Swamp. After traversing Lowndes County, the road headed north into Montgomery. Today, except for an expansion from two lanes to four, Interstate 80 remains unlit and relatively untraveled. A few patches of cotton can still be seen from the road between mile markers 98–100.

Because of its remoteness, which offered unlimited opportunities for white hecklers or worse, security for the Selma to Montgomery March of 1965 was elaborate. Soldiers and guardsmen checked the fields and bridge abutments for bombs and walked concentric circles around the campsites before allowing the marchers to camp. Judge Frank Johnson, in accordance with a plan submitted by Movement lawyers, had specified that only three hundred marchers would be allowed on the two-lane portion and that they should march on the left side facing traffic, two abreast and narrowing to single file at the bridges. Governor Wallace railed at the decision as the work of a "mock court" and informed President Johnson that Alabama did not have enough personnel to police the march. The president promptly federalized nineteen hundred Alabama national guardsmen and assigned two thousand army personnel, as well as the FBI and U.S. marshals, to guard the route. Thirty C-130 transport planes could be heard rumbling into Selma the night before the march, and army jeeps drove through Selma's streets to and from the local armory.

Marchers walked for five days along the highway from March 21 to 25, 1965. In charge of their protection was Brigadier General Henry V. Graham, who in 1963 had convinced Governor Wallace to step aside on the schoolhouse steps of the University of Alabama after he had barred the entrance of a black student. Although Movement lawyers had assured Judge Johnson that all logistics were taken care of, not all the supplies were adequate. Marchers got sick from drinking poor-quality water from a Roto-Rooter truck until the National Guard supplied another one. Here are some impressions from the march:

Day 1, March 21: From the beginning there were white racist taunts. As Jim Letherer, an amputee on crutches who walked the entire distance, passed,

(continued on next page)

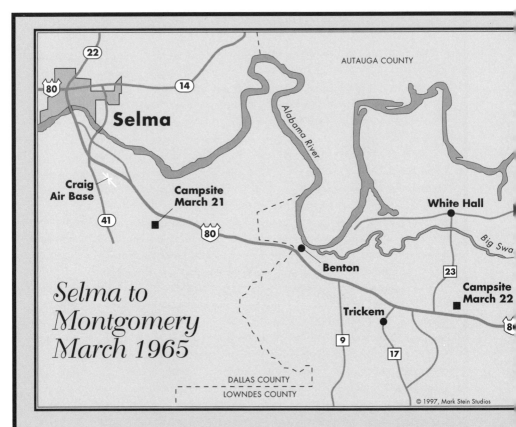

Selma to
Montgomery
March 1965

© 1997, Mark Stein Studios

bystanders shouted a military-style "Left. Left. Left . . ." A ton of food from the Green Street Baptist Church in Selma was brought in new garbage cans for dinner: pork, beans, and spaghetti. In all, marchers went about seven miles on the first day and camped near Southside High School on land owned by David Hall, a black farmer. Students from a seminary in Berkeley, California, pitched four large tents. In deference to a white obsession with the prospect of interracial sex, men and women slept apart. That night the temperature fell below freezing in the glow of campfires.

Day 2, March 22: After awaking to frosty ground and oatmeal, marchers entered Lowndes County and walked fifteen miles to a farm owned by Rosie Steele. During this stretch Stokely Carmichael, a SNCC staffer, periodically broke away from the march to talk about registering to vote with blacks who had gathered by the road-side. This groundwork later grew into a postmarch drive in Lowndes County. At Trickem Fork one woman waited in a crowd for the line of marchers to show, threw her arms around King, and proudly announced to her friends: "I done kissed him!" The marchers bedded down in a pasture dotted with white-faced cattle.

Day 3, March 23: Marchers walked eleven more miles in the rain past the half-

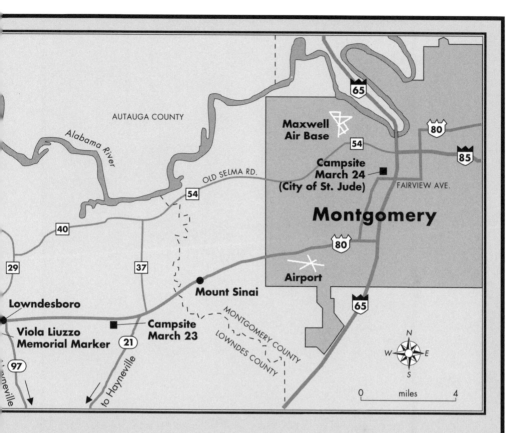

way point to a farm owned by Robert Gardner. King had stayed in a pink and white heated mobile home each night but had marched most of the way from Selma and had severe blisters. This was as far as he went, and he departed for a fund-raiser in Cleveland, Ohio. Activists built small earth burial mounds with little signs that said SEGREGATION on them. Fresh-cut hay did little to firm up the soggy campsite. Dinner was barbecued chicken, hash, peas and carrots, and a candy bar.

Day 4, March 24: Marchers walked twelve miles, entering Montgomery County and arriving at the City of St. Jude, a Catholic compound. More than ten thousand people arrived for a jamboree of speeches and entertainment provided by such celebrities as Harry Belafonte, Dick Gregory, Joan Baez, Peter Paul and Mary, Sammy Davis, Jr., Johnny Mathis, and Alan King.

Day 5, March 25: Marchers swept into Montgomery and stopped at the state Capitol.

A few hours after the rally in Montgomery, Viola Liuzzo, a white Detroit housewife, and Leroy Moton, a young black SCLC volunteer, drove marchers back to Selma in her Oldsmobile. They were driving back to Montgomery along Highway

(continued on next page)

Memorial marker for Viola Liuzzo near Highway 80 in Lowndes County, 1995. (Townsend Davis)

80 when they were seen by Klansmen in another car. The Klansmen chased Liuzzo's car near Lowndesboro at one hundred miles per hour and then shot twice into her car. Liuzzo died instantly, and the car careened into four strands of barbed wire. Moton played dead in the wreckage until the Klansmen moved on; then he flagged down another Movement shuttle for assistance. By the next day the FBI had nabbed four suspects in the killing, aided by an informant who had infiltrated the Klan and was actually in the assailants' car at the time of the shooting. After a mistrial and an acquittal before local juries in Lowndes County, federal prosecutors on December 3, 1965, convicted two men of violating Liuzzo's civil rights; each received the maximum ten-year sentence. It was the first civil rights conviction for a racial murder in the modern South. Today Viola Liuzzo's commemorative gravestone stands on a hill near the highway on the eastbound side between mile markers 113 and 114. She is buried in Detroit. In 1996 Congress designated Interstate 80 between Selma and Montgomery a National Historic Trail, qualifying it for federally funded development.

Perry County, Alabama

The Martyrdom of Jimmie Lee Jackson

Zion United Methodist Church
Martin Luther King Memorial Parkway, Marion

A terrifying night march that began here on February 18, 1965, intensified the voting rights campaign and shifted its focus from the Dallas County Courthouse in Selma to the state Capitol in Montgomery. Although it was far more violent than Bloody Sunday in Selma, it has received less attention because no photographs or footage have survived.

Even for college graduates like Albert Turner, a black bricklayer and longtime organizer, registering to vote in Perry County then was out of the question. But under the leadership of Turner and a fiery woman named Lucy Foster, blacks started to try in the early 1960s. Efforts to register centered on a local black fraternal organization, the Rising Star Association, that was founded in the late 1920s by Hampton D. Lee, owner of Lee's Funeral Home. Rising Star met near here at a social hall until SNCC and SCLC workers endorsed a more aggressive stance and forced it to meet elsewhere for safety reasons. The police had maintained a hands-off approach to local organizing until February 3, 1965, when seven hundred black schoolchildren were arrested during a march in downtown Marion and started to attract the national press. At one point, half the town was in jail somewhere in the county.

Night marches were the Movement's riskiest way to up the ante. Plans for a night march in Marion attracted dozens of state trooper cars, each bearing Confederate battle flags on the front license plate, and reinforcements from Sheriff Clark in Dallas County. The day before, marchers had met at this church and walked around the courthouse undisturbed. On the evening of February 18, 1965, SCLC's C. T. Vivian gave a rousing speech at the church and left by the back door while the marchers proceeded out the front.

Albert Turner led a line of marchers out of the church and headed for the Perry County jail, where SCLC activist James Orange was held. Although the marchers had planned only to sing at the jail and turn back, some officers thought they were starting a jail break. The line had not finished exiting the church when state troopers blocked it in front of the post office, extracted activist Willie Bolden, and deposited him on the courthouse steps across the street.

Then they shot out the streetlights and wildly beat the marchers, pursuing them all over town. They also laid into anyone who was black, whether associated with the march or simply coming home from work. Troopers beat two UPI photographers and smashed their cameras; Richard Valeriani, a correspondent for NBC, was beaten with an ax handle and hospitalized with six stitches. Some marchers were arrested and brought bleeding to the jail, where Orange first heard about the melee. The rest doubled back and went in the back door of the church. When troopers tried to follow them in, marchers beat them back with furniture.

One of those injured behind the church was eighty-year-old Cager Lee, past president of a branch of the Rising Star Association and one of the first black registrants in Marion. His grandson Jimmie Lee Jackson, twenty-six years old, had brought him to the mass meeting here that night. Jimmie Lee had returned to Marion from Indiana to be with his family. He liked to cook, hunt, and shoot pool. The previous winter he had also gone to the courthouse to register. That night Jimmie Lee was in Mack's Cafe, a sandwich place where his sister and mother worked down the hill from the church just in front of Lee's Funeral Home. When Jimmie Lee tried to get his grandfather to a doctor and resisted an attack on his mother, troopers cornered him in the cafe and shot him in the stomach as he was pinned against a cigarette machine.

Jackson ran from the cafe through a gauntlet of billy clubs and fell in front of what was then a bus station and is now the church parking lot. He died in Good Samaritan Hospital in Selma eight days later, inspiring calls for the long march to Montgomery. A historical marker behind the church serves as a reminder of the tragic death. No one was ever prosecuted for it, although Al Lingo, who commanded the Alabama state troopers, admitted in court that the assailant was a state trooper.

The first of several memorial services for Jimmie Lee Jackson was held here on February 28, 1965. SCLC's mercurial James Bevel cited an Old Testament passage to support a march to the Capitol steps in Montgomery, an idea also voiced by local activist Lucy Foster. Albert Turner and several others from Marion took part in the Bloody Sunday march the following week. Turner still lives in Marion, working as an insurance salesman and county commissioner.

The funeral procession for Jimmie Lee Jackson outside Marion, March 3, 1965. (UPI/Corbis-Bettmann)

Jimmie Lee Jackson Gravesite

Heard Cemetery, off Highway 14

At a memorial service for Jimmie Lee Jackson at the Zion United Methodist Church, King stood over the casket and asked: "Who murdered Jimmie Lee Jackson?" His answer: "He was murdered by the irresponsibility of every politician from governors on down who has fed his constituents the stale bread of hatred and spoiled meat of racism." After the service more than seven hundred people filed behind a slow-moving hearse in the rain for more than three miles up Highway 14 to the Heard Cemetery, a slave graveyard in a pine clearing. Jackson was laid beside his father, who had died less than six months before in a car accident.

Today Jackson's grave still stands here, with a headstone financed by the Perry County Civic League that bears the shotgun pocks of passing vandals. SCLC conducts an annual service and pilgrimage here each February. The section of Highway 14 that runs in front of it has been renamed Martin Luther King Memorial Parkway. It runs about eighty-five miles through the heart of the Black Belt and is probably the longest road in the nation so named.

Mount Tabor Baptist Church

North Perry County, Alabama (Highway 29)

Coretta Scott married Martin Luther King, Jr., here on June 18, 1953, at her family's church. She wore a blue pastel waltz gown and insisted ahead of her time that *obey* be omitted from the wedding vows. When the reception was over, the newlyweds drove to the closest thing in the area to a hotel for blacks, a local funeral parlor.

The house of her father, Obadiah Scott, who had accumulated hundreds of acres as a farmer and whose daughters worked in the field, is up the hill next to his recently boarded-up grocery store. As a young girl Coretta lifted bags of feed and boxes her sister could not budge and kept up with the fastest harvester in the fields. King's first biographer wrote of her childhood frolics with her brother, "Willie and Coretta would roam the woods, wading in their favorite creeks, imaginatively fishing with a worm on a pin, catching crawfish with their bare hands."[19]

Lowndes County, Alabama

Birth of the Black Panther

White divinity student Jonathan Daniels had little preparation for full-time activism in Lowndes County save his Christian faith and his study of the absurd in the writings of Camus.

Lured south from New Hampshire by the TV accounts of Bloody Sunday in March 1965, Daniels came to a county in which field labor, long a way of life, had diminished after decades of mechanization. Most households lacked a car or a washing machine; four out of five had no telephone. In 1960 the median family income was $1,364, the lowest in the state and nearly half that of neighboring Dallas County. Even by Black Belt standards, black residents were low on the economic ladder: Farmhands got $3 to $6 a day in planting season. Blacks outnumbered whites four to one, but about ninety families owned 90 percent of the land in the county.

From 1873 to 1875, black Congressman James T. Rapier represented Lowndes County. But Alabama's constitutional changes in 1900 imposed literacy tests, property requirements, and poll taxes to disenfranchise the blacks who had swelled the voting rolls during

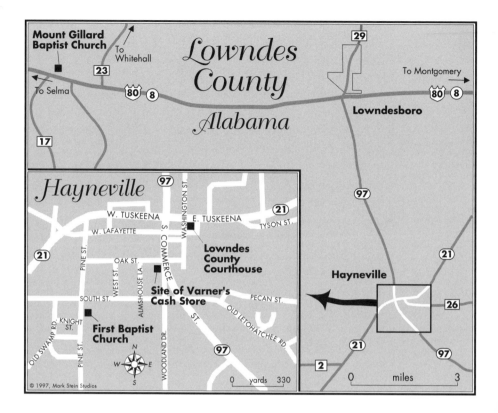

Reconstruction. Lowndes County had fifty-five hundred black voters registered in 1900; a year later the number was forty-four. By 1965 *all* blacks had been purged from the voting rolls, and a requirement that every new voter be vouched for by someone already registered perpetuated this condition. Blocked from voting, blacks also were excluded from jury service.

Some blacks had tried to register in the late 1950s, but the Lowndes County Movement grew as a quiet parallel to the Selma voting rights campaign of 1965. On March 1 a group of thirty-seven blacks appeared at the Lowndes County Courthouse at the center of the Hayneville town square, asking to register. Martin Luther King, Jr., joined them, inquired about the process, and was told to mind his own business. The office was abruptly closed.

On March 15 another group arrived and was directed to the county jail two blocks away, where a supposedly defunct gallows lurked near the registration table. This time local activists John Hulett and a blind preacher, Rev. J. C. Lawson, passed the test to become the first black registrants in Lowndes County in the twentieth century. Those not registered had failed to answer questions such as "What part does the Vice President play in the Senate and House?" and "What legal and legislative steps would the states of Alabama and Mississippi have to take to combine into one state?" On March 19, 1965, local residents who had some economic independence from whites founded the Lowndes County Christian Movement for Human Rights at Frank ("Bud") Haralson's store (now gone) in the town of White Hall.

Four days later the Selma to Montgomery marchers came through on Highway 80, drawing lines of sharecroppers to the roadside. Soon after the march was over, Stokely Carmichael, Bob Mants, and other SNCC workers moved into Lowndes County, thinking of it as the domino that could topple the Black Belt's old ways. They went from porch to porch, sometimes by mule, encouraging farmers and loggers to register. That spring blacks continued to show up to register at the county jail in Hayneville, and registrars agreed to suspend the voucher and literacy requirements.

Jonathan Daniels, an Episcopalian divinity student, was one of the few northerners who stayed behind after the Selma to Montgomery March. Although SNCC was wary of white activists by July 1965, Daniels nonetheless became the first white volunteer in Lowndes County. A mild-mannered man who drove a Plymouth, he wore his clerical collar and work boots to meet with prospective voters, attended mass meetings, and tried to convince the Dan River Mills textile plant to hire more blacks in skilled positions.

On August 14, 1965, SNCC organizers led the county's first mass demonstration against segregated facilities in the town of Fort Deposit. They fanned out to local stores and cafes, carrying signs that said: NO MORE BACK DOORS, and WAKE UP! THIS IS NOT PRIMITIVE TIME. Whites circled the marchers in cars bearing the bumper sticker "Open Season." As the marchers picketed the stores on that hot morning, Daniels and his coworkers were surrounded by white men and arrested for parading without a permit. They were carted in a dump truck to the county jail in Hayneville. It was Daniels's first, and only, jail term.

On August 20 Daniels and the others were released without explanation and walked a short distance to a cash store to get some cold drinks and await a ride. Daniels and Rev. Richard Morrisroe, a white priest from Chicago, were shot in front of the store. Daniels died instantly, and Morrisroe was hospitalized for months. Their assailant was tried and acquitted in September for the shooting of Daniels. Although the county had had its share of lynchings and was known as Bloody Lowndes before the voting campaign, the unpunished deaths of Daniels and Viola Liuzzo five months earlier solidified the nickname.

Meanwhile blacks tried to use their new voting power. Lowndes County, along with three other Black Belt counties and four other counties in the South, was chosen for initial enforcement of the Voting Rights Act in 1965 because registering was still extremely difficult for blacks. SNCC and local activists canvassed without the aid of voting lists, a proper directory, or much in the way of transportation, to get people to try the new procedure. By mid-September 1965, aided by federal registers set up at the post office in Fort Deposit, 1,328 blacks had registered. By the time of the general election in November 1966 blacks already constituted a majority of the eligible voters.

On April 2, 1966, blacks organized the Lowndes County Freedom Organization (LCFO), an independent political party designed to put blacks in office during the 1966 election. Its symbol was a pouncing black panther, connoting a strong response to provocation and a particular threat to the white rooster symbol of the Alabama Democrats, which carried a banner "White Supremacy for the Right" on it. The filing fees for political candidates suddenly were jacked from fifty to five hundred dollars, but the LCFO was still determined to back local people for office.

Seeking to set up a separate political party in Lowndes, the activists found creative ways to reach an untutored population. They coined a jingle, "Vote for the Panther and Go Home." They created comic books describing the duties of all the local offices: school board member, coroner, tax assessor, tax collector, and sheriff ("He collects fines in the county for bootlegging, traffic violations, etc."). Another comic book traced the political enlightenment of a Mr. Blackman, who complains that black folks use their mouths only for eating and saying, "Yes suh." Eventually Mr. Blackman goes to the courthouse to register, attends mass meetings, and becomes sheriff of the county on the panther ticket.

Less than three months after its founding the LCFO nominated a slate of independent candidates, but they lost. During the Meredith March

1966: From Farmer to Black Panther

A journalist quoted this black farmer in her story about the emerging Lowndes County Freedom Organization:

"We been walkin' with dropped down heads, with a scrunched-up heart, a timid body in the bushes. But we ain't scared any more. Don't meddle, don't pick a fight, but fight back! If you have to die, die for something, and take somebody before you."[20]

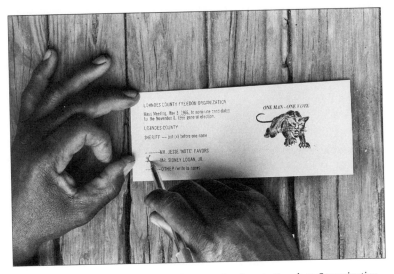

Filling out a nomination ballot for the Lowndes County Freedom Organization, with its black panther logo, 1966. (© 1997 Flip Schulke)

through Mississippi in 1966, the panther appeared on signs that said, MOVE ON OVER OR WE'LL MOVE ON OVER YOU. That same year Bobby Seale and Huey Newton founded the Black Panthers in California, using the Lowndes County symbol to represent their militant approach. After its candidates had won only minor offices in 1968, LCFO was merged with the National Democratic Party of Alabama (NDPA), a statewide black independent party.

Door-to-door canvassing in the Black Belt finally led to the election of Lucius Amerson as sheriff of Macon County in fall 1966, the first black to hold that office in the region since Reconstruction. He was followed in July 1969 by Thomas Gilmore, sheriff of Greene County, and in 1970 by John Hulett, sheriff of Lowndes County. These campaigns were marked by bitter white resistance. In Greene County the chairman of the NDPA bought up all the buckshot at the local hardware store as a precautionary measure. Sheriff Hulett presided over the modernization of a Lowndes County department that owned no police radio when he arrived. He also noticed that blacks began to carry shotguns in their truck cab racks just as whites had, and as time went on, he saw that both blacks and whites used those racks more for fishing equipment than for guns. He retired in 1993 after twenty-three years in office.

Sheriff Hulett's son, John E. Hulett, was elected mayor of Hayneville in 1988. By then the county commission was also majority black.

Today Jonathan Daniels is recognized as a martyr in the Episcopal Church calendar on August 14, the day of his arrest in Fort Deposit.

Mount Gillard Baptist Church
Trickem Fork (off Highway 80 at Route 17)

On March 25, 1965, white housewife Viola Liuzzo was killed on the highway a few miles away from here after participating in the Selma to Montgomery March. Coming on the heels of an exuberant and violence-free march that had passed before the church's front door, Liuzzo's death was a sobering reminder of the risks of activism. That Sunday, three days later, 150 people arrived here for the first mass meeting in Lowndes County.

The gathering was a breakthrough because teachers and other community leaders, who had either ignored the Movement or worked behind the scenes, came out in open support. Although it began as a memorial and protest of the murder, the event evolved into regular meetings of the Lowndes County Movement to push for voter registration. The church was remodeled in 1987 and was used for a mass meeting during the Selma to Montgomery March reenactment in 1995.

Site of Varner's Cash Store
Hayneville (near intersection of Routes 21 and 97)

In the 1960s a wood-frame store here with its Coke sign overhead and Pepsi thermometers flanking the door was about the only store in town that blacks felt comfortable patronizing. In fact on August 20, 1965, a black activist released from jail had just bought cigarettes here when Jonathan Daniels and three others decided to

Qualifications

From an organizing booklet put out by the LCFO in 1967:

"They have told us that we are not 'qualified' to practice politics, that we are not 'qualified' to run our lives! Everyone knows if he will think about it that each and every grown man and woman is just as 'qualified' as anyone else to decide what he wants his life to be like. There may be some information that some of us need in order to decide how to go about making our lives what we want them to be, but we can get that information and we can learn it just as well as anyone else."[21]

get a drink while waiting for their rides. Daniels approached the store with Ruby Sales, a Tuskegee student. Walking behind him were Reverend Morrisroe and Joyce Bailey, a black Fort Deposit girl who had been arrested on her nineteenth birthday. After a week in the county jail without fans or air conditioning and bad food a Coke must have sounded pretty good to them. According to Sales, you could "feel the heat coming out of the pavement."

On that Friday afternoon the sight of a pair of scruffy young white men each walking beside a teenage black girl got the attention of Tom Coleman. Coleman, whose father had been sheriff in the 1910s, when Hayneville was a gambling haven, often played dominoes at the courthouse with the sheriff and deputies and was usually willing to lend a hand with law enforcement.

By the time Daniels and Ruby Sales reached the screen door, Coleman was standing at the door with his shotgun. He told them "to get off this property, or I'll blow your goddamn heads off." Daniels asked if he was threatening him and pushed Sales out of harm's way. Then, from six to eight feet away, Coleman pointed his twelve-gauge shotgun at Daniels and fired, hitting him in chest. Sales, who had fallen to the floor, was covered with Daniels's blood and played dead. As Morrisroe grabbed Joyce Bailey and ran, Coleman fired again, hitting Morrisroe in the back and side. Bailey and Sales escaped, and Coleman then went to the courthouse and turned himself in, leaving Daniels draped over the concrete platform in front of the store and Morrisroe felled in the dirt road.

A week later Episcopalian ministers from New Hampshire attended a service for Daniels in Selma and journeyed to the cash store to honor one of their own. Morrisroe survived the attack. Today the store is an insurance office, and the county jail remains behind it.

Lowndes County Courthouse

Washington Street, Hayneville

Like nearly every county courthouse in the South, this one sits at the center of a leafy town square with a towering obelisk to the Confederacy at one end. In the 1950s it had plank floors and a cage for prisoners. The tall windows were thrown open in the hot months, inviting bugs or birds to fly in and circle under the tin ceiling. In 1965 the courthouse still had three rest rooms: WHITE MEN, WHITE WOMEN, and COLORED.

Trials in Lowndes County typified small-town justice at the time. The jury pool was picked by a county commission of three that weeded out people deemed either incompetent or too valuable else-

John Hulett, founding member of the Lowndes County Freedom Organization and later sheriff, on the portico of the Lowndes County Courthouse in Hayneville, 1996. (Jessica Allan)

where to serve on a jury. Blacks were not even on the rolls, but the commission also excluded people under twenty-one and over sixty-five, women, the disabled, and illiterates without property. In practice those selected for the jury box were mostly a few hundred middle-aged white men with time on their hands. Eight of them had been called to serve thirteen times or more in the eight years before the trial of Tom Coleman. Coleman himself had been a juror a dozen times in as many years.

Into this system in May 1965 went the case of Collie Leroy Wilkins, tried for the shooting of Viola Liuzzo on Highway 80. The jury deadlocked; a mistrial was declared. Four months later the same prosecutors and judge convened in the same courtroom to try Tom Coleman for the shooting of Jonathan Daniels. The prosecution seemed to have a good case for murder. Coleman had admitted the shooting and had done it in broad daylight in front of several witnesses. No weapons had been found at the scene that could be traced to the victims, and an argument of self-defense was a stretch considering that the victims were just out of jail and had no reason to threaten Coleman.

As the courtroom filled on the first day of the trial, September 27, 1965, it was clear that Coleman's case would be no calm review of events at the cash store. Coleman was charged with the lesser charge of manslaughter, despite the intervention of the state attorney general Richmond Flowers, who had pushed for a murder charge. As potential jurors were picked, Tom Coleman's own name came up at random. "Might as well strike him," someone helpfully suggested. Finally a dozen white men, all of whom knew Coleman or his family, were selected. The three defendants from the Liuzzo trial sat in the audience along with dozens of friends and reporters, who spilled out onto folding chairs.

After the prosecution's evidence the defense needed just fifty-three minutes for its case. In addition to a claim of self-defense, Coleman's attorney succeeded in branding Daniels as a shady outsider in clerical garb who carried a book called *The Fanatic* and kept company with young black girls. The jury came back the next day with an acquittal and filed out, each juror shaking Tom Coleman's hand. Coleman got his final reprieve when the case against him for shooting Morrisroe was dismissed and no further charges were brought. He eventually went back to his construction job and continued playing dominoes at the courthouse into retirement.

Meanwhile blacks continued to register to vote here and in Fort Deposit, although a swastika was painted on the town water tower right behind the courthouse and a cross was burned on the town square lawn the night after Coleman's arrest. The day Daniels was shot, seventy-one blacks had registered under the eye of federal registrars. By September 1965 blacks voters nearly equaled white voters in the county.

First Baptist Church
Pine Street, Hayneville

Although at first reluctant to open its doors to Movement meetings, this church held a memorial service for Jonathan Daniels. It also served as the county's first real polling place for blacks in the modern era. By law, nominations for local offices had to take place at or near the courthouse, but even after the Voting Rights Act was passed, the Lowndes County Courthouse was the last place blacks would be allowed to meet. The location was switched to the grounds of First Baptist six blocks away, and residents overcame prevailing fears to come and drop paper ballots in cardboard boxes on May 3, 1966, for the independent LCFO party with its roaring panther emblem. Nine hundred new black voters met outside the church to nominate an independent slate for local offices. Although the panther candidates lost in the general election that fall, the vote was a remarkable achievement considering that not one black had been registered in Lowndes County a year earlier.

Arkansas

Little Rock, Arkansas

Federal Troops Escort the Little Rock Nine

Central High School
Park Street (between Fourteenth and Sixteenth Streets)

Above the entrance of massive Central High School, four stone figures are meant to represent ambition, personality, opportunity, and preparation. Together these qualities are a collective profile of the nine black high school students selected to pass through the front doors for the first time in 1957.

Central High has always resembled a fortress. When it was built in 1927, it was the largest high school in the nation, two blocks long and one block deep. The school was so vast that the returning students routinely tricked the new students into purchasing elevator tickets, although the only way to reach the seven floors of the building was by climbing flights of stairs.

Little Rock quickly became the first major test of federal power to enforce the *Brown* decision. The nearby town of Hoxie had managed to integrate in 1955, and Little Rock was set to phase in integration after a federal court order required it. But Orval Faubus had been

Central High School in 1996. (Townsend Davis)

elected governor in 1954 with staunch opposition to integration as his rallying cry. On Labor Day, September 2, 1957—two days before the start of the new school year—he sent canvas-topped trucks filled with Arkansas national guardsman to surround the school.

Daisy Bates, the state NAACP president, had planned for all nine black children to meet at the corner of Twelfth Street and Park, but on the morning of September 4 only eight appeared. Student Elizabeth Eckford had not heard of the plan because her family did not have a phone. An angry crowd of white spectators showed up at the school that morning, and when Mrs. Bates and several local ministers attempted to usher the eight students through the lines, they were stopped cold by the guardsmen. Eckford, who approached the line at another point, was on her own. Wearing sunglasses and a white checked dress and carrying a notebook in her hand, she repeatedly tried to pass through the line while a crowd of white onlookers hounded her from behind. She finally gave up and sat down at a city bus stop. She was surrounded by whites who spit epithets at her until a reporter and the wife of a local professor came to her aid and got her onto a bus out of the area.

On September 23 the black students again attempted to enter the school, this time by the side entrance on Sixteenth Street. The crowd had expected them in the front, so the students succeeded in entering the school for a few hours. But the mob attacked several reporters on the scene, and the local police chief determined the children had to be sent home for their own safety.

President Eisenhower had followed the unrest from a golf course in Newport, Rhode Island. To him such flouting of a federal court order required a strong reaction. After the mob had prevailed a second time, he nationalized the Arkansas National Guard and ordered a thousand troops from the 101st Airborne "Screaming Eagle" Division of the 327th Infantry Division to assist in carrying out the Court's integration order.

Army station wagons showed up at Mrs. Bates's house on September 25 to escort the students to the school once more. One of the nine children said, "For the first time in my life, I feel like an American citizen." The parents and Mrs. Bates watched anxiously from the living room. At the school Major General Edwin Walker had explained his mission to the entire student body gathered in the auditorium and said that no interference would be tolerated. At 9:22 A.M. the students pulled up to the school entrance, surrounded by soldiers, and walked up the staircase and through the front door as 350 paratroopers with rifles stood at attention around the school's perimeter.

That year the Little Rock Nine, as they were known, negotiated the cavernous, mazelike corridors of the school with one soldier each to serve as their bodyguards. They endured nearly continuous abuse, and several eventually moved to other cities because of it or because their parents lost their jobs as a result of the crisis. Governor Faubus, in a move widely imitated throughout the South, later closed the school to all students for an entire year rather than integrate. But on May 27, 1958, Ernest Green became the first of the nine to graduate in a ceremony at Quigley Stadium. Each of the nine went on to attend college.

Today the school exterior remains essentially as it was in 1957, although a floral plaza in front of the steps has replaced a decorative pool. The student body today is majority black, and the school continues its academic and athletic dominance in the state.

Daisy Bates House
1207 West Twenty-eighth Street

Daisy Bates and her husband, L.C., built and moved into this house in the summer of 1956. She was president of the state NAACP, and he founded a weekly paper focusing on racial justice,

The Little Rock Nine: Life at Central High and Beyond

Nine children integrated Central High School in the fall of 1957:

Minnijean Brown: Eleventh grader. Dreamed of singing in the glee club. Taunted frequently, she was suspended and later expelled for dumping her cafeteria tray on her tormentors. Afterward white students passed out cards that read, "One down, eight to go." Became a writer and citizen of Canada.

Elizabeth Eckford: A quiet student who sewed her own clothes. The image of her walking alone into the jaws of a hostile crowd was captured in famous photo and news accounts. Became a social worker and, alone among the nine, continued to live in Little Rock.

Ernest Green: The only senior in the group. In 1958, 125 national guardsmen monitored his graduation, the first for a black student at Central High. Became a managing director of Lehman Brothers investment bank.

Thelma Mothershed: Eleventh grader with a heart condition that caused her to collapse several times during the stressful first term at Central High. Became a teacher.

Melba Patillo: Daughter of a teacher, she went on to become a TV reporter and wrote a memoir of her childhood and the Little Rock crisis entitled *Warriors Don't Cry.*

Gloria Ray: Was forced to "dance" as whites threw firecrackers at her feet in the hallways of Central High. One student tried to lasso her with a rope. Later became a publisher and moved to the Netherlands.

Terrence Roberts: His family moved to California after repeated abuse. Became a professor at UCLA.

Jefferson Thomas: Quietly endured hallway beatings. His father was arrested for keeping a concealed weapon during the integration of Central High. With Carlotta Walls, became the last of the nine to graduate from Central High in 1960.

Carlotta Walls: One classmate followed her around and called her names while stepping on her heels. Became a realtor in Denver.

the *State Press.* She was jailed after writing a story about a hand-picked jury in a labor case involving striking black workers. In August 1957 a rock came flying through the large front window with a note attached: "Stone This Time. Dynamite Next."

During the integration of Central High Mrs. Bates became the protector of the Little Rock Nine. She talked with the parents, listened to the students' tales of daily abuse, and called state or

The Little Rock Nine in the home of Daisy Bates, September 1957. (UPI/Corbis-Bettmann)

national politicians for help. She received most of the fan and hate mail that poured in for the students once the issue was covered by the media, and she hosted the media here as well. The nine students often convened here to plan their next move or subject themselves to the popping flashes of news cameras. The house was guarded by trainees from a local barbershop.

Today every inch of wall space in the house is taken up with awards and tributes, with piles more in the basement. Mrs. Bates moves about in a wheelchair and was honored by being asked to carry the Summer Olympic torch in 1996 when it passed through Little Rock on its way to Atlanta.

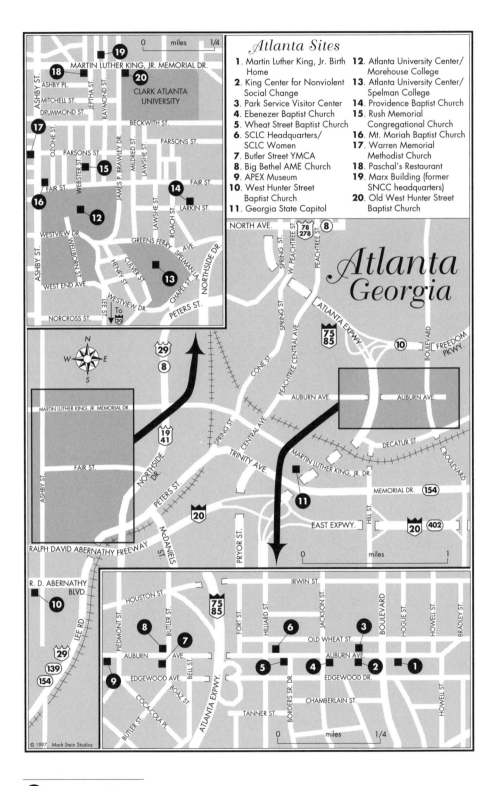

Atlanta Sites

1. Martin Luther King, Jr. Birth Home
2. King Center for Nonviolent Social Change
3. Park Service Visitor Center
4. Ebenezer Baptist Church
5. Wheat Street Baptist Church
6. SCLC Headquarters/ SCLC Women
7. Butler Street YMCA
8. Big Bethel AME Church
9. APEX Museum
10. West Hunter Street Baptist Church
11. Georgia State Capitol
12. Atlanta University Center/ Morehouse College
13. Atlanta University Center/ Spelman College
14. Providence Baptist Church
15. Rush Memorial Congregational Church
16. Mt. Moriah Baptist Church
17. Warren Memorial Methodist Church
18. Paschal's Restaurant
19. Marx Building (former SNCC headquarters)
20. Old West Hunter Street Baptist Church

Atlanta
Georgia

© 1997, Mark Stein Studios

Georgia

Atlanta, Georgia

Leadership from Sweet Auburn to West Hunter

Atlanta has boasted of its reputation as "Too busy to hate" ever since the phrase was coined by its longtime mayor William Hartsfield in the 1950s. Its political leaders always emphasized reconciliation and trusted a small group of black and white leaders to resolve racial tensions. Atlanta served as home to the civil rights organizations SCLC, SNCC, and the Southern Regional Council, which each mounted campaigns from Louisiana to Virginia. For all but five years of his life, Martin Luther King, Jr., lived here, the city of his birth, preaching at his father's Ebenezer Baptist Church, writing his books, and getting what little relaxation he could manage between crises beckoning from other cities.

Before the Movement Atlanta was as fundamentally governed by the Jim Crow code of segregation as any other city in the South. A race riot in 1906 left twenty-six blacks dead and streetcars overturned, raising calls for an organization to address racial injustice. The NAACP grew out of those protests in 1909, and its only founding black officer was W. E. B. Du Bois, a sociology professor at Atlanta University. In summer 1946 blacks in Atlanta agitated for civil rights after whites had killed two black couples in a brutal road-side lynching in Monroe, Georgia, a mere fifty miles east of the city. Throughout King's life, whether it was as a child forced to stand on a segregated bus or as a father who could not take his children to a whites-only amusement park called Funtown, he often pointed to his hometown to show how partial racial progress actually was. Stone Mountain, just northeast of Atlanta, always was considered a Klan stronghold.

Over the years the seeds of racial change grew up predominantly in two Atlanta neighborhoods: the cluster of historically black colleges on the west side of town and the former black business district along Auburn Avenue to the east. In 1942 Benjamin Mays, president of Morehouse College, and Rufus Clement, president of Atlanta University, were among the black leaders who gathered in Durham, North Carolina, for a regional conference on racial injustice, which was sharpened by the prospect of black servicemen being sent into combat in World War II. The conference decried the wide range of racial wrongs that became a menu for protest in the coming decades: exclusion of blacks from voting and juries, police brutality, and inequality in education and salaries.

Stirred by such manifestos and the prospect of black voters beginning in 1944, city officials began to allow the first cracks in segregation in the late 1940s. Atlanta hired eight black policemen in 1948, at first empowering them only to hold rather than arrest white suspects but later according them full duties. After the U.S. Supreme Court's decision requiring desegregation of public schools "with all deliberate speed," in 1955 Atlanta slowly began the process of doing so; it took until the early seventies to achieve full integration. Five respected black men decided to test out the public North Fulton golf course in late 1955 and played without incident.

Atlanta's first racial protest outside the courtroom came in January 1957, when a group of local black preachers rode in the white section of city buses and were arrested. Later that month King convened a conference of young activist preachers at Ebenezer Baptist Church to plot the future of integrated public transportation. The group, which became known as the Southern Christian Leadership Conference, went on to organize challenges to everything from poverty to locally imposed voting barriers. After he moved back to Atlanta from Montgomery in early 1960, King used Atlanta as his base of operations.

Students from the west Atlanta campuses in 1960 realigned the goals of the Movement in Atlanta toward the removal of racial prej-

The King family: "Daddy," Alberta, Coretta, and Martin, Jr., with their four children, in Atlanta in 1964. (Max Scheler/Black Star)

udice from all walks of life. Not long after the first college student sit-ins were reported at a Woolworth's in Greensboro, North Carolina, in February 1960, black students began to eye the plush downtown department stores as potential targets. At first heeding the advice of their elders on the faculties of Atlanta University and Morehouse College, the students published an "Appeal for Human Rights" demanding immediate equal rights. Then, in March, they started their first sit-ins, targeting the premier store Rich's. "If we can topple Rich's," reasoned student leader Lonnie King, "all we have to do is just kind of whisper to the others." The tactic of requesting service at white-only lunch counters was so novel that some reporters called them sit-downs.

The students honed their operation over the summer and sent waves of student volunteers to sit at white sections and to picket those stores that refused to serve or hire blacks on a equal basis. Businesses were hard pressed, and several closed for months at a time. After endless negotiations between black attorney A. T. Walden and white lawyers representing a group of stores, a partial agreement to desegregate was announced in March 1961.

The "Blue Bomb" and the Presidential Election of 1960

King's jailing for joining the students who sat in at Rich's in October 1960 not only prompted high-level discussions in Atlanta but also set the stage for a phone call that rippled through the U.S. presidential race.

At the time the race between Richard Nixon and Senator Jack Kennedy was very tight. Nixon had met King briefly in his capacity as Eisenhower's vice president, but Kennedy was a stranger to the King family. While held on the sit-in charge, King was transferred from Atlanta to a jail in De Kalb County, where he had been put on probation for a preexisting traffic charge. When the county judge found King had violated the terms of his probation by trespassing at Rich's, he was given a four-month sentence and immediately transferred to the maximum security state prison at Reidsville, more than two hundred miles south and east (still there).

In the heat of the campaign Jack Kennedy took an aide's advice and called Coretta King, who was pregnant with her third child, from Chicago to express his sympathies. Shortly thereafter Robert Kennedy called the De Kalb County judge to argue that the civil rights leader was entitled to bail pending an appeal. Meanwhile King wrote his first letter from jail to his wife, requesting some books, a handful of sermons, and a radio. The next day he was released.

The Kennedy gestures did much to attract "Daddy" King and other black voters to the Kennedy camp, which capitalized on the incident by distributing a campaign flyer on blue paper that highlighted the difference between "No Comment Nixon versus a Candidate with a Heart, Senator Kennedy." The flyer, known as the blue bomb, was distributed to black churches the Sunday before the election. In the end Kennedy carried the states of Illinois, Michigan, and South Carolina with a large measure of black votes. The phone call to Mrs. King also marked the beginning of on-again, off-again contact between the Kennedy administration and the Movement, which became most pronounced during times of crisis, such as during the Freedom Rides of 1961.

In 1962 Ivan Allen, a bow tie–wearing white moderate, became Atlanta's mayor, and Leroy Johnson became the first black senator in the Georgia legislature since Reconstruction. Allen was the first southern mayor to endorse the Civil Rights Act of 1964. Several of Atlanta's restaurants and hotels refused to bow to the new order. Downtown restaurants, such as Leb's Deli, Ship Ahoy, Krystal, and Morrison's (all now gone), were subjected to another round of student sit-ins, which in turn drew groups of Klansmen in robes onto Peachtree Street. Rabid segregationist Lester Maddox, who headed a group called GUTS (Georgians Unwilling to Surrender), used his

College students in the female detention room after simultaneous protests at restaurants downtown, March 15, 1960.
(UPI/Corbis-Bettmann)

restaurant The Pickrick (formerly at 891 Hemphill Avenue NW) to publicize protests against the civil rights bill on huge racist signs. When the bill passed and was tested by some black customers, Maddox drove them from the premises at pistol point. The Heart of Atlanta Motel (formerly at 225 Courtland Street) provided the test case under which the U.S. Supreme Court declared the Civil Rights Act of 1964 constitutional. After that Atlanta's businesses finally were open to all, more than four years after the local student movement had begun. In 1964 King was awarded the Nobel Peace Prize and, after much agonizing among Atlanta's glitterati, was honored in a tribute dinner at the city's first fully integrated gala.

Archsegregationist Lester Maddox outside his restaurant, The Pickrick, after black students attempted to integrate it, August 14, 1964. (UPI/Corbis-Bettmann)

In the late 1960s the Georgia statehouse became a stage to test the limits of political speech. Julian Bond, a member of SNCC and a Movement leader during his student days at Morehouse College, won election in 1965 to the Georgia House of Representatives from a neighborhood on Atlanta's west side. After his election but before the term began, SNCC issued a statement, which Bond endorsed, protesting against the draft and the excesses of the Vietnam War. Legislators were so outraged that they refused to seat Bond, forbidding him to stand and swear the oath of office on January 10, 1966. This gesture brought demonstrations ringing the Georgia Capitol and eventually a decision from the U.S. Supreme Court affirming Bond's right to the seat, despite his expressions of dissent. Bond later received a nomination for vice president at the Democratic National Convention in Chicago in 1968, only to withdraw it because at age twenty-eight he fell well below the constitutionally required age of thirty-five.

Racial rifts continued to tear at the fabric of the city that was so proud of its ability to mend them. In September 1966 a police shooting of a black car theft suspect sparked riots in the predominantly black Summerhill neighborhood near Grant Park. In November the people of Georgia voted segregationist Lester Maddox into the governor's mansion, a gubernatorial term during which Maddox continued his racist grandstanding.

On April 4, 1968, the city and the nation were plunged into sorrow after King was assassinated at a motel in Memphis, Tennessee. City officials feared a renewal of street violence, which gripped dozens of U.S. cities. Atlanta did not explode, but people poured into the street for the funeral on April 9, when hundreds of thousands walked down Auburn Avenue from the Ebenezer Baptist Church to a service at Morehouse College. King's body was borne in a mule-drawn wagon, meant to symbolize SCLC's next major campaign, the Poor People's March to Washington. King was buried temporarily at Southview Cemetery. A few weeks later his close friend Rev. Ralph Abernathy led the march in King's name.

During the 1960s Atlanta gained a baseball stadium, a subway system, and an influx of seventy thousand new black residents. By 1969 blacks had won five of sixteen city council seats and three of nine positions on the board of education. Finally, in 1973, thirty-five-year-old Maynard Jackson was elected Atlanta's first black mayor. Jackson, a grandson of the former don of Auburn Avenue John Wesley Dobbs, redistributed political power to neighborhood councils, laid plans for a new airport, and aggressively promoted affirmative action in city contracts and hiring. His two terms were a study in how reforms are tempered by the agenda of the business elite.

In the 1970s and 1980s Movement veterans dominated Atlanta politics. Andrew Young, former SCLC executive vice-president, was elected to represent Atlanta's Fifth Congressional District in 1972, becoming the first black representative to go to Washington from Georgia since Reconstruction. He also served as ambassador to the United Nations under President Carter and two terms as Atlanta mayor from 1981 to 1989. In 1986 Movement veterans John Lewis, former SNCC chairman, and Julian Bond squared off in a hard-fought battle for Atlanta's Fifth Congressional District. Lewis prevailed and has been reelected six times, serving as a Democratic party whip and, since the Republican majority was elected in 1994, as an unofficial foil to House Speaker Newt Gingrich, who represents the 90 percent white Sixth District just north of the city. Other Movement figures, including Benjamin Mays, Lonnie King, and Hosea Williams, have continued to weave through Atlanta politics, speaking out on racial balance in the schools, opportunities for minority contractors, the impact of freeway construction, and other community issues of the post-Movement era.

"Sweet Auburn" Avenue

Auburn Avenue between Courtland and Randolph Streets

At its peak a dozen or so blocks along Auburn Avenue were the backbone of a black business district that *Forbes* magazine in 1956 dubbed "The Richest Negro Street in the World." It was originally named Wheat Street, after white merchant Augustus Wheat, but residents successfully petitioned the city council in 1893 to have it changed to Auburn. Its black-owned institutions were the envy of the entire South: banks, insurance companies, contractors, the *Atlanta Daily World* (a black daily newspaper since 1932), nightclubs, and three prominent churches that did not shy from worldly prosperity (Ebenezer Baptist, Wheat Street Baptist, and Big Bethel AME). In explaining the street's nickname, John Wesley Dobbs, a leading black Mason and voting campaigner in the 1930s, said, "It takes sugar to sweeten things, and, as you know, it takes money to buy sugar."

During the Movement Auburn was still a main drag. Both overall-clad SNCC workers and buttoned-down SCLC preachers ate and met at B. B. Beamon's restaurant (formerly at 233 Auburn); the first SCLC office was at the Savoy Hotel (formerly at 239 Auburn); SNCC had its first offices here (at 197 and 135 Auburn); and Coretta Scott King worked as a teller at Citizens' Trust Bank (formerly 212 Auburn) just after she was married. All these institutions have since vanished, but today the APEX (African-American Panoramic Experience) Museum, features a video on the history of Auburn Avenue and rotating exhibits on black culture at 135 Auburn. One of its most dramatic moments came on April 9, 1968, when a mule-drawn wagon carried King's body down Auburn Avenue and across town. Several of his trusted colleagues from the Movement led the massive procession, gripping the wagon as they walked.

Since its decline as a commercial center in the 1960s and 1970s Sweet Auburn has taken on new life as a historic district designed to preserve the remnants of King's childhood. The street received a makeover for the 1996 Summer Olympics. The National Park Service, operating out of an office at 522 Auburn, conducts tours of the house where King was born and has restored some of the shotgun houses on the same block.

Martin Luther King, Jr., Birth Home (Williams House)

501 Auburn Avenue

King grew up in a busy home. His grandfather Rev. A. D. Williams bought this Queen Anne–style house in 1909. When his daughter married Martin ("Daddy") King, Sr., the newlyweds moved in, and all three of their children were born in the upstairs bedroom: Christine, Martin, Jr., and Alfred Daniel (A.D.). Grandmother Williams occasionally conducted choir practice in the foyer while Daddy King met with those citizens interested in voting in the parlor. Other family members frequently stayed in any remaining bedrooms.

As a boy Martin, Jr., was subject to strict Baptist rules, and his parents assigned him chores, such as keeping the basement furnace supplied with coal. Bible verses were recited at the dinner table. But he was still allowed to play the board game Monopoly, roller-skate, ride a bike, and play basketball at the YMCA down the street. During one frolic he slid down a banister and knocked his grandmother down; he was so upset he jumped out a second-story window, landing unharmed. After Grandmother Williams's death in 1941 Daddy King moved to his dream house, a yellow brick structure three blocks north of the old house on Bishop's Row. That block has since been swallowed by a freeway.

The house where King was born, photographed in 1995. (Townsend Davis)

Martin, Jr., Reports on One Fine Snowy Day

Using a child's typewriter, eleven-year-old Martin, Jr., wrote a number of letters to his father, who at the time was preaching at a revival in Ohio. In his letters the young King often recounted funerals and other news from Ebenezer Baptist Church, family news, and how much money he was making on his newspaper delivery route. Here is one of King's letters, with its original spelling:

"24 January 1940   Atlanta, Ga.

"Dear Daddyy:

    "Just a few lines to let you know that I am feeling fine and hope you are the same. We are having some snow and the last report we heard the snow was a little more than ten and a half inches and we are really having a fine time make-ing snow men and throwing snow balls. And the policemen made everybody clean off their sidewalks and Christine and I cleaned off and it was a hard job. I received your letter and I am glad you liked my typeing. I am keeping the fire burnning but Mr. Gibson had to put some coal im the basement because it gave out. We can not go to school until Monday because it is to bad.

"Your truly,

"Martin Luther King"[22]

Martin, Jr., maintained strong ties to his home. During his first extended stay away from home at a farm in Connecticut when he was fifteen, he wrote to assure his father that he was behaving and to request that his mother send some of her fried chicken and rolls. After attending three all-black schools and skipping two grades, Martin, Jr., graduated from Booker T. Washington High School and began at Morehouse College in 1944. During his college years he lived at home and commuted to Morehouse by bus. Throughout his life Daddy King was a constant presence, at times lending support to his son's campaigns by picketing and speaking in his engagingly blunt style and at other times cautioning his son to pay more heed to his own safety. Daddy King died in 1984.

Martin Luther King, Jr., Center for Nonviolent Social Change

449 Auburn Avenue

Since 1971 King has been buried here in a marble tomb with an eternal flame set among cascading fountains. The King Center, although primarily administrative, has a gift shop and a lobby dis-play of King's clerical robe, his Nobel Peace Prize (awarded in 1964), and the congressional roll call for the bill that created the Martin Luther King, Jr., federal holiday in 1983. Across the street is the Park Service Visitor Center (450 Auburn), which features six thematic alcoves on King and the Movement bisected by a paved road, meant to symbolize the Movement's many marches. The King Center, for many years run by King's widow, Coretta Scott King, is currently headed by their third child, Dexter King.

Ebenezer Baptist Church
407 Auburn Avenue

Ebenezer Baptist Church has remained small and stable for more than seventy years while Atlanta's glittering skyline has grown up to the west of its neon sign. Three generations of men from King's family pastored this church, leading it through expansion, hope, and tribulation during the Movement.

The church was founded by Rev. John A. Parker in 1886 and was originally on Airline Street. Under Rev. Alfred Daniel Williams, it moved to its present location in 1914 and into the present sanctuary in 1922. Williams was treasurer of the National Baptist Convention and president of the local NAACP chapter.

His son-in-law, Martin Luther King, Sr., grew up on hardscrabble farmland in Stockbridge, Georgia, and made his way as a circuit preacher. Although his education consisted of one teacher for all grades who taught without books or pencils, Daddy King received a degree from Morehouse College and married Alberta Williams, A. D. Williams's only surviving child and a graduate of Spelman College. In 1931 Daddy King became pastor of Ebenezer, rescuing the church from near bankruptcy and establishing it as the house of worship for the economic and educational elite. His firm control of church affairs became the model his son, Martin, Jr., later emulated when pastoring his first church, Dexter Avenue Baptist Church in Montgomery, Alabama. Daddy King also led early efforts to get black citizens to vote and to equalize the salaries of black and white teachers.

Martin, Jr., gave his first sermon at Dexter at age eighteen and became an assistant pastor in 1948, when he was still in college. After graduate school he moved to Montgomery and became a lead spokesman for the bus boycotters in 1955–56. He convened about sixty of the South's active black preachers at Ebenezer in January 1957 to talk about plans for integration of public transportation, a group that became SCLC. Four years later Ebenezer served as a coordinating center for the Freedom Rides.

In 1960 King joined his father at Ebenezer as copastor, allowing

King at the Ebenezer Pulpit

In the late 1960s King increasingly confided in his home congregation in a way that differed from his prepared statements to the press. He often used the Ebenezer pulpit to express his worries about death threats and personal shortcomings. The sermons were faithfully recorded by his wife, Coretta, on a tape machine, which is currently on display at the King Center. Here are four excerpts from sermons delivered in his home church:

On the Social Gospel (March 3, 1963)[23]

"I'm sick and tired of seeing Negro preachers riding around in big cars and living in big houses and not concerned about the problems of the people who made it possible for them to get these things. . . . The church that overlooks this is a dangerously irrelevant church. It's all right to talk about 'silver slippers over yonder,' but men need some shoes to wear down here. It's all right to talk about streets flowing with milk and honey over yonder, but let's get some food to eat for people down here in Asia and Africa and South America and in our own nation who go to bed hungry at night. It's all right to talk about mansions in the sky, but I'm thinking about these ghettos and slums right down here. Only religion that professes to be concerned about the souls of men and is not concerned about the economic conditions that cripple the soul, the social conditions that corrupt the soul, is a dry, dead, do-nothing religion in need of new blood. The danger of those who follow this idea that God is going to do everything is that they will end up with a purely otherworldly religion. They will separate religion from life. And they will separate the God of religion from the God of life and religion will have no relevance in the everyday affairs and agonies of men."

On Nonconformity (January 16, 1966)[24]

"Once the philosopher Nietzsche said, 'Every man is a hammer or an anvil.' I want you to decide this morning what you're going to be. Are you going to be an anvil, molded by the patterns of society? Are you going to be a hammer, molding the patterns of society? To put it another way, what are you going to be this morning, a thermometer or a thermostat? . . . Now this morning we as Christians must decide whether we will be thermometers, merely registering the temperature of society, or whether we will be thermostats, transforming the temperature of society. 'Be not conformed to this world. Be ye transformed by the renewing of your mind.'"

On Swimming and Faith (March 3, 1963)[25]

"I was with a friend of mine on a distant island. There we were out there trying to swim and I saw that he had an ease about his swimming. And he said to me, 'Martin, wait a minute. I want to get over to you the way to really swim. You are straining too much.' And I came to see at that moment that you learn to swim by faith. He said, 'Now, you've got to learn how to swim by using the dead man's float. Just stretch your arms straight out, and put your legs straight back and head lying straight down in the water and just float awhile.' And I tried it and I discovered that I couldn't sink. Only when I started struggling with the water did I sink. But when I would lay myself right there, arms straight forward and legs straight back and head straight down I just floated along. And I discovered that moment that this is the meaning of faith. It is not struggling for something but it is lying your all, your being, you existence out on the eternal, cosmic waters of the divide, and He will hold you up. Through storms, and winds, through rain and agony, He will hold you up."

On Vietnam (April 30, 1967)[26]

After making several impromptu remarks supporting the right to oppose the Vietnam War, King in 1967 came out squarely against the war in a speech at Riverside Church in New York on April 4, 1967. Many people within and without the Movement, including his father and NAACP leaders, disagreed with him. He delivered a version of this speech at Ebenezer, departing from his usual practice of preaching without notes to read from a written statement:

"There is at the outset a very obvious and almost facile connection between the war in Vietnam and the struggle I and others have been waging in America. A few years ago, there was a shining moment in that struggle. It seems as if there was a real promise of hope for the poor, both black and white, through the poverty program. There were experiments, hopes, a new beginning. Then came the build-up in Vietnam and I watched the program broken as if it was some idle political plaything—our society gone mad on war—and I knew that America would never invest the necessary funds or energies in rehabilitation of its poor so long as ventures like Vietnam continued to draw men and skills and money like some demonic, destructive suction tube. You may not know it, my friends, but it is estimated that we spend five hundred thousand dollars to kill each enemy soldier while we spend only fifty-three dollars for each person classified as poor. . . . [W]e have been repeatedly faced with a cruel irony of watching Negro and white boys on TV screens as they kill and die together for a nation that has been unable to seat them together in the same school room. . . . Somehow this madness must cease—we must stop now! . . . I speak for the poor of America, who are paying the double price of smashed hopes at home and death and corruption in Vietnam. . . . I speak out against this war because I am disappointed with America. There can be no great disappointment where there is no great love. I am disappointed with our failure to deal positively and forthrightly with the triple evils of racism, economic exploitation and militarism. We are presently moving down a dead-end road that leads to national disaster."

him more time to devote to SCLC campaigns. His sermons ranged from Mother's Day advice on how to teach children to love to his controversial opposition to the Vietnam War. In March 1968, just before his assassination, the last SCLC staff meeting was held at Ebenezer to discuss the troubled campaign in Memphis. King's last undelivered sermon was titled "Why America May Go to Hell."

After his death the haunting sound of King's own voice echoed through Ebenezer on April 9, 1968. A mere two months earlier he had taken to its pulpit and imagined his own funeral, saying he wanted to be remembered as a "drum major for justice" and to "leave a committed life behind." These taped words were played at the service to an openly weeping audience of 750 people who packed the church. Ushers were dressed in somber morning coats and striped pants, while many of the Movement workers, who were preparing for the Poor People's March, wore jeans to the funeral to express solidarity with the focus on alleviating poverty King had been emphasizing before his death. Afterward Reverend King's younger brother, Alfred Daniel (A.D.), took King's place until his own premature death in an accident in his swimming pool in 1969. Their mother, Alberta King, who devoted her life to the Ebenezer choir and the celebration of church music, was shot and killed in 1974 while playing the organ at an Ebenezer service by a deranged gunman from Ohio. The murderer, Marcus Chenault, died in prison in 1995.

Since Daddy King's retirement in 1975, Rev. Joseph L. Roberts has served as Ebenezer's pastor and head of its many community programs. Ebenezer's New Horizon Sanctuary, a new church that will feature eight teaching windows on black history and triple the old seating capacity, is scheduled to open across the street near the Visitor Center.

Southern Christian Leadership Conference Headquarters

334 Auburn Avenue

Since 1965 SCLC has run its many campaigns from this building, formerly home to one of the largest groups of black Masons. After an exploratory meeting at Ebenezer Baptist Church in January 1957 SCLC was founded on February 14, 1957, at a church in New Orleans. To avoid direct competition with the NAACP, it did not solicit individual memberships but relied on the ebb and flow of donations to survive; frequent brushes with insolvency resulted.

King headed the organization from its founding until his death in 1968, managing to keep together a stable of strong personalities ranging from the fiery Hosea Williams to the courtly Andrew Young.

The SCLC headquarters was initially set up by the indomitable Ella Baker in the Savoy Hotel on Auburn Avenue, followed by offices at 208 Auburn and 41 Exchange Place downtown under Rev. Wyatt Tee Walker. SCLC coordinated a range of programs, including voter registration across the South, the massive demonstrations in Birmingham known as Project C in 1963, the March on Washington in 1963, and the Poor People's Campaign of 1968. Most of its efforts were focused on cities other than Atlanta, although King made brief appearances in 1964 on behalf of striking black workers at the Scripto pen company, which had plants in the Auburn neighborhood. In 1968 Rev. Ralph Abernathy, King's handpicked successor, took over SCLC and led the Poor People's March to Washington behind the mule-drawn farm cart that had headed King's funeral procession.

Since 1977 SCLC has been headed by Rev. Joseph Lowery, one of

King and the SCLC staff meet at B. B. Beamon's restaurant on Auburn Avenue.
(© 1997 Flip Schulke)

the organization's founding preachers. He has kept the organization active in health care, racially charged legal cases, civil rights legislation, affirmative action, and gun buybacks to reduce violence. Although SCLC has been straining financially, a spin-off group called SCLC Women, founded in 1979 and headed by Lowery's wife, Evelyn, has mastered the art of the matching grant. SCLC Women has promoted education about civil rights through such efforts as erecting a monument in Lowndes County, Alabama, to Viola Liuzzo, a Detroit housewife killed after the Selma to Montgomery March in 1965. In 1995 SCLC Women moved into the Tabor Building at 328 Auburn Avenue, which features a civil rights photo collection exhibited in the stairwell.

The building also housed radio station WERD, the first black-owned radio station, which hit the airwaves in 1949. Its opening slogan was "We are here, we are here, and we ain't going nowhere." When King wanted to make an announcement from the SCLC office below, he banged on the ceiling with a broomstick. The radio announcer would introduce him, lower the microphone outside the window, and dangle it so King could pull it in and make the announcement.

Wheat Street Baptist Church
359 Auburn Avenue

Rev. William Holmes Borders used to preach with a microphone attached to a cord that was, in the words of a longtime congregant of this church, "about a hundred feet long—and he used every inch of it." In the 1940s Borders's pillar-to-post preaching style and resonant voice attracted a young Martin Luther King, Jr., to the church's formidable balcony. Inside the wide, stained glass sanctuary, completed in 1939, Borders served as pastor for fifty years until his retirement in 1988, in turn praising the worldly accomplishments of church members and then chastising them for not being more committed to civil rights. He was a learned and biting critic of segregation and hosted a radio program called "Seven Minutes at the Mike."

While all Atlanta was enthralled with the 1939 movie premiere of *Gone with the Wind*, Borders criticized the film as a romanticized view of slavery. When black servicemen were lynched in nearby Monroe, Georgia, in 1946, he presided at the funeral and set up a fund to catch the killers and to protest the halfhearted investigation that followed. In January 1957, with the Montgomery bus boycott concluded only weeks earlier, he led a group of preachers onto the white sections of Atlanta's city buses, launching what was called the Triple L Movement ("Love, Law, and Liberation"). His church became a haven and rallying point for protesting students from the west side campuses when they were turned away from the state Capitol in May 1960. His poem in praise of black achievers called "I Am Somebody," composed in 1943, has been adopted by civil rights leader Jesse Jackson as a trademark refrain.

Wheat Street today continues its talent for combining the dollar and the divine; its past accomplishments include the construction of a large housing complex and shopping center and the formation of a credit union.

Butler Street YMCA

20–24 Butler Street

When the U.S. Supreme Court outlawed all-white primaries in 1944, Mayor William Hartsfield ventured for the first time into the nerve center of black Atlanta, the Butler Street YMCA. He met with black leaders and urged them to join the voting rolls. Within two months eighteen thousand blacks had done so. From that point on the Y became a mandatory stop for politicians seeking opinions from black leaders as well as the place for planning local initiatives.

Under the motto "Food for Taste and Food for Thought for Those Who Hunger for Information and Association" the Hungry Club Forum has met here to discuss civic affairs since the 1940s. The first black police officers in the city initially were stationed here. The Y hosted many civic events, from SCLC's early fund-raisers to SNCC conferences to meetings with the police chief about brutality toward blacks. When Mayor Ivan Allen drafted his testimony in favor of the Civil Rights Act of 1964, he came to the Y to run it by black leaders first.

King used the Y as a place to swim, unwind, and get an occasional massage.

Atlanta University Center

West Atlanta

At the turn of the century the *Atlanta Constitution* reported: "On every hill top in the neighborhood of Atlanta there is a Negro college or university, comfortably, if not amply, endowed." From the polite petitions against the most flagrant abuses of Jim Crow in the 1910s to the street protests of the 1960s, the students and faculties of the historically black colleges here have always had a hand in pushing for change. The Atlanta University Center (AUC) consists of a cluster of institutions that have shared ideas and resources since their founding: Morehouse, Spelman, and Morris Brown colleges, Clark College and Atlanta University (now Clark Atlanta University), and the Interdenominational Theological Center.

Throughout their history they produced a large number of the country's black Ph.D.'s and ministers, as well as the blueprints for reform. W. E. B. Du Bois served on the sociology faculty at Atlanta University after the publication of *The Souls of Black Folk* in 1903 and stayed until he began working for the NAACP's clarion publication *Crisis.* Benjamin Mays, president of Morehouse, and Rufus Clement, president of Atlanta University, were often at the forefront of efforts to achieve racial equality during World War II.

For a young man with aspirations to leadership in Atlanta and beyond, graduation from Morehouse College (830 Westview Drive SW) was for many years a rite of passage. Spelman College (entrance at 350 Spelman Lane), across the street, prepared young women for the civic duties and social graces necessary to join the black social elite. Spelman College originated in the basement of Atlanta's Friendship Baptist Church and benefited from large philanthropic donations from the Rockefeller family. Morehouse was founded in Augusta, Georgia, in 1867, moved to Atlanta as the Atlanta Baptist Seminary in 1879, and was renamed Morehouse in 1913.

King's grandfather Rev. A. D. Williams was a Morehouse man, graduated in 1898. His wife, Jennie Parks, went to Spelman, as did their only daughter, Alberta Williams. Martin ("Daddy") King also went to Morehouse before assuming the pastorship of Ebenezer Baptist Church, so it was a natural choice for young Martin, Jr. After graduating, he went on to Crozer Theological Seminary in Pennsylvania and received a Ph.D. at Boston University.

The first student sit-ins in Greensboro, North Carolina, in February 1960 caught on quickly on Atlanta's west side. Students from all the AUC schools issued a joint statement in local newspapers in March 1960 that introduced a new militancy to Atlanta's famously civil discourse on race relations. "We do not intend to wait placidly for those rights which are already legally and morally ours to be meted out to us one at a time," they declared. "Today's youth will not sit by submissively, while being denied all of the rights, privileges and joys of life." Although Mayor Hartsfield said the statement was constructive, Governor Ernest Vandiver said it was "calculated to breed dissatisfaction, discontent, discord, and evil."

Students began with sit-ins at government offices on March 15, 1960, which resulted in seventy-seven arrests under an antitrespassing statute the Georgia legislature had just passed. Initial negotiations were fruitless, and the students perfected their protest operation over the summer. They set their sights on desegregating Rich's department store, the jewel of the downtown shopping district at Broad and Alabama streets. At Rich's, which had a crystal-clear enclosed walkway that carried shoppers between stores, one could get anything from "a packet of pins to a passage to Paris." Although many black professionals had charge accounts there, they were not allowed to eat at the lunch table, and few black workers rose above menial positions within the store.

The students, who were getting nowhere with the private petition-

---

Speaking Out: Martin Luther King, Jr., in College

Martin, Jr., was far from a serious college student, but he was very social and active outside the classroom. In four years at Morehouse, his only A was in his junior-year Bible class. In the rest of his classes, a mix of biology, sociology, literature, French, philosophy, and a course in freshman hygiene, he received a combination of mostly Bs and Cs. He was seen on campus sporting smart coats and a wide-brimmed hat, and he joined the debating team, glee club, and the Morehouse chapter of the NAACP. His talent for public speaking was evident, however, and he won second prize in oratorical contests in both 1946 and 1948, when he was just beginning to preach at Ebenezer Baptist Church. In a letter to the Atlanta Constitution *during the summer of 1946, after a series of brutal lynchings in nearby Monroe, Georgia, he showed early eloquence and outrage:*

"I often find when decent treatment for the Negro is urged, a certain class of people hurry to raise the scarecrow of social mingling and intermarriage. These questions have nothing to do with the case. And most people who kick up this kind of dust know that it is simple dust to obscure the real question of rights and opportunities. . . . We want and are entitled to the basic rights and opportunities of American citizens: the right to earn a living at work for which we are fitted by training and ability; equal opportunities in education, health, recreation, and similar public services; the right to vote; equality before the law; some of the same courtesy and good manners that we ourselves bring to all human relations."[27]

ing favored by their elders, finally convinced King to join them for a full-fledged march downtown. On October 19, 1960, they walked from the west side campuses down Hunter Street (now Martin Luther King, Jr., Drive) and appeared at the sixth-floor Magnolia Room at Rich's. Their arrests started daily waves of protest that eventually resulted in color-blind service at Atlanta's restaurants and hotels.

The October 19, 1960, sit-in resulted in King's first night in prison, spent at the Fulton County jail (formerly 157 Decatur Street). Although he had been arrested several times before and released, this time he joined the students in serving out his jail term to dramatize injustice rather than posting bail money. It was the first time Mrs. King had to explain to their two young children returning from nursery school why their father was in jail. The jailing took on added significance when King's transfer to De Kalb County to face penalties on another charge became a last-minute issue in the 1960 presidential campaign.

After King was killed on April 4, 1968, it was fitting that both Spelman and Morehouse would help lay him to rest. For two days his body lay in a open casket in Sisters Chapel, named for John D. Rockefeller's mother, Laura, and her sister, Lucy, on the Spelman quadrangle. Thousands of mourners filed by, leaving tears on the Plexiglas covering of his body that had to be wiped clean several times during the procession. After a memorial service at Ebenezer on April 9, King was eulogized by Benjamin Mays, president of Morehouse during King's college days and a King mentor, on the portico of Harkness Hall at Morehouse. Today a statue of King with his right arm extended stands in front of the Martin Luther King, Jr., International Chapel on Westview Drive across from the Spelman parking lot.

West Hunter Street Baptist Church
1040 Ralph David Abernathy Boulevard SW

For almost thirty years Rev. Ralph D. Abernathy, King's most trusted friend and Movement confidant, pastored this church, originally situated on West Hunter Street (now Martin Luther King, Jr., Drive). Their partnership began in Montgomery in the 1950s, when King pastored Dexter Avenue Baptist Church and Abernathy pastored First Baptist Church across town. When King moved to Ebenezer Baptist Church in Atlanta in 1960, Abernathy soon followed. Abernathy, after first serving as pastor at Eastern Star Baptist Church in Demopolis, Alabama, and First Baptist in Montgomery,

West Hunter Street Baptist Church, formerly pastored by Rev. Ralph Abernathy, photographed in 1995. (Townsend Davis)

began to preach at West Hunter in November 1961. West Hunter was well established but open to progress; its previous pastor, Rev. A. Franklin Fisher, was among the ministers arrested for attempting to integrate Atlanta's buses during the Triple L campaign in 1957.

Abernathy accompanied King on every major civil rights campaign from St. Augustine, Florida, to Chicago, Illinois, occasionally ending up in jail with him. He roomed with King at the Lorraine Motel in Memphis and was only steps away from his friend when King was gunned down in April 1968. It fell to Abernathy to coordinate memorials to King from this church and to carry the torch as SCLC's president from 1968 to 1977, starting with the Poor People's March to Washington. Abernathy served as pastor here until his death in 1990. He is entombed in Lincoln Cemetery on Simpson Road in west Atlanta. His inscription reads, "I tried." The church was formerly at 775 Hunter Street (now Martin Luther King, Jr., Drive) in a stone building (now used by another congregation) with a distinctive rose window. West Hunter Street Baptist Church moved to its present location in 1973 and is pastored by Rev. T. DeWitt Smith, Jr.

West Hunter was one of several churches in west Atlanta that hosted Movement activities, including Mount Moriah Baptist Church (200 Ashby Street SW), the site of a SNCC meeting before the sit-in at Rich's; Providence Baptist Church (659 Larkin Street SW), where student protesters ran a shuttle service for picketers downtown; and Rush Memorial Congregational Church (150 James P. Brawley Drive SW), where students were trained in nonviolent protest techniques. Warren Memorial United Methodist Church (181 Ashby Street SW) was the site of a dramatic mass meeting on March 10, 1961, when the terms of an initial agreement governing downtown stores were announced. Students were disappointed that it would not go into effect until the following fall and loudly blamed their elders until King made an impassioned plea for unity that saved the agreement and resulted in a temporary halt to street demonstrations.

Paschal's Restaurant

830 Martin Luther King, Jr., Drive SW (formerly West Hunter Street)

After west Atlanta's clean-cut students experienced their first arrests and were released on bond, they went to Paschal's near the colleges for a free chicken dinner. After that the restaurant became so popular as a Movement joint that Rev. Ralph Abernathy declared, "A new America has been mapped within the walls of Paschal's."

Founded by two brothers, Robert and James, as a sandwich shop on Hunter Street in 1946, Paschal's opened as a state-of-the-art motel and restaurant in 1959, just as the Movement was gaining mass appeal. In those days two pieces of chicken, yams, and green peas cost about ninety-nine cents. In 1960 the brothers added La Carrousel, a nightclub that booked the likes of Wes Montgomery and Aretha Franklin. Both SCLC staff and students met here under the watchful eye of Orah Sherman, hostess for more than thirty years. Until it closed in 1996, the Paschal brothers ran the place together; Robert tended to the kitchen while his younger brother, James, managed the business office.

Paschal's was one of the last remaining businesses from the heyday of Hunter Street, a lively campus-based complement to Sweet Auburn during Movement days. Militant and articulate SNCC workers ate down the street at Frasier's Cafe (formerly at 880 Hunter). Mixed in with the Dairy Queen and the Deluxe One Hour Odorless Cleaners were the key community centers: the old West Hunter Street Baptist Church, the NAACP regional office, the Pullman Porters Social Club, and the offices of the *Atlanta Inquirer*. The *Inquirer,* edited by Clark College humanities Professor Carl Holman,

James Paschal in 1995 in the restaurant he founded with his brother Robert called Paschal's on former West Hunter Street. (Townsend Davis)

started publishing in July 1960 as an alternative to the *Atlanta Daily World,* which did not support the student sit-ins. Staffed primarily by such student activists as Julian Bond and John Gibson, the *Inquirer* most closely expressed the high expectations of the students and the progressive faculty. Hunter Street, which today is economically hanging by a thread, was renamed Martin Luther King, Jr., Drive in the 1970s. In 1996 Paschal's was purchased by Clark Atlanta University.

Marx Building

6–8½ Raymond Street

From October 1962 until it was disbanded, SNCC made its headquarters here just off Hunter Street. The building was named for a local tailor, not for the philosopher with whose writings many of the college-educated staff were familiar. Here James Forman and the rest of the SNCC staff struggled with a sporadic supply of telephones, typewriters, and darkroom equipment to lead and keep track of civil rights campaigns in a dozen southern states. One winter, Forman ended up in the hospital when the heat went out. In its organizing prime the building was mint green, and inside, the staff often smelled home cooking from nearby Alex's Barbecue Heaven.

Although it managed to generate a steady stream of press releases and support new programs with few resources, the SNCC staff also was notorious for conducting marathon staff debates at the head-quarters. If you were off to a movie, as one Movement photographer remembers, "you usually had twelve people who went with you and spent two hours discussing which movie to see." Later during SNCC's Black Power phase SNCC Chairman Stokely Carmichael was arrested here for his involvement in the Atlanta Summerhill riots. Cleveland Sellers, SNCC program secretary, also was arrested here and jailed for refusing to submit to the draft during the Vietnam War. When times were rough, a perpetual pot of hot dogs and beans, an economical Movement fuel, was kept on a stove in the back of the office. Today the building is standing, but not inhabited.

Albany, Georgia

Putting the Plantation to the Test

Mounting a challenge to age-old customs takes practice. The Movement tested out nearly every nonviolent tactic in the southwest town of Albany, Georgia, sometimes simultaneously. A combination of voter registration, boycotts, sit-ins, marches, lawsuits, and urgent pleas to Washington had never been tried on a large scale until a local Albany Movement joined forces with SNCC and SCLC in 1961. The results were mixed for the national Movement, as the campaign surged on and off for six years. But activists learned critical lessons about the dynamics of nonviolence and hastened the arrival of desegregation to a town that was as firmly entrenched in the old ways as anywhere in Alabama or Mississippi.

Nestled in the midst of peanut and pecan farms, not far from President Jimmy Carter's hometown of Plains, Georgia, Albany was first and foremost planters' country. In earlier times it was a trading center for slaves and cotton. All around it were properties owned in the modern era by such families as the Woodruffs and the Mellons and bearing old plantation names: Mercer Mill, Pineland, Wild-meade, and Chickasawhatchee. Situated on the banks of the Flint River, Albany was home to more than fifty-five thousand "happy people," as one publication put it, with the Coats & Clark thread plant as its largest industry. In those days the area south of

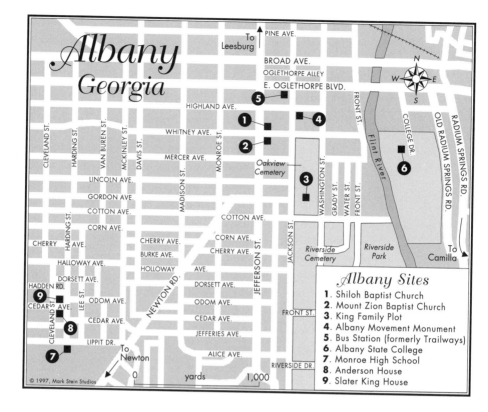

Albany Georgia

To Leesburg

PINE AVE.
BROAD AVE.
OGLETHORPE ALLEY
E. OGLETHORPE BLVD.
HIGHLAND AVE.
WHITNEY AVE.
MERCER AVE.
LINCOLN AVE.
GORDON AVE.
COTTON AVE.
CORN AVE.
CHERRY AVE.
BURKE AVE.
HALLOWAY AVE.
DORSETT AVE.
HADDEN RD.
ODOM AVE.
CEDAR AVE.
LIPPIT DR.
To Newton

CLEVELAND ST.
HARDING ST.
VAN BUREN ST.
MCKINLEY ST.
DAVIS ST.
MONROE ST.
MADISON ST.

Oakview Cemetery

WASHINGTON ST.
GRADY ST.
WATER ST.
FRONT ST.

FRONT ST.
Flint River
COLLEGE DR.
OLD RADIUM SPRINGS RD.
RADIUM SPRINGS RD.

COTTON AVE.
CORN AVE.
CHERRY AVE.
HOLLOWAY AVE.
DORSETT AVE.
ODOM AVE.
CEDAR AVE.
JEFFERIES AVE.
ALICE AVE.

JACKSON ST.
JEFFERSON ST.
NEWTON RD.

Riverside Cemetery
Riverside Park
To Camilla

FRONT ST.
RIVERSIDE DR.

CHERRY AVE.
HARDING ST.
HALLOWAY AVE.
DORSETT AVE.
CEDAR AVE.
LEE ST.
CLEVELAND ST.

© 1997, Mark Stein Studios

0   yards   1,000

Albany Sites
1. Shiloh Baptist Church
2. Mount Zion Baptist Church
3. King Family Plot
4. Albany Movement Monument
5. Bus Station (formerly Trailways)
6. Albany State College
7. Monroe High School
8. Anderson House
9. Slater King House

Oglethorpe Boulevard was a largely unpaved area of about eleven blocks square known as Harlem. There was only one hotel for blacks (now gone), and news of the black community was carried in the black weekly paper, the *Southwest Georgian* (still in business today). The daily *Albany Herald* took a segregationist stance under the leadership of James Gray, a force in the Democratic Party and family friend of the Kennedys. Even the tax forms for blacks were a different color from those for whites.

Underneath what one resident called the "sea of pseudotranquility" simmered discontent with segregation. Local black leaders started to discuss ways to break it down in the 1940s. The Voters League was created in 1947, and by 1958 a remarkable 19 percent of eligible black voters had registered. News of the strong stand taken by the ACMHR in Birmingham, Alabama, in the late 1950s prompted a number of local black citizens to start organizing: Slater and C. B. King, Marion Page, Bo and Goldie Jackson, Rev. Samuel Wells, E. D. Hamilton, and Dr. William Anderson. In 1959 an NAACP Youth Council was created under Thomas Chatmon. After a high school student sat in the white section of a movie house, thirty-five Monroe High School (900 Lippitt Drive) students tried it, leaving when a police officer arrived. In early 1961 black citizens put forth a mild petition asking for discussion of racial issues by the city commission and pointing out the need for paving and sewage facilities in black residential areas.

At the same time SNCC decided in August 1961 to focus voter registration efforts on Albany. When SNCC's Charles Sherrod, twenty-two, and Cordell Reagon, eighteen, set up shop in Albany that October, students were curious. They gave the activists the admiring label of Freedom Riders, although some adults crossed the street to avoid them. Sherrod, Reagon, and SNCC worker Charles Jones made the rounds of the pool halls and basketball courts to attract young people to their workshops. In November the progressive Slater King took over leadership of the local NAACP, and on November 17, 1961, a hodgepodge of adult organizations and SNCC banded together to form the Albany Movement; Dr. Anderson was president, Slater King vice-president, and retired railroad worker Marion Page secretary. Although there was agreement on the need for the organization, the local Movement at that moment had no practical strategy.

Meanwhile the younger generation was not waiting around for orders. In the wake of the Freedom Rides the federal Interstate Commerce Commission had issued a ruling that all interstate transportation facilities be desegregated. On November 1, 1961, the day that order went into effect, nine students gathered in the white section of the Trailways Station on the corner of Oglethorpe Boulevard and Jackson Street in the north corner of Harlem in Albany's first open street protest. Threatened with arrest, they left and later filed affidavits with the ICC. During Thanksgiving travel on November 22 three high school students from the NAACP Youth Council were arrested for sitting in the white section of the bus station dining room, and later that day Bertha Gober and Blanton Hall, SNCC protégés and students from Albany State College, were arrested for trying out the white waiting room. Three hundred students protested their convictions and jail term the next day.

The first mass meeting of the Albany Movement was held in their honor on November 25 at Mount Zion Baptist Church. The Movement also opened two other veins of protest: the first mass march on November 27 protesting the expulsion of Gober and Hall from Albany State and a boycott against businesses that placed ads in the

A Crowd Gathers at the Trailways Eatery

In his first experience in a long career of writing about the Movement, white reporter Pat Watters covered the first mass march in Albany for the Atlanta Journal *on November 27, 1961. Here he describes the march, which started at Shiloh Baptist Church and ended at the Trailways Bus Terminal restaurant:*

"The little band of the brave walked silently to the bus station, and there awaiting their 'demonstration,' twenty-five state troopers in yellow raincoats held big billy clubs, and the white paddy wagons of the Albany police idled nearby. The demonstrators were joined by a tall, slim black youth jauntily wearing a blue beret, and they entered the lunch room of the bus terminal. It had been the scene of previous arrests of the 'outsider' freedom riders which precipitated the great Albany Movement, whose stirring, beginnings, I was witnessing. A waitress came hurriedly out of the lunch room, her apron still on, her middle-aged white face full of a consternation that might be fear, might be rage, probably both, and she hurried across the street into a beauty parlor. . . . In memory they are held, like a photograph: the balding, thin, middle-aged proprietor of the lunch room, in shirt sleeves and wearing his apron, his eyes excited behind rimless glasses, his broad mouth tight . . . talking with him, four Albany policemen, swollen to menacing proportion in all the militaristic paraphernalia of their uniforms and weaponry . . . the crowd of Negroes, several hundred, not of the movement, but drawn to its actions, standing warily all around the borders of the bus terminal, watching. . . .

'Take 'em out,' the proprietor finally said in a tight, angry voice to the police, and they moved rapidly into this place of confrontation, itself a powerful symbol, this place of heavy chipped china, grease-encrusted grill, with grits served always with the eggs and bacon, with funeral home and insurance company calendars on the wall. . . ."[28]

Albany Herald. Several other students also were expelled; some of them became SNCC staffers.

Albany at the time had an unusual police chief in Laurie Pritchett. He was not above condemning any "nigger organization" that would disrupt Albany, but he understood better than most that racial violence, particularly if magnified by the media, would make things worse for the old order in Albany. He studied Gandhian dynamics and talked with Movement leaders regularly to anticipate maneuvers, at one point even appearing in the pulpit of Shiloh Baptist Church to plead for calm. He made the arrests of Movement protesters an orderly, dispassionate ritual, although out of the view of the cameras there were several rough arrests. He also demonstrated an ease with the rhetoric of the Movement, bowing when marchers prayed and one time even requesting that jailed protesters sing the modified freedom song then in vogue, "Ain't Gonna Let Chief Pritchett Turn Me Around." He shrewdly portrayed Albany as either under control or a boiling cauldron, depending on the audience.

On Sunday, December 10, 1962, SNCC executive secretary James Forman led a biracial group on a train ride from Atlanta. They were promptly arrested at the Albany train station for trespassing, setting off a series of rallies and jailings. By the end of that week five hundred protesters had been arrested for sympathetic marches on charges of parading without a permit. They filled not only the jail in Albany but also the ones in Camilla, Leesburg, and Newton. Governor Ernest Vandiver sent 150 highway patrolmen to the area.

Lured by the ardent crowds the Albany Movement was attracting, King came to Albany on December 15 for a series of mass meetings at Shiloh and Mount Zion that were attended by 1,500 people. The following afternoon he led a double-file group of 264 blacks to City Hall along what had become the common march route: east from the churches on Whitney Avenue, then north on Jackson Street past Oglethorpe Boulevard and Broad Street toward the group of government buildings along Pine Avenue. Armed guardsmen lined Jackson Street, and Dr. Anderson said to them, "If you strike anyone in this line, strike me first." In those days the city jail faced Pine Avenue, with palm trees out front and a side alley on Jackson Street where marchers were herded. Once they were arrested, Chief Pritchett treated King and Abernathy like prize catches, holding them under armed guard at his office before shipping them out to the Sumter County jail in Americus. King said he wanted to stay there through Christmas to draw a spotlight to the Albany campaign.

Two days later the leaders of the Albany Movement announced a surprise settlement with the city that pleased neither SNCC, whose hard work had been eclipsed, nor SCLC, which was just getting started in Albany. In exchange for halting demonstrations, the city orally agreed to desegregate bus and train stations, release all demonstrators, including King, on bond, and hear black complaints at the first meeting of the city government of 1962. None of the concessions except the release of the prisoners was honored, and King left Albany until his trial in February, when he was convicted of disorderly conduct and parading without a permit. Meanwhile the Albany Movement tried two more tactics: a bus boycott, which

Mayor Asa Kelley appeals to demonstrators to disband before they are arrested in front of City Hall, December 1961. (UPI/Corbis-Bettmann)

drove the city to discontinue bus service, and a boycott of selected white businesses.

During this period of frequent mass meetings and mass arrests freedom songs were first recognized as an integral part of the Movement. Rutha Harris and Bernice Johnson were members of choirs in their local churches, and they often led mass meetings in rousing renditions of "Ain't Gonna Let Nobody Turn Me Around" and "Woke Up This Morning with My Mind Set on Freedom." According to one activist, the songs "became as much a way of life as breathing and eating and sleeping." During marches the sight of students being crammed into paddy wagons or whisked off the street often was accompanied by the sound of them singing and clapping. Singing was so pervasive that the *New York Times* sent its folk music critic down to Albany in December 1961 to make an earnest study of it. Later a group called the Freedom Singers, featuring several performers from Albany, toured the country to raise money for the cause with their inspiring a capella numbers.

A second wave of protest in Albany began with the return of King and Abernathy in July 1962 for their sentencing on the parading conviction, which resulted in a fine of $178 or forty-five days'

Albany: The Singing City

Two distinct groups of songs were common during the Movement: topical songs, about particular events, and freedom songs, which addressed the common experiences of the racial struggle. Freedom songs, such as "Oh Freedom," often used the call-and-response format of black church music. Topical songs developed from songs of protest during slavery, the Progressives in the late nineteenth century, and union movement songs of the 1930s and 1940s. In both instances singers freely mixed verses and made up new ones or substituted words to fit the current situation. Sometimes an existing pop tune was completely made over with new lyrics; thus the tune "Hit the Road, Jack," by Albany native Ray Charles, became "Get Your Rights, Jack."

Below are the lyrics for a verse of a topical song called "Oh Pritchett, Oh Kelley," named for Albany's police chief and mayor, and sung to the tune of the spiritual "Oh Mary, Oh Martha." It was written by Albany student Bertha Gober:

Oh Pritchett, Oh Pritchett
   Oh Kelley, Oh Kelley
Oh Pritchett open them cells.

I hear God's children crying for mercy Lord
I hear God's children praying in jail
Bail's getting higher
   praying in jail
Bond's getting higher
   praying in jail.[29]

---

hard labor. They chose to do the time, but within two days the fines had been paid by an unidentified "well-dressed Negro man," police said, and they were required to go free. King groused at the "subtle and conniving tactics" used to undermine the Movement's plans and to sow internal dissent. Abernathy said at a mass meeting that evening, "I've been thrown out of lots of places in my day, but never have I been thrown out of jail." It turned out later that someone close to Albany Mayor Asa Kelley had paid the fine.

The next two weeks brought overlapping tides of crisis. Marchers fanned out and tested public facilities from the Carnegie Library to the bus station to lay the groundwork for desegregation lawsuits. Aware of King's promise to "turn Albany upside down," federal Judge Robert Elliot issued an injunction forbidding further marches on July 20. This put King in a quandary over whether to obey a court order that appeared patently unconstitutional. After meeting with his aides at Dr. Anderson's home on Cedar Avenue, he announced to the press gathered in the backyard that he would obey it for now. SNCC leaders then took him to task for dictating sudden changes of direction and destroying the organic grass roots protest in Albany they had so carefully nurtured.

The judge's order did not include one local preacher, Rev. Samuel Wells. Though not an officer of the Albany Movement, he had attended board meetings and been very active. On July 21 he appeared at Shiloh Baptist Church before a mass meeting and stirred the crowd. He got a thunderous response to his statement "I can hear the blood of Emmett Till coming from the ground!" Without asking anyone to follow, he simply walked out the front door of the church, and 160 people followed him down Jackson Street toward Oglethorpe Boulevard, where marchers had been stopped by police in the past. They all knelt, then were arrested and held for eighteen days while King watched from the sidelines. Jailers took all the bedding out and made protesters sleep on the cement floor.

On July 24 the federal injunction was overturned on appeal. Many in Albany were shocked to hear that Slater King's pregnant wife, Marion, had been knocked down and kicked while bringing food to protesters held at the Mitchell County jail in Camilla the previous day. That prompted rock throwing at police in Harlem and an offer from the governor of twelve thousand national guardsmen to restore order.

The next day King declared a moratorium on marches to serve as a Gandhian day of penance for breaking the code of nonviolence. On July 27 he led a prayer vigil in front of City Hall, landing himself in the Albany jail for the third time. On July 28 attorney C. B. King went to the Dougherty County courthouse to check on rumors (which turned out to be true) that a white SNCC protester was being abused in jail. The lawyer was told to leave and was beaten with a walking stick by Sheriff D. C. Campbell. Pictures of him bloodied and bandaged appeared in the local papers and kept tension crackling.

Meanwhile King served one of his longest jail sentences, a full two weeks. His wife, Coretta, came to Albany and brought their children Yoki and Marty for their first jail visit. They played with their father in the corridors. By the time King was released on August 10, Judge Elliot had issued another injunction against marching, but enthusiasm for marching had been dampened in King's absence.

Life in the Albany Jail

In a daily diary published in Jet *magazine during his two weeks in jail, King recounted life on the inside:*

"**S**unday, July 29—Everything was rather quiet this morning. We had our regular devotional services among all the prisoners. I read from the Book of Job. We hold services every morning and evening and sing whenever we feel like it. Since only Ralph [Abernathy] and I are in a cell together, we can't see the other prisoners, but we can always hear them. Slater [King] is two cells away. Marvin Rich, Ed Dickenson and Earl Gorden (some white demonstrators) are across the hall in another cell block but they join us in services. After devotion, I started reading some of the books I had with me.

"They brought us the usual breakfast at 8 o'clock. It was one link sausage, one egg and some grits, two pieces of bread on a tin plate with a tin cup of coffee. We were astonished when the jailer returned at 10 minutes after 10 this morning with a plate of hash, peas and rice and corn bread. He said it was supper and the last meal we were going to get that day because the cook was getting off early. Soon, the Rev. Mr. Walker came over with Dr. Roy C. Bell from Atlanta and Larry Still, a writer from *Jet*. Roy inspected Ralph's teeth and said he would arrange with Chief Pritchett to get us some 'food packages.' I told him this was needed because we would starve on the jail house food. The Albany Jail is dirty, filthy, and ill-equipped. I have been in many jails and it is really the wors[t] I have ever seen.

"Monday, July 30—I spent most of the day reading and writing on my book on Negro sermons before our hearing in Federal court started. The heat was so unbearable. I could hardly get anything done. I think we had the hottest cell in the jail because it is back in a corner. There are four bunks in our cell, but for some reason, they never put anybody in with us. Ralph says every time we go to the washbowl we bump into each other. He is a wonderful friend and really keeps our spirits going. The food seemed to be worse than usual today. I could only drink the coffee.

"I talked with Wyatt and he told me the demonstrations were still going as planned. . . . Lawyers King and Donald L. Hollowell of Atlanta came to see me before the hearing started. We discussed how the Albany battle must be waged on all four fronts. A legal battle in the courts; with demonstrations and kneel-ins and sit-ins; with an economic boycott and, finally, with an intense voter registration campaign. This is going to be a long summer."[30]

King then left Albany, attempting to hand the reins back to the Albany Movement and SNCC. Although many reforms were achieved locally, SCLC could point to few concrete gains after its largest commitment of money and staff time to date for any one city.

Charles Sherrod (far right) organizing in Terrell County, 1962. (Danny Lyon/Magnum Photos)

SCLC leaders established ground rules for future ventures into seg-regated communities: get promises in writing, make and stick to lim-ited goals, and control the flow of arrests. SCLC also learned that economic pressure was more effective than direct political pressure in those areas where black votes had not yet exerted significant leverage, a lesson later implemented in Birmingham.

In late 1962 the struggle by local citizens was far from over. The city commission finally heard a set of grievances but said it could not act on them while they were the subject of a federal lawsuit. On August 11 the city shut down the library and two parks rather than integrate them. There was news of repeated destruction of wood-frame churches in surrounding counties. On August 12, 1962, Shady Grove Baptist Church in Lee County was burned down, lead-ing the sheriff after a cursory inspection to declare it the result of an electrical storm. SNCC had conducted a voter registration meeting there just four days before. On August 15 and 16, 1962, King toured the area, lambasting the lightning theory and saying that church bombing represented degeneration to a "tragic level." In September two other churches were burned, this time in the Terrell County town of Sasser: Mount Mary Baptist Church and Mount Olive Baptist Church. The FBI found evidence of arson, although Sheriff Z. T. Matthews insisted there was none. Three nights after King came to survey the wreckage, I Hope Baptist Church in Terrell County also was torched; that fire resulted in a rare conviction of four white men for arson. Movement funds went to replace the burned churches with simple structures.

On March 6, 1963, fearing federal intervention, the city commission voted to repeal the segregation ordinances and reopened the public library. Since nothing prevented private swimming pools from being segregated, *Herald* editor James Gray convinced the city to sell him one of the pools at Tift Park and reopened it for whites only. Marches, picketing, and a wade-in at the pool during summer 1963 resulted in dozens more arrests and a police roundup of SNCC leaders. More grave charges faced SNCC workers in nearby Americus, where they were jailed on charges of insurrection, a capital crime.

Yet another violent incident from the countryside came back to haunt Albany in 1963. In July 1961 Sheriff L. Warren ("Gator") Johnson of Baker County had shot and wounded a black man, Charlie Ware, while he was handcuffed. When a civil suit for damages was brought against Johnson, an all-white jury in April 1963 found him not liable. One of the jurors on the case was Carl Smith, who owned a store in Harlem (formerly on the 300 block of Highland Avenue) that had been picketed earlier for refusing to hire black clerks. On April 20 about one hundred students picketed his store, urging a boycott for his role in the acquittal of Sheriff Johnson that succeeded in forcing him out of that location within two days. This brought a federal investigation into a group of Movement leaders known as the Albany Nine and charges of juror intimidation and perjury, although the picketing happened after the Johnson trial was already over.

This investigation marked an about-face for the Justice Department. DOJ had brought its first voting rights case in nearby Terrell County in September 1958 and had filed a brief opposing Judge Elliot's injunctions against marching in Albany in 1962. President Kennedy himself had made sympathetic statements during the Albany campaign, and a Kennedy aide had once again called Coretta Scott King while her husband was in jail. But when the Albany Nine investigation started, FBI agents grilled Movement workers. "They swarmed this place over," one of the nine remembers. The nine included Dr. Anderson, other leaders of the Albany Movement, and Joni Rabinowitz, a white SNCC worker and the daughter of a radical

New York lawyer. They were tried in a courthouse in Macon and convicted, although the convictions were later set aside because the jury was not racially representative of the community.

By that time it was clear that Albany had been through irreversible changes. In 1962 Thomas Chatmon ran for a position on the city commission and lost, despite a strong showing. This setback started a series of voter registration drives that made black voters a force in the mayoral, gubernatorial, and congressional elections that followed. The Civil Rights Act of 1964 was implemented without serious incident. After police shot and killed a fifteen-year-old black boy in April 1964, the community demanded police reforms. In October 1964 Albany hired six black police officers.

In 1994 Tropical Storm Alberto dumped huge amounts of rain on southwestern Georgia, and the overflow of the Flint River covered twenty-three square miles, sprung coffins from graveyards, and caused more than a hundred million dollars' worth of damage in Dougherty County. The rebuilding effort was heralded as a model of racial cooperation.

Shiloh Baptist Church

325 Whitney Avenue

The pastor here during Movement days was, and today still is, Rev. Horace C. Boyd. He attended seminary at Morehouse in

Shiloh Baptist Church, 1996. (Townsend Davis)

Atlanta, and when he settled in Albany in 1959 and his wife began school at Albany State, he had no idea the Movement was coming to his church. Along with its twin across the street, Mount Zion Baptist, Shiloh was one of two major black churches in Albany. The Shiloh sidewalk was a natural send-off point for marchers headed downtown via Jackson Street. As a veteran who knew some of Atlanta's black civic leaders, such as Benjamin Mays and Daddy King, Boyd agreed to let the church be used for everything from Movement meetings to sleeping quarters. In those days the church had no air conditioning, the choir loft was about a third its current size, and the baptismal font sat in front of the pulpit. For most meetings people were "in the midst of jamming and cramming" in the pews, in the vestibule, and along the walls, the pastor remembers. On the outside hung a neon-lit cross, and three crosses embedded in brick highlighted its pointed roof.

On December 15, 1961, Shiloh was the site of one of the most inspiring mass meetings King had attended since the Montgomery boycott of 1956. He flew from Atlanta and was driven straight from the Albany airport to Shiloh, which had loudspeakers mounted on the outside to carry the proceedings into the street and to Mount Zion, on the opposite corner of Whitney Avenue. He heard the singing inside Shiloh pouring into the streets: "Integration is on its way / Singing glory hallelujah / I'm so glad." When he entered the church, he was engulfed by chants of "Freedom." Energized by the crowd, he told them: "They can put you in a dungeon and transform you to glory; if they try to kill you, develop a willingness to die." When he was asked to join in the march the next day that would result in certain jailing, he could hardly refuse.

When Chief Pritchett came to the church to speak in July 1962 after a spate of rock throwing during one of King's jail terms, some of the congregants applauded efforts to maintain order, and some jeered. During tense times the police were outside between the two churches day and night, and the church was open around the clock.

Shiloh was also the site of the announcement by Albany activist Marion Page in December 1961 that the city had agreed to certain limited reforms, which were not realized until years later.

Mount Zion Baptist Church/Albany Civil Rights Movement Museum

324 Whitney Avenue

Rev. E. James Grant, a Morehouse alumnus and classmate of Daddy King's, opened this church to some of the most gripping meetings of the Albany Movement. Albany's citizens began meeting here on November 25, 1961, three days after the arrest of black high school students at the bus station. When King first arrived in Albany in the evening of December 15, 1961, he spoke first at Shiloh Baptist Church, then walked across the street to an equally fervent overflow crowd at Mount Zion, went back to Shiloh, then returned to Mount Zion for a fourth address, getting surer and stronger each time.

Today Mount Zion is being converted into a civil rights museum that will feature the work of SNCC photographer Danny Lyon.

Albany Movement Monument
West Highland and Jackson Streets

Four black granite slabs with historical chronologies and quotations surround a fountain at the Albany Movement monument, set between the former black business district and the graveyard on Jackson Street. The names of local Movement people are etched in white stones around a brick periphery. Some of those listed have gone on to renown; others, such as former Albany State student Bertha Gober, have receded from public view. The monument was unveiled on November 20, 1992.

Rev. Samuel B. Wells in front of a monument to the Albany Movement, 1995.
(Townsend Davis)

Dr. William Anderson House

914 Cedar Avenue

Osteopath William G. Anderson and his wife had known Martin Luther King, Jr., since his high school days. They were selected to telephone him during the first weeks of street protests to ask him on behalf of the Albany Movement to come and address a mass meeting in December 1961. Although neither King nor SCLC had plans for Albany, King's speeches that night initiated his nearly two-year involvement with the Albany campaign.

Dr. Anderson was among Albany's professional men who joined the Criterion Club, a social group that had created a local Voters League in 1947. He also was among those who petitioned the city government for a biracial commission to examine desegregation. At the founding meeting of the Albany Movement on November 17, 1961, Anderson, who was from nearby Americus and a novice at civil rights organizing, was chosen to lead the marches down Jackson Street and into jail. The Kings often stayed at this house, which was watched during the visit by two detectives from the Albany Police Department.

When Albany's campaign heated up again in the summer of 1962, Dr. Anderson was jailed along with King for conducting a prayer vigil. When King decided to stay in jail and cancel an appearance on the television show "Meet the Press," Dr. Anderson appeared in his stead, helping refocus the attention of the Kennedy administration on southwestern Georgia. The pressures of the Albany campaign, which included the publication of his address and phone number in the *Albany Herald* and frequent death threats, eventually prompted Dr. Anderson to withdraw from Movement activity. He lives in Detroit today.

King Family Plot, Oakview Cemetery

200 Cotton Avenue

No family put more on the line for the Movement than the Kings of Albany (no relation to the Atlanta Kings). Allen James King was from Jackson County, Florida, born in 1872, a drayman who, according to family lore, had to move after a dispute with a white man on a road. He settled in east Albany. His son Clennon Washington King arrived at the Tuskegee Institute penniless and paid his way through school as a chauffeur for Booker T. Washington. He was so devoted to the institution's founder that he kept a photograph of him by his bedside and was heard to declare, "Everything I am and hope to be I owe to Pa Booker." He married Margaret Allegra Slater of Milledgeville, Georgia, a light-skinned black woman who was cut off by her family for marrying a darker man. He settled in Albany as a postman, cofounded a voters league and the local NAACP, and owned the *Southwest Georgian,* a black weekly newspaper.

Clennon King and his wife raised seven children, among them son Chevene Bowers (known as C.B.) King. He graduated from Fisk University in Nashville and Western Reserve in Cleveland and was at one point the only black trial attorney in south Georgia. His office at 221½ Jackson Street (now the Ritz Cultural Center) opened in October 1954. He traveled to other courts in Georgia, license in hand, appearing in courthouses that still assigned black spectators to Jim Crow balconies. He was known for his extraordinary motivation, preparation, and courtly demeanor, and he always knew two ways out of whatever town he was appearing in.

C. B. King represented many who were on the front lines of the Movement, from Martin Luther King, Jr., to the Albany State students at the bus station to Charlie Ware, whose shooting in Baker County was an emblematic miscarriage of justice and the precursor of the Albany Nine controversy. C. B. King also negotiated on behalf of the Albany Movement and filed suits to desegregate Albany's public schools and to equalize the pay for schoolteachers and city workers. C. B. King ran for Congress in 1964, a race that attracted twenty-five hundred new black voters. He received a significant six thousand votes, although he finished fourth out of six candidates. He also ran for governor of Georgia in 1970 and was the first black candidate for that office; he came in third and forced a runoff between Jimmy Carter and Carl Sanders. He died in 1988.

His younger brother Slater Hunter King was an insurance and real estate broker who lived across the street from Dr. Anderson (at 1304 South Cleveland Street) in what was then the emerging neighborhood of Lincoln Heights. Relatively secure in his support from black customers, Slater King was among the more militant voices in Albany and succeeded Dr. Anderson as head of the Albany Movement. He led one of the first prayer vigils at the courthouse on December 13, 1961, and was jailed several times thereafter for marching (he called on his brother C.B. for legal representation). He mounted an unsuccessful bid for mayor in 1963, the first black citizen to do so. He died in 1969 in a car accident.

The Kings' eldest son was Clennon Washington, Jr., a flamboyant man who in 1958 applied without success to the University of Mis-

Epitaph for a Movement Lawyer

C. B. King wrote his own epitaph, which reads:

"**L**et what good there has been in the lives we've lived be a model to lives yet unspent and those that come after.

"Let our occasional deeds of courage and the lofty hopes and dreams which marked our earthly vigil be your inheritance to gird you in your reach for the uncertainties of forever.

"Let our past visions of tomorrow's fulfillment be for you this moment's heeded challenge, and

"Let it be in your farewell that you will have kept aglow the fragile sparks of life's trusts to illumine the way and make safe the legions of Hannibal that will follow."

sissippi before James Meredith's admission in 1962. Then an instructor at Alcorn Agricultural and Mechanical College in Mississippi, he arrived on the Ole Miss campus alone and was eventually declared insane for his efforts. He was institutionalized at Whitfield, a segregated Mississippi asylum, and it took his brother C.B.'s advocacy to get him out. He is still living.

Today C. B. King and his father are buried in the King family plot, which is located on the second north-south dirt path west of Washington Street in a clearing. Slater King is buried at Roselawn Cemetery on Martin Luther King, Jr., Drive.

Albany State College

504 College Drive

This college was a fermenting ground for activism in southwestern Georgia. Discussions about integration took place in 1961 before the Albany Movement was formed, and three students wrote the *Albany Herald* to protest a racist comment on a radio show. On November 27, 1961, four hundred students followed behind SNCC leader Charles Jones to march in protest against the trial of the five students arrested at the bus station, marking the first mass march in Albany. In January 1962 forty students, including Miss Alabama State College, were suspended for having demonstrated the previous month.

Later Albany State students helped teach dozens of adults the basics of voter registration and the electoral system in citizenship schools in 1962.

Savannah, Georgia

Local Movement by the Sea

In the waning days of the Civil War Savannah capitulated so gracefully to the arriving troops of General William T. Sherman that rather than burn it to the ground, he went to one of Savannah's prominent homes and sent a telegram to President Abraham Lincoln offering the city up as a handsome Christmas present. So also did Savannah in the 1960s ultimately accept the demands of the Movement rather than dig segregationist trenches that would have brought certain bloodshed. The strength and breadth of the local campaign for civil rights achieved such rapid progress that local leaders requested that Martin Luther King, Jr., stay away for fear of upsetting their momentum.

In those days Union Station was on West Broad Street (now Martin Luther King, Jr., Boulevard), the main street of the black community. It was lined with barbers, confectioners, pawnbrokers, beauticians, restaurateurs, insurers, and photographers (most now gone). The West Broad Street YMCA, where Movement workshops were held, was at 714 West Broad between Hall and Gwinnett streets, and the bricklayers' local was two blocks away. Many Baptist churches that were used for Movement meetings, such as Mount Zion and Bolton Street Baptist churches, and the *Savannah Tribune*, then the nation's oldest black newspaper, also were on West Broad. Under Savannah's genteel veneer lay the same attachment to Jim Crow that could be found in any other southern city. When Jackie Robinson was playing minor-league baseball for the Brooklyn Dodgers' farm team and came for a game against the Savannah team at Grayson Stadium, the family of the general for whom it was named said it would take his name off the stadium if Robinson were allowed to play. The team canceled its game.

The local branch of the NAACP laid a solid foundation for the Movement. When an exhibition displaying the original Constitution and the Declaration of Independence came through Savannah on a Freedom Train in 1948, the NAACP Youth Council passed a resolution declaring the segregated viewing lines set up in Savannah a "shameful disgrace." Leadership of the branch passed in 1950 from the esteemed pastor of First African Baptist Church, Rev. Ralph Mark Gilbert, to Westley Wallace (W. W.) Law, who had worked for

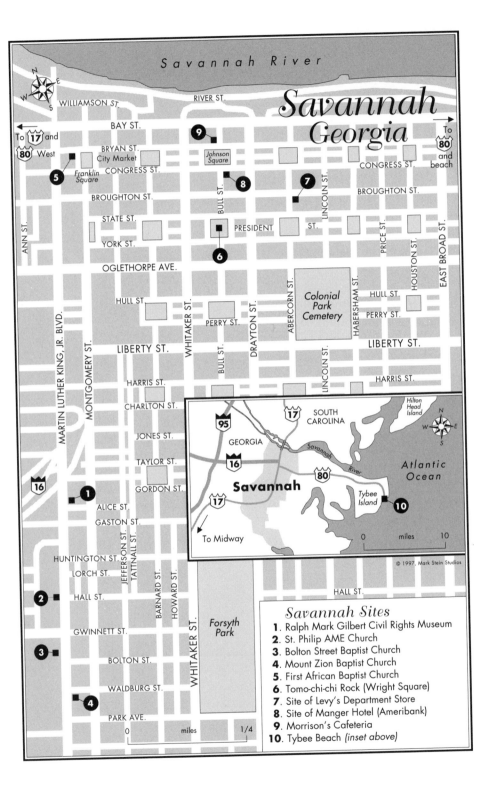

Savannah
Georgia

Savannah River

WILLIAMSON ST.
RIVER ST.
BAY ST.
To **17** and **80** West

BRYAN ST.
City Market
CONGRESS ST.
CONGRESS ST.

Franklin Square
5

Johnson Square
9
8
7

BROUGHTON ST.
BROUGHTON ST.

STATE ST.
PRESIDENT
ST.

YORK ST.

ANN ST.

6

OGLETHORPE AVE.

HULL ST.
Colonial Park Cemetery
HULL ST.

PERRY ST.
PERRY ST.

BULL ST.
WHITAKER ST.
DRAYTON ST.
ABERCORN ST.
LINCOLN ST.
HABERSHAM ST.
PRICE ST.
HOUSTON ST.
EAST BROAD ST.
MONTGOMERY ST.
MARTIN LUTHER KING, JR. BLVD.

LIBERTY ST.
LIBERTY ST.

HARRIS ST.
HARRIS ST.

CHARLTON ST.

JONES ST.

16

TAYLOR ST.

GORDON ST.
1
ALICE ST.

GASTON ST.

HUNTINGTON ST.

LORCH ST.

2
HALL ST.
HALL ST.

GWINNETT ST.
Forsyth Park

3
BOLTON ST.

WALDBURG ST.

4
PARK AVE.

JEFFERSON ST.
TATTNALL ST.
BARNARD ST.
HOWARD ST.
WHITAKER ST.

0   miles   1/4

Inset map:

95
17
SOUTH CAROLINA
Hilton Head Island

GEORGIA

16

Savannah River

Savannah

80

Atlantic Ocean

17

Tybee Island
10

To Midway

0   miles   10

© 1997, Mark Stein Studios

Savannah Sites

1. Ralph Mark Gilbert Civil Rights Museum
2. St. Philip AME Church
3. Bolton Street Baptist Church
4. Mount Zion Baptist Church
5. First African Baptist Church
6. Tomo-chi-chi Rock (Wright Square)
7. Site of Levy's Department Store
8. Site of Manger Hotel (Ameribank)
9. Morrison's Cafeteria
10. Tybee Beach (inset above)

the group since he was a teenager. In an effort to spread the word about NAACP activities, which were not reported reliably in the local daily paper, the branch sponsored Sunday afternoon mass meetings at local black churches beginning in March 1960 and every week for more than a year. At that time young blacks in Savannah wanted to emulate the student sit-ins in North Carolina that had begun in February 1960.

On March 16 black students sat down at eight lunch counters at downtown stores and refused to move until they were served, resulting in three arrests. The local Movement called for a total boycott of downtown stores until they served all customers, hired blacks above the menial level, desegregated drinking fountains and rest rooms, and addressed their black customers with courtesy titles. Students sat quietly at the counters reading their textbooks and picketed outside with signs that said YOU CAN BUY A $50 SUIT, BUT NOT A 10 CENT CUP OF COFFEE and WE WANT A MOUTHFUL OF FREEDOM. The Savannah boycott lasted from March 1960 to July 1961, one of the longest of the entire Movement and longer even than the bus boycott in Montgomery.

The Jewel by the Sea

In April 1960 Douglas Kiker, a writer for the Atlanta Journal, *summed up Savannah through white eyes:*

"This is Georgia's oldest city, one of its largest, certainly its most beautiful—and undoubtedly its most troubled at the moment. Spring is in its full red, lavender and white blossom and bloom here now and tourists are flooding in from the north with their cameras, and feel anxious to lose themselves in the moss, oaks and the profuse azaleas and camellias—as common here as field straw in Piedmont—and to tour leisurely the stately old homes and churches and colonial market squares.

"Savannah society is traditionally self-contained and aloof from the rest of Johnny-come-lately Georgia. Savannah aristocrats nod coolly to Atlanta, smile at Charleston, but bow only to London and Florence (for their traditions of beauty, respectively).

"But Savannah is caught up in an all-consuming racial problem just now. Sit-downs seem to come and go in the South, but they have entered their second straight month here, with no sign of a let-up, and the city's figured 100,000 citizens are tired and exasperated."[31]

In April 1960 the city council forbade picketing of two or more people against a business. The law prompted a candid remark by the outgoing mayor: "I don't especially care if it's constitutional or not." The boycott forced into bankruptcy five major stores that refused to integrate, and a local paper noted that blacks marching in an Easter Day parade "apparently were wearing last year's outfits." By October of that year student-led groups had tested nearly every corner of Savannah with "wade-ins" at the beaches, "kneel-ins" at white churches, "ride-ins" on the buses, "stand-ins" at theaters, and what one activist termed a "piss-in" at a segregated rest room. Six black youngsters were arrested for playing basketball in traditionally all-white Daffin Park near Grayson Stadium on charges of breaching the peace. A lawsuit was filed to challenge the convictions, which carried a one-hundred-dollar fine or five months in prison each, and they were overturned by the U.S. Supreme Court as unconstitutional.

In June 1961, with the boycott still in force, Savannah's bus company promised to hire black drivers for some of its routes. That summer activists tested the previously all-white swimming pools of Daffin Park. By October 1961 certain public facilities, such as the buses, golf courses, and restaurants, were desegregated in a comprehensive agreement reached with the city government. The boycott was lifted. In December of that year a group of blacks from Savannah rode in the white passenger section of the Savannah to Atlanta train, the Central of Georgia Railroad's *Nancy Hanks.* During their integration of the first statewide train in Georgia, the club car was closed, but white passengers offered them newspapers, cigarettes, and Christmas greetings.

Just as in Atlanta, however, resistance generated a second round of protests, this time demanding complete integration in all facets of city life. Local movie theaters first integrated, then reverted to segregation under public pressure in June 1963. This backsliding sparked daily workshops in nonviolent protest, followed by large noontime marches on the stores of Broughton Street and occasional night marches. Although Savannah enjoyed a relatively peaceful emergence from segregation, several protesters faced police dogs and tear gas, were roughed up, and were jailed on extremely high bond during this more militant phase of demonstrations. Activist Hosea Williams was held for sixty-five days in jail. Large numbers of black marchers took to the streets, resulting in the burning of at least one store and prompting a harsh crackdown and seventy-five arrests alone in one night in July. The city passed an outright ban on marches, and Governor Carl Sanders placed National Guard troops on alert.

By fall 1963 Savannah's taste for crisis had soured, and the bricks of segregation were crumbling. In August the city had announced another desegregation pact, and this one stuck when it was implemented in October. The NAACP called off a planned Christmas boycott. In September 1963 twelve black students enrolled as seniors at Savannah High School, and seven entered the Robert W. Groves High School in west Chatham County. By the time King gave his New Year's address in Savannah's Municipal Auditorium in 1964, he was praising Savannah as "the most desegregated city south of the Mason-Dixon line."

The key to the Savannah campaign was the local NAACP, led by W. W. Law. His job as a postal worker kept him in constant contact with people all over the city, and he worked late into the night at the NAACP office on West Broad Street. The NAACP maintained a list of every black home with a phone and kept people informed by making one hundred copies of the list and assigning each volunteer a single page to cover. Also indispensable to the campaign was the dynamic leadership of Hosea Williams, a chemist at the U.S. Agriculture Department, and Benjamin Van Clark, a local high school student. Williams delivered rousing speeches from atop Tomo-chi-chi rock on Wright Square in front of the county courthouse during his lunch hour that prompted mass marches and "lay-ins" at Morrison's Cafeteria and rallies in Johnson Square. He also led night marches in 1963 and spearheaded the Chatham County Crusade for Voting (CCCV), which mounted an impressive registration campaign with the aid of a "Ballot Bus" to take people to the polls. Van Clark, the bold nineteen-year-old head of CCCV's youth division, led as many as three marches a day downtown. They included a mock funeral for segregation during which demonstrators carried a casket and wore black clothing. Van Clark was jailed twenty-five times and then, after a march in July 1963, disappeared from the city.

Also key was the leverage of black voters, which had been heightened by voter registration drives. Fully 57 percent of eligible black citizens were registered to vote by 1960, a higher percentage than among whites. This strength allowed the black population, constituting about a third of the city's total, to influence the election in 1960 of white moderate Mayor Malcolm Maclean, who promptly appointed a black official to each city council board and authority. Savannah was one of the first southern cities to see black political candidates, starting with the unsuccessful bid of Juanita Williams

(Hosea's wife) for Superior Court clerk in June 1961. It also was among the first cities to convert from an at-large to a district election system, in which officials were elected on the basis of votes from their neighborhoods rather than city-wide and which gave blacks a better chance for office. In 1966 Bobby Hill became the first black state legislator from Savannah since Reconstruction. In 1995 Savannah elected its first black mayor, Floyd Adams, Jr.

Since the 1970s W. W. Law has been the driving force behind an effort to understand black history and preserve historic structures in Savannah. A model for preserving its stately antebellum homes and tree-lined squares in the 1980s, Savannah has in the 1990s turned more attention to preserving its black heritage.

First African Baptist Church
23 Montgomery Street (Franklin Square)

Rev. Ralph Mark Gilbert, pastor here from 1939 to 1956, served as president of the Savannah branch of the NAACP from 1942 to 1950 and of the state NAACP from 1942 to 1948. He led the drive to establish the West Broad Street YMCA and oversaw the breakthroughs of the 1940s: the hiring of the first black police officers, the push for equal teacher salaries, and black voting in primary elec-

Frontispiece of the First African Baptist Church, 1995. (Townsend Davis)

tions. He increased the local NAACP membership to three thousand and invited prominent activists such as Atlanta's Walter White to speak at the church. The pastors who succeeded him, Rev. Curtis J. Jackson (1956–61) and Rev. William Franklin Stokes (1963–73), both supported boycotts and marches at a time when many preachers demurred. First African was the send-off point for the first sit-ins downtown on March 16, 1960. The church basement was used for meetings at which Savannah's youths were urged to turn in their weapons and to focus on the power of the ballot.

Founded in 1773, First African is the oldest autonomous black church in North America. The present building was built in 1859, and for years it was known simply as the brick church because it was the first building of its kind erected by black workers for their own use. The original pews are in the basement, and below a diamond-shaped series of holes in the floor lies a hiding place used to house runaway slaves.

Site of Levy's Department Store
201 East Broughton Street

Three NAACP youths—Carolyn Quilloin, Joan Tyson, and Ernest Robinson—were arrested for sitting in at the Azalea Room here on March 16, 1960, during Savannah's first direct-action protest. They were convicted under a hastily passed Georgia antitrespassing law and received a sentence of one hundred dollars or five months in jail. On March 26 Levy's was the first of the many stores on Broughton Street to become the target of the fifteen-month boycott. Today the building is vacant.

Site of the Manger Hotel
36 Bull Street

The Manger Hotel (now the Ameribank building) was the site of an integration test led by Hosea Williams and of the 1963 agreement to desegregate all public facilities. This settlement was comprehensive and involved not only the Movement leaders, the mayor, and representatives of the holdout movie theaters but also bankers, hotel operators, and an Episcopal bishop.

Ralph Mark Gilbert Civil Rights Museum
460 Martin Luther King, Jr., Boulevard

This three-story brick building, built in 1914 by black Atlanta contractor Robert Pharrow, first housed the Wage Earners Loan and Investment Company, one of the oldest black lending institutions in

W. W. Law in front of the Ralph Mark Gilbert Civil Rights Museum, formerly the NAACP headquarters in Savannah, 1995. (Townsend Davis)

the nation. "Most Beautiful Negro Bank in the Country," crowed the *Savannah Tribune* when it opened, noting its Victor screw-door safe, mahogany furniture, ladies' retiring room, and stately chandelier with twelve bulbs. The building became the home office of the Guaranty Life Insurance Company, whose founder, Walter Scott, headed a NAACP delegation that protested the shameful condition of black schools.

During Movement days the building was a magnet for the activity of West Broad Street, housing the NAACP after it moved there from 1214½ West Broad above a shoe repair shop. Lawyers Clarence Mayfield and Eugene Gadsden each had an office in this building, as did the dentist John Jamerson, Jr. (all active in the Movement). The basement housed a barbershop. Gadsden was the first black lawyer admitted to the Savannah Bar Association in December 1965 and later served as a Superior Court judge.

Since 1994 Chatham County has provided more than two million dollars to renovate and convert the building into a museum.

Bolton Street Baptist Church
821 Martin Luther King, Jr., Boulevard

By chance the first mass meeting of the Savannah Movement was held here on Sunday, March 20, 1960, at 4:00 P.M. because it was the only city church not holding a service or other program that afternoon. Those gathered unanimously voted to boycott downtown stores, and some tossed their charge cards from Levy's department store down from the church balcony to show their support. The second mass meeting was held at St. Philip AME Church (613 West Martin Luther King, Jr., Boulevard), which also became a Movement meeting place.

Tybee Island Beach
I-80 at Butler Avenue

In the early 1960s the sight of black people dipping in the Atlantic Ocean was unheard of, one Movement veteran recalls. On August 17, 1960, a group of NAACP youths led the first Atlantic "wade-ins," modeled on the first of their kind in the Gulf of Mexico in Biloxi, Mississippi. They swam for ninety minutes until eleven of them were rounded up and arrested, a protest that resulted in the eventual desegregation of Savannah's premier beach. They staged another wade-in in July 1963 during the summer revival of demonstrations. When the 1964 Civil Rights Act was passed, they also tested the motels along the strip and were warmly received.

Three black youths arrested for attempting to integrate Tybee Island beach, July 1963. (UPI/Corbis-Bettmann)

Dorchester Academy Boys Dormitory

U.S. 84, two miles west of Route 17 (next to Midway Congregational Church), Midway, Georgia (Liberty County)

In summer 1961 SCLC aide Andrew Young was casting about for a suitable place to house the Movement's citizenship schools, which taught courses on voter registration. A natural choice was the Highlander Folk School in Monteagle, Tennessee, which had hatched the program and handed it over to SCLC. Unfortunately Highlander had just been shut down by Tennessee authorities on a trumped-up bootlegging charge. So Young, a Congregationalist minister, petitioned the board of the United Church of Christ for permission to use Dorchester Academy to teach activist civics. The board agreed, and for the next four years local Movement leaders from Virginia to Texas received instruction here in the Citizenship Education Program.

Under former Charleston schoolteacher Septima Clark, Dorchester became the center for both citizenship class training and voter registration programs, which were funded by major philanthropies, such as the Field Foundation. Classes started with thirty-four people from Louisiana, Georgia, and South Carolina on July 17, 1961. Students, farmers, retirees, housewives, dressmakers, and restaurateurs all came here on buses to fill in gaps left by Jim Crow educations and lifetimes of continuous labor. In the classes adult students learned the basics of literacy, government, and voting.

Discussion might begin with the words *Citizen* or *Constitution* on a blackboard and lead to an explanation of the voting rules in each state. In math class, seed and fertilizer amounts were used in equations, while reading lessons came from everyday texts such as the newspaper or road signs. Aided by King's whirlwind recruiting trips through the South and by recruiting and teaching by SCLC staffer Dorothy Cotton, Dorchester trained hundreds of volunteers in 1962. They in turn founded ninety-five similar schools in their home communities. Fannie Lou Hamer, Annelle Ponder, and L. C. Dorsey from Mississippi were just three local leaders who took training at Dorchester back to the plantations of the Delta. Overall the program trained more than two thousand teachers, both at the Dorchester Center and at other locales in the South.

Dorchester also was a welcome retreat for SCLC staffers recovering from the last campaign or planning the next one. Rev. Wyatt Tee Walker's four-part master plan for Project C, SCLC's 1963 Birmingham campaign, was first unveiled to the staff here. It was also a place to reflect on the lessons of fast-paced events that had taken place in Albany, Georgia, and the Freedom Rides in Alabama. In the nearby fields here preachers still in white shirts and thin black ties played softball, with King pitching from the mound. Like Highlander, Dorchester's prominence as a planning center led to suspicions that it was a Communist cell.

The columned brick building, formerly the boys dormitory, is the last remaining structure of the Dorchester Academy, which educated black children from Liberty County and other coastal counties under the auspices of the American Missionary Association until public education for blacks became more widespread after the Depression. Inside it are a mural celebrating black heritage and an exhibit on the history of Dorchester.

Mississippi

Transformation of the Magnolia State

In a speech in Yazoo City in June 1966 Rev. King said Mississippi had a "strange affinity for the bottom." The state had a reputation for brutal enforcement of a racial code dating back to plantation times. Countless activists have spoken of swallowing hard upon seeing the WELCOME TO THE MAGNOLIA STATE signs at the Mississippi border. Life was difficult for black Mississippians who wanted to change their own communities. Mississippi historically had the worst record on racial violence, education, infant mortality, and living standards for its black residents.

This ghoulish portrait of race relations in Mississippi was largely deserved when the Movement started. Mississippi's chasm between the wealth and opportunities afforded blacks and whites posed obstacles for the traditional Movement methods of boycotts, marches, and voter registration, particularly in economically underdeveloped areas such as the Delta. Testaments to nonviolence in Montgomery and Atlanta were often considered impractical or even suicidal here. In addition to running up against a tradition of armed self-defense, activists found at best tepid support among the majority of local ministers. Although King made several speeches all across the state, SCLC never had a significant presence here. By the end of 1964 Dave Dennis of CORE, although a believer in non-

A sprinkler in the Mississippi Delta, 1995. (Townsend Davis)

violence, was not alone in thinking that strict adherence to non-violence in Mississippi was "a waste of good lives." Several activists were shamelessly slain, a grim echo of Mississippi's distinction as the leading state for lynchings in the 1930s and 1940s.

Despite the difficulties, some of the greatest long-term accomplishments of the Movement ultimately were won in Mississippi. Pathbreaking voter registration drives, combined with federal legislation, had resulted by the 1990s in the highest percentage of black officeholders and voters of any state in the nation. The concept of the Freedom Schools, and other experiments resulting from the infusion of volunteers during Freedom Summer of 1964, laid the groundwork for revisions in public school curricula nationwide. Activists who traversed the back roads brought to light widespread health and educational deprivation that later resulted in a vastly improved social safety net in the state.

As blacks pursued the right to vote in the 1950s, it became harder to attain. The state instituted a two-year residency requirement and a two-dollar annual poll tax. Under Jim Crow legislation enacted in 1890, applicants often were required not only to read and write out a portion of the Mississippi Constitution, which had 285 sections, but also after 1954 to explain it to the satisfaction of the local registrar. This was often impossible for blacks facing a hostile white official. After 1954 the number of black voters in Mississippi dropped from twenty-two thousand to a mere twelve thousand. As of 1960, all the counties in the Delta, and most of those counties stretching down to the Louisiana border along the Mississippi River, were black-majority counties. Although voting-age blacks enjoyed a two to one advantage in some of these counties, only a handful were registered. About 5 percent of blacks were registered in the state overall.

After the *Brown* decision Mississippi was beset by uncertainty. Some black educators saw an opportunity to upgrade their institutions and supported Governor Fielding Wright's plan to make good on "separate but equal" as a way to avoid the Supreme Court's mandate. NAACP chapters sprang back to life, and new ones sprouted under the leadership of the state president, Emmett J. Stringer. At the NAACP's urging, parents submitted petitions requesting school desegregation in Mississippi's cities, starting in Vicksburg in 1955. After a series of racial killings in 1955 the NAACP conducted an antilynching campaign under the slogan "M is for Mississippi and Murder."

Meanwhile the Mississippi legislature crafted ever more creative ways to preserve the old regime: strict segregation in transportation, a breach of the peace law carrying a thousand-dollar fine and six months in jail, a requirement that libraries carry white supremacist literature, and the creation of an investigative body called the Sovereignty Commission in 1956. The legislature also added a requirement that potential voters' names be published in the local newspaper and allowed challenges to their applications on the basis of moral character. Hand in glove with governmental restrictions were the efforts of the white Citizens' Council to marshal businesses, creditors, and suppliers against anyone pushing for change.

The first open attack on segregation in Mississippi came on the Gulf Coast ten weeks after the student sit-ins in Greensboro, North Carolina, in 1960. When Dr. Gilbert Mason and his friends ventured onto the public beach in Biloxi in April 1960, they were attacked by a mob armed with chains, bats, and pipes while the police looked on. An earlier NAACP petition to desegregate the beaches had resulted in the firing of two of its signers and a cross burning. DOJ then sued to desegregate the beaches, but black swimmers had already integrated them by the time the suit was won.

After the arrival in Jackson of the Freedom Riders in May 1961 CORE, SNCC, and the NAACP all became active in the state, pursu-

Segregation's Spies: The Sovereignty Commission

The Mississippi State Sovereignty Commission was created by the state legislature in 1956 to protect Mississippi from "encroachment" by the federal government. In reality the federal threat to segregation was still a long time coming, and the commission staff spent most of its time rooting out the plans and backgrounds of anyone suspected of aiding the Movement. It accumulated files on more than ten thousand people and groups. It even provided secret microphones shaped like wristwatches, which were wired through the sleeve to shoulder-holstered tape recorders, for those who wanted to tape-record Movement figures.

No racial matter was too trivial for a commission write-up. Investigators responded to a Biloxi couple who worried that their daughter just off to college was dating a black man. Other times they investigated the heritage of children reputed to be of mixed race. A white chiropractor relocating from Ohio to Indianola was worth a look because he had black patients and a single mother for a secretary. They monitored academics, organizers, and activist preachers. The commission circulated descriptions and license plates of Movement cars to local sheriffs, and its reports were sent directly to Governor Paul B. Johnson.

The commission combined its web of informants with creative anti-Movement propaganda. It designated speakers to tour the North with the message that race relations were fine and that most blacks actually preferred segregation. It requested that the Jackson newspapers run unflattering stories about the Movement and drop the title "Reverend" from the names of Movement preachers on the theory that they endorsed atheistic communism. Blacks knew that some in their midst were cooperating with the commission; certain "Uncle Toms" were identifiable by their new cars and other luxuries.

The commission was phased out in 1973, buried with a legislative order to destroy all the files. The ACLU and a coalition of Movement parties sued to save the files in 1977 as proof that the state had violated myriad constitutional rights. The case languished in federal Judge Harold Cox's court until an appeals court demanded a ruling. In 1989 Judge William Barbour ruled that the files should be opened, but further delays resulted when a subgroup of plaintiffs expressed concern that blanket disclosure would invade the privacy of people swept into the commission's broad net. Meanwhile the *Jackson Clarion Ledger* examined some of the files and published a series of articles on them called "Mississippi's Secret Past" in 1990. The files currently are in the process of being made public under the conditions of a court order.

ing different agendas. CORE's focus was interstate travel, as it had been during the Freedom Rides. SNCC was interested in building voter registration in rural counties. The NAACP continued to focus on petitions and legal suits. Dozens of local voters leagues encouraged registration in their communities. All gathered under the umbrella of COFO, the Council of Federated Organizations, which was first chartered under the eye of Aaron Henry in Clarksdale and was reconfigured in February 1962 as a coordinating body for Movement efforts in the state. As part of COFO, CORE oversaw Movement activities in central and east Mississippi while SNCC supplied the majority of fieldworkers statewide.

In the summer of 1963 an entirely new form of protest presaged the transformation of Mississippi politics through the strength of the black vote. After planning by COFO, several hundred black Mississippians who were not officially registered cast shadow ballots at makeshift polling places in their communities in the Democratic primary in August. The shadow balloting came to be known as the mock vote. In a runoff for governor later that month twenty-seven thousand blacks statewide—more than were actually registered—

COFO workers in Belzoni during the mock vote in October 1963. (Matt Herron/ Take Stock)

did the same thing. At a protoconvention in Jackson on October 6 the arrayed COFO forces nominated Aaron Henry to head a ticket for governor with white Tougaloo College chaplain Rev. Ed King as his running mate. Organized in merely a month, the campaign garnered an amazing eighty-three thousand mock votes, which were cast at black churches and businesses all across the state despite intense intimidation. This turnout laid to rest the widespread belief among whites that blacks simply were uninterested in voting.

In 1964 racial tremors in Mississippi reached earthquake proportions. A revival of Klan vigilantism left smoking crosses and torched churches all across the state. There were sixty-one cross burnings on

So, You Want to Be a Freedom Summer Volunteer?

Signing up as a Freedom Summer volunteer brought some unique orientation materials in the mail. "We hope you are making preparations to have bond money ready in the event of your arrest," read the first paragraph of a memo to accepted applicants in 1964. "Bond money for a single arrest usually runs around $500." Prospective volunteers were instructed on the rules governing Mississippi license plates, and they were told to bring only one dressy outfit. "Men should not bring Bermuda shorts," another memo specified.

In addition to absorbing all the orientation materials on Freedom Schools and voter registration, the volunteers were asked to bring any office or educational equipment they could get their hands on: typewriters, stencils, magazines, comic books, chalk, inner tubing ("gasoline stations are only too happy to give away old inner tubes"), and even colored telephone wire ("ask your telephone company") for art projects. At a minimum each Freedom School teacher was expected to bring twenty-five pens and pencils, paper, tape, and a first-aid kit. With Freedom School budgets of nineteen hundred dollars per month per school, such donations were essential.

At the Movement orientation in Oxford, Ohio, the volunteers learned the rules of survival gleaned from four years of activism in Mississippi. For sit-ins, at which they were likely to be pushed or beaten, glasses, pens, watches, and sandals were out. They were instructed to know all routes in and out of town, stay five miles below the speed limit, not sleep near the windows, not expose their hosts to unnecessary danger by giving out their address, and, most important, not go places alone, especially at night.

In the end the volunteers had to find their own way. They survived on their wits and on lessons learned from their hosts, Movement cohorts, and daily experiences.

April 24 alone. Even before hundreds of white students ventured into Mississippi during that summer, three young activists had been shot dead and buried under an earthen dam south of Philadelphia, Mississippi. Movement activists chartered their first political party, the Mississippi Freedom Democratic Party (MFDP), at a convention in Jackson in April.

That summer brought the great experiment in biracial activism known first as the Summer Project and later as Freedom Summer. The Movement's purpose during the summer was twofold: to mount a serious challenge to the Democratic Party presidential delegation through the candidates of the newborn MFDP and to supplement existing education in black communities through the Freedom Schools. COFO organizers who had been working on the ground in Mississippi for several years led the way, aided by a group of college students. The students, many of whom had not worked as activists before, were predominantly white liberals from the North or California; nearly half were female. Of the 650 or so student volunteers, only 26 were from the South. Blacks made up less than 10 percent of the new recruits.

The students attended orientation at weeklong sessions at the Western College for Women in Oxford, Ohio, starting on June 13, 1964. On June 20 the first wave boarded a bus for Mississippi while the rest continued training. Six or seven men rode in a separate car headed for Meridian. The next day three of them—James Chaney, Andrew Goodman, and Mickey Schwerner—disappeared after visiting a burned church in Neshoba County. The second group of volunteers in Ohio were briefed on this chilling development and were given the option to back out. Few did so. With a tip from an informant federal agents discovered the bodies of the three victims on August 4 under ten tons of soil near the county fairgrounds. Nationwide anxiety turned to mourning.

Despite the fate of Chaney, Goodman, and Schwerner, activists established Freedom Schools, voter registration drives, and community centers in more than forty locations across the state. Not surprisingly, the documented incidents of violence were enough to fill a file cabinet: eighty beatings, sixty-seven bombings of churches, homes, and businesses; hundreds of arrests. A touring Movement troupe called the Free Southern Theater performed a play called *In White America* at dozens of Freedom Schools across the state. A separate caravan of folk singers, including Pete Seeger, the Chad Mitchell Trio, and the SNCC Freedom Singers, also toured the state.

Just Another Day at the COFO Office

The murders of Chaney, Goodman, and Schwerner were just three of a series of attacks on Movement workers during the summer of 1964. COFO, from its headquarters in Jackson, kept a running summary of incidents, great and small, in the counties where it was active. Every day brought reports of threats, false arrests, and violence, at times leavened with Keystone Kops–like episodes as law enforcement and white citizens fell over one another to harass Movement workers. Here is a report from one day during that summer, June 23, the day the car used by Chaney, Goodman, and Schwerner was found:

"Philadelphia: Missing car found burned; no sign of three workers. Car was on list circulated statewide by Canton White Citizens Council.

"Jackson: Shots fired at home of Rev. R. L. T. Smith. White man escapes on foot, reportedly picked up by a city truck. (Smith's home is under 24-hour guard.)

"Moss Point: Knights of Pythias Hall firebombed. Arson attempt on side of building. Damage slight. Used for voter rallies.

"Moss Point: Two summer volunteers picked up as they leave café, relax on private lawn. Taken by police at 85 m.p.h. without lights at night to Pascagoula jail. Held in 'protective custody' overnight and then released.

"Jackson: Civil rights worker held eight hours after receiving $5 change for a $20 bill.

"Jackson: White car fires shot at Henderson's cafe. Negroes pursue. Three shots fired, hitting one Negro in head twice.

"Clarksdale: Local pastor, a civil rights leader, arrested for reckless and drunk driving. He is a total abstainer.

"Statewide: Negroes try to attend Democratic Party county conventions. Participation systematically discouraged.

"Ruleville: *Look, Time* reporters covering voter rally at Williams Chapel, chased out of town by car at speeds up to 85 m.p.h. Early next morning, nine Negro homes, cars hit by bottles thrown from similar car."[32]

The other aspect of Freedom Summer was preparation for the Democratic National Convention in Atlantic City in August 1964. The COFO forces sought to show that blacks had been boxed out of the electoral machinery that selected the thirty-four delegates from Mississippi to cast nominating votes for president at the convention. After they were excluded from the selection process that resulted in an all-white Mississippi delegation, blacks set up an identical process under the banner of the MFDP and sent their own delegates to

Atlantic City to challenge the legitimacy of the all-white delegation.

Just as the fruits of its labor began to ripen, COFO disbanded in July 1965 in a meeting at Tougaloo College in Jackson. Governor Paul Johnson called for a repeal of the restrictive voting requirements, which was passed in a special session. The federal Voting Rights Act was passed and signed on August 6, 1965, mandating what black Mississippians had been fighting for: a racially neutral voting process. This goal became a reality, although DOJ initially only sent registrars into eight Mississippi counties and avoided some areas where racial exclusion had been most flagrant and violent.

A Day in the Life of the Volunteer

Some of the most important work was the rounds made by the volunteers to sign people up for the MFDP. Here volunteer Les Johnson describes his encounter with a new world:

"**C**anvassing is very trying, you walk a little dusty street, with incredibly broken down shacks. The people sitting on porches staring away into nowhere—the sweat running down your face! Little kids half-naked in raggy clothes *all* over the place—this is what you face with your little packet of 'Freedom Forms.'. . . The walls are inevitably covered with a funeral hall calendar, a portrait calendar of President Kennedy, old graduation pictures. Maybe a new cheap lamp from Fred's dollar store.

"You meet an afraid, but sometimes eager, curious face—one which is used to . . . saying 'Yes Sir' to everything a white man says. . . . You see their pain, the incredible years of suffering etched in their worn faces; and then, if you convince them to sign, you leave. You walk down the deteriorating steps to the dirt, to the next house—the next world and start in on your sales pitch again, leaving behind something which has broken you a little more. Poverty in the abstract does nothing to you. When you wake up to it every morning, and come down through the streets of it, and see the same old man on the ground playing the accordion, the same man selling peaches out of a basket too heavy for his twisted body, the same children, a day older—a day closer to those men—after this every day, poverty is a reality that is so outrageous you have to learn to . . . become jaded for the moment—or else be unable to function."[33]

The Freedom Schools: Charting a New Educational Path

The Freedom Schools were a response to the unequal and out-dated public school education available to most blacks. In 1960 black students completed an average of only six years of school, compared with eleven for whites. The state spent about four times as much for white students as for blacks, with even more skewed ratios in rural areas. The Freedom Schools were designed to provide traditional instruction in reading, writing, and arithmetic along with an awareness of black history and politics. More broadly, their purpose was to help students begin to question inequality.

The idea took concrete form in a proposal by SNCC field sec-retary Charles Cobb. The program director was Staughton Lynd, a Yale historian formerly at Spelman College in Atlanta, who adopted a cooperative model of education. Students were encouraged to shape the curriculum and to bring their unique experiences into the classroom. By the end of Freedom Sum-mer fifty Freedom Schools with nearly twenty-five hundred high school–age students were up and running from Moss Point on the Gulf Coast to Holly Springs near Memphis. Some students continued to attend in the fall after regular school.

It was a big change from their regular schooling. Teachers and students addressed one another by their first names. They often arranged chairs in a circle, and students were not required to raise their hands before trotting off to the bathroom. Along with classes in basic math and remedial reading, the students were encouraged to write essays about conditions in their neighborhoods, including racism. They read poems by Langston Hughes and used a text published by SNCC called *Negroes in American History: A Freedom Primer.* Students gath-ered in Meridian for a convention, declaring support for the Civil

Once black voting strength took hold in the late 1960s, open race baiting disappeared from campaign speeches and the number of black officeholders began to swell. Robert G. Clark, a teacher from Holmes County, became the first black legislator to go to Jackson in 1967. The MFDP joined a coalition of black and white moderates called the Loyal Democrats of Mississippi, who succeeded in chal-lenging the regular Democratic delegation in Chicago in 1968 on the

Rights Act of 1964 and condemning apartheid in South Africa. Many of them later became active in boycotts, voter registration drives, and other Movement activities. The novelty of the approach was not lost on local whites. "They call them schools," reported a Hattiesburg newspaper, "but there aren't any report cards, bells, or football teams."

Although their impact was not immediately apparent, the Freedom Schools were among the most lasting contributions of Freedom Summer. Many children look back on those classes now as eye-openers that allowed them to imagine an integrated world. The emphasis in class on student participation, hands-on learning, black history, and community activism was later adopted in some form in nearly every school in the country.

Freedom School teacher Edie Black and a class in Mileston. (Matt Herron/ Take Stock)

basis of the customary exclusion of blacks from the process. Although it had limited leverage to push Movement positions, it nonetheless completed the effort that had begun with homemade ballots and cardboard voting boxes in 1963 and had seized center stage at Atlantic City in 1964. By 1968 nearly 60 percent of eligible blacks were registered to vote. By 1980 blacks constituted nearly half the electorate and were a majority in sixteen counties.

The Delegation Challenge by the MFDP in Atlantic City

The appearance of the MFDP in Atlantic City was charged with emotion and caused President Johnson his only genuine political headache at the 1964 convention. Barred from the convention floor, the MFDP delegation marched along the Atlantic City boardwalk carrying huge sketches of Chaney, Goodman, and Schwerner, who had just been found dead in east Mississippi. The MFDP challenge, if unorthodox, had appeal not only because blacks had been excluded unfairly from the process but also because they were prepared to support President Johnson. White delegates were ready to defect from the party in favor of Goldwater. The delegations of Oregon, Michigan, and New York had pledged their support for the challengers. However, it was clear that President Johnson would rather let the white delegation stay seated and vote against him than replace it with the MFDP challengers and risk incurring the wrath of huge chunks of the South.

At a dramatic hearing of the credentials committee on August 22 Martin Luther King, Jr., testified for the MFDP, as did Aaron Henry, Rita Schwerner, Rev. Ed King, and Fannie Lou Hamer. Mrs. Hamer gave a gripping account of injustice in the

MFDP delegation demonstrating on boardwalk of Atlantic City during the Democratic National Convention, August 1964. (Bob Adelman/ Magnum Photos)

Delta. "Is this America?" she asked. "The land of the free and the home of the brave, where we have to sleep with our telephones off the hooks because our lives be threatened daily because we want to live as decent human beings, in America?" President Johnson hastily called a press conference in order to eclipse her emotional testimony, but the networks broadcast it later in the evening to a prime-time audience.

The credentials committee soon came forth with a half-hearted offer: The MFDP would be allowed two at-large delegates and was promised a fairer selection process next time around in 1968. After wrenching consultations among the Movement forces in Atlantic City, the MFDP rejected the offer. In the words of Mrs. Hamer, "We didn't come all this way for no two seats." The MFDP, upon its return to Mississippi, then ran four candidates for Congress in another challenge to the nomination process, and sixty thousand unofficial votes were cast in the national election. This mock vote highlighted the need for stronger federal voting rights legislation, which came to pass in the Voting Rights Act of 1965. MFDP candidates ran legally but failed to win any of the 1966 primary races despite the addition of one hundred thousand new black voters to the rolls in two years.

In 1986 Mike Espy, a mild-mannered attorney from a Delta funeral home family, became the first black member of Congress from Mississippi since Reconstruction. He was so popular that his picture could soon be found hanging next to King's in many homes. He was subsequently elected to two more terms, attracting substantial white support. He joined the Clinton cabinet as secretary of agriculture in 1992 but resigned in 1994 after allegations of impropriety. Bennie Thompson, a black activist since his days at Tougaloo College in the early 1960s, has represented the Second Congressional District ever since. There are a few Movement organizations still at work in Mississippi, and many community organizers work for Head Start and other social services agencies. Hollis Watkins, an activist who as a teenager started registering people to vote in McComb, runs Southern Echo, a leadership training group that endorses the goals of indigenous activism first pioneered by SNCC and CORE.

Mississippi Burning and Its Critics

Released in 1989, *Mississippi Burning* was the first Hollywood feature about the Movement in Mississippi. Predictably enough, it provoked controversy. It was based on the FBI's investigation into the Chaney-Goodman-Schwerner murders and starred Gene Hackman and Willem Dafoe. In the movie the FBI agents are responsible for bringing the assailants to justice, while the role of black activists in the investigation and the Movement in general is downplayed. At the time Movement people particularly objected to the portrayal of the FBI in a crusading role in the Philadelphia case, which in reality was more than offset by a decade of lackluster investigations into racial killings and hostile surveillance of Movement activities. One activist said the movie was "about as real as Santa Claus." Another refers to it today as simply "that bad movie."

Criticism went far beyond name-calling. A special academic conference was held at Tougaloo College in 1989 to discuss stereotypes and misconceptions raised by the movie. The *Jackson Clarion Ledger* used the movie as the rationale for a four-month series of articles about race relations not only in Philadelphia but all over the state. The movie made the cover of *Time*, sending reporters poking around the state asking then-and-now questions and causing a reformist governor to lament the recycling of unflattering images. *Mississippi Burning* had been only the last of a series of portrayals authored mostly by white northerners that consistently underplayed the role of black activists or otherwise got things wrong. Many Movement workers who had participated in the production of the film vowed not to aid another such media project without greater control.

Several of them formed the Mississippi Community Foundation, a sort of Movement cartel under which they pledged not to give interviews or otherwise aid documentary projects about Mississippi and to channel their efforts into their own versions of history. Although work has begun on a more authentic Movement film underwritten by the foundation, it has not yet been completed.

Jackson, Mississippi

Capital in the Eye of the Storm

Mississippi's capital city was a crossroads for those who upheld segregation and those who vowed to dismantle it. At a congressional hearing in December 1946 Jackson area black veterans and leaders from across the state testified about flagrant voting abuses by a champion race baiter, Senator Theodore Bilbo. The parade of well-dressed black witnesses summoned from the back row of a segregated hearing room in Washington, D.C., marked the beginning of a coordinated campaign against racism.

Jackson also was the birthplace of the Dixiecrat revolt of 1948, when segregationist southern congressmen defected from the Democratic Party. A Truman administration report called "To Secure These Rights" had advocated the elimination of segregation. But at the Democratic National Convention that year the Mississippi delegation and part of the Alabama delegation walked out rather than support an integrationist plank. Mississippians then voted for a breakaway ticket of Strom Thurmond of South Carolina for president and Mississippi Governor Fielding Wright as his running mate. Although Truman won the election, the Dixiecrats remained an influential bloc in Congress, specializing in sandbagging civil rights bills for the next two decades.

Despite the efforts of Medgar Evers and other activists in Jackson, steps toward equal rights in the 1950s were small as the result of the limited leverage of the NAACP and the inability to reach a wider audience. In September 1955 Thurgood Marshall's televised appearance on the "Today" show to talk about the *Brown* case went unseen by Jackson residents because the local NBC affiliate, WLBT, refused to broadcast it and told the audience the station was experiencing "technical difficulties." Jackson also was home to Mississippi's only daily newspapers, the *Clarion Ledger* and the *Jackson Daily News,* owned by brothers Robert and Thomas Hederman and unrelentingly hostile to the Movement. The black-run *Jackson Advocate* began as a crusading voice against segregation in the 1940s, but under mercurial editor Percy Greene, who assisted the Sovereignty Commission and criticized the NAACP, it changed positions in the 1950s and defended the status quo.

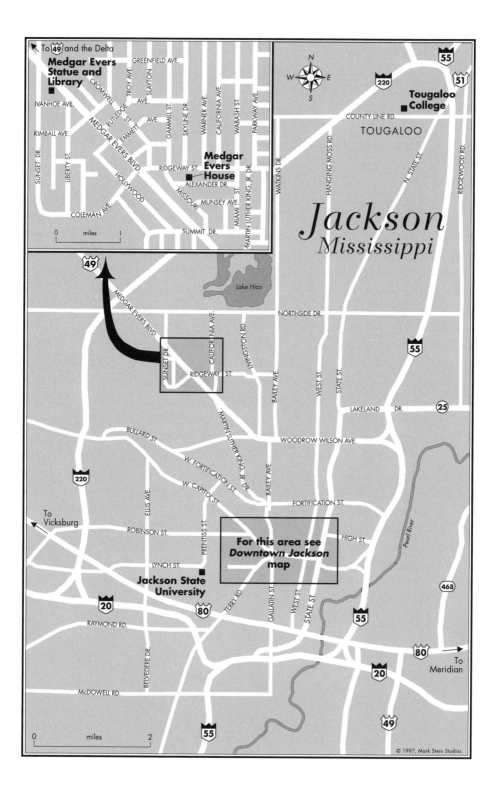

To 49 and the Delta

Medgar Evers
Statue and
Library

GREENFIELD AVE.

IVANHOE AVE.

KIMBALL AVE.

Medgar
Evers
House

RIDGEWAY ST.

ALEXANDER DR.

SUMMIT DR.

CROMWELL ST.

TROY AVE.

SLAYTON AVE.

RUTLEDGE ST.

EMMETT AVE.

MEDGAR EVERS BLVD.

HOLLYWOOD

COLEMAN AVE.

SUNSET DR.

LIBERTY ST.

GAMMILL ST.

SKYLINE DR.

WARNER AVE.

CALIFORNIA AVE.

WABASH ST.

PARKWAY AVE.

MISSOURI

MIAMI

MARTIN LUTHER KING, JR. DR.

MUNSEY AVE.

0   miles   1

49

MEDGAR EVERS BLVD

Lake Hico

NORTHSIDE DR.

SUNSET DR.

RIDGEWAY   ST.

CALIFORNIA AVE.

LIVINGSTON RD.

BAILEY AVE.

WEST ST.

STATE ST.

55

LAKELAND   DR.

25

BULLARD ST.

MARTIN LUTHER KING, JR. DR.

WOODROW WILSON AVE.

W. FORTIFICATION ST.

W. CAPITOL ST.

BAILEY AVE.

FORTIFICATION ST.

220

ELLIS AVE.

To
Vicksburg

ROBINSON ST.

PRENTISS ST.

For this area see
Downtown Jackson
map

HIGH ST.

Pearl River

LYNCH ST.

Jackson State
University

20

80

RAYMOND RD.

BELVEDERE DR.

TERRY RD.

GALLATIN ST.

WEST ST.

STATE ST.

55

468

80

To
Meridian

20

McDOWELL RD.

0   miles   2

55

49

N
W   E
S

220

55

51

Tougaloo
College

COUNTY LINE RD.

TOUGALOO

HANGING MOSS RD.

WATKINS DR.

N. STATE ST.

RIDGEWOOD RD.

Jackson
Mississippi

© 1997, Mark Stein Studios

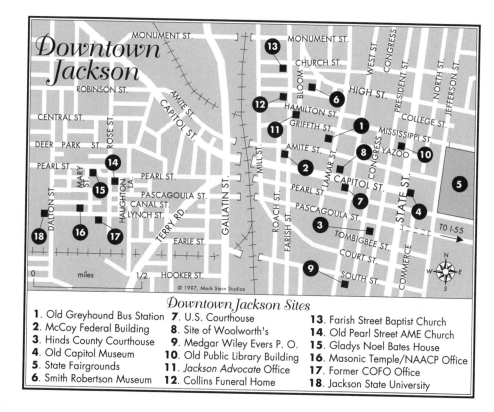

Downtown Jackson

Downtown Jackson Sites

1. Old Greyhound Bus Station
2. McCoy Federal Building
3. Hinds County Courthouse
4. Old Capitol Museum
5. State Fairgrounds
6. Smith Robertson Museum
7. U.S. Courthouse
8. Site of Woolworth's
9. Medgar Wiley Evers P. O.
10. Old Public Library Building
11. *Jackson Advocate* Office
12. Collins Funeral Home
13. Farish Street Baptist Church
14. Old Pearl Street AME Church
15. Gladys Noel Bates House
16. Masonic Temple/NAACP Office
17. Former COFO Office
18. Jackson State University

In spring 1960 students from Jackson's black colleges started a campaign to boycott the stores on Capitol Street that was aimed at improving the treatment of black customers and protesting the lack of black clerks. The following year nine students at Tougaloo College, members of the NAACP Youth Council, made the first desegregation test in Jackson. Their target: the main branch of the public library on State Street, a facility far superior to a separate branch for blacks. In full view of a waiting press corps the students entered the library on March 27, 1961, flipped through the card catalog, and managed to begin reading a few library books before police arrested them for breaching the peace. The library building at 301 State Street still stands across from the current main branch, the Eudora Welty Library, and is used as an administrative building by the city of Jackson.

The arrest of the Tougaloo Nine, as they were called, sparked student efforts. Jackson State College students first staged a prayer meeting in front of their own library, then marched to the city jail, where the Tougaloo students were detained. They were scattered by

Capitol Street, c. 1959. A dramatic sit-in took place at the Woolworth's on the left in May 1963.

police with dogs and tear gas, one of the first civil rights marches subjected to these methods. The Tougaloo Nine trial was a segregated spectacle in the municipal courtroom that resulted in hundred-dollar fines, suspended sentences, and assignments for the students to write one-thousand-word essays on juvenile delinquency. Students went on to test the Jackson zoo, parks, and swimming pools while black businessmen challenged segregation in public transportation. Just before Christmas Rev. R. L. T. Smith announced his candidacy for Congress, the first by a black candidate in Mississippi since Reconstruction. Smith made an eloquent and unprecedented appeal on Jackson TV for an end to "outworn slogans and the screaming epithets of bigotry."

After the Freedom Riders ended their journey in Jackson in May 1961, several activists stayed behind to coordinate waves of subsequent riders. Tougaloo students, Jackson State College students, and students from the Nashville student Movement worked to harness the enthusiasm for direct tests of segregation generated by the Tougaloo Nine. They urged groups of students, black and white, to test the segregated sections of transportation facilities. For the next several months people arrived by train from Memphis and New Orleans for that purpose. By summer's end more than three hundred people had submitted to arrest, and organizers James Bevel and Bernard Lafayette had been sentenced to six months in jail for orchestrating the tests.

In 1962 the NAACP North Jackson Youth Council announced a Christmas boycott of downtown merchants to protest the continuing code of segregation in shopping and hiring. On December 12, 1962, the students, together with their adviser, Tougaloo sociology professor John Salter, picketed the Woolworth's on Capitol Street and submitted to peaceful arrests. Meanwhile students secretly went from house to house, distributing leaflets hidden in their coats and umbrellas that urged people to stay away from downtown. The *Jackson Daily News*, never at a loss for vivid imagery when it came to racial issues, editorialized that the demonstrations were directed by northern puppeteers and were "about as useless as a reading lamp in a coffin."

Six months of boycotting left its mark. The city fathers initially rejected the Movement demands, so a more intensive campaign began the following spring with the student sit-in at Woolworth's on May 28, 1963. The abuse heaped on the passive students drew national press attention and convinced the NAACP leaders to follow the students' lead. On May 31 a Friday afternoon march of 600 schoolchildren set off from the Farish Street Baptist Church in the largest demonstration Jackson had yet seen. It was met with an equally determined line of law enforcement officers, who rounded up 450 protesters and carted them to the stockades at the State Fairgrounds. In a rare appearance on the picket lines Roy Wilkins, head of the national NAACP, joined Medgar Evers, head of the state NAACP, and both were arrested in front of Woolworth's in June. The city of Jackson successfully curtailed open demonstrations with a lawsuit that same month.

Then, on June 12, 1963, a chilling murder struck a quiet residential section of the city. After a late-night meeting at the New Jerusalem Baptist Church, Medgar Evers drove home and was gunned down as he walked to his front door. His funeral at the Masonic Temple on Lynch Street produced a massive outpouring of mourners, one of the largest gatherings in the history of Jackson. After the service about ten thousand people walked silently from the temple to the Collins Funeral Home on Farish Street, and the city council temporarily lifted its ban on marching. The marchers

The Trials of Byron de la Beckwith

It took eleven hours to find a vintage 1918 Enfield rifle in a cleared patch across from Medgar Evers's house on Guynes Street and nine days to trace the weapon to a white Greenwood man named Byron de la Beckwith. It took thirty years to put Beckwith behind bars for the murder of one of the South's tireless civil rights leaders.

Beckwith, known to his friends as Delay, was a salesman and ex-marine who clung obsessively to the remnants of a Confederate heritage. By the time Beckwith's father died when he was five, the immediate family was deep in debt and past glory existed only in his imagination. He was raised by cousins and an uncle, dropped out of Mississippi State College, and became a salesman for a tobacco and candy distributor in Greenwood. He was a charter member of the Citizens' Council and a connoisseur of racist literature.

Beckwith was first arrested for the murder of Evers at his home in Greenwood and taken to the Jackson city jail on June 21, 1963. The prosecution's case rested on Beckwith's fingerprint, found on the weapon, and his history as a gun-loving racist with a need for attention. He had a fresh scar above his eye from the kick of a rifle shot. And he freely admitted that he carried thirty to forty guns in his car at any given time and was an accomplished shot.

At the trial in January 1964 Beckwith reveled in his starring role. He dressed snappily in a suit, French cuffs, and handkerchief, smiled and joked with the court officers, and startled the prosecutor by offering him a cigar in the jury's presence. He waved to the press corps in the balcony. After the presentation of evidence the jury came back deadlocked. Beckwith was retried in June, and again the jury could not reach a verdict.

His release and welcome home in Greenwood were worthy of a heavyweight champion. Crowds cheered him along the highway as he rode home with a sheriff's escort. He received friends and admirers at the Leflore County Courthouse and was made an auxiliary police officer. From then on Beckwith made a habit of showing up at civil rights hot spots, such as the Leflore Theater in Greenwood after it was integrated in 1964 and Greenwood's Broad Street Park during the Meredith March in 1966. In 1967, riding his wave of popularity, Beckwith announced his intention to run for lieutenant governor.

Meanwhile the murder case remained dormant. In 1967 Myrlie Evers published her stirring memoir *For Us, the Living*, which began with the sentence "Somewhere in Mississippi lives the man who murdered my husband." She moved to California and remarried. Beckwith went back to being a salesman, this time in Florida. While traveling in Louisiana, he was arrested and convicted of carrying explosives. He returned briefly to Greenwood, then moved to Signal Mountain, Tennessee, near Chattanooga. The case seemed to have become a dim memory.

Then a series of events in the late 1980s brought it back with searing intensity. A leak of some of the Sovereignty Commission files revealed that the commission had screened jurors for the defense, raising the possibility of jury tampering. A young white prosecutor named Bobby DeLaughter got interested in the case. And although the transcript of the first trial was missing from the courthouse, Myrlie Evers found a copy in a trunk. The rifle had somehow ended up in the closet of a local judge, who was also the prosecutor's father-in-law. The media hurricane created by the movie *Mississippi Burning* gave the Evers case added urgency.

A new trial began in January 1994 in Jackson with a majority-black jury. Beckwith, by then seventy-three, sat blankly through the trial, at times removing his hearing aid. Some of the witnesses from the first trial, wobbly and well into retirement, once again mounted the witness stand. Dead or unavailable witnesses spoke through the transcript of the 1964 trials. Myrlie Evers, after three decades of grieving, came back from California to testify for a third time. In his summation the prosecutor made it clear that the case was an unhealed wound to the state. "It's right, it's just, and Lord knows, it's just time," he said. After five hours of deliberation the jury returned a guilty verdict. Beckwith is currently serving time in a Hinds County prison in Raymond.

came face-to-face with a line of helmeted officers. Although several marchers experienced abuse and responded by pelting the officers with debris, cooler heads prevailed, and the march disbanded peacefully. After intervention by the Kennedy administration the city government agreed to hire black policemen and to address the grievances first raised by the boycott. It was years before it actually made good on its promises, and the concessions robbed the local Movement of its momentum.

During Freedom Summer in 1964 the COFO state headquarters on Lynch Street coordinated a dizzying array of programs and monitored the steady onslaught of violent incidents and reprisals against Movement workers across the state. All the while the "Thompson Tank," a thirteen-thousand-pound tank with mounted machine guns and inch-thick bulletproof glass named after the mayor, stood at the ready should demonstrations get out of hand. At the same time the Civil Rights Act of 1964 mandated open service to all. The plush Robert E. Lee Hotel on North Lamar Street was closed to the public, though it still offered free rooms to state legislators. CLOSED IN DESPAIR, read the sign on the door. Two strong signals heralded a new era as Jackson began to feel the cost of heel digging on race. The

Jackson Chamber of Commerce urged compliance with the Civil Rights Act, and a new governor, Paul Johnson, metamorphosed from Ross Barnett's enforcer at Ole Miss into a proponent of racial moderation. Johnson declared in his inaugural speech, "Mississippi is part of this world, whether we like it or not."

In the second phase of its 1964 convention challenge the MFDP protested the composition of the all-white Mississippi congressional delegation. In one of the largest marches since the Evers funeral, five hundred demonstrators set out from Morning Star Baptist Church on June 14, 1965, behind MFDP chairman Lawrence Guyot and made it to the state Capitol for the first time. Afterward nearly all the marchers were arrested and shipped off in vans and trash trucks to the fairgrounds, where they were subjected to the harsh conditions of a makeshift prison camp. In the following week the number of marchers arrested climbed to more than a thousand.

Jackson erupted in protest once more in May 1967 after the shooting of activist Ben Brown by Jackson police during student rioting on Lynch Street. Two Tougaloo students were disciplined for using a school bus to retrieve their classmates from a rally at Jackson State College, and this only spurred more protest. It prompted Tougaloo students to boycott classes and block the campus gate. Lynch Street again became a flashpoint in 1970, when Mississippi state highway patrolmen, called in to quell unrest on the Jackson State campus, shot and killed two students on opposite sides of Lynch Street. Later the two Tougaloo students who had commandeered the bus for protests attained high office: Bennie Thompson as a member of Congress and Constance Slaughter-Harvey as Mississippi assistant secretary of state.

Gladys Noel Bates House

1037 West Pearl Street

In 1948 Gladys Noel Bates, a black science teacher at Smith Robertson School (now the Smith Robertson Museum at 528 Bloom Street) and a Tougaloo graduate, brought a lawsuit that became the first open racial challenge in Mississippi. At the time she was paid $120 a month, half of what her white counterparts with identical qualifications were earning. When the NAACP agreed to represent the black teachers in a lawsuit, Mrs. Bates stepped forward to be the named plaintiff.

She was well suited for a frontline role in one of the NAACP's first Deep South lawsuits. Her father, A. J. Noel, was one of the founding members of the Jackson NAACP, and she joined the youth chapter and registered to vote upon her return home from teaching in North Carolina and Kosciusko, Mississippi. Her father built the house on its current site in 1924.

After Mrs. Bates first became involved in the lawsuit, retribution was predictably swift. Her colleagues at the school "scattered like mice running from a cat" when they saw her coming down the hall, although some offered discreet support. Both she and her husband, John M. Bates, Sr., also a teacher, were fired. After alarmist headlines in the Jackson newspapers, someone shot into the house, attempted to burn it, and left burning crosses nearby.

Representing Mrs. Bates were the NAACP's Robert Carter, later a federal judge, and Constance Baker Motley, who had just passed the bar and later became the first black woman on the federal bench. The suit prompted the state to order an equalization of salaries in public schools and eventually to implement it after lengthy resistance. Mrs. Bates's parents continued to be active into the 1960s, housing Freedom Riders when they came to Jackson in 1961. She moved with her husband in 1960 to Denver, where she still lives.

Greyhound Bus Station

219 South Lamar Street

Although New Orleans was their original destination, the Freedom Riders traveling by bus got only as far as Jackson. After violence, political jousting, and security arrangements held up the riders in Montgomery for several days, a Trailways bus headed straight for Jackson under heavy guard on May 24, 1961. City police ushered the bus into the Trailways Station in Jackson, where twelve passengers disembarked and headed for the white lounge, some of them in dire need of relief after the nonstop trip of 260 miles without a bathroom. Their next stops were a paddy wagon and a jail cell, where they were held on charges of disturbing the peace. Unbeknownst to them, the Kennedy administration had agreed to allow local police to make the arrests contrary to federal law as long as order was maintained.

A second bus, carrying CORE head James Farmer and fifteen other passengers, pulled into this Greyhound station later that day and met the same fate. Attorney General Robert Kennedy, who had been drawn into active mediation of the disputes attending the Freedom Rides, called for a cooling-off period. Farmer responded that any further cooling would plunge blacks into a "deep freeze." That fall the ICC banned segregated sections at interstate transportation facilities.

The Trailways station has been torn down and is now the site of the Russell C. Davis Planetarium (201 East Pascagoula Street). The blue Greyhound Station, which has been remodeled as an architect's office, maintains its original appearance and still features a sprinting neon greyhound on the roof.

Hinds County Detention Center

407 East Pascagoula Street

The Hinds County jail became a rite of passage for several Freedom Riders, marking their conversion from bold students to Movement veterans. After their arrests in May 1961 they each got a two-hundred-dollar fine and a sixty-day suspended sentence. They chose to serve out their sentences to focus attention on the injustice of the charges and to fill the jails. Forty-one-year-old James Farmer, the head of CORE, served thirty-nine days in jail alongside young Freedom Riders and lost twenty-two pounds. Many of those jailed later assumed leadership roles in the Movement; they included John Lewis, James Bevel, Diane Nash, Stokely Carmichael, C. T. Vivian, and Bernard Lafayette.

Because of overcrowding, the Freedom Riders eventually served out their sentences in the state penitentiary. First they were taken to a prison farm in Raymond, Hinds County, where Rev. C. T. Vivian was beaten for refusing to "sir" his jailers. Then, on the orders of Governor Ross Barnett, they were sent to Parchman Penitentiary, a maximum-security facility in Sunflower County set in the cotton fields of the Delta, where prisoners tilled the land in stripes. At Parchman the Freedom Riders served a prison term that became a Movement crucible. Parchman was notorious for brutal plantation-style incarceration. Although the Freedom Riders were not subjected to routine violence, as some feared, many served their first hard time in prison. The women were asked to exchange all their belongings, including the bobby pins in their hair, for striped skirts, and men were given shorts that were several sizes too big.

At Parchman contact with the outside world was limited, so they held devotional services and passed notes between segregated cells through a messenger. Those who insisted on singing freedom songs had to give up their mattresses or subject themselves to a hosing down. On the governor's birthday they got ice cream and cake. Fat cats in business suits, including the governor himself, came to see them on display like animals in a zoo. In fact one Freedom Rider with a toothache was offered the ministrations of a veterinarian equipped with a large instrument for pulling horse teeth. Movement leaders who were imprisoned at Parchman later looked back with pride at having plumbed the depths of Mississippi's penal system, leaving them able to carry their formative experience together into many communities all across the South.

U.S. Courthouse (James O. Eastland Building)
245 East Capitol Street

The chambers of U.S. District Judge W. Harold Cox, who showed segregationist sympathies but ultimately was forced to follow civil rights precedents, were here. Cox, a college friend of Senator James Eastland's and the son of a sheriff from Sunflower County, was appointed by President Kennedy. In his courtroom DOJ faced an uphill battle in voting rights cases and criminal cases involving whites who harassed Movement workers, including the killers of Chaney, Goodman, and Schwerner. As late as 1964, while sitting in judgment on a voting case originating in Canton, Judge Cox routinely referred to prospective black registrants as "niggers" and wondered in open court: "Who is telling these people they can get in line and push people around, acting like a bunch of chimpanzees?" Cox ruled, nonetheless, that the Madison County registrar was required to process fifty voting applications a day, which comported with DOJ's legal position. In the same building in March 1964 Judge Sidney Mize ordered desegregation of Mississippi's public schools.

The courthouse also is home to a controversial mural in the fourth-floor courtroom, a thirty-by-thirteen-foot tableau of plantation life in Mississippi. It was painted by Ukrainian artist Simka Simkhovitch in 1938 as part of the WPA's program to put artists to work decorating U.S. post offices (twenty-seven in Mississippi alone). At the center of the painting stands a two-story brick courthouse with four columns, surrounded by magnolia, livestock, and pine trees. A benevolent planter stands in front of it with one arm around a mother, who is cradling a child. He is surrounded by images of labor. To the left a black woman is stooping to pick cotton and a black man is strumming a banjo under the watchful eye of a white overseer. Surveying the scene is a robed judge, who cradles a lawbook and appears to defer to the central figure of the planter.

This mural, although not unusual for the WPA genre, began to appear increasingly anachronistic as the courthouse became the forum for Movement cases, starting with the teacher salary case of 1948. Cases on school desegregation, voting, and racial intimidation were all argued under its gaze until it was draped with a curtain at the request of Movement lawyers in the early 1970s. The mural was briefly unveiled for a ceremony marking the installation of Judge Cox's portrait at the courthouse after his death in 1988. That provoked yet another round of controversy, and since then it has remained behind the curtain and is not viewable by the general public.

Woodworth Chapel, Tougaloo College

500 County Line Road

In 1946, after all-white primaries were declared illegal, Tougaloo chaplain William Albert Bender took black students to vote in his precinct in nearby Ridgeland. He was barred at the door by a deputy sheriff with a drawn pistol, and a cross was burned on the Tougaloo campus.

Bender represented the beginning of a tradition of Tougaloo faculty and students who jeopardized their safety for the Movement and provided one of the only sanctuaries in the state for its activities. The college was backed by the New England–based United Church of Christ, which gave it unique freedoms, and it had deep roots in the abolitionist American Missionary Association. Ernst Borinski, a Tougaloo sociology professor who had escaped from the Nazis in the 1930s, initiated periodic racial discussions between the students of Tougaloo and nearby white Millsaps College.

At the center of Movement activity on campus was Woodworth Chapel, named for Tougaloo's president from 1887 to 1912, Dr. Frank Woodworth. John Mangrum, another Tougaloo chaplain, advised the student NAACP youth chapter during the Tougaloo Nine protest in 1961. The Freedom Riders were housed in Tougaloo dorms later that year and often met in the chapel to sing and exchange ideas. The Tougaloo students, in addition to pressing SNCC and COFO programs, came up with creative ideas of their own. In the summer of 1963 students and faculty began a series of kneel-ins in Jackson's white churches. When students were turned away from a concert at the Jackson Auditorium in November 1963, they persuaded the artists not to appear in a segregated facility but to perform at Tougaloo instead. By making the rounds of the city's religious and cultural institutions, the students showed the patent inadequacy of the sit-in settlement with the city authorities reached after the summer protests of 1963.

One of the participants in the seminal Borinski discussion groups was Rev. Ed King, a graduate of Millsaps College who returned to Jackson as Tougaloo's chaplain in 1963. Along with colleague John

Salter, Ed King immersed himself in all aspects of the Movement. He ran for lieutenant governor in the mock vote of 1963, supported the MFDP at the Democratic National Convention in 1964, and ran as an MFDP congressional candidate in 1966. While he was chaplain, Joan Baez gave a concert to an integrated audience of five hundred here in March 1964. During this period the chapel bell routinely was rung to call a meeting after students were released from prison.

Tougaloo was unusual in its tolerance of Movement activity, and so was its president, Dr. A. D. Beittel. Dr. Beittel, who was installed in 1959, visited the Tougaloo Nine in jail in 1961. When in 1963 he heard that three Tougaloo students had initiated the first sit-in at the Woolworth's on Capitol Street and were being heaped with abuse, he went down to the store and joined them at the counter. His

(Left to right) John Salter, Joan Trumpauer, and Anne Moody sitting in at Woolworth's on Capitol Street, May 28, 1963. (AP/Wide World Photos)

involvement prompted threats to revoke Tougaloo's charter and led to his early retirement in June 1964.

The last leg of the Meredith March in 1966 proceeded through the Tougaloo gates on its way to downtown Jackson.

Site of Woolworth's
124 East Capitol Street (now a parking garage)

Just as it had been in Greensboro three years earlier, the long lunch counter at Woolworth's became the favored place to launch Jackson's highly publicized sit-ins. On May 28, 1963, three Tougaloo students—Pearlena Lewis, Memphis Norman, and Anne Moody—slipped in the back door and took their seats at the counter. "I'd like to stay here with you," one white woman said to them, "but my husband is waiting."

After a lunchtime crowd gathered, Norman was pulled from his stool by an ex-police officer, kicked, beaten, and then arrested. Two whites—Lois Chaffee, a Tougaloo professor, and Joan Trumpauer, a student activist—took his place at the counter. A crowd of hostile whites gathered in the store, shouting out insults and showering the foursome with catsup, mustard, and cigarettes while they sat impassively. John Salter, the Tougaloo professor and adviser to the protesters, was pummeled in the store and had pepper water splashed in his face. Finally, after three hours of hateful hazing, the store manager closed the store and the protesters were led away by police escorts. Vivid photographs of the assault later became the basis for a life-size sit-in exhibit at the National Civil Rights Museum in Memphis.

Old Capitol/State Historical Museum
100 South State Street

This building served as the state Capitol from 1839 until 1903. It anchored the east end of Capitol Street, later the scene of Movement marches and boycotts that stretched from the Old Capitol to the railroad station, including the sit-in at Woolworth's in 1963. At one point the mayor pledged to line this street with a thousand police officers. Since 1961 the Old Capitol has housed the State Historical Museum, which includes a small, rich civil rights exhibit, one of the first in the country when it opened in 1984. Included is the wooden sign of COFO and the MFDP, which was mounted atop the office in the Neshoba County town of Philadelphia in the mid-sixties, and the slippers activist Joan Trumpauer wore in the Hinds County jail.

State Fairgrounds

1207 Mississippi Street

The annual state fair has long been a showcase for prize livestock, cooking, and crafts. Attendance in the 1960s was strictly segregated: Whites attended the first week of the fair, blacks part of the second week. Part of SNCC's Freedom Rider follow-up campaign in 1961 was a picket line at the fairgrounds gate to urge a boycott of the fair until it was desegregated, which put a dent in attendance. Police sent six German shepherds snarling into the crowd and arrested seven students for obstructing the street. Split attendance at the fair eventually was ended after the boycott became an annual event over the next two years.

When the first street demonstrations hit Jackson in May 1963, the fairgrounds had another purpose: They became a substitute for overcrowded jails. Demonstrators of all ages were brought here and held under unsanitary conditions. The grounds were again used for detention in June 1965, when the MFDP organized a mass march protesting the exclusion of black candidates from the electoral process. Surrounded by barbed wire and monitored by searchlights at night, prisoners were kept in the livestock exhibition spaces and ate out of common food barrels. During this period the local papers referred to it as the Fairgrounds Hotel.

Livestock pens at the State Fairgrounds in Jackson, 1995. (Townsend Davis)

Medgar Evers House

2332 Margaret Walker Alexander Drive (formerly Guynes Street)

When Medgar and Myrlie Evers bought this house on his GI mortgage in 1957, the neighborhood was a new subdivision for black families. Missouri Avenue was the dividing line between black neighborhoods to the north and white neighborhoods to the south. Several neighbors expressed concern that violence against the Evers family would be visited on their houses by mistake. But when violence did arrive, the killer had the right address.

Medgar Evers devoted his life to challenging racism. On his twenty-first birthday in 1946 he led a line of veterans to the courthouse in his hometown of Decatur, Mississippi, to register to vote. He had been stationed as a soldier in France, where integration was so natural that he carried on a romance with a white woman. Afterward he went to Alcorn College on the GI Bill and married a piano-playing student from Vicksburg, Myrlie Beasley. They moved to Mound Bayou, where he worked for T. R. M. Howard's Magnolia Mutual Insurance Company, rising at dawn to begin his house-to-house sales pitches in Clarksdale. He came home full of stories of black families strapped by poverty, exploitation, and hopelessness. In December 1954 he jumped at the chance to become the NAACP's first full-time field secretary in Mississippi.

He began working for the NAACP just as it rose to face the new crises brought on by *Brown*. The NAACP in Mississippi had shriveled to 129 members in six branches in 1944. The largest chapter had been in Jackson, where members still declined to meet in the same place twice in a row. By 1955 the NAACP was fully engaged in assisting black families battered by the retaliation of the Citizens' Council against signers of school petitions and by a sobering string of racial killings. The rest of the decade brought a continuous stream of white vengeance. Usually Evers reported the facts to the police and watched fruitless investigations fade into forgetting.

Evers was both a loyal organization man, crisscrossing the state for the NAACP, and a crusader. He named his firstborn son Darrell Kenyatta, after the Kenyan guerrilla leader. He insisted that the family buy groceries from the black-owned supermarket rather than white-owned Kroger's, where prices were lower. He volunteered his children for the lawsuit challenging Jackson's segregated schools. And he kept a backbreaking travel schedule right up to his death, gunning his powder blue 1962 Oldsmobile down highways to shake pursuers and periodically resorting to a disguise of army fatigues and boots.

Even before he became the NAACP point man, Evers was a moving target. He had turned down the chance at a corner lot on Guynes Street because it would have exposed the family to easier attacks. Threatening phone calls often required that he and his wife take the phone off the hook and walk away, leaving the caller to spew insults into the wall. The children were taught to stay away from windows and hit the floor at the sound of anything suspicious, and Evers often swiveled out of bed half awake to grab a rifle from under the bed at the sound of unknown visitors. One night someone threw a Molotov cocktail into his car parked in the carport beside the house, setting a blaze that his wife extinguished with a garden hose.

Upon returning home on June 11, 1963, from an NAACP meeting, Evers was getting out of his car in the driveway with an armful of shirts bearing the slogan "Jim Crow Must Go." His wife and children inside, who had stayed up to watch a presidential speech on civil rights, heard two pops in succession: the slam of the car door and a gunshot that hit Evers in the back before he could reach the door. Using a deer rifle with a telescopic sight, the shooter had crouched in a honeysuckle bush across the street and fired a single shot through the back of Evers's white shirt. The shot ripped through his chest, through a front window, and bounced off the refrigerator and a coffeepot before settling in a kitchen cabinet. Evers's wife and three children hit the ground. When they ran out to find him near the front door, Evers was facedown in a pool of blood with the house keys clenched in one hand. He died an hour later.

After an emotional funeral march in Jackson, Evers was given a soldier's burial in Arlington National Cemetery in Washington on June 19, 1963. A bronze statue of him stands on the grounds of the Medgar Evers Branch Library a short distance from the house. In 1994 Congress named Jackson's new main post office branch after him. The house has been donated to Tougaloo College but is temporarily boarded up.

Masonic Temple/NAACP Office
1072 Lynch Street

After the *Brown* decision the black Masons of Jackson were eager to have lead counsel Thurgood Marshall as a guest speaker. In those days the Masons had more than four hundred lodges around the state. Traditionally the auditorium at Jackson State College, known as the City Auditorium, was the largest gathering place for blacks.

But after the city banned an appearance by Marshall there, the Masons put plans for their own auditorium on a fast track. It was opened on May 30, 1955, with Marshall as the inaugural speaker. From then on common sights outside the temple were the patrol cars of police officers, who routinely took down the license plate numbers of Movement cars. The temple was used for everything from gatherings of the NAACP state chapters to fund-raisers by Lena Horne and Jackie Robinson to workshops in nonviolence conducted by CORE during the street demonstrations of 1963.

Upstairs in room 10 was the office of Medgar Evers, the first NAACP field secretary in the state. There his wife, Myrlie, handled administrative affairs while he went all over the state appearing at churches and meeting halls. He maintained an almost comic level of formality at the office, insisting that he and his wife address each other as Mr. and Mrs. and allowing no public displays of affection even after everyone else had gone home.

The funeral of Medgar Evers on June 15, 1963, brought Movement people here from all over the state. Four thousand mourners on folding chairs packed the temple hall in record heat while Evers

James Farmer of CORE addresses an NAACP rally at the Masonic Temple during the trials of the Freedom Riders, August 13, 1961. (UPI/Corbis-Bettmann)

lay in an open casket. T. R. M. Howard praised Evers's work in the Delta and said "he loved the NAACP with every fiber of his being." Roy Wilkins praised his voter registration work and excoriated politicians who were blocking civil rights legislation in Congress. The service was so tightly controlled that the NAACP even dictated what dress Mrs. Evers wore.

This hall also was the site of the COFO convention in October 1963 at which the concept of a Freedom Vote among unregistered blacks took shape. The hall again was packed for the MFDP convention on August 6, 1964. In the preceding months blacks had caucused and tried their hand at presidential politics, many for the first time, all across the state before they came to Jackson to select a delegation of blacks and whites to go to Atlantic City. In a full-fledged convention romp, complete with placards for each county, a mixture of the SNCC vanguard, the NAACP-era old guard, and newly energized farmers and laborers chose a delegation led by Lawrence Guyot, Aaron Henry, Fannie Lou Hamer, Annie Devine, Victoria Gray, and Rev. Ed King. Ella Baker, a veteran organizer and cofounder of SNCC four years earlier, cautioned the audience not to let politics distract from the goal of community improvement.

On August 11, 1968, many of the MFDP veterans met here again in an interracial coalition with the Loyal Democrats of Mississippi. This group challenged the delegates at the Democratic National Convention again, this time in Chicago. There they were seated and were supported by the same people who had turned them away four years earlier.

Today the temple still houses the current head of the NAACP Mississippi branches. Myrlie Evers, after moving to California, returned to Jackson to witness the long-delayed conviction of her husband's killer in 1994. She was elected national NAACP chairman of the board of directors in 1995.

Old Pearl Street AME Church
925 West Pearl Street

After the electrifying sit-in at Woolworth's on May 28, 1963, this church hosted a rousing mass meeting of one thousand people and extended a warm greeting to the demonstrators. When word spread that Mayor Allen Thompson had at first agreed to the Movement's demands and then reneged, the entire audience volunteered to march downtown. Today the building houses the Zion Travelers Baptist Church.

One of Jackson's most moving mass meetings, held the night after Medgar Evers was killed on June 12, 1963, also was held here. Formerly equivocal preachers roared defiance. Interorganizational rifts temporarily subsided. Myrlie Evers, her husband dead less than twenty-four hours, urged people to carry on the fight in his memory. "I come to you tonight with a broken heart," she said. "I come to make a plea that all of you here, and those of you who are not here, will, by his death, be able to draw some of his strength, some of his courage, and some of his determination to finish this fight."

Pearl Street's pastor, Rev. G. R. Haughton, headed the delegation that obtained the city's first concessions to the Jackson Movement. On June 18, 1963, at a mass meeting at College Hill Baptist Church (1600 Florence Avenue) shortly after the Medgar Evers funeral, those in attendance voted to accept the mayor's offer to hire more black police and sanitation workers and to hear future grievances in exchange for halting the demonstrations that had peppered the city for three weeks. Although it fell far short of complete desegregation, it was the first concrete reform flowing from the Tougaloo protest of two years earlier.

Farish Street

Farish Street today is a shell of its former self, a formerly thriving black business district of which two churches, two funeral homes, and the *Jackson Advocate* are the survivors. Before it moved into the Masonic Temple on Lynch Street, the NAACP had an office at 507½ Farish Street above Big John's, which served tasty pig's ear sandwiches. This building later housed the MFDP, the Medical Committee for Human Rights, a Head Start office, and several public-interest legal groups. The NAACP legal staff had offices upstairs in the two-story building at 538 Farish, while attorneys R. Jess Brown and Jack Young, who constituted half of the black Mississippi bar, had offices down the street. They handled Movement cases from the sit-ins to the school challenges. The *Mississippi Free Press*, which was printed in Holmes County by muckraker Hazel Brannon Smith and shipped to Jackson each week, operated out of No. 538½. Everyone ate at Steven's Kitchen, a brick building at 604 Farish that is no longer a restaurant but still bears the inscription "Welcome to Steven's."

Farish Street was the scene of throngs of mourners who followed behind the white hearse carrying the body of Medgar Evers on June 15, 1963. Police motorcycles escorted the marchers as they headed silently into town from the Masonic Temple in 101-degree heat, some shaded by umbrellas. When the casket passed by a line of police, some removed their blue riot helmets.

The mourners first marched to the Collins Funeral Home (415 Farish Street), observing the terms of a city permit. Then a group of young people began to sing "No More Bullets" to the tune "Oh Freedom," followed by "This Little Light of Mine." They clapped and sang while they walked back the way they came and streamed past police motorcycles. Marchers were blocked by heavily manned barricades at the intersection of Farish and Capitol streets, the gateway to downtown. When police began to clear the area by force, a few people responded by tossing bottles at them. Brave efforts by SNCC and CORE workers and DOJ attorney John Doar convinced the marchers not to vent their anger further and to return home.

Clarie Collins Harvey, in addition to running the Collins Funeral Home, founded a group called Womanpower Unlimited, which furnished Movement protesters with food, lodging, and a way to contact their families. Mrs. Harvey later served on the board of the Southern Regional Council and was the first black trustee of Millsaps College. Down the street at 100 West Capitol Street stands the Dr. A. H. McCoy Federal Building, the first federal building named for a black American. McCoy was a Jackson doctor who headed the state NAACP.

Farish Street Baptist Church
619 North Farish Street

At a momentous meeting in July 1954 black leaders came together to urge the governor to enforce the *Brown* decision. This was a marked shift from previous demands, which merely requested more humane forms of segregation and improved, if still separate, schools. After long and heated debate, the older generation of black leaders stunned Mississippi's white politicians by declaring themselves "unalterably opposed" to any effort to circumvent *Brown*.

The pastor during Movement days, Rev. S. Leon Whitney, supported the Movement and was bitten by a police dog when he attended the trial of the Tougaloo Nine in 1961. His church was the site of a meeting in 1963 when black leaders finally backed the sit-ins at downtown stores. This church also was the send-off point for an unprecedented march of six hundred Jackson high school students on May 31, 1963. On a Friday afternoon students arrived at the church and heard a lecture on nonviolence from Whitney, who gathered up everything that could be construed as a weapon, from a toothpick to a pocketknife, in the church collection plates. The students then marched two abreast and carried American flags as far as Capitol Street, where they were arrested and taken to the State Fairgrounds in garbage trucks.

COFO Office

1017 Lynch Street

At this nerve center of Freedom Summer WATS (wide-area telephone service) line operators kept in hourly touch with COFO offices across the state. It was a complex operation, encompassing voter registration, the convention challenge, security arrangements, housing, paychecks, and keeping track of the location of every volunteer scattered in three dozen outposts. A posted sign attested to the near impossibility of this task: NO ONE WOULD DARE BOMB THIS OFFICE AND END ALL THE CONFUSION. Although a busy center during Freedom Summer, it fell into decline by December 1964.

On May 11, 1967, in the midst of unrest on Lynch Street sparked by the arrest of a Jackson State College student for speeding, Movement worker Ben Brown was shot and killed not far from this office near the corner of Mount Olive Cemetery. Brown, a Jackson native, had been inspired by the Freedom Rides and had been involved in nearly every Movement program in Jackson since then. He had marched down that same street as part of the Evers funeral cortege, worked to register voters, served time in the State Fairgrounds as part of the MFDP demonstrations against the state legislature in 1965, and worked for the Delta Ministry, a church-based relief group. That night Brown went for a sandwich to Lynch Street, a short walk from his apartment, where he encountered a stand-off between bottle-hurling students and police. Police fired over the heads of the crowd, but one or two officers leveled their guns and caught Brown with shots in the head and back. He died the next morning on his twenty-second birthday. No assailant has ever been prosecuted. The city council in 1995 designated a park on Mill Street between Whitfield and Fairbanks streets as Benjamin Brown Park.

Jackson State University

1400 John R. Lynch Street

As a historically black state-funded college, Jackson State College was not in a position to challenge segregation openly. That did not stop its students, though. Taking their cue from students at Tougaloo College across town, Jackson State students in 1961 led a prayer vigil in front of their library to express solidarity with the Tougaloo

Nine that brought out seven hundred supporters. They also marched to the city jail, boycotted classes to protest the abolition of the student government, and helped engineer the Freedom Ride challenges at transportation facilities in summer 1961.

Originally called Natchez Seminary and established by the northern American Baptist Home Mission Society of New York during Reconstruction, the college was moved to Jackson in 1883. It was originally set on what is now the Millsaps College campus and relocated to Lynch Street in 1903. Lynch Street was named for John Roy Lynch, speaker of the Mississippi House during Reconstruction and a three-term black congressman.

Lynch Street, heavily traveled, ran through the heart of campus. Alexander Hall in 1970 was a women's dormitory that faced Lynch Street and housed about nine hundred students. A five-floor staircase with windows faced the street. On May 13, 1970, after several days of student protest against the killings at Kent State and the Vietnam War, students began pelting passing cars with rocks. Jackson police then barricaded Lynch Street at both ends of the campus. Expecting more violence the following night, one thousand national guardsmen were readied. After students again began abusing passing cars and set fire to a dump truck, a combined force of police and patrolmen moved in. A rumor of sniper fire provoked thirty-eight officers to open fire, unleashing more than one hundred rounds of ammunition in the direction of Alexander Hall and Roberts Hall across the street. Jackson State junior Phillip Gibbs and high school student James Earl Green were found dead on the ground, and four were injured inside Alexander Hall.

Today a memorial sits in the courtyard in front of Alexander Hall, which still has visible damage from the gunfire. Lynch Street has since been blocked off at the campus.

Site of Mount Beulah Center (Bonner-Campbell College)

18449 Old Highway 80 West, Edwards

Mount Beulah was formerly the campus of a black junior college founded in 1870, that merged with Tougaloo College. The first statewide Movement training was conducted here in 1963 under the leadership of SNCC field secretary Bob Moses and Bernice Robinson, the pioneering citizenship school teacher from Charleston, South Carolina. They planned voter registration workshops to be held that summer in Ruleville, Greenwood, and other areas of the Delta.

Mount Beulah also was the headquarters of one of the most

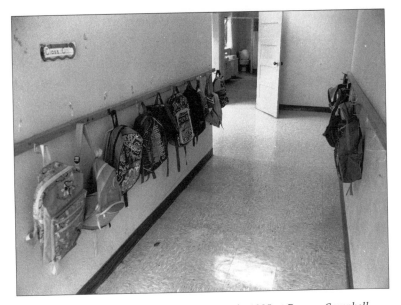

Book bags of students in a Head Start program in 1995 at Bonner-Campbell College (formerly Mount Beulah Center), where the preschool program originated. (Townsend Davis)

durable of the antipoverty programs, the program for preschoolers from poor families called Head Start. The children were provided with two hot meals a day, medical care, and a constructive learning environment. In its first summer in 1965, Head Start operated eighty-four centers in twenty-four counties, serving about six thousand children.

The Delta Ministry, a missionary antipoverty group under the National Council of Churches, also was housed here. Delta Ministry staffers were among the seven hundred people who attended a conference here on January 29, 1966, to discuss the lack of jobs, housing, and food in the hard-pressed areas of the state. Two days later a group from the conference drove past guards at the Greenville Air Force Base and occupied an empty building. They eventually were ejected but not before expressing bitter dissatisfaction with the Johnson administration's handling of antipoverty programs. In 1968 Mount Beulah also was one of the send-off points for the Poor People's March to Washington. Today, as Bonner-Campbell College, the campus hosts minister's conferences, retreats, and Head Start programs.

Head Start and the Great Society

In 1965 with the passage of the Voting Rights Act, many Movement people channeled their efforts into the antipoverty programs of Lyndon Johnson's Great Society, twenty million dollars of which were devoted to Mississippi. Mississippi became the focus of a raucous battle over the Child Development Group of Mississippi (CDGM), which was constructed nearly overnight and relied upon the community work already done by members of COFO and the MFDP. CDGM, which administered the Head Start preschool education program, rankled lawmakers, particularly Mississippi Senator John Stennis. He saw the federal government as underwriting the work of subversives posing as charity workers. Although many of the CDGM administrators had been active in the Movement, the mandate that such a program involve the "maximum feasible participation of the poor" meant that most of the staff were people from the neighborhoods, some of whom had been involved in the Movement and some of whom had not. The program ran into rough waters when it was discovered that CDGM had paid the bail of its staffers who had been arrested for demonstrating on behalf of the MFDP in Jackson. As a result of this and other allegations of mismanagement, the CDGM headquarters was moved from Mount Beulah in Edwards to an office building in Jackson.

The program was cut in half during its second season in November 1965. After a toddlers' "play-in" in Washington in February 1966, when forty-eight black children appeared with their teachers before the House Education and Labor Committee, the program was restored. Administration was shifted in the fall to a more moderate white-controlled nonprofit corporation called the Mississippi Action for Progress (MAP), and CDGM was denied funding. This brought the Movement forces out once again for a massive protest in Jackson on October 8, 1966, and a sustained lobbying campaign saved CDGM for one more round. By the end of 1967 CDGM had been taken over by state agencies, under which Head Start continues to operate. Even under a Republican governor, Head Start is a fixture in the social services network, and its vans are visible in many struggling neighborhoods across the state.

McComb, Mississippi

Moses Leads the First Mass Voting Drive

McComb, set in the piney woods of south Mississippi near the Louisiana border, developed as a railroad town that bred strong streaks of independence in its people. It was named for a railroad man, Henry Simpson McComb, and the Illinois Central Railroad was the primary employer for blacks and whites, who were members of separate unions. Union men and members of the NAACP laid the groundwork for the bold plans of SNCC, which selected McComb for its first mass voter registration campaign.

Local railroad crane operator C. C. Bryant became head of the Pike County NAACP in 1954. After the Greensboro sit-ins of 1960 students from Burglund High School wanted to sit in at Woolworth's in McComb, but the NAACP considered that move too inflammatory and preferred to recruit new members quietly. Mere membership in the NAACP was considered dangerous, and local leaders did not yet endorse the methods of direct confrontation then being popularized by the Freedom Riders and SNCC. At the time 15 police officers were enough to watch over the 14,500 residents of McComb, nicknamed the Camellia City.

All that changed when Bryant invited Bob Moses to launch a pioneering voter registration project in McComb in July 1961. During extensive canvassing of black churches and homes, Bryant and Moses introduced the voter registration form to many families for the first time and raised money through five- and ten-dollar donations. About 250 black residents had previously registered. After SNCC workers Reginald Robinson and John Hardy joined the effort, Moses held the first registration class in the black Masonic Hall in McComb. Two teenagers from nearby Summit, Hollis Watkins and Curtis Hayes, publicized the classes. In August Moses escorted four students down to Magnolia to take the voting test at the Pike County seat. Three of them passed.

The first sign of trouble appeared two weeks later, when Moses attempted the same thing with two prospective registrants in the town of Liberty, the seat of neighboring Amite County. Billy Jack Caston, the sheriff's cousin, stopped them in the street and beat Moses to his knees with a knife butt. Moses, who had not resisted

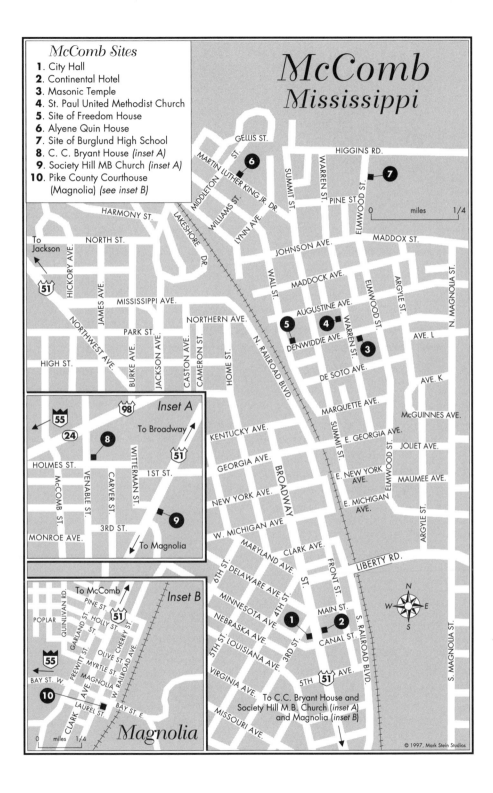

the assault, required nine stitches to close his wound; Caston was acquitted of criminal charges. News of this incident attracted student activists to McComb and mobilized local high school students. They tested out integration at a Woolworth's counter on Main Street and the Greyhound Bus Station for the first time. They were jailed for a full month before they were bailed out.

Then a series of violent incidents drew in the federal government and temporarily stalled the McComb Movement. Two young activists were assaulted in September by local officials in neighboring towns: Travis Britt was beaten while trying to register in Liberty, and John Hardy was pistol-whipped for doing the same in Tylertown, the seat of Walthall County. DOJ, which was responsible for protecting voting rights, sued to stop the prosecution of Hardy, who had been arrested for disorderly conduct. It was one of only two

White Supremacy in Brookhaven (Lincoln County)

Lamar Smith, sixty-three, was a farmer and a veteran who had urged fellow blacks to register to vote and had campaigned against an incumbent county supervisor. On August 13, 1955, nine days before a runoff election, he was approached by white men on a courthouse lawn in Brookhaven and shot down in front of a crowd of Saturday visitors. The sheriff saw a man with blood on his clothes leave the scene, but no witnesses came forward, and the case was never prosecuted. In this case, as in others, Ruby Hurley and other NAACP staffers found witnesses and gathered evidence, submitted them to the FBI (which at the time had no office in Mississippi), and watched as nothing was done.

Brookhaven also was the hometown of Judge Tom Brady, who in 1955 wrote and distributed one thousand copies of *Black Monday*, the most influential of the anti-*Brown* polemics. Richly illustrated with racist folklore, it painted integration as the first step in a short slide to communism. Brady compared blacks' contribution to the American Revolutionary War with "that of a well-broken horse" and wrote that no amount of training "can convince him that a caterpillar or a cockroach is not a delicacy." *Black Monday* quickly gained cult status among white supremacists.

Ten years later in Brookhaven the statewide White Knights of the Ku Klux Klan was founded on February 15, 1964, by Sam Bowers, a Laurel man who ran a vending business called Sambo Amusement Company. This rebirth marked a revival of organized Klan violence after nearly a decade of increasing gains by the Movement and retaliation by the white Citizens' Council.

times during the Movement that DOJ blocked local prosecutions of activists attempting to exercise their constitutional rights.

On September 25, 1961, Herbert Lee, a black farmer and registration worker, was shot dead by a white member of the Mississippi legislature, E. H. Hurst, near a cotton gin in Amite County. Hurst was the father-in-law of Billy Jack Caston, the man who first beat Bob Moses in Liberty and whom Moses had warned DOJ about only hours before the shooting. Hurst's defense was that Lee had attacked him with a tire iron, a claim denied by Louis Allen, a black logger who had witnessed the shooting. Although Hurst never was prosecuted, Allen lived with death threats for the next two and half years. Federal authorities were unable or unwilling to do more than investigate and express concern about Allen's safety, despite constant entreaties from Movement people to protect him. On January 31, 1964, the day before he had planned to move to Milwaukee, Allen was shot outside the gate of his house and died. This tragic sequence taught many in the Movement that the federal government held limited sway over local law enforcement.

Meanwhile students returning to school in fall 1961 breathed new life into the McComb Movement. Two Burglund High School students, Ike Lewis and Brenda Travis, were suspended for their sit-in arrests over the summer. Students then led a spontaneous mass march, the first one in McComb, on October 4, 1961. The students had intended to march seven miles to the county seat in Magnolia but thought better of it when they attracted a hostile crowd and saw the afternoon light fading. They returned to town on Broadway Street and were stopped by a line of police standing shoulder to shoulder. Someone called a hearse to the scene. One white man driving by was so amazed that he drove his car through a plate glass window. A student hopped up onto the steps of City Hall and began to pray. He was arrested.

One by one marchers took turns mounting the steps until the police waded in and arrested all of them. A mob of hostile onlookers singled out Bob Zellner, a white SNCC worker, and gave his eyeballs a determined gouging. Police eventually arrested 116 people and charged SNCC activists with contributing to the delinquency of minors. The activists were convicted on October 31 and sentenced to four to six months at the Pike County jail in Magnolia. More tests of the Greyhound station later that fall succeeded with the benefit of police protection, although a white mob assaulted the press instead. The students' actions encouraged adults to say in the open what they had complained about behind closed doors for years.

Although racial violence had occurred in McComb before 1964, that summer brought a surge of terror to match anything visited on Birmingham or the Delta. On June 22 three houses of black activists were bombed, including that of C. C. Bryant, whose guards drove off the bombers with a shotgun. After eight COFO staffers arrived in July, a staggering series of attacks fell not only on Movement people and homes but also on black churches that had deliberately avoided the cause. On August 30 Alyene Quin's cafe was raided and forced to close on false liquor possession charges; her home was seriously damaged by an explosion in September. Police intimidation reached an all-time high, and some Movement workers were hauled in for interrogation several times a day. In a typical incident vandals soaked the carpet runner leading to the altar of a black church with diesel fuel and lit it with the aid of crumpled newspapers and back issues of *Reader's Digest.*

By October the local paper had lost track of the number of violent attacks, inviting readers to "Make Your Own 'Incident' Count" and

Alyene Quin at a meeting of the Mississippi Community Foundation in McComb, 1991. (Matt Herron/Take Stock)

Robert Parris Moses Comes Full Circle

The SNCC model of community change derives largely from the enigmatic, dedicated spirit of Bob Moses and his formative experiences in McComb. His first trip to Mississippi was in July 1960. By the time he left in late 1964, he had endured beatings and jailings and had demonstrated the structural nature of racial injustice. His goal was both to lead and to follow the tempo of change set by local residents. The image of Moses as a young activist living on a shoestring in a black community in order to amplify its own local Movement was emulated in communities from Florida to Virginia.

Moses was born in New York City, son of a janitor at a Harlem armory. Although his grandfather had been a Baptist circuit preacher in Tennessee, South Carolina, and Virginia, Moses came across in the South as a cerebral northerner. "We thought he was a Communist because he was from New York and wore glasses and was smarter than we were," recalled Julian Bond. He earned a philosophy degree from Harvard and taught mathematics at a New York school until news of the sit-ins in Greensboro in 1960 pulled him southward. SNCC, then only a few months old, assigned him to scout out Mississippi. After consulting local leaders in the Delta, he settled on McComb as the site of its first voting drive in the summer of 1961.

In McComb philosophy collided with reality. He discovered in going door to door how ingrained fear of political participation was. His ventures to the courthouses of Pike, Walthall, and Amite counties resulted in beatings, trials bristling with hostile spectators, and a five-week stay in the Magnolia jail until bail could be raised. Unlike some SNCC workers who relished confrontation with southern sheriffs as a way to embolden local people, Moses viewed such confrontations as unpleasant necessities for change. His belief in community-driven initiatives was realized when

(continued on next page)

Bob Moses, who led SNCC's first voting drive in McComb, pictured here during Freedom Summer training in 1964. (Steve Schapiro/ Black Star)

McComb students began sit-ins and led a bold march to City Hall without his prompting.

His manner of speaking contrasted sharply with that of high-flying preachers. At mass meetings he related both savage injustices and sweet triumphs in the same measured monotone. On many occasions he wore bib overalls and sneakers. His quiet charisma won him a loyal Movement following.

A campaign the following year in Greenwood, Mississippi, brought home to him the twin injustices of poverty and educational deprivation. A SNCC food relief program spurred hundreds of blacks, many of whom could not read or write, to appear at the courthouse for the first time. Moses reasoned that since many blacks in the rural South had been forced to leave school at a young age for field labor, the government should either provide sufficient education for them or abolish citizenship testing for voting. During 1962–64 he endorsed the biracial efforts of Freedom Summer at a time when black activists were questioning the utility of white volunteers in the Movement.

The events of 1964 were disillusioning for Moses. The promises of DOJ protection, FBI investigation, and representation for the MFDP at Atlantic City all had proved hollow. Even after the passage of the Civil Rights Act of 1964 most public places in the South were still segregated. So too were the public schools a decade after *Brown*. Five people who had worked closely with Moses for voting rights had been killed. As the media clamored for biographical tidbits on Moses and played on his biblical name, he became more oracular. He changed his name to Robert Parris, his middle name, in December 1964 and returned to his original focus on teaching. Even during the heady days of the MFDP political campaigns, Moses had emphasized literacy as a key to change.

After receiving a draft notice in 1966, Moses went to Canada and worked odd jobs for several years. In 1969 he moved to Tanzania, a Movement outpost, where he returned to the classroom to teach math. Under an amnesty program during the Carter administration he returned to the United States in 1977 and settled in Boston. In 1982 he used a MacArthur "genius" grant to create the Algebra Project, a program for improving the math skills of inner-city students that draws on the organizing tradition of SNCC and his muse, the organizer Ella Baker.

offering its best guess (twenty-four). The backlash also fell on whites who gave the slightest harbor to the Movement, including Red and Malva Heffner, who were made pariahs in their hometown and were forced to leave their home at 202 Shannon Drive. The saga later was chronicled in a book by white Greenville journalist Hodding Carter entitled *So the Heffners Left McComb*.

Blacks fought back by organizing in their neighborhoods. They opened Freedom Schools under the direction of Ralph Featherstone, and more than one hundred students signed up. They held mass meetings at St. Paul United Methodist Church for a voting drive in fall 1964. Despite a raid on the COFO workers' living quarters, organizers distributed three thousand leaflets for a Freedom Day rally at the courthouse in Magnolia. A few dozen blacks who showed up at the courthouse were permitted to take the voting test, although the registrar continued to process applications at a snail's pace. Armed guards and well-lit driveways became the norm for many Movement homes and businesses.

After the bombing of black cafe owner Alyene Quin's home, unrest along Old Summit Road and press reports of an unchecked rampage began to affect McComb businesses. President Johnson met in Washington with Mrs. Quin and two other McComb women, and the meeting resulted in the first arrests for the violence. Oliver Emmerich, editor of the local *Enterprise-Journal,* called for calm; his plea earned him smashed windows at the newspaper office, crosses burned on his lawn, and a circulation boycott. On November 18, 1964, 650 white citizens published a statement in the paper advocating an end to the campaign of terror and certain racial reforms. At the same time some of McComb's most visible institutions began to admit blacks where they had formerly been forbidden: Woolworth's (formerly 205 Main Street), the Greyhound Bus Station (formerly 206 Canal Street), the Continental Hotel (still at 113 South Broadway), the Holiday Inn (Interstate 55), and the Palace Theater (109 Main Street). By the late 1960s blacks constituted a majority of voters in Pike County, and in 1995 voters elected the county's first black sheriff, Fred Johnson.

Masonic Hall (Eureka Lodge No. 5)

630 Warren Street

On August 7, 1961, Bob Moses taught the first SNCC-sponsored voter registration class in Mississippi on the second floor here. C. C. Bryant, a local Freemason, had been interested in voter education and arranged for use of the space. The hall also hosted a rally featuring NAACP field secretary Medgar Evers and was the stopoff point for the student marchers from Burglund High School in October 1961. After the students were arrested at City Hall and Movement leaders left town on bail, the activists left a sign on the door that read SNCC DONE SNUCK.

In those days a black-owned grocery store, the Burglund Super Market, occupied the first floor. When police came looking for SNCC activist Charles Jones after the Burglund students' march to City Hall, he donned a bloody butcher's apron and started chopping meat. Thus disguised, he was met by DOJ attorney John Doar, who had flown into McComb from Washington to monitor the situation. The building was among those bombed in the violent summer of 1964. Today it is unoccupied.

St. Paul United Methodist Church
711 Warren Street

At the urging of member Alyene Quin, this church hosted the first Movement meetings and regular voter registration classes in McComb. Some of the Nonviolent High classes also were held here for students boycotting classes at Burglund High School. Later it housed a Head Start program.

Alyene Quin House
304 Martin Luther King, Jr., Drive (formerly Old Summit Road)

Alyene Quin grew up in Biloxi and had been a registered voter there since 1953. She moved to McComb in the mid-1950s and took over a cafe called South of the Border (now closed) at 500 Summit Street. Several times she had gone to the courthouse in Magnolia to pay poll taxes and had tried to register without success.

Mrs. Quin's cafe was the site of a critical meeting in August 1964, when McComb was shaken regularly by bombs and Klan attacks. The covert meeting was attended by local black business people and civic leaders, who resolved to assist the recently arrived COFO staff, set up housing and food committees, and put up fifty dollars each for a community center in McComb. Later Mrs. Quin's white landlord told her to quit feeding Movement people at the cafe, so she began serving food out of her home. She also was instrumental in getting St. Paul United Methodist Church reopened to Movement mass meetings in fall 1964. She later was jailed with her children for swimming at a public park, and she organized food runs to the jail in Magnolia when others were jailed.

On September 20, 1964, while Mrs. Quin was attending an MFDP meeting in Jackson, a group of Klansmen drove past the house several times, tossed about a dozen sticks of dynamite toward the porch, and fled in their cars. They then went fishing on the Bogue Chitto River. The powerful explosion wiped out the front

St. Paul Methodist Church, where mass meetings and Freedom School classes were held, photographed in 1995. (Jessica Allan)

porch, collapsed the roof, and rattled glasses on the table of a cafe several blocks away. Quin's two young children, Jacqueline and Anthony, were injured but not killed in the blast. This attack on a pillar of the black community brought out an angry crowd. The street was blocked in both directions, and order was restored only after the deployment of one hundred highway patrol officers and after COFO leaders urged calm with a bullhorn. In a common but ludicrous twist the sheriff accused Mrs. Quin of bombing her own house, and the COFO leaders and many local black citizens were charged with criminal syndicalism, a serious offense formerly brought against radicals of the labor movement.

The next day, at the urging of Washington columnist Drew Pearson, who had taken an interest in the siege of McComb, Mrs. Quin traveled to Washington with two other women involved in the McComb Movement, Matti Dillon and Ora Bryant. The three met briefly with President Johnson. A week later, after redoubled FBI and police effort, the bombers were arrested. In October 1964 nine white men pleaded guilty to explosives charges and were given suspended sentences. The judge reasoned they were from good families, had been provoked by Movement activities, and were "just starting out," although the average age of the defendants was thirty years old, and one was forty-four.

The plans for a community center materialized in 1971 as the

Martin Luther King community center (601 Martin Luther King, Jr., Drive). It is down the street from Mrs. Quin's house, where she still lives.

Site of Freedom House
702 Wall Street (now an empty lot)

On July 5, 1964, COFO project director Jesse Harris opened the Freedom House here, a wood-frame house where six black and two white organizers lived. In a typical description the local paper described white activist Dennis Sweeney as "unkempt, unshorn, unshaven in grimy sports clothes and sneakers." The house was bombed on July 8, two days after a visit from Congressman Don Edwards of California, whose son was volunteering elsewhere in the Freedom Summer project. Sweeney and activist Curtis Hayes were injured, but COFO kept organizing through the summer. After the bombing, Episcopalian Bishop Paul Moore held an ecumenical service in front of the damaged structure, using an ironing board and sheet as a makeshift altar. A few months later COFO staffers were charged with running an eatery out of the Freedom House without a license. Movement workers also operated a radio center out of a former barbershop next door, and the relief group Delta Ministry had an office across Denwiddie Street. The site is now an empty lot.

Burglund High School
1000 Elmwood Street

Inspired by a Medgar Evers speech, students formed their own NAACP Youth Council here in 1958. Students questioned why their own teachers, accomplished scholars in their subject areas, could not register to vote. Three years later Burglund students led the first mass march in McComb in solidarity with two classmates who had been punished for their protest activities. On October 4, 1961, the students stacked their books on the schoolhouse steps and walked from the Burglund gates down Summit Street to the Masonic Temple. There they raised protest banners and marched down to the City Hall steps to pray, where police arrested them. For fifteen-year-old student Brenda Travis, it was her second arrest for demonstrating, and the judge shipped her off to a reform school eighty miles away. Some children were doubly punished when they discovered that not only were they arrested, but also their parents were dead set against their involvement in the Movement and spanked them in public.

SNCC workers created a Nonviolent High for those students who continued to boycott Burglund and who refused to sign a pledge not to march. Nonviolent High's makeshift classes were a prototype of the Freedom Schools that emerged several years later. Other protesting students attended classes at Campbell College, an AME institution in Jackson. Today Higgins Middle School occupies the school grounds.

Society Hill MB Church
4098 Highway 51 South

This church, where C. C. Bryant was a deacon and Rev. Ed Taylor was pastor, assisted Bob Moses in the formative stages of the voter campaign by providing a mimeograph machine to reproduce voting forms. The wood-frame church close to Highway 51 was bombed on September 20, 1964, about a half hour after Alyene Quin's house had been hit. The church was rebuilt as a brick structure set back from the road.

C. C. Bryant House
1533 Venable Street

NAACP stalwart C. C. Bryant has lived here for more than fifty years. He had an adjacent barbershop about thirty yards away (now torn down), where Movement people came for haircuts or to meet people. Here they read books about Africa and heard talk about police brutality in the early days of the Movement. One poster in the shop bore a picture of two black youths with the caption "We're going to register. What is your excuse?" The barbershop was bombed in April 1964; the house itself was bombed that June. From that point on, Movement guards watched Bryant's property from nearby posts. Bryant still lives here.

Pike County Courthouse/Jail
Magnolia

Although previously allowed to register at regional offices around the county, voters from McComb were required to register at the circuit clerk's office in Magnolia, eight miles away, to be eligible to vote in state elections. This system, designed by the state legislature in the 1950s to discourage black voting, was still in place in the 1960s, when Bob Moses and SNCC began organizing in McComb. They journeyed frequently to Magnolia and often ended up in the county jail, which is on the same grounds as the courthouse.

After the Burglund High School march to City Hall in October 1961, Moses was tried and found guilty of disturbing the peace. In

Letter from a Pike County Jail

A letter from Bob Moses to SNCC compatriots in November 1961 described the atmosphere inside the Pike County jail. Because they could not raise fourteen thousand dollars in bail bonds, Moses and several other organizers spent thirty-nine days in jail:

"**W**e are smuggling this note from the drunk tank of the county jail in Magnolia, Mississippi. Twelve of us are here, sprawled out along the concrete bunker; Curtis Hayes, Hollis Watkins, Ike Lewis and Robert Talbert, four veterans of the bunker, are sitting up talking—mostly about girls; Charles McDew ('Tell the story') is curled into the concrete and the wall.

"Later on Hollis will lead out with a clear tenor into a freedom song; Talbert and Lewis will supply jokes; and McDew will discourse on the history of the black man and the Jew. McDew—a black by birth, a Jew by choice and a revolutionary by necessity—has taken on the deep hates and deep loves which America, and the world, reserves for those who dare to stand in a strong sun and cast a sharp shadow.

"In the words of Judge Brumfield, who sentenced us, we are 'cold calculators' who design to disrupt the racial harmony (harmonious since 1619) of McComb into racial strife and rioting. . . . 'Robert,' he was addressing me, 'haven't some of the people from your school been able to go down and register without violence here in Pike County?' I thought to myself that Southerners are most exposed when they boast.

"It's mealtime now: we have rice and gravy in a flat pan, dry bread and a 'big town cake': we lack eating and drinking utensils. Water comes from a faucet and goes into a hole.

"This is Mississippi, the middle of the iceberg. Hollis is leading off with his tenor, 'Michael row the boat ashore, Alleluia; Christian brothers, don't be slow, Alleluia; Mississippi's next to go, Alleluia.' This is a tremor in the middle of the iceberg—from a stone that the builders rejected."[34]

jail he and other activists bided their time by singing, reading, and playing chess with cigarette butts. Young white children were brought to the jail to see what real radicals looked like. When one of them asked jailed SNCC leader Charles McDew to "say something in Communist," he delighted her by reeling off a phrase in Yiddish. When Movement workers, McComb residents, and students parked a bus near the courthouse in March 1965 and marched silently around the building seven times, they were arrested and placed in bare cells at the county farm.

Oxford, Mississippi

Jeeps on the Campus of Ole Miss

The arrival of James Meredith in 1962 dissolved a 114-year tradition of all-white education at the University of Mississippi. Fierce attachment to that tradition, fanned by defiant rhetoric from the governor, temporarily transformed the idyllic campus into a battleground. U.S. marshals, national guardsmen, and army soldiers were called in to quell unrest that erupted in fall 1962. The show of force was the furthest the federal government had gone since *Brown* to dismantle state resistance to integration.

The idea of a black undergraduate rested uneasily at Ole Miss, a guardian of the Lost Cause. In the 1930s the university lost its accreditation after it became the political plaything of rabid segregationist Governor Theodore Bilbo. In 1956 a white cleric invited to

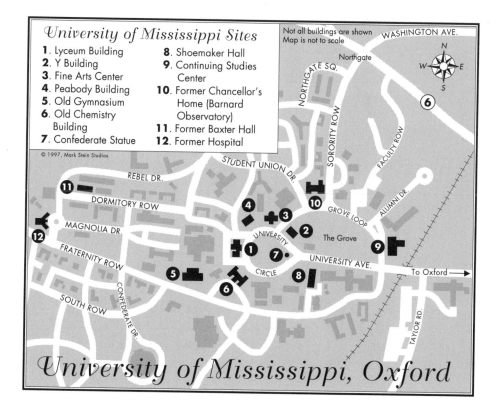

University of Mississippi Sites

1. Lyceum Building
2. Y Building
3. Fine Arts Center
4. Peabody Building
5. Old Gymnasium
6. Old Chemistry Building
7. Confederate Statue
8. Shoemaker Hall
9. Continuing Studies Center
10. Former Chancellor's Home (Barnard Observatory)
11. Former Baxter Hall
12. Former Hospital

Not all buildings are shown
Map is not to scale

© 1997, Mark Stein Studios

University of Mississippi, Oxford

speak at a campus religious program was promptly disinvited after it was discovered that he was donating half of his prize money from an appearance on the "$64,000 Question" to the NAACP. Will Campbell, later a Movement figure affiliated with the National Council of Churches, raised eyebrows as director of campus religious life by inviting young black journalist Carl Rowan to campus that same year.

James Meredith, who grew up in Koskiusko, Mississippi, as one of ten children, challenged this tradition. After eight years in the air force, Meredith enrolled at Jackson State College in 1960. He then applied to Ole Miss and received the assistance of the NAACP's legal staff and state head Medgar Evers. The other major civil rights groups considered integration at Ole Miss secondary to marches, boycotts, and voter registration drives. But the NAACP legal staff had championed desegregation in education since its lawsuits against white-only colleges and graduate schools in the 1940s, an effort that had culminated in the *Brown* decision. The rejection of Meredith's application forced him into court, where he was represented by Derrick Bell and Constance Baker Motley. A federal court ordered the admission of Meredith on September 13, 1962.

Resistance quickly mounted to a feverish pitch. In a televised address Governor Ross Barnett pledged that no school would be integrated on his watch and said that those who agreed with him should be prepared to go to jail before drinking "from the cup of genocide" that integration represented. With few exceptions Mississippi politicians echoed this sentiment. Barnett elicited frenzied applause when he took the field at an Ole Miss football game on September 29 to cry, "I love Mississippi! I love her people! I love her customs!" As the day of Meredith's scheduled admission approached, retired General Edwin Walker, who had commanded the U.S. Army troops that enforced President Eisenhower's integration of Little Rock's Central High School in 1957, announced that he had changed his mind about the wisdom of integration and called for a showdown at Oxford.

On Sunday, September 30, 1962, bands of cars bedecked with Rebel flags circulated through the town of Oxford while "Dixie" saturated the radio waves. That afternoon Meredith, protected by a small armed guard, already was hidden in a dorm room at Baxter Hall on the edge of the campus. A crowd of students gathered on the central lawn, the Circle, with the Lyceum as its centerpiece, and hurled bricks and bottles at a line of federal marshals on duty. When the Mississippi Highway Patrol withdrew from the area, the crowd, fortified by armed outsiders, grew more hostile. Even as President Kennedy delivered a televised speech calling for calm, the situation on campus deteriorated. After federal marshals had been injured by gunfire, Robert Kennedy ordered the army mobilized from Memphis, where it had been on alert. The troops arrived at 2:00 A.M., relieving the hard-pressed marshals and occupying the entire campus and town of Oxford.

Two people were killed in the murky circumstances of the evening. A French journalist named Paul Guihard, who in his afternoon dispatch had described the chaotic atmosphere enveloping the campus, was shot in the back and killed near the Peabody Building. On the opposite side of the Circle, Ray Gunter, a jukebox and pinball repairman who worked at the university, was shot in the head and killed near a corner of what is now Shoemaker Hall. The overall accounting was grim: 160 injured marshals, 200 arrests, and a formerly pristine campus littered with debris, tear gas canisters, and three charred cars. Meredith registered the next day.

The event traumatized the university. Thirty-seven professors resigned, and student enrollment dropped. The charged atmosphere required faculty, staff, and students to obtain passes to travel to and from the campus, and they were asked to present them so often that some wore them dangled from their necks. Army tents were pitched on a campus playing field. Some twenty thousand troops, more than the population of Oxford itself, patrolled the campus and town for

---

The "Never, No Never" Song

The Jackson Daily News *printed the lyrics to this segregationist rallying cry with the suggestion that they be clipped and sung at the Ole Miss versus Kentucky football game the night before Meredith's arrival on campus:*

Never, never, never, never, No-o-o Never Never Never
We will not yield an inch of any field
Fix us another toddy, ain't yieldin' to nobody
Ross's standin' like Gibraltar, he shall never falter
Ask us what we say, it's to hell with Bobby K
Never shall our emblem go from Colonel Reb to Old Black Joe.[35]

the rest of the year in jeeps stenciled with insignias reading "USAFOX" (U.S. Armed Forces, Oxford). Operation Rapid Road, as it was called, cost the army $2.5 million.

Meredith's presence gradually became less controversial, but there was always the threat of danger. On Valentine's Day 1963 he played golf with two white faculty members on the university course. "The walkie talkies used by the marshals and the military weren't exactly conducive to good golf," one player wrote. "How this guy keeps up his spirit, having to put up with constant surveillance 24 hours a day, and putting up with the rest of the human race, is beyond my comprehension." In June 1963 a second black student, Cleveland McDowell, enrolled at the law school without incident. By the time of Meredith's graduation in August 1963—to which he wore a NEVER button upside down in the style of Movement activists at the time—his presence barely caused a ripple in the crowd. Still, it was nearly a decade before black students were accepted in large numbers at the school.

U.S. marshals posted at the Lyceum during the Ole Miss disturbances, September 30, 1962.
(Charles Moore)

In 1970 Ole Miss started an Afro-American studies department, and black student enrollment has steadily increased since the 1970s. The first black fraternity house appeared on Fraternity Row in 1988; the house was burned by vandals that August and subsequently rebuilt. Currently more than 10 percent of students are black.

The Lyceum

University Circle

At this antebellum administrative building James Meredith registered for class on Monday, October 1, 1962, after a riot had laid waste to the campus the night before. Used as both a Union and Confederate hospital during the Civil War, the Lyceum again was pressed into service one hundred years later as a recovery area for wounded officers and journalists. Today its white columns still bear visible chips from the bullets and debris let loose that terrifying evening.

At about 4:15 P.M. on September 30 U.S. marshals dispatched from Memphis lined up in front of the Lyceum under the command of Chief Marshal James McShane. Their purpose was to serve as a decoy so that Meredith could quietly slip into his dorm room at the rear of the campus. The decoy worked all too well, and within a half hour a crowd of rowdy students assembled near the Circle. When more marshals arrived in white Ford Falcons, students burst out from the bushes and smashed the car windshields with bricks and construction materials scavenged from the site of a new science building. The Circle, and the adjacent area known as the Grove, were filled with hostile students, who formed a wavering, semicircular line and made periodic lunges and shouted insults at the marshals. False rumors swirled that a female student had been killed. After one of the marshals had been struck with a piece of pipe, they were ordered to release tear gas and pulled on their gas masks. One science professor's first reaction was to rush to the Peabody Building next door to protect his laboratory rats from tear gas. By nightfall the students were replaced by rowdies who had come from all over the state and as far as Mobile and Birmingham to raise hell. The streetlights all had been knocked out, and military floodlights illuminated the entrance, by now shrouded in tear gas.

Rioters continued to mill around while the marshals conversed with one another through the metallic muffle of gas masks. Mississippi highway patrolmen withdrew from their posts and drove down University Avenue, shouting encouragement to the mob. Sniper fire

James Meredith, flanked by James McShane (left), chief U.S. marshal, and John Doar (right), assistant attorney general for civil rights, on his way to register at Ole Miss after the riots on campus. (Charles Moore)

caught one marshal in the neck and seriously wounded him. Still, the marshals held their fire. The Lyceum corridors were lined with injured marshals and members of the press, and federal officials relayed the desperate situation to Washington from phones inside. Mississippi national guardsmen arrived at about 10:10 P.M., by which time the campus echoed with the popping of gunfire. Someone sent a bulldozer from a construction site toward the Lyceum and bailed out while it was still in gear, pointing it toward the steps with the plow blade raised. It nearly reached the curb before a marshal jumped up and disengaged it.

After a series of delays army units finally began to arrive at about 2:00 A.M. They unloaded at Sorority Row and marched in V formation with fixed bayonets past showers of debris up to the Lyceum to the unrestrained applause of the relieved marshals. Sixteen thousand army troops eventually quelled the crowd. About two hundred people were later apprehended; less than a sixth of them were Ole Miss students. At 8:00 A.M., with the Circle strewn with rubble and pockets of tear gas still causing students to cough, James Meredith mounted the Lyceum steps holding a handkerchief to his face and registered.

A Captain's View from a Jeep

Captain Murry C. Falkner, a national guardsman and nephew of novelist William Faulkner, commanded the first officers to arrive at the Lyceum when rioting was near its worst. Here, in an army report, he describes the scene:

"It appeared the Grove was full of people and the street on which we were to drive was a sea of people. The only lights were at the Lyceum and the glow from a burning automobile. As we passed the Geology Building and the Confederate Statue, a 2x6 piece of lumber was thrown at my jeep. Fortunately, it missed its target! From here to the Lyceum Building was absolute Hell! People would not move out of the street. They threw bricks, concrete, everything and anything they could find—including words. I leaned over to my driver and screamed for him to put the jeep in second gear and not to slow down or stop for anything. . . .

"As my lead jeep passed the 'Y' [the Old Chapel, which housed a YMCA], there were 3 concrete benches spaced across the street. My driver and I saw them at the same time and, fortunately, we dodged them. A brick came through my side of the windshield and glass shattered over us. We straightened out in the street again and I noticed something white coming toward my face from the right of my jeep. [By] reflex action I threw up my left arm to shield my face. . . . [It] broke three bones [in my arm] and cut my wrist. The number three jeep in line hit one of the benches, a 2½-ton truck got another, and the trail jeep got the third one. This only provided more Ammo for the mob. All vehicles took a terrific beating from the debris that was thrown. My driver and several other men were hit as we drove on toward the Lyceum.

As we approached the Lyceum, the marshals laid down a volley of tear gas for us to drive through. . . ."[36]

The next morning Falkner found seven bricks and a Molotov cocktail in his jeep and a bullet hole in the radiator.

Baxter Hall

Dormitory Row West

This building, constructed in 1948 as a men's dorm, was named for Hermann Baxter, a former student body president killed in World War II. In 1962 and 1963 it housed another veteran, James Meredith, who was protected by two dozen guards on his first night at the college while a mob, unaware of his presence, roamed the campus. It currently is a telecommunications center.

When he began attending class, Meredith was accompanied by three U.S. marshals who tracked his every move by radio, calling each other Peanut; Meredith was referred to as Cargo. A DOJ attorney tagged along for Meredith's first ten days. At night three marshals stood guard in a room adjacent to Meredith's and connected by a small kitchen. One of them was awake at all times. An alert platoon bivouacked in a gully behind the dorm, known as the Hole, ready to respond to any incident. At first Meredith was taunted by white students and forced to eat alone in the cafeteria, but hostility gradually diminished. Meredith had little direct involvement in the Movement after his graduation from Ole Miss until 1966, when his March against Fear into the Mississippi Delta prompted the last of the Movement's marathon marches.

The Mississippi Delta

Outposts in the Land of the Lost

Shrouded in mystique, the Delta evokes a host of images. Geographically it is the potato-shaped area in northwestern Mississippi constituting the floodplain between the Mississippi and Yazoo rivers, stretching northward from Vicksburg to Memphis. Formerly swamp and forest, the flat, rich tracts of Delta soil were first cleared and farmed after Reconstruction, blossoming into seas of white cotton. Tens of thousands of black workers tilled the land while a handful of whites, who controlled the economy and the ballot box, owned it. The Delta has always been known for its tough conditions, feudal justice, and rich tradition of blues music. Writers have piled metaphor upon metaphor to describe it, everything from a "strange and detached fragment thrown off by the whirling comet that is America" to "the most southern place on earth."

White political domination was so open that planters often convened their black workers to tell them whom to vote for. More common still was the notion that voting at all was a betrayal of blacks' primary loyalty to the plantation. Mechanized farming reduced the demand for field labor after World War II, and this led to an exodus to Chicago and other points north. Emigration of those with portable job skills reduced the middle-aged ranks and left children and the elderly to carry on. In 1960 the U.S. poverty line was three

At the dedication of the Mileston Community Center, Holmes County, 1964. (Matt Herron/Take Stock)

thousand dollars, and three quarters of all Delta families fell below it. The median income for black families was below two thousand dollars. Even those black families above the poverty line were hardly guaranteed a decent standard of living.

The Delta always was famously resistant to social change. "Disturbing ideas crawl like flies around the screen of the Delta," wrote one native observer in the 1930s. "They rarely penetrate. It is only when the price of cotton is affected that the Delta takes cognizance of the outside world." Nonetheless Dr. T. R. M. (Theodore Roosevelt Mason) Howard founded the Regional Council of Negro Leadership (RCNL) in the Delta town of Cleveland in 1951 to support black businesses and forge links among the Delta cities of Cleveland, Clarksdale, Greenville, and Greenwood. Dr. Howard had moved to the all-black Delta town of Mound Bayou from Kentucky in the 1940s and was chief surgeon at the Knights and Daughters of Tabor Hospital. He founded the Magnolia Life Insurance Company, lived lavishly, and sponsored appearances by Thurgood Marshall and Mahalia Jackson at barbecues at his house. He led a campaign to boycott gas stations that would not provide rest rooms for blacks, distributing bumper stickers that read, "Don't Buy Gas Where You Can't Use the Rest Room." It was not exactly a stake in the heart of segregation, but mounting a racial campaign of any kind took enormous courage. After a sustained backlash against him and his business, and a draft notice at age forty-seven, Dr. Howard moved to Chicago.

Systematic retaliation against active blacks became the mission of the Citizens' Council, founded in Indianola in 1955. An early example of its effectiveness was its response to an August 1955 petition to desegregate the schools in Yazoo City signed by fifty-three black citizens. The council bought newspaper advertisements prominently displaying the signers' names and pressured their employers, suppliers, and acquaintances to fire them or cut them off. A woman who had signed was not allowed to buy twelve dollars' worth of groceries at the A&P. One by one the signers withdrew their support for the petition until only two remained, and they had already left town. The scene was duplicated in many communities across the South, effectively stymieing the NAACP's effort to desegregate the schools through the pleas of local black citizens.

In the 1950s organized efforts by the RCNL and the NAACP made way for the door-to-door efforts of SNCC and CORE. Aaron Henry of Clarksdale was on a committee formed in May 1961 to meet with Governor Barnett during the tense journey of the Freedom Riders, a group later reconstituted as COFO. Activism broke out in Henry's hometown of Clarksdale in November 1961, when two black marching bands were banned from the annual Christmas parade. Black residents initiated a boycott of downtown stores under the slogan "If we can't parade downtown, why should we trade downtown?" Henry was arrested for leading the boycott, and his wife lost her teaching job.

In 1962 Movement forces concentrated on the Delta city of Greenwood. The withdrawal of a supplemental government food program there caused widespread hunger, and SNCC and CORE struggled to fill the void. When in 1963 activists Ivanhoe Donaldson and Ben Taylor drove a truckload of food and medicine from Michigan destined for Greenwood, they were arrested in Clarksdale and spent several days in jail on charges of smuggling narcotics. The "drugs" turned out to be over-the-counter medical supplies, such as aspirin and bandages. The journey was one of twelve relief runs activists made that winter. Other projects focused on promoting Gandhian self-sufficiency. In a 1963 experiment sponsored by Dave

White-Collar Klan: The Citizens' Council

Whites in Indianola formed the premier group in the South devoted to maintaining segregation, the Citizens' Council, often called the White Citizens' Council. The group was organized in July 1954 by Robert ("Tut") Patterson, a Delta planter and former paratrooper who reviled the idea of racially mixed schools (his daughter was then about to enter first grade). At a town hall rally in Indianola seventy-five whites, including the mayor and city attorney, formed the Citizens' Council as a way to defend the southern way of life without resorting to the brutality of the Ku Klux Klan.

Seeping into respectable society through civic groups such as the Rotary or Kiwanis clubs, the group endorsed political and economic intimidation of black activists. These tactics reached into every recess of civic life, prompting not only firings and demotions but also the manipulation of draft notices and tax audits and the termination of supplies, credit, insurance, and utilities. The council published white supremacist tracts and sponsored reverse Freedom Rides with promises of free transport and pocket change to convince blacks to migrate to the North. After desegregation of the public schools had begun in Mississippi, the council issued guidelines on how to start a private school and sponsored several such "academies." These tactics went hand in hand with physical threats against the Movement, which, if not openly endorsed by the council, were encouraged by its actions.

By October 1955 the council had twenty-five thousand members in Mississippi and had established a headquarters in Winona. It also had a growing presence in Alabama and other states. For the next decade the council pressed for white resistance in boardrooms, newsrooms, government offices, churches, and the upholstered living rooms of polite society all across the South. It made black families pay a heavy cost for even the most minor support for integration, a cost arguably heavier overall than the sporadic cross burnings and bloody night rides of the Klan. Its influence faded with the succession of blacks to political and economic leadership, coupled with the passage of federal laws in the 1960s forbidding retaliation for political activism. The last reported Citizens' Council meeting was held in the town of Black Hawk, near Greenwood, in 1987.

Dennis of CORE, known as the Home Industry Cooperative, eighteen Ruleville women raised money for the Movement by making quilts and rugs for sale.

In 1962 Greenwood became the first place in the Delta where large numbers of blacks turned up at the county courthouse to register to vote. In an area where only about forty had tried to do so in the previous seven years, hundreds lined up to register. The next year Delta blacks cast the lion's share of Freedom Votes in the mock election of 1963 and supplied many of the troops for the challenge to the Mississippi Democratic delegation the following year. Nearly half the Freedom Summer projects of 1964 were in the Delta, including the model community center in Mileston, Holmes County. Meanwhile SNCC mounted voter drives in towns such as Ruleville and Drew. After the death of Martin Luther King, Jr., in 1968, the mule-drawn wagon at the head of the Poor People's March set out from the Delta town of Marks, reputed to be one of the poorest towns in America.

Once registering became more routine, several election cycles passed before raw numbers of voters resulted in the election of black officials. After a well-organized campaign in Holmes County Robert Clark broke through in 1967 under the MFDP banner. He became the first black Mississippi representative in the twentieth century, winning by a mere 116 votes. In twenty-one other communities blacks won local offices from clerk to coroner. By 1971, 300 blacks were campaigning for office statewide, and in 1977 the Delta had its first black mayor of a formerly white town, Eddie Carthan of Tchula. Congress proved harder to crack partly because the Mississippi legislature had redrawn congressional districts in order to dilute the black vote. The legislature achieved the same effect by requiring that some county positions be elected at large instead of by geographic district. Clark lost two tough races for Congress in the majority-black Second District in 1982 and 1984.

Finally in 1986 Mike Espy, a thirty-two-year-old lawyer from Yazoo City, became the district's member of Congress, the first black representative from Mississippi since Reconstruction. His brother Henry became mayor of Clarksdale in 1989. In the 1980s the city and county governments of the Delta were run in part by black officials who constituted either a majority or a significant minority of local governing boards.

Despite political advances, the Delta struggles economically today. Efforts to attract new business, a $750 million catfish industry, and the appearance of dockside casinos along the Mississippi River have not eliminated a heavy reliance on agricultural subsidies and welfare payments. Several groups carry on the Movement spirit. The MFDP still meets occasionally in Holmes County, the place where it went the furthest. The Delta Foundation promotes black businesses, as it has since 1969, through low-interest loans. Mississippi Action for Community Education (MACE) subsidizes low-cost housing and sponsors an outdoor blues festival each September. The

Delta Health Center in Mound Bayou, founded in 1965 as the first prepaid health clinic in the nation, continues to furnish basic health services to the region's poor under the direction of former share-cropper and Movement protégé Dr. L. C. Dorsey. The Delta Ministry, no longer a project of the National Council of Churches but still continuing its charitable mission, now operates out of Greenville under Movement veteran Owen Brooks.

Site of Aaron Henry's Drugstore

213 Martin Luther King Street (formerly Fourth Street), Clarksdale

Aaron ("Doc") Henry, known as the grand old man of civil rights, was a unifying force in the Delta. He led the Mississippi NAACP, worked under the COFO banner, and headed the ticket of the MFDP in its bid to convert activism into electoral achievement. He was one of the few who bridged the gap between the relative caution of the NAACP old guard and the confrontational tactics of the student organizers.

Henry was a World War II veteran who had trained as a pharmacist at Xavier University in New Orleans and worked as a porter at a Clarksdale hotel. His drugstore, where he displayed the Declaration of Independence and the Emancipation Proclamation in the window, doubled as a Movement headquarters. Near the soda fountain lay piles of NAACP applications and information about poll taxes and voting. When Henry was elected president of the state NAACP in 1960, he readily acknowledged the need for new tactics and the prospect of jail sentences, a break from the usual NAACP party line.

In March 1963 vandals broke the windows of the drugstore and later set off an explosion that damaged the roof. The same month, while Detroit black Congressman Charles Diggs was visiting the Henry home, someone set the house on fire. That summer Clarksdale's government buildings and phone company were picketed after the city refused to hear any of the black community's grievances. Henry, then forty-one years old, was arrested and assigned to the garbage detail. It was one of about thirty arrests for him.

That fall Henry ran for governor in the Movement's first coordinated attempt to demonstrate statewide black voting power in the South. The Freedom Vote of 1963, as the mock vote was called, dealt only with potential voters, but Henry treated it as any other political campaign by endorsing COFO's platform and delivering whirlwind stump speeches across the state. He testified on behalf of the MFDP in Atlantic City in 1964. He later became the pivotal member of a coalition of moderate Democrats who succeeded in integrating the

Aaron Henry in his drugstore in Clarksdale, October 1963. (Matt Herron/ Take Stock)

Mississippi Democratic party in 1968, and he served in the state legislature from 1980 to 1995. His drugstore burned down in 1993, a likely arson. Henry died in 1997.

Amzie Moore House

614 South Chrisman Avenue, Cleveland

Known in the Delta as the Czar because of his omnipresence, Amzie Moore was a vital link between local people interested in change and outsiders wanting to help.

Moore, an army veteran and postal worker, became president of the Cleveland branch of the NAACP in 1950s and built it into the second-largest branch in the state. He constantly coaxed those blacks who lived comfortably as teachers and preachers to invest themselves in attacking segregation. He drew strength from the example of his grandfather, a slave who acquired 640 acres of land and died at age one hundred and four.

Moore had registered to vote in 1936 and was active in the RCNL. He ran the only gas station with rest rooms for blacks along the 225-mile stretch between Vicksburg and Memphis.

When Bob Moses in 1960 went looking for a location in which to start a SNCC voter registration project, he first came to this house. From that point on Moore's home was where Movement workers went to get oriented for taxing work in the Delta, to hide from police, or to recuperate after a nerve-racking campaign. Moore housed up to a dozen SNCC organizers at a time, feeding them cheese and peaches or keeping a pot of spaghetti and meatballs simmering. The house was also well lit and stocked with guns. Upon returning from the Delta, Movement workers reported that their stay with the Moores featured a constantly ringing phone. The house was one of several distribution centers during the Movement-led food donation effort of 1962–63. Today the house is occupied by another family.

Moore died in 1982. His grave lies in Westlawn Memorial Gardens on Mullins Road between Chrisman Avenue and Winnie Drive in the central-west part of the cemetery. The headstone features his picture and the inscription "My soul is at rest."

Hartman Turnbow House

Off Highway 49, Mileston, Holmes County

Hartman Turnbow's family owned land here since Reconstruction. On April 9, 1963, Turnbow was one of fourteen Holmes County residents who went to the county seat in Lexington and made the first attempt by blacks in recent memory to register. His

Gravestone of Amzie Moore in Cleveland, 1995. (Townsend Davis)

house, a veritable arsenal of small arms near the railroad tracks, was an indispensable Movement haven.

Shortly after he registered, someone tried to firebomb his house with cans of gasoline, damaging the couch and ceiling. Turnbow chased the attackers away with rifle shots. Turnbow, Bob Moses, and three other SNCC workers were arrested for arson of the house, charges that were later dropped. The house also was attacked during the election season of 1964, when Turnbow was active in the MFDP. Today another family lives here.

Mileston Community Center

Off Highway 49, Mileston, Holmes County

This community center, one of the few left in Mississippi, embodied the spirit of Freedom Summer in 1964. One goal of that summer was to build a dozen community centers that would serve as all-purpose libraries, recreational facilities, health clinics, and job-training hubs. This building was constructed by Abe Osheroff, a white organizer and carpenter from California. At the time more than fifty vol-

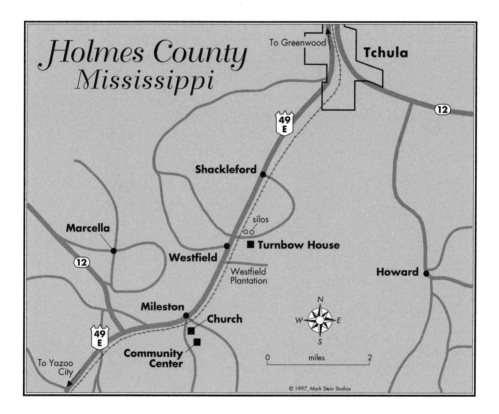

Holmes County Mississippi

To Greenwood

Tchula

49 E

12

Shackleford

Marcella

silos

Turnbow House

Westfield

Westfield Plantation

Howard

12

Mileston

Church

N

W E

S

49 E

Community Center

To Yazoo City

0   miles   2

© 1997, Mark Stein Studios

unteers were working in Holmes County under young activist Hollis Watkins. After receiving bomb threats, the Movement organized armed guards to protect the center and nearby homes where volunteers were housed.

Mileston was an ideal organizing center because in 1940 the federal government had bought five failing plantations comprising ninety-five hundred acres and offered the land to black sharecroppers. More than a hundred families bought property under low-cost mortgages backed by the government, partially liberating them from white control. A typical farm comprised sixty acres of land, a house and barn, seed, mules, and basic tools. One of thirty model programs nationwide, it helped found a community that supported a community store, a new school, and a cotton gin. Today the community center building is still standing but is badly deteriorated and hidden in foliage.

Rev. George Lee Gravesite

Green Grove Missionary Baptist Church, 602 Church Street, Belzoni

In spring 1955 Dr. T. R. M. Howard sponsored a mass meeting of thirteen thousand people under a huge tent in Mound Bayou. *Ebony* called it the largest civil rights gathering in Mississippi "since Booker T. Washington dedicated the town's oil mill" fifty years earlier. One of the speakers was Rev. George W. Lee, an NAACP member, preacher, and printshop owner from Belzoni. Lee urged the audience to register to vote so that the Delta could have its own black member of Congress. Two weeks later, while driving in Belzoni, Lee was shot in the face by whites in a passing car; he died before he could receive medical treatment. Movement activists considered it the kind of broad daylight murder that could happen to any of them, and it was one of the first racial killings that provoked an all-fronts response from the NAACP. A memorial marker stands at the intersection of West First Street and George Lee Avenue in Belzoni, and he is buried in this church grayeyard.

Lee had helped register ninety-two black voters in the previous year along with his friend Gus Courts, a Belzoni grocer and head of a local NAACP chapter. Six months after Lee was killed, the sixty-five-year-old Courts was shot and wounded in front of his store, prompting local police to point to the black community as the collective suspect. Courts recovered and moved to Chicago.

Sunflower County Courthouse

Indianola

People came to register here from all over Sunflower County, which ran fifty miles from north to south. On the south side of the courthouse stood waist-high yellow sunflowers, and a ubiquitous white courthouse gang made it intimidating for blacks to approach any of the building's four entrances. Fewer than two hundred of thirteen thousand eligible black voters in the county had registered when the Movement started here.

Fannie Lou Hamer tried to register here on August 31, 1962. She was one of eighteen who attempted to register that day, the first Movement action of significant size in the county. Most of those who arrived with her by bus were evicted from the registration office, but Mrs. Hamer and a black man were allowed to stay and fill out the forms. She was asked about de facto laws referred to in a section of the Mississippi Constitution. "I knowed about as much about a facto law as a horse knows about Christmas Day," she later said. Her application was denied on the spot.

As the bus made its way back to Ruleville, six or seven trucks followed. The bus was stopped just outside Indianola, and its driver was arrested and taken to the county jail. The charge: driving a bus too similar in color to a yellow school bus. The passengers rustled up the thirty dollars needed to bail him out later that day. The same night W. D. Marlow, owner of the plantation where Mrs. Hamer worked and lived, sent her packing after she refused to withdraw her application.

Indianola heated up again during the summer of 1964, when four hundred people attempted to register during a COFO drive that spread from Ruleville to the towns of Indianola and Sunflower. Only ten passed the test. Residents continued to cast shadow votes for the MFDP even after a Movement home and freedom house were bombed and police used force to break up a rally. A group of teenagers tried to integrate the Indianola Public Library (201 Cypress Drive) and were turned away.

In 1965 blacks picketed the courthouse for the first time. Backed by a court order, blacks registered in significant numbers here that same year.

Fannie Lou Hamer House and Gravesite

721 Fannie Lou Hamer Drive (formerly James Street), Ruleville

Fannie Lou Townsend Hamer was born in 1917 and grew up in the fields of the Delta. She became a Movement heroine for her

Charles McLaurin Goes to Sunflower County

Charles ("Mac") McLaurin was a teenager in the summer of 1961, when he first heard of the Movement. Freedom Riders were staging continuous protests at bus stations in Jackson, and Movement organizers frequented local pool halls and restaurants. They presented civil rights work as a macho alternative to running with a gang. McLaurin signed up, protested against the segregated state fair in Jackson, and trained for voter registration work in 1962.

His posting was Sunflower County in the Delta. Sunflower intrigued him. Not only did he want to see a field of real sunflowers, but he also liked the idea of challenging powerful Mississippi Senator James Eastland, who owned a plantation in the county, in his own backyard. McLaurin was twenty years old when he set out on his first Movement assignment.

His immersion in the community of Ruleville was vintage SNCC. First, he found steadfast hosts in Joe and Rebecca McDonald, who were not easily intimidated by drive-by shootings and frequent visits by local law enforcement. Before organizing a single meeting, McLaurin visited churches, played basketball, went drinking on Saturday nights. He mowed yards for fifty cents apiece just to get a chance to discuss voter registration. No one could claim to have worked in the Delta without a hands-on experience with cotton, so he spent one day chopping cotton with a hoe. The next day his upper body was so sore he had to roll himself out of bed.

Charles McLaurin at a church in Sunflower County, 1995.
(Townsend Davis)

Most organizing then was done on foot. Perhaps thirty black families in Ruleville had cars, so on Saturdays the town was packed with people who had walked from Doddsville and other outlying areas. A top priority was encouraging local people not to knuckle under to routine intimidation. When Movement workers were picked up and taken downtown for police ques-

(Continued on next page)

tioning, they insisted on walking back under their own steam rather than ride in a police car. After the community center where they met had been burned down, they continued to meet in small groups in people's homes.

By mid-August 1962 it was time to try voter registration. McLaurin accompanied three middle-aged women to the courthouse in Indianola. At the time he had never even been to the courthouse, and he watched with pride as the women marched up the steps with heads held high before being turned away. Two weeks later McLaurin repeated the journey with Fannie Lou Hamer and seventeen others by bus from Ruleville, and he waited outside while Mrs. Hamer and another person tried to register for the first time. Mrs. Hamer, earthy and fearless, was just what SNCC was looking for, and she began drawing the ten-dollar-a-week SNCC salary in December 1962 for her efforts. Later McLaurin accompanied Mrs. Hamer to her first SNCC meeting in Nashville, and she later came to treat him like a son.

By this time McLaurin was well on his way to adopting the peripatetic ways of a full-time SNCC worker. He was liable to appear anywhere in Mississippi in dark sunglasses, which he wore all the time to hide his fear. He gave a speech on the courthouse steps in Greenville in 1963 that resulted in a jail sentence of ninety days; the conviction was reversed on free speech grounds. In 1964 he and four other activists driving to a SNCC meeting in Atlanta were pulled over by the highway patrol near Columbus, Mississippi, beaten, and treated to a harrowing night at the Lowndes County jail.

McLaurin also tried his hand at running for political office. In 1971 he ran for a state senate seat held by a white Cleveland attorney and lost. Afterward he stayed on and worked in Indianola. Today Mac is a well-known figure in the county. He has been in Indianola for more than two decades now and works as assistant director of public works, making his rounds in a truck and weighing the thought of another run for office.

steely will. The youngest of twenty children, she began picking cotton at age six on a plantation. She worked the same backbreaking hours as the rest in the field, from "can to can't," and later became a timekeeper on the plantation of W. D. Marlow. Only miles away, but aeons apart, lived James Eastland, the ranking segregationist in the U.S. Senate during the 1960s. He owned a fifty-four-hundred-acre plantation near Doddsville, a few miles south of Ruleville. By 1964 so much had changed that there was talk of Mrs. Hamer challenging Eastland for his Senate seat.

She first heard about voting while attending a civil rights meeting at William Chapel in Ruleville. She quickly adopted the Movement, and it her, lending her booming voice and a keen eye for injustice. "Mrs. Hamer became a person who could not only bring people together," said SNCC worker Charles McLaurin, "but who could say things that would make people move."

After her first failed attempt to register in August 1962 forced her to leave her home on the plantation, she took refuge at a guest house in Ruleville. She passed the voting test on her second try in December 1962. About the same time she moved into a rented home at 626 East Lafayette Street in Ruleville, near William Chapel. She began to travel for the Movement and served as a popular speaker and a SNCC field secretary. Her first trip in April 1963 was to the Dorchester Academy in Georgia for citizenship training. She went back east in May to the citizenship school on Johns Island,

---

McLaurin on Organizing

Charles McLaurin's "Notes on Organizing," a report based on his experience in Ruleville and Indianola, became a classic primer for future activists. In it he identified two ways to begin organizing:

"**A**n invited person goes to live with X person in Y community. Mr. X carries the person to church on Sunday. He introduces him to his friends and neighbors. You are there to do a job which at this time is undefined; so you act friendly, smiling and greeting the ladies as they approach you. Then, with your warm, friendly face you say to the people, 'I want to do something for this community.' That afternoon you are asked out to someone's home for dinner. Go, because this is one time you will be able to talk with a family, or maybe several families. Remember, try to answer all questions asked of you at this point because you are on trial. You must impress, as well as express.

"An *uninvited* worker faces many difficulties; first, he is unexpected and in many cases unwanted by the do-nothing leaders of the community. He is a stranger to people, and therefore, he is alone in a strange place. If he is to be successful, he must become a part of the community. . . .

"If you just talk and ask questions, some of them may talk about Chicago or welfare checks; this is good, this is what is on their minds presently. . . . Apathy will disappear when you give the people some responsibility. . . . You must be friendly, reliable, and most of all trustworthy. . . . When the people trust you and trust your judgment, suspicion will be a thing of the past."[37]

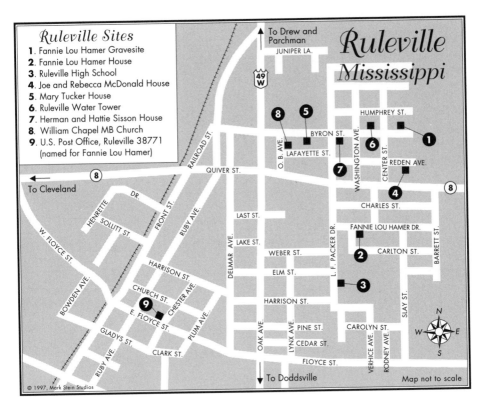

Ruleville Sites

1. Fannie Lou Hamer Gravesite
2. Fannie Lou Hamer House
3. Ruleville High School
4. Joe and Rebecca McDonald House
5. Mary Tucker House
6. Ruleville Water Tower
7. Herman and Hattie Sisson House
8. William Chapel MB Church
9. U.S. Post Office, Ruleville 38771
   (named for Fannie Lou Hamer)

Ruleville Mississippi

Map not to scale

South Carolina. Returning from that trip, she and two other Movement workers were beaten in a notorious incident at the Winona jail. Her account of this incident formed the core of her short but riveting testimony at the Democratic Convention in Atlantic City. The Montgomery County jail (217 Sterling Avenue, Winona), where the incident happened, remains a jail today.

The first time Mrs. Hamer cast a ballot, she voted for herself as a congressional candidate for the MFDP in 1964. She challenged Jamie Whitten, a twelve-term segregationist with a firm grip on federal agriculture policy governing the Delta. She lost in a landslide because of the still-minuscule number of registered black voters. In 1964 the Hamer house became a Freedom Summer headquarters. Students white and black lugged their trunks to James Street, filled the house with Movement chaos, and taught classes on the lawn near the pecan tree.

Mrs. Hamer also worked with the Delta Ministry and the National Council of Negro Women to develop housing and a day-care center

Grave of Fannie Lou Hamer in Ruleville, 1995. (Townsend Davis)

in Ruleville. In 1969 she founded a 680-acre agricultural cooperative called the Freedom Farm, located in north Sunflower County not far from the Marlow plantation where she had worked for eighteen years. The co-op grew beans, peas, okra, potatoes, and peanuts and raised hogs for members to eat. It also sold cotton and soybeans.

Mrs. Hamer's prominence in the Movement led to honorary degrees from several colleges and a critical role in the 1968 challenge to Mississippi's all-white Democratic delegation. She gave her name and time to a lawsuit to desegregate the schools of Sunflower County and ran unsuccessfully for the state senate in 1971. Battling ill health, she continued to make appearances and work for the Movement. One day in 1972, after picketing a white grocery store that had mistreated a black customer, she collapsed and was admitted to the hospital. Five years later, on April 14, 1977, she died of cancer at a hospital in Mound Bayou.

Mrs. Hamer was buried on land formerly held by the Freedom Farm and now the property of the city of Ruleville. She had died virtually penniless, so Owen Brooks and other activists raised money for the funeral. Her headstone reads: "I am sick and tired of being sick and tired." Her husband, Perry, a farm worker known as Pap who later worked for Head Start, died in 1992 and is buried beside her. The Ruleville post office was named for her in 1994, and her name is still wistfully mentioned by black and white leaders who saw her as the embodiment of commitment. The house is now inhabited by one of Mrs. Hamer's grandchildren.

Joe McDonald House
909 Reden Street, Ruleville

Charles McLaurin, Landy McNair, and Charles Cobb first arrived here on August 19, 1962, to recruit new voters, exposing their hosts to certain danger. It wasn't long before gunshots were fired at the house. When the mayor of Ruleville came by the McDonalds' house to confiscate a rifle after the shooting, activists told McDonald that the seizure was illegal. Not long after, McDonald, a field laborer, walked down to the mayor's office, demanded the rifle back, and, to the amazement of his neighbors, came home with it. Despite intimidation, McDonald continued to work for voter registration in Ruleville and in Drew, the next town up Highway 49, during Freedom Summer in 1964.

The Tucker house on Byron Street was put to a similar use. Fannie Lou Hamer stayed there after she had been ejected from the Marlow plantation; it was sprayed with gunfire ten days after her arrival. The shots did not harm Mrs. Hamer or the Tuckers but instead injured two young girls who were staying there. In Herman and Hattie Sisson's house (822 North Division Street), two college girls were injured by gunshots from roving night riders.

William Chapel Missionary Baptist Church
O.B. Avenue at Lafayette Street, Ruleville

One of several ways to undercut the Movement in Ruleville was to revoke the tax-exempt status of this church, its primary meeting place. City officials also cut off the water and successfully pressured an insurance company to cancel the church's casualty policy. A firebomb slightly damaged the chapel after a rally in June 1964. Even so, the church held mass meetings here every Friday at 7:30 P.M.

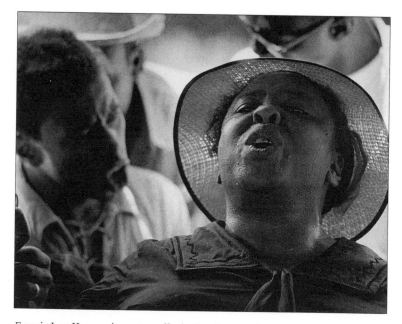

Fannie Lou Hamer sings at a rally during the Meredith March, June 12, 1966.
(Charmian Reading)

In this church Fannie Lou Hamer first heard that blacks could register and vote, and here she was memorialized after her death in 1977. Her funeral was attended by five thousand friends, acquaintances, and Movement leaders, and an overflow crowd also paid its respects at Ruleville High School (360 L. F. Packer Drive). She was eulogized by Georgia Congressman Andrew Young, then just appointed ambassador to the United Nations by President Jimmy Carter. Young led the singing of a spiritual Mrs. Hamer sang hundreds of times and used as a vocal trademark, "This Little Light of Mine."

Young's Gro and Market (formerly Bryant's Grocery and Meat Market)

Money, Leflore County

The unpunished murder of Emmett Till in 1955 was branded indelibly into the memories of many young people across the South, both horrifying and galvanizing a generation. Youngsters who saw Till's misshapen body in photographs in *Jet* magazine later became the ardent staffers of SNCC and referred to the Till case as their political awakening. Today the country store where the tragedy began is still standing, barely, between a gas station and a part-time post office beside a set of railroad tracks.

Young's (formerly Bryant's) Gro and Market in Money, where Emmett Till ventured before he was killed for his boldness, photographed in 1995. (Townsend Davis)

In 1955 Emmett Till was a cocksure fourteen-year-old who spoke with a stutter, a result of a childhood bout with polio. His mother was a native of Tallahatchie County who had moved to Chicago; for his summer vacation she sent him to visit his great-uncle Mose Wright, a sixty-four-year-old sharecropper. Wright lived three miles east of Money. His mother had warned Till to act deferentially toward whites. But at about 7:30 P.M. on August 24 Till's friends dared him to speak to the white woman inside this store, and he took them up on it.

Money back then was a hamlet with a post office, school, gas station, and cotton ginning station. The Bryant store stood in the middle of Money with a Coke sign hanging out front. That evening Till went inside and bought two cents' worth of bubble gum from Carolyn Bryant, the owner's wife. Accounts of what happened next vary, but one version was that Till said, "Bye, baby," and whistled at her, although rumors quickly spread that he had been more forward than that.

Three days later Roy Bryant set out with his half brother, J. W. Milam, to defend his wife's honor. They found young Till at the home of Mose Wright and took him away in their pickup. They beat the boy, shot him once in the head, strapped him with barbed wire to a seventy-five-pound cotton gin wheel, and threw him into the serpentine Tallahatchie River. On August 31 a fisherman discovered

The Delta

the body at Pecan Point on the river some twelve miles north of Money and three miles west of Philipp. The remains were identified and sent back to Chicago, and after Mrs. Till insisted on an open-casket funeral, *Jet* magazine's gruesome pictures of the partly decomposed body elicited chills of horror and cries for action nationwide.

Tallahatchie County Courthouse
Town Square, Sumner

Despite the efforts of Judge Curtis Swango to maintain judicial decorum, the Till trial, held here in 1955, was a wild, racially charged media circus. More than seventy journalists descended on Sumner. By order of the judge, all who attended, including Till's mother, were frisked for weapons. Several temporary phones were installed in the lobby, which resounded with clattering typewriters. Meanwhile the television networks, although banned from the courtroom proceedings, sent daily film back to New York via a tiny airfield in nearby Tutwiler.

In those days the second-floor courtroom had green-plastered walls and tall windows with shabby pull shades. The usual seating capacity was 108, but the courtroom was so packed that on the third day the judge ended the session early, worried that the court had become a firetrap. Beginning on the first day of trial, September 19, all participants were subjected to rigid segregation. Black spectators, such as James Hicks of the *Amsterdam News*, L. Alex Wilson of the *Tri-State Defender*, and Congressman Charles Diggs, sat at a fold-up card table outside the usual spectator rail in a rear corner. Outside, excited local merchants raffled off a car. The town limits sported a booster's sign: A GOOD PLACE TO RAISE A BOY.

All five attorneys practicing in Sumner offered their services to the defense free of charge. An all-white jury was drawn from slips of paper in the judge's straw hat. Even in this majority-black county, there were no registered black voters, which was a requirement for jury service.

The trial lacked the solemnity of a murder case. As described by the NAACP's Ruby Hurley, who attended the trial, the defendants ate ice-cream cones and played with their children in court "just like they were out at a picnic." Each defendant had two sons under the age of five. Dressed in suspenders and neckties, the little boys shot toy pistols at one another (and the prosecutor) and rattled the courtroom rail pickets. Because of the heat, which "brought on much hat fanning," Judge Swango allowed spectators to remove their coats and smoke while a porter made the rounds with ice water. Two ceiling fans rotated ineffectually above the bench.

Emmett Till's mother, Mamie Bradley, who had been born two miles from Sumner in the town of Webb, identified her son by the silver signet ring he had picked out before leaving Chicago. Mrs. Bryant testified that a black boy had grabbed her hand and asked her for a date. As was the custom, Mrs. Bryant was addressed as "Mrs."; Till's mother as "Mamie." The dramatic climax of the trial came when Mose Wright, thin and bent, rose from the witness stand to point out defendants Milam and Bryant as the abducters of Till that night, temporarily silencing the courtroom. One defense attorney told the jurors that their "forefathers would turn over in their graves" if they convicted Milam and Bryant.

On Friday, September 23, the jury stayed out an hour and seven minutes and came back with acquittals for both men. Friends pressed forward to congratulate them, and they lit up cigars. Most outsiders expressed outrage. Representative Adam Clayton Powell of New York called for a boycott of everything made in Mississippi, and the NAACP made the murder its front-burner issue. On January 24, 1956, an article by William Bradford Huie in *Look* magazine filled in the grisly details that had been omitted at the trial. After the acquittal the two men were insulated from another prosecution by double jeopardy, and when Huie offered to pay them about four thousand dollars for their story, they agreed. Huie's tell-all exposé revealed how Bryant and Milam had abducted the boy, killed him, and disposed of his body.

After blacks boycotted the Bryant and Milam businesses in the Delta for fifteen months, the store in Money was closed, and both men had difficulty getting jobs and credit in their community. Roy Bryant moved to Texas to work as a boilermaker and returned to run a general store in Ruleville before he died. J. W. Milam first joined his half brother in Texas, then did construction work in Greenville. He died on New Year's Eve in 1981. Mamie Till is still living in Chicago.

Greenwood, Mississippi

Hard Lessons in the Delta

Greenwood Leflore, a peculiar slaveowner and Unionist, lent his name to both Leflore County at the eastern edge of the Delta and its primary city, Greenwood. Leflore, half Indian and half French, had been chosen as a Choctaw chief but later betrayed his tribe by ceding much of the Choctaw land to the federal government in the Treaty of Dancing Rabbit Creek in 1830. Later the Movement had a sustained presence here, generating mass enthusiasm of the sort given more publicity in Albany or Birmingham. Greenwood was seen as a key not just to the county but to a five-county area that could set an example for the entire Delta.

When the Movement began taking hold in Greenwood, nearly two thirds of the county residents were black, yet only a fraction

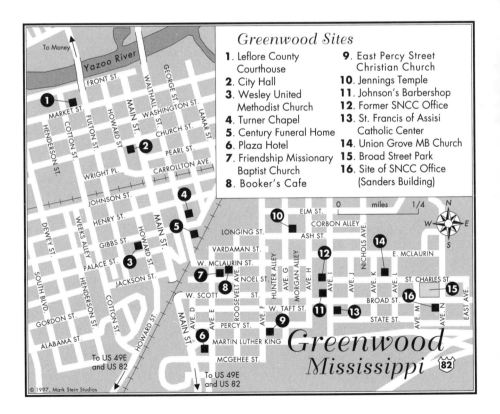

Greenwood Sites

1. Leflore County Courthouse
2. City Hall
3. Wesley United Methodist Church
4. Turner Chapel
5. Century Funeral Home
6. Plaza Hotel
7. Friendship Missionary Baptist Church
8. Booker's Cafe
9. East Percy Street Christian Church
10. Jennings Temple
11. Johnson's Barbershop
12. Former SNCC Office
13. St. Francis of Assisi Catholic Center
14. Union Grove MB Church
15. Broad Street Park
16. Site of SNCC Office (Sanders Building)

Greenwood Mississippi

© 1997, Mark Stein Studios

had registered to vote. The city was still a cotton hub, moving eight hundred thousand bales a year. It was the state headquarters of the Citizens' Council, and Judge Tom Brady delivered a speech to the Sons of the American Revolution here that he later expanded into *Black Monday,* a book that acquired cult status among segregationists. The stately houses on Royal Boulevard were separated from the black neighborhood by the river and the railroad tracks. The NAACP chapter in Greenwood was founded in 1952, but voting under the old system of poll taxes and trick questions was limited to those few economically secure enough to avoid certain retaliation.

In June 1962 Bob Moses arrived in Greenwood with twenty-three-year-old Sam Block, who had grown up in Cleveland, Mississippi, and attended Mississippi Vocational College in nearby Itta Bena. Local leader Cleveland Jordan, who had tried to register in the 1950s, showed them around and arranged for use of the Elks Hall (Scott Street and Avenue F) for initial meetings. Their gatherings stirred up fear of a backlash. Block was forced not only to seek another venue for meetings but also to find another home, which temporarily turned out to be a local junkyard.

Only a few came forward to help them. Rev. Aaron Johnson opened the doors of his First Christian Church (now East Percy Street Christian Church) for Greenwood's first mass meeting. Black photographer Robert Burns lent office space at 616 Avenue I. Dewey Greene, a veteran attending college at Block's alma mater, also lent a hand. A pool hall owner gave ten dollars. By August four people were ready to attempt to register at the Leflore County Courthouse. For his efforts Block was dragooned and beaten by white men on the street.

After a lull that lasted through the end of 1962, the Movement got a chance to recharge its campaign by responding to a calculated squeeze by government officials. Seasonal workers since 1957 had benefited from a government surplus program that distributed basic foodstuffs, such as flour and dried milk, in the winter months. In July 1962 the county canceled the program, a blow that fell heaviest upon black sharecroppers. Movement workers filled the void by distributing donated food from the SNCC office and urged recipients to register to vote. That winter food lines stretched up to six hundred people long.

On February 19, 1963, the day nine thousand pounds of donated supplies were scheduled to arrive from Chicago, four buildings in Greenwood were burned, including a dry cleaner near the SNCC office. After protesting that the Movement was the target of violence, Sam Block was arrested for breach of the peace. He was offered a plea bargain frequently presented to Movement organizers all over the South: a light sentence in exchange for leaving town. Block turned it down, was convicted, sentenced to six months in jail, and released pending an appeal.

On February 28 tension mounted further when white men in a Buick shot into a car carrying Bob Moses, Randolph Blackwell (an Atlanta activist in town to observe the revived voting campaign), and a young driver from Jackson, Jimmy Travis. The shooting, which occurred on Highway 82 seven miles west of Greenwood just east of Mississippi Vocational College (now Mississippi Valley State University), left Travis hospitalized with a bullet in his spinal cord. Wiley Branton, a black attorney from Little Rock who headed the national Voter Education Project, complained bitterly to the Kennedy administration and called on activists around the state to converge on Greenwood. The Movement staff in town soon swelled to forty people.

Opportunity and danger were the order of the day in March 1963. There was a second arson attempt on the SNCC office and

Greenwood Police Chief Curtis Lary confronts organizer Sam Block near the Leflore County Courthouse, April 2, 1963. (UPI/Corbis-Bettmann)

another drive-by shooting of SNCC workers. On March 26 Dewey Greene's house (at Howard and Henry streets) was riddled with buckshot. Meanwhile the city police force nearly doubled in size with the addition of many volunteers. After a meeting at Wesley United Methodist Church to honor Dewey Greene, James Forman and Bob Moses of SNCC led a march to City Hall on March 27, 1963,

Dick Gregory: Movement Provocateur

Comedian Dick Gregory had a special affection for the Delta and a flair for dramatic assistance to the Movement. His quips were famous for their razor's edge. "A white moderate in Mississippi," he once said, "is a cat who wants to lynch you from a *low* tree."

Gregory was as prone to flamboyant action as he was to vivid language. In 1962 he responded to the food shortage in Leflore County by chartering a plane with seven tons of food and then helping unload it himself in Clarksdale. He assisted Clyde Kennard, the first black applicant to Mississippi Southern College, who was held in a Mississippi prison on trumped-up charges and was released and treated for cancer in a Chicago hospital before he died.

Gregory came to Greenwood in 1963 as mass meetings began attracting large crowds. His biting satire of white politicians and equivocators within the black community alternatively made audiences either squirm or shout in agreement. He called local press coverage "disgraceful" and railed at Governor Barnett: "By his crooked tactics and his crooked standards, he has made us better than him." He chided local Baptist preachers for not hosting the Movement and urged members to look such pastors in the eye and walk out. "Give 'em their church," he said. "Give it to 'em empty, and let the good white folks come and fill it up for them." After Greenwood police first brought dogs to counter the demonstrators, he declared, "We will march through your dogs. And if you get some elephants, we'll march through them. And bring on your tigers and we'll march through them!" He left the phone number of the Greenwood jail with his friends at home in Chicago because he knew he would be staying there.

In Birmingham in 1963, dressed dapperly in a gray suit and vest, Gregory again marched and mouthed to great effect. The next year, when he was informed of the disappearance of COFO workers Chaney, Goodman, and Schwerner, his only question was, "What airport do I fly to?" He then accompanied Movement leaders to the Neshoba County Courthouse in Philadelphia, Mississippi, and later offered a twenty-five-thousand-dollar reward to anyone who could find the three slain workers. In Selma in 1965 both he and his wife marched to the courthouse months before the arrival of SCLC and King. Predictably, Gregory was among the first to join the Meredith March in 1966.

Today Dick Gregory still performs and raises money for civil rights causes.

the first street march of the campaign. It attracted a line of police who met the marchers at the City Hall steps with an eager German shepherd and arrested ten Movement leaders. The next day a similar march was stopped upon returning from City Hall, and police let loose German shepherds that nipped at the protesters' legs.

Word of these demonstrations and police countermeasures fueled the Greenwood campaign. Mass meetings overflowed with new recruits. A steady stream of people volunteered to go to the courthouse to register, although many were still rejected. On March 30 the Justice Department, in an unprecedented move, filed a lawsuit to stop the harassment of the protesters. In Washington, D.C., Mississippi Senators Eastland and Stennis took turns denouncing the feds and the Greenwood Movement. To avoid a clash between federal and local authorities, DOJ then withdrew its lawsuit in exchange for the release of SNCC workers from jail and a resumption of the surplus food program. Marches continued through the summer, and standoffs were so common that high school students knew the circuit clerk, Martha Lamb, and certain police officers by name.

The following year brought Freedom Summer, and after SNCC made Greenwood its regional headquarters, the town came to resemble a low-tech war zone. When protester Silas McGhee attempted to integrate the Leflore Theater after the passage of the Civil Rights Act in July 1964, he was pelted with wadded paper and later attacked. McGhee, whose mother had hosted the Movement on her farm, returned to the theater with his brother Jake seven more times, facing similar abuse each time. When he appeared at a Freedom Day rally at the courthouse on July 16, he was kidnaped by three white men, who drove him to a plumbing shop and beat him. So intense was police scrutiny of the McGhees that at one point in August the entire family—the mother and all three sons—faced an assortment of minor criminal charges. Silas McGhee later was elected to the SNCC executive staff. That same month many from Greenwood participated in the MFDP Leflore County convention and the district convention in Greenville. Students organized a boycott of a store owned by a white police officer who had dragged a pregnant black woman down the street.

After the Voting Rights Act of 1965 was passed, federal registrars were installed in the Greenwood post office, and the Greenwood Voters League urged citizens to take advantage of the new law. Only then did large numbers of blacks register for the first time. The first black sheriff's deputy in Leflore County, Charles Cooley, was hired in 1971, and he went on to a twenty-five-year career in law enforcement. In 1979 and 1985 lawsuits forced the county and the city respectively to elect state representatives from geographic districts instead of at large. Today both governments are racially balanced, although the black neighborhoods are still in the midst of a continuing effort to upgrade the quality of housing. Now more than thirty years old, the Greenwood Voters League is run by David Jordan, a city councilman, state senator, and son of activist Cleveland Jordan.

Century Funeral Home
East Gibbs and Walthall Streets

The body of Emmett Till was brought here before being sent back to Chicago in 1955. Greenwood police officer C. A. Strickland photographed the body, and some black children playing nearby, who

Simon Garrett, who worked at the Century Funeral Home and helped recover the body of Emmett Till, in 1995. (Townsend Davis)

later became Movement activists, sneaked a peek at it. Century also handled the funeral of Fannie Lou Hamer, paid for by Movement donations. The home was founded in 1938 by Henry Espy, whose grandson Mike Espy in 1986 became the first black member of Congress from Mississippi since Reconstruction.

COFO/SNCC Offices

1. 616 Avenue I, between St. Charles and Broad Streets
2. McLaurin Street between Avenues F and G
3. 708 Avenue N (the Sanders Building)

SNCC first set up shop in a two-story brick building at 616 Avenue I. At the time it was considered a success to get three people to stick to their promise to attempt to register at the courthouse. During summer 1962 three SNCC workers who saw a carload of armed whites heading for the office escaped out a bathroom window and clambered down an antenna to safety. Bob Moses and Willie Peacock, who had driven over from Cleveland when they heard trouble was brewing, arrived at 3:30 A.M. to find the office ransacked and empty. Rather than seek safer shelter or attempt a nighttime search, they simply slept in the office, demonstrating the level of chaos SNCC people learned to live with daily. Their landlord, the photographer Robert Burns, was subsequently charged falsely with bigamy and asked them to leave.

SNCC next worked out of an office near a dry cleaner on McLaurin Street. Sam Block and Willie Peacock were driving near this office on March 6, 1963, when whites drove up to their car and fired shots through the front windows. Block and Peacock escaped with minor injuries from the flying glass. On March 24 the SNCC office was badly damaged by fire. As was common for such incidents Movement workers were accused of setting the fire themselves to elicit sympathy for their cause.

In March 1963 SNCC moved again to 708 Avenue N in a building (now a vacant lot) off Broad Street Park. It was transformed from a run-down barn into a two-story Movement hive, with its all-important WATS line and the bustle of a military headquarters. Organizers ran food distribution, voter registration, and educational programs as well as a kitchen on the first floor. SNCC also distributed seeds for a Freedom Garden. By summer 1964 SNCC supporters were shipping boxes of books to the office. Some foreign embassies, many from Africa, donated maps and other materials about their countries. Eventually the office on Avenue N housed a Movement library

COFO worker sorting ballots at the COFO office at 708 Avenue N, 1964. (Bern Keating/Black Star)

on the second floor that rivaled the local public library. Two cats lived there: one named Freedom and one named Now.

Booker's Cafe
211 West McLaurin Street

At one of the last remaining Movement joints here, run by Mildred Wright, you can still fill up on pig tails, chicken, and other home cooking.

East Percy Street Christian Church
(Disciples of Christ)
100 East Percy Street

Rev. Aaron Johnson, a former soldier from Carroll County and pastor since 1959, was the first preacher in Greenwood to open the doors of his church (formerly First Christian Church) to Movement meetings in 1962. He did it because he not only believed in the goals of the activists but also did not want young people who were attracted to their program (his daughter, for one) to be hanging out at seedier locales. When the congregation dwindled to about twenty

Rev. Aaron Johnson, who kept his church open for Movement meetings, in front of the East Percy Street Christian Church, 1995. (Townsend Davis)

regular members, Johnson still kept the church doors open. He even married two Movement volunteers under a canopy of flowers and Freedom Summer flyers at the COFO office. In those days Johnson's church was made of wood; the church has since been rebuilt in brick.

Johnson still preaches at the church and also cuts hair at his barbershop on the northwest corner of Avenue I and Broad Street.

Plaza Hotel and Liquor Store
301 Martin Luther King Drive

Built in 1948, this fifty-five-room black hotel hosted blues players, Negro League ballplayers, and the black press during the Emmett Till trial in 1955. Eddie ("Deadeye") Cochran, former local NAACP president and founding member of the Greenwood Voters League, ran the place. Movement meetings were held here before churches would allow them, and Cochran helped bail protesters out of jail. The hotel was damaged by fire in 1974, and only the liquor

Eddie ("Deadeye") Cochran, voting activist, in his liquor store, formerly the Plaza Hotel, in 1995.
(Townsend Davis)

store remains. In 1995 Cochran was shot and killed during an attempted robbery of his store.

Wesley United Methodist Church

800 Howard Street

Wesley Chapel, led by Rev. Israel Rucker from 1960 to 1968, first provided support for the Movement's food relief effort and later became the send-off point of the first mass march in Greenwood in 1963. As the largest meeting place for blacks in Greenwood, it had hosted graduation ceremonies for the local black high school, housed homeless people during the Depression, and served as an emergency shelter during tornado season.

The first march on March 27, 1963, began as a mass meeting to protest the violence that had culminated in the shooting at Dewey Greene's home. When Rev. David Tucker of Turner Chapel led a group of prospective voters to the county courthouse the next day, they were met upon their return by a line of one hundred officers near the church. A German shepherd loosed on Rev. Tucker left him with a bloodied leg, but the violence backfired. Local people credit this incident with transforming the Greenwood Movement from a small-scale voting drive to a citywide campaign.

The church has been a provider to the black community since it was organized in 1870, housed in the present building since 1921.

Union Grove MB Church

615 St. Charles Street

Under Rev. B. T. McSwine this church opened its doors to the Movement early on and housed a Freedom School office. McSwine also was one of the preachers who posted property bonds to bail out protesters.

Turner Chapel

717 Walthall Street

Organizers met here and at Wesley Chapel during the height of the Greenwood Movement. It was pastored by Rev. David L. Tucker. Tucker and Endesha Ida Mae ("Cat") Holland, then a young congregant, reformed ex-prostitute, and citizenship school teacher, led the first mass march in Greenwood in March 1963. After Tucker was bitten by a police dog while marching downtown, he urged his fellow ministers to register to vote and warned that emotional preaching without action was merely "sounding brass and tinkling cymbals."

Friendship Missionary Baptist Church

220 Noel Street

Friendship was one of the first Baptist churches in Greenwood to open its doors to the Greenwood Movement and to host citizenship and Freedom School classes. After the shooting of protester Silas McGhee on August 16, 1964, one hundred angry activists gathered here and then headed for the SNCC office on Avenue N. Police in full riot gear blocked off both ends of the street where the office was located and dispersed the crowd in one of the most volatile street protests of the campaign.

St. Francis of Assisi Catholic Center

708 Avenue I

Father Nathaniel Machesky allowed the Movement to distribute food and clothing from this building, one of several ways in which the Catholic Church here supported the Movement.

Leflore County Courthouse

310 Market Street

This neoclassical revival courthouse built in 1906 on the banks of the Yazoo River was the destination of many marches, beginning with one on March 27, 1963. Protesters were taken either to the city jail (behind the current City Hall), the county jail, or the county farm; sometimes they were transported in a school bus painted black with screens across the windows.

The Meredith March of 1966: Last of the Great Movement Treks

The March against Fear began as a solo walk by James Meredith and ended with the ascendancy of black nationalism, and the slogan "Black Power."

Starting out at the Peabody Hotel in Memphis on June 5, 1966, Meredith walked down Highway 51 (which today parallels Interstate 55), intending to travel 225 miles. He was equipped with only his pith helmet and an ebony walking stick given to him by an Egyptian village chief. Meredith had gained renown for his admission to Ole Miss in 1962 but since then had not been vocal on civil rights issues and had declined to coordinate his march with any Movement group. His purpose was to show that blacks in the new era could walk, and register to vote, without fear. The first day he walked 12 miles to the state border dividing Tennessee and Mississippi.

The next day he got 16 miles into Mississippi before he was shot by a white

James Meredith at the outset of his March against Fear in June 1966. (Vernon Merritt/Black Star)

Memphis man hiding in the brush on the side of the highway just south of Hernando. Meredith fell to the pavement with more than sixty birdshot pellets in his body in front of a handful of reporters. He was rushed to William F. Bowld Hospital in Memphis and survived with no permanent injuries. Movement groups pledged to continue the journey and to use it as a call for stronger enforcement of the Voting Rights Act.

The Movement phase of the march contained two distinct flanks: SCLC staffers and King carried on the tradition of freedom songs and nonviolent prayers, while the SNCC staff, led by its newly elected chairman, Stokely Carmichael, insisted that the armed Deacons for Defense accompany the marchers for protection. During the day Mississippi highway patrolmen lined the highway and prevented further ambush attacks. Along the way four thousand new black voters registered to vote in towns across northern Mississippi. Below are a few highlights:

June 7, Highway 51 near Hernando: After visiting Meredith in the hospital and receiving his consent to continue marching, King, Floyd McKissick of CORE, and Stokely Carmichael marched south.

June 14, Grenada: Marchers arrived at the courthouse square, where an SCLC staffer placed an American flag atop a statue of Jefferson Davis. Local blacks also registered to vote, nearly tripling the total in the county. Marchers then headed southwest along Route 7.

June 16, Greenwood: Marchers were arrested after attempting to camp at a public school contrary to city orders. After their release a rally was held at Broad Street Park. Stokely Carmichael vented his frustration by leading repeated chants of "Black Power!" Later King called the slogan "an unwise choice" for a rallying cry because of its violent connotations. Meredith himself, who rejoined the march after his recovery, praised King and the NAACP but confessed his own feeling that "nonviolence is incompatible with American ideals." The march proceeded down Highway 49 past Belzoni.

June 21, Philadelphia: King and a group of marchers broke away from the march to join a commemorative service in Philadelphia for Chaney, Goodman, and Schwerner on the second anniversary of their deaths. They marched downtown while police ejected hostile onlookers from roadside trees. Near the county courthouse they held a prayer session while the sheriff and the deputy sheriff, awaiting trial on federal charges related to the killings, looked on. On the way back to a black neighborhood, marchers were pelted with debris and insults. That night, in Yazoo City, King gave an impassioned defense of nonviolence at a rally where both "Black Power" and "Freedom Now" were chanted.

June 23, Canton: The site of CORE's major organizational effort in the state. At McNeal Elementary School, marchers were again denied permission to pitch tents, only this time they tried to occupy the grounds. Sixty state troopers first fired tear gas into the crowd, then waded into it. Wielding truncheons and gun butts, they cleared the area in fifteen minutes. Unlike the similar charge of troopers in Selma the previous year, the Canton incident provoked little national outrage. Marchers retreated to the Asbury Methodist Church to recover.

June 26, Tougaloo College, Jackson: Like St. Jude in Montgomery, the haven on the edge of town. Here celebrities gathered for a rally before the final approach to Jackson. Prankish SNCC workers affixed "Black Power" bumper stickers to police cars. Two thousand people, some in red, white, and blue hats and other patriotic garb, set out from the campus gate and walked the final eight miles down Highway 51 into downtown Jackson.

June 26, State Capitol, Jackson: King and Carmichael spoke to a crowd of fifteen thousand people.

After the march Meredith graduated from law school, worked briefly at a Wall Street law firm, and moved back to Mississippi in 1971. He ran a bar and a tree farm and moved to a formerly all-white suburb of Jackson. From 1989 to 1991 he worked for Senator Jesse Helms of North Carolina, a former segregationist, in order to gain access to the Library of Congress for research on a book he was writing. Throughout his career he has maintained a vision of racial equality based on the preeminence of Africa and an appreciation of the structural advantages afforded white people. Today he lives in Jackson.

During the Meredith March in 1966 some one thousand people followed King, Stokely Carmichael, and Hosea Williams to the courthouse, where they prayed before continuing west toward Itta Bena. By 1968, 73 percent of eligible black voters in the county had registered.

Meredith Arrives at the Hernando Town Square

This firsthand account written by Meredith appeared in the Saturday Evening Post *after the march:*

"The thing I remember most clearly is coming over a rise, with the harsh Mississippi sun baking the pavement of Highway 51, and seeing the town of Hernando lying before me like some Hollywood director's idea of a small town in the American South: a few small stores, some old decaying mansions and many, many unpainted board houses where the Negroes lived. It was the first town I had come to in Mississippi. I saw white faces at windows, and white men standing in front of their shops or staring blankly from the lawns of their homes. I didn't see any Negroes. At least, I didn't see them anywhere around the main street. But they were waiting for me when I walked into the main square of the town. Some of them had been there for two hours, standing together on the far side of the square. There were young men and old, children with pure young faces and old men bent with age. Most were wearing the long blue overalls of cotton-field workers, and they did not seem to know what to do. Some looked away, some stared at the ground. All of them were aware of the group of whites, silent and sullen, who watched us from the far side of the square. . . .

"I urged them to register to vote, because that was one of the keys to the future, and they said, 'We're gonna register, we're gonna register.' And then we went around to a cafe to have something to eat. I was eating a cheeseburger and drinking a glass of milk, when an old Negro farmer came over and pressed a dollar bill in my hand. He had probably never earned more than $300 in a single year. 'You just keep that,' he said. 'You just keep that.' I still had that dollar bill in my pocket a few hours later when my back was riddled by shots fired from ambush."[39]

Broad Street Park

Broad Street between Avenues M and N

During the Meredith March, marchers pitched tents here (where the swings are now located) after they were turned away from Stone Street Elementary School on June 16, 1966. Stokely Carmichael, who was jailed for trying to set up camp at the school, spoke at a rally in the park shortly after his release from jail not far from the SNCC office where he had worked two years before. He advocated burning down the courthouses of Mississippi to "get rid of the dirt." He also started a chant of "We want black power!" that brought shouts of agreement from the crowd and later took hold as the slogan of a new militancy.

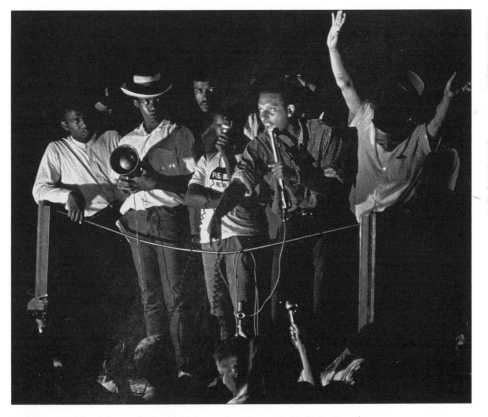

Stokely Carmichael demanding "Black Power" on June 17, 1966, in Broad Street Park in Greenwood during the Meredith March. (Bob Fitch/Black Star)

Meridian, Mississippi

The Final Days of Chaney and Schwerner

Segregation in Meridian was enforced by the respectable white community while tight-knit Klan factions in Lauderdale and Neshoba counties planned selective missions of violence. This combination presented formidable obstacles to Movement organizers, a fact noted by Mickey Schwerner himself in early 1964 after only a few months' experience in the area.

Schwerner, a white CORE field secretary, and James Chaney, a black Meridian native, returned to east Mississippi in June 1964 after they heard that their initial plans there had gone awry. Mount Zion Methodist Church, northeast of Philadelphia, which had agreed to host a Freedom School, had been raided by the Klan. When they learned that the Klan had beaten church members and

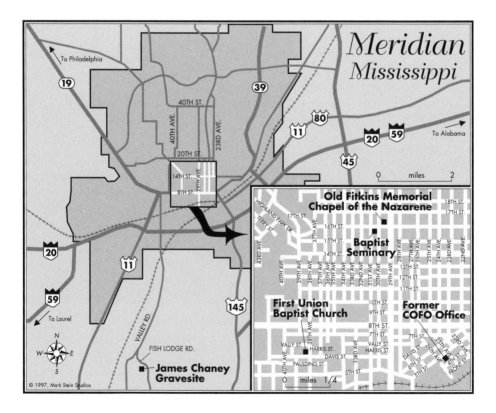

burned the wood church to the ground on the same night, the organizers drove from Freedom Summer training in Ohio to Meridian on June 20 to investigate.

Schwerner, twenty-four, was a Cornell graduate who, with his wife, Rita, had been working for CORE in Mississippi since January. They had settled in Meridian (at 1308 Thirty-fourth Avenue) and created the first Movement community resource and recreation center in the state. Chaney, a twenty-one-year-old plasterer, was returning home, where he had first gotten wind of the Movement in 1963. The trip to Ohio had been his first journey to the North. He had worked in the Delta and as a new staff member of CORE had canvassed Neshoba County with Schwerner. Making the trip with them was Andrew Goodman, twenty, a white student who had heard Clarksdale organizer Aaron Henry speak at Queens College in New York City and was making his first visit to Mississippi as a Freedom Summer volunteer.

After checking in at the Meridian COFO office the next day, the three visited the ruins of the Mount Zion Methodist Church, were arrested for speeding on the way back, and were jailed in Philadelphia. They were released at ten-thirty that night and got about ten miles down Highway 19 toward Meridian when they were pulled over again by a sheriff's deputy. This time they were handed over to the Klan, brutally murdered, and buried. Their bodies were recovered six weeks later southwest of Philadelphia under a man-made

The Meridian COFO office and community center, where Mickey and Rita Schwerner worked, in 1964. (Vernon Merritt/Black Star)

earthen dam. Even the funeral arrangements bowed to segregation. Mickey Schwerner's parents were denied their request to bury their son beside his black cohort, James Chaney, in Meridian. Goodman and Schwerner were buried separately in New York City.

On December 4, 1965, after an extensive investigation, federal prosecutors arrested Neshoba County Sheriff Lawrence Rainey, Deputy Sheriff Cecil Price, and nineteen others. They were charged with violating the civil rights of the three slain workers under a Reconstruction-era law. After a series of delays, the trial was held in the federal post office building in Meridian (2100 Ninth Street), starting on October 6, 1967. John Doar, DOJ's most experienced civil rights attorney, led the prosecution. The defendants stayed remarkably relaxed through the trial. A famous photograph of them at their arraignment shows Rainey, surrounded by laughing supporters, reaching into a pouch of Red Man chewing tobacco to add to an already bulging chew in his cheek.

With the aid of Klan informants prosecutors laid out for the all-white jury the plan to execute the three civil rights workers. As early as April 1964 the Lauderdale County klavern of the Klan had discussed killing Mickey Schwerner, known as Goatee for his tufted chin. At the trial a prosecution witness explained how the deputy sheriff had coordinated the release of the civil rights workers with a group of Klansmen lying in wait in Philadelphia. He described how the workers were forced out of their car, shot at close range, carried to the earthen dam near the fairgrounds, and buried with a bulldozer that same evening. Seven Klansmen were found guilty of civil rights violations on October 20, 1967. Deputy Sheriff Cecil Price was convicted and sentenced to six years in jail; his boss, Sheriff Rainey, was acquitted. Sam Bowers, Imperial Wizard of the White Knights of the Mississippi Ku Klux Klan, also was convicted and spent six years in federal prison before his release in March 1976. It was the first successful federal prosecution of racial violence in Mississippi.

Racial change came to Meridian after a local campaign of sit-ins and boycotts, which began before the murders and laid the groundwork. Since 1977 blacks have served in city government and have pushed for economic opportunity through the Meridian Action Committee, headed by Rev. Charles Johnson.

First Union Baptist Church

610 Thirty-eighth Avenue

James Chaney was mourned by seven hundred people at a solemn service here on August 7, 1964. Before the service mourners marched silently, two by two, from four separate churches at dusk and met here to pay their respects. Fannie Lee Chaney and her younger son Ben sat in the front row, a phalanx of media in front of them and hundreds of mourners gathered outside. Printed on the program was part of a poem by Paul Laurence Dunbar: "He died in action with his armor on!" In a moving and bitter speech Dave Dennis of CORE admitted that the steady stream of racial brutality in Mississippi had left him feeling vengeful. "I'm not going to stand here and ask anyone not to be angry, not to be bitter tonight," he said. "We've defended our country. To do what? To live like slaves." He lashed out at those who sat by complacently in the face of such injustice. "God damn your souls!" he cried.

Under Rev. Richard Sylvester Porter, pastor from 1959 to 1974, the church allowed Movement meetings where citizens discussed poll taxes and voting. Because of cross burnings and other threats, the church was guarded by volunteers with shotguns. Later the church opened the first Head Start program in Meridian.

James Chaney Gravesite (Okatibbee Cemetery)

Fish Lodge Road off Valley Road

James Earl Chaney was buried here in the early evening on August 7, 1964. He was remembered in a small family service before the large memorial service at First Union Baptist Church. Chaney

James Chaney's grave outside Meridian, 1995. (Townsend Davis)

had lived a life of activism that started with his wearing forbidden NAACP buttons made of paper during his days at Harris High School and ended at age twenty-one during an investigation into a racial bombing. He knew his community cold, worked doggedly on voter registration in the Delta, and possessed valued skills as a driver who could get a carload of Movement workers out of a jam.

Chaney's grave stands apart from the others in front of an eternal flame on a small hill near the Okatibbee Missionary Baptist Church. The headstone reads: "There are those who are alive, yet will never live. There are those who are dead, yet will live forever. Great deeds inspire and encourage the living."

COFO/CORE Office
2505½ Fifth Street

On the upper floor of this two-story white building above Fielder & Brooks drugstore Chaney, Goodman, and Schwerner were last seen by their Movement colleagues. After driving all night from Ohio and arriving here, they set out on June 21, 1964, for the Mount Zion Methodist Church fifty miles north. They left instructions with volunteer Louise Hermey to call COFO headquarters in Jackson and the FBI, a routine Movement precaution, if they did not return by 4:00 P.M. It was her first day on the job, and she dutifully called. When 5:30 P.M. came and went with no sign of them, COFO workers called all the area jails, looking for them. That set off a chain reaction of calls that eventually reached the Justice Department in Washington and prompted a massive manhunt.

Several months before the deaths the office had become a model Freedom Summer office and community center. Rita Schwerner had transformed five dingy rooms on the second floor into a library with thousands of donated books, fresh paint and blue curtains, a Ping-Pong table, and a phonograph. Mickey Schwerner had held voter registration classes here twice a week while his wife organized popular sewing classes and storybook reading for children. They each received ten dollars a week from CORE for their efforts.

Meridian Baptist Seminary
Sixteenth Street and Thirtieth Avenue

This three-story brick building on a hill was once the "palace of the Freedom School circuit," hosting a hundred Freedom School delegates at their convention on August 8, 1964, the day after the Chaney funeral. Under a hand-painted sign reading FREEDOM IS A CON-STANT STRUGGLE, students mixed discussion groups and workshops with a Saturday night play. They heard speeches by some of the Movement's leading lights, including A. Philip Randolph, James Forman, and Bob Moses. The students even considered a fall class boycott to spur public schools to adopt some of the features of the Freedom Schools they attended that summer.

The seminary, formerly one of the prominent educational institutions for blacks in east Mississippi, offered black history courses for high school students during the 1920s and 1930s. It closed in 1972. Across the street from it is the former site of the Fitkins Memorial Chapel of the Nazarene (2914 Sixteenth Street, now New Jerusalem Church), which was a refuge for Schwerner and Chaney. They occasionally met there or napped under the huge tree on the corner. The church's pastor, Rev. Charles Johnson, was one of the few preachers who encouraged them to pursue their mission.

Philadelphia, Mississippi

A Search Leads to an Earthen Dam

The disappearance of the three civil rights workers in 1964 sparked a local Movement here that centered on a short strip of Carver Avenue. In those days most blacks lived on the gravel roads north of Highway 16 and west of the railroad tracks in a neighborhood known as Independence Quarters. Although federal Prohibition had been repealed in 1935, Neshoba County supported a healthy bootlegging trade through the 1960s while remaining dry under state law.

Sheriff Lawrence Rainey, elected in 1963, was notoriously rough on blacks. He sported a military swagger and often cruised through the neighborhood to make his presence felt. He instituted a curfew; blacks had to be off the streets by 9:00 P.M. By early 1964 racial tension here was rising. On April 5, 1964, twelve crosses burned in Neshoba County, five of them in Independence Quarters and one on the county courthouse lawn. Klan literature started showing up on people's doorsteps.

On a humid Sunday, June 21, 1964, while most of the county was at church, Chaney, Goodman, and Schwerner drove from Meridian

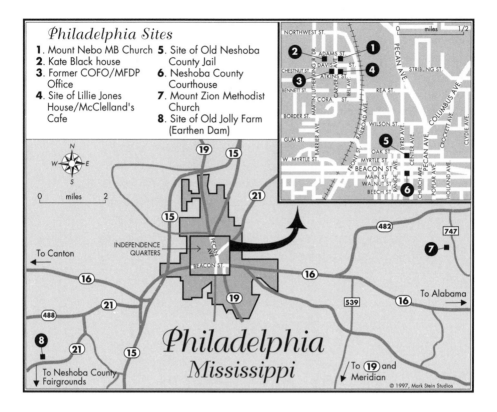

Philadelphia Sites

1. Mount Nebo MB Church
2. Kate Black house
3. Former COFO/MFDP Office
4. Site of Lillie Jones House/McClelland's Cafe
5. Site of Old Neshoba County Jail
6. Neshoba County Courthouse
7. Mount Zion Methodist Church
8. Site of Old Jolly Farm (Earthen Dam)

Philadelphia
Mississippi

© 1997, Mark Stein Studios

to inspect the damage at Mount Zion Methodist Church in Neshoba County. On their way back Chaney, the driver, was pulled over for speeding by Deputy Sheriff Cecil Price just inside the eastern city limits of Philadelphia at about 4:00 P.M. The three were held in the county jail until about 10:00 P.M., when they were released. Price followed the activists' 1963 blue Ford station wagon down Highway 19 toward Meridian, then a short way southwest on Highway 492 toward Union in hot pursuit. Then the civil rights workers disappeared.

A popular theory in the ensuing weeks maintained that their disappearance was a hoax perpetuated by the Movement to give momentum to the Freedom Summer campaign, then just beginning. This speculation, widely circulated in the press, gained subscribers the day after the disappearance when the station wagon was pulled from Bogue Chitto swamp near the Mount Zion church without any sign of the passengers. The county was soon flooded with federal investigators and the press, who occupied the ground floor of the Benwalt Hotel (238 Byrd Avenue North, now an old-age home called the Philadelphian) near the Neshoba County Courthouse.

Recovery of the Ford station wagon driven by James Chaney, north of Philadelphia, June 23, 1964. (Steve Schapiro/Black Star)

Movement workers conducted their own night searches of the fields and woods of Neshoba County.

As the summer dragged on, FBI MISSING flyers with three blank-faced photos of Chaney, Goodman, and Schwerner became a numbingly familiar sight. Finally, on August 4, 1964, the FBI found the bodies at Old Jolly Farm under fifteen feet of earth about five miles southwest of Philadelphia near the county fairgrounds off Route 21. It was six days before the county fair, the signature event of the area, was to open. When the dam was uncovered, all three were found to have been shot, Schwerner and Goodman once and Chaney six times. The property was owned by Olen Burrage, owner of a trucking company, who denied any knowledge of the killings. The site of the earthen dam is unmarked today, except for a NO TRESPASSING sign.

Despite the tragedy, COFO was determined to continue the effort that had begun at Mount Zion Methodist Church in the spring. That summer Martin Luther King, Jr., visited Independence Quarters, where he shot pool and urged local residents to press on with civil rights efforts. "Some preacher, this Martin Luther King," fumed a white letter writer to the local paper. "He comes into a community like Philadelphia where people are hungering for some good news: instead of a Bible, he uses a cue stick."

COFO opened an office on Carver Avenue in August 1964. Kate Black's house (255 Adams Street) housed four Movement workers, two black and two white, during Freedom Summer. Hoodlums shot into the house, but she escaped unharmed. Police took her husband, who also was politically active, on gratuitous rides through the neighborhood in a caged truck. For months activists took small groups down to the courthouse to register.

In January 1965 the first black patrolman was seen on Carver Avenue, followed by another in July. The first mass march in Neshoba County was held on the one-year anniversary of the killings, when seventy-five people marched from the COFO office on June 21, 1965. In a procession that was nearly unthinkable only months before, the marchers walked downtown and out Highway 16 to the Mount Zion Methodist Church, an arduous eight-mile journey in the hot sun. Dinner was served, and a memorial service was held on the church grounds. That demonstration began the process of getting paved streets in black neighborhoods and desegregation at the courthouse. By year's end, 320 blacks, backed by the Voting Rights Act of 1965, had registered at the courthouse, while another 400 had registered at a special federal registration center at the post office.

The second anniversary of the killings on June 21, 1966, brought King and others from the Meredith March to Philadelphia. They walked two miles from Independence Quarters toward the court-house, attracting hostile onlookers. King and Abernathy spoke to a crowd at the county jail on Myrtle Street. Then the marchers reassembled in front of the Neshoba County Courthouse. A large crowd of whites peppered King's speech with jeers and firecrackers. Sheriff Lawrence Rainey and Deputy Cecil Price, who were awaiting trial on charges of violating the civil rights of Chaney, Goodman, and Schwerner, stood behind him. When King said he thought the murderers were in their midst at that very moment, someone shouted, "They're right behind you!" and the white crowd cheered. On the way back to Independence Quarters, marchers and camera crews were pelted with debris, and young whites in a convertible leaned on the car horn and gave the march a good buzzing. King later said Philadelphia was one of the worst towns he had ever marched through, bringing him face-to-face with "the real possibil-ity of the inevitability of death."

In the late 1960s, with the aid of federal housing loans, the wooden houses of Independence Quarters were replaced by brick ones. The public schools were desegregated in 1970, and a public park was built in 1971 to serve the black community. On the twenty-fifth anniversary of the killings, Mississippi Secretary of State Dick Molpus, a white man whose family ran a lumber business in Philadelphia, spoke at an interracial ceremony at Mount Zion Methodist Church, delivering a message of regret for the killings and calling for future racial cooperation.

In the 1990s legalized gambling, formerly a favorite whipping boy of local preachers, supplied an economic injection to the county. Choctaw Indians had long inhabited Neshoba County and had survived as a smaller minority group wedged between black and white. In 1994 the Choctaws opened a forty-thousand-square-foot neon palace called the Silver Star Hotel and Casino on Highway 16 four miles west of Philadelphia. Today it is by far the largest employer in the county.

Mount Zion Methodist Church

County Line Road, Neshoba County (Longdale)

Church member Cornelius Steele, who had first tried to vote in 1952, invited Chaney and Schwerner to speak in May 1964 about summer plans here after it was agreed that the church would be used as a Freedom School. Blacks had owned their own land in this area, known as Longdale, since 1879, and a wood-frame church had stood on this spot since 1899.

Mount Zion Methodist Church, which was burned down in 1964 and where the three workers went to investigate before they were killed, in Longdale, outside Philadelphia, 1995. (Townsend Davis)

On June 16, 1964, during a routine board of stewards meeting, the Klan stormed the church and savagely beat three black congregants. That night the Klansmen returned and burned it down, leaving nothing but a forty-year-old bell, the smell of kerosene, and rubble "strewn about like the bones of some prehistoric creature," as one Movement worker later put it. Chaney and Schwerner returned here to secure affidavits about the raid and beatings. Their trip from Meridian out to Mount Zion on June 21 was their last: They were jailed, released, and killed later that night.

The church was rebuilt and rededicated in February 1966, and a plaque near the front door and three crosses outside pay tribute to the three who were slain. The bell remains outside as a memorial.

Neshoba County Courthouse
401 Beacon Street

On September 14, 1964, while the murder investigations were going on, eighteen blacks from Neshoba County showed up at the courthouse to register, the first visible act of the COFO project here. Cars whirled around the square as crowds of people clogged the surrounding streets to watch and yell catcalls. The prospective voters lined up single file and entered the courthouse one at a time. Three of them eventually passed the test. Meanwhile police arrested Alan Schiffman, a COFO worker known around town as COFO Red for his red hair.

Before federal enforcement of voting rights, blacks who tried to register here were subjected to conundrums common in registration offices all around the South ("How many bubbles in a bar of soap?"). Registrars had complete discretion to determine what constituted a correct answer. During the voter registration drives of 1965 an elderly woman, frustrated by the continuing requirement of being able to interpret the state constitution to the satisfaction of the registrar, said, "It meant what it said, and it said what it meant." Even after the Voting Rights Act of 1965, registration did not immediately become a routine process.

Site of the Old Neshoba County Jail
422 Myrtle Street

In a one-story red-brick building here Chaney, Goodman, and Schwerner were incarcerated on the afternoon of June 21, 1964. Schwerner and Goodman were held in a cell with a white man arrested for drunkenness while Chaney was kept in a rear cell with a black man charged with vagrancy. They were fed a chicken dinner but were not allowed to use the phone. When COFO workers called at about 5:30 P.M. looking for them, the woman minding the desk said they were not there. At about 10 P.M. all three were released after paying a twenty-dollar fine. Deputy Price sent them on their way, saying, "Now, let's see how quick y'all can get out of Neshoba County."

Mount Nebo Missionary Baptist Church
257 Carver Avenue

The only memorial in Philadelphia to the three slain Movement workers stands in front of this church, where mass meetings were held and where the congregation pushed for the vote. This church also participates in an annual exchange program, set up by a church in Philadelphia, Pennsylvania, in 1964, to promote racial under-standing.

At a ceremony two years after the slayings, on June 24, 1966, King led a memorial service here, followed by a march to the court-house downtown. The church also was the headquarters for a coun-tywide boycott in 1966 to protest repeated incidents of police brutality. The memorial to the three slain workers was dedicated in 1976 through a fund-raising effort led by local activist Lillie Jones.

COFO/MFDP Office
242–44 Carver Avenue

Unlike many communities where activists often attempted to operate in secret, the COFO office here was visible for all to see. It was marked by a large COFO sign, showing black and white hands linked together, which was mounted atop this office and now is on display in the Old Capitol Museum in Jackson.

The office was set up under the leadership of COFO's Ralph Featherstone on August 13, 1964—one week after the burial of James Chaney—to coordinate the first Freedom Schools in Neshoba County. Featherstone sought to continue the efforts begun by the three slain civil rights workers who had begun organizing before the summer. COFO workers here initially were harassed by a group of white men and the sheriff's office, which questioned the validity of the lease and took surveillance photographs. The project was housed here for part of 1964 and into 1965. Movement workers came to refer to the nightly parade of drive-by insults and police lights as the Comedy of Terrors.

The building was originally owned by Calloway Cole of Longdale

Lillie Jones with COFO worker Alan Schiffman outside her house on Carver Avenue, with the Neshoba County COFO/MFDP office in the background, 1965. (Florence Mars/Courtesy Mississippi Department of Archives and History)

and later by Amos McClelland, the leading businessman on the section of Carver Avenue known as the Hill. He also owned a cafe across the street called McClelland's (245 Carver Avenue), which still exists. COFO meetings were held downstairs, and the COFO workers lived upstairs. The office housed the all-important phone and mimeograph machine. In the 1950s the building had housed a hotel run by Charles Evers, brother of Medgar, during his days as a fast-talking DJ. Evers also ran a taxi company and urged blacks to register to vote until he left town for Chicago in 1956. The building is now a day-care center.

Site of Lillie Jones House
241 Carver Avenue

Lillie ("Aunt Lil") Jones, energetic, talkative, and dynamic in her late sixties, surveyed and encouraged the Movement from her porch rocking chair here, across the street from the COFO office. Her husband came from one of several black families that had owned land in Longdale since Reconstruction. Aunt Lil's house was at the crest of the Hill. It was an ideal lookout post for cars coming down the street, "a mudhole in winter and a dustbowl in summer," as one local historian put it. Jones aided the Movement by working locally and traveling to Ohio and Michigan to raise money for the cause. While in her eighties, she spearheaded the effort to install the memorial in front of the Mount Nebo Baptist Church down the street, which was dedicated on December 12, 1976. Her house has been torn down, and the land is owned by the Goodway Baptist Church. She died on December 9, 1983, and is buried in the Mount Zion Methodist Church cemetery.

Hattiesburg, Mississippi

Vernon Dahmer's Courageous Stand

Hattiesburg, a post–World War II boomtown, represents both the heights and the depths of the Movement. In 1964 the Freedom Schools, which later became models for community assistance programs and innovative ways to teach history to young people, had their widest reach here. But Hattiesburg also was home to one of the most recalcitrant white registrars in the South and bears the burden of the murder of black businessman Vernon Dahmer, Sr.

The southeast corner of the state had its share of brutal racial slayings. Mack Charles Parker was lynched in Poplarville, to the south of Hattiesburg, in 1959. U.S. Army Corporal Roman Duckworth was shot in a bus as it pulled into his hometown of Taylorsville to the north in 1962.

Signs of change appeared when young organizers Hollis Watkins and Curtis Hayes, who had cut their teeth on campaigns in their native Pike County, began working to register black voters here in 1962. They operated under the wing of Vernon Dahmer, Sr., and the local NAACP, headed by electrician J. C. Fairley. Together they formed the Forrest County Voters League, which convinced handfuls of people to try to register at the Forrest County Courthouse. Most were turned down, and several who were school bus drivers lost their jobs.

For the next five years the black business district on Mobile Street and the county courthouse were the scenes of repeated pickets and arrests pertaining to the right to vote. After the statewide mock vote

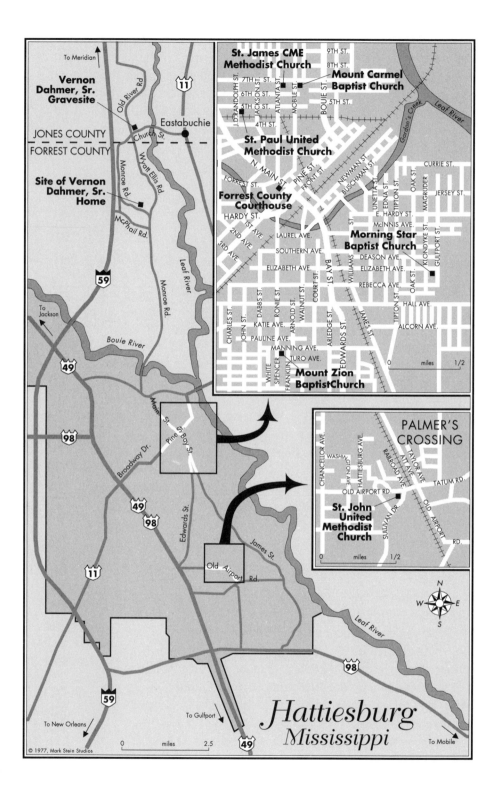

of November 1963, Hattiesburg became the site of the first Freedom Day demonstration in front of the courthouse. The event was designed to highlight exclusionary voting practices that had already been ruled illegal several times. This kind of picket line was imitated in many towns across Mississippi, dispelling the fear typically associated with appearing at the county seat. On January 21, 1964, fifty-one clergymen joined a band of two hundred people and stood in front of the courthouse during a Freedom Day march. Police monitored the gathering and asked black men for their draft cards but declined to break it up. The registrar, then under the media spotlight and dressed in a black suit for the occasion, allowed twelve blacks to take the voting test that day.

Meanwhile south of the city, in a black community called Palmer's Crossing, both adults and children were experiencing a new kind of learning. Building on the model established in South Carolina, Victoria Gray began teaching adult citizenship classes in homes and churches, touting reading and registering as the first two steps to true integration. During Freedom Summer in 1964 Hattiesburg also led the state in Freedom School enrollment with six hundred elementary and high school–age children in classes held in local churches. At the same time teaching led to action. Volunteer teacher Sandra Adickes was arrested in August 1964, after six of her students attempted to check out books from the public library and to sit at a segregated lunch counter.

The Case of Clyde Kennard

In 1959 Clyde Kennard, a farmer and former army sergeant, became the first black to apply for admission to Mississippi Southern College (now the University of Southern Mississippi). Kennard had already completed three years at the University of Chicago and had moved back to Mississippi to help his mother run a chicken farm. Not only was he turned down, but he was also arrested while on campus for his interview after police had planted liquor in his car. Ten days later he was arrested again for storing twenty-five dollars' worth of chicken feed that a black teenager had stolen from a warehouse and placed in his unlocked henhouse. He was sent to Parchman Penitentiary for seven years on the latter charge and was forced to work in the fields even after he was diagnosed with cancer and had lost forty pounds. His imprisonment became a cause célèbre in the Movement, and Governor Barnett ordered his release in 1963, a few months before his death at age thirty-six.

Sandra Adickes and her Freedom School class in Palmer's Crossing, summer 1964. (State Historical Society of Wisconsin)

In 1966 black businessman and farmer Vernon Dahmer, Sr., who had actively encouraged voter registration, was killed in a firebomb attack on his home north of the city. His death produced mass marches in Hattiesburg and promises of swift action from everyone from local prosecutors to President Johnson. With the aid of the testimony of one of the Klansmen who attacked the house, Billy Roy Pitts, three white men were convicted of murder and one of arson. In addition, DOJ filed suit under the 1965 Voting Rights Act, but no one was convicted. Today the Dahmer family, encouraged by the 1994 conviction of Medgar Evers's killer after two prior mistrials, is pressing prosecutors to reopen the case against suspects arrested for, but never convicted of, the crime.

Vernon Dahmer Gravesite
Shady Grove Baptist Church, 101 Church Street

Vernon Dahmer, Sr., was the great-grandson of white slaveholder John Kelly and a slave. After emancipation Kelly left to his slave

Vernon Dahmer, Sr., on his tractor north of Hattiesburg, 1964.
(George Ballis/Take Stock)

children, who had cared for him in old age, substantial tracts of land northwest of Hattiesburg bordering the Leaf River. The area became an integrated community of farmers known as the Kelly Settlement.

By the 1940s Vernon Dahmer was using 340 acres of that land for cotton farming, a grocery store, and a sawmill. Whites and blacks alike hauled pine logs to his mill to be sliced into lumber and finished at a planer mill a few hundred feet from his house. Dahmer had a natural work force in his six sons, and on a Sunday afternoon he was the local Pied Piper, carting fifteen to twenty children from the area in his truck down to the river for a swim. Kids often hung around Dahmer's grocery store under a soda pop sign that read BARQ'S, IT'S GOOD. Although Dahmer had only a tenth-grade education, he had read widely and told his sons as they worked beside him about Adam Clayton Powell, Walter White, and other black activists of the 1940s and 1950s.

Dahmer did business with his white neighbors and lent them his equipment, but when he got involved in the Movement in the 1960s and drove people down to the courthouse to register, he grew more careful. Inviting Freedom Riders to his home in 1961 prompted routine death threats on the phone. Dahmer took to driving his cotton picker with a loaded shotgun in one arm and shut the machine down whenever a car went by in twilight. He and his wife slept in shifts so that the house was guarded through the night.

After the Voting Rights Act of 1965 was passed, the local sheriff allowed people to pay their poll taxes at certain appointed areas outside the city. Dahmer volunteered his store for this purpose and offered to pay for those who couldn't afford the two-dollar fee. When the head of the local NAACP warned him of danger, he said, "There's no saving without sacrifice."

On Monday, January 10, 1966, at about 2:00 A.M., shortly after it was announced on the radio that the Dahmer store would be used as a poll tax center, two carloads of Klansmen pulled up to his house. Dahmer was home with his wife, Ellie, and three young children, Betty, Dennis, and Harold. The assailants first set fire to the store, from which Dahmer's eighty-three-year-old aunt barely escaped in time to avoid injury. Then they shot into the house and tossed jugs of gas and a flaming rag through the broken windows. In short order the eaves of the roof were burning and the living room was a ball of fire. One of the Dahmer children recalls the sound of bald tire rims grinding in the gravel as the Klansmen maneuvered to escape. Dahmer grabbed a rifle and, while shooting back at his attackers, set about getting his family, still in nightclothes, out the back windows of the house. Badly burned and suffering from severe smoke inhalation, Dahmer was the last one out; his daughter Betty had burns on her arms and forehead. By the time the Fire Department came, the house had burned down to the foundation. Dahmer died that afternoon in a local hospital.

The memorial service for him, held at this church, was attended by about five hundred people, including NAACP head Roy Wilkins. Dahmer had been a member and taught Sunday school here. He was buried along with his father, George Dahmer, and other descendants of the Kelly family in the church cemetery.

Sixteen Klansmen—fifteen from nearby Laurel—were charged with murder; four were convicted. Klan leader Sam Bowers was

The eldest four sons of Vernon Dahmer (left to right: George, Martinez, Vernon, Jr., and Alvin) inspect the remains of their home, which burned and killed their father on January 10, 1966.
(Courtesy Vernon Dahmer, Jr.)

tried no less than four times for his alleged role: twice for murder and once each for arson and for federal civil rights violations. All four prosecutions ended in mistrials. Bowers eventually served a six-year sentence in connection with the murder of Chaney, Goodman, and Schwerner in Neshoba County.

The remains of the Dahmer planer mill are off Monroe Road, north of McPhail Road, in an area of the Kelly Settlement where several members of the Dahmer family still live. The Dahmer house was rebuilt with money from the local Chamber of Commerce. Dahmer's wife, Ellie, retired after a long career as a schoolteacher in 1987. She served as Forrest County election commissioner in the 1990s and still lives in the Kelly Settlement.

Forrest County Courthouse
641 Main Street

Theron Lynd, the massive circuit clerk, was a strict enforcer of racially exclusive voting procedures. Since the 1940s he had each of the 285 sections of the Mississippi Constitution written on a note card. When a prospective voter came to register, Lynd plucked one card out of the file, then asked the applicant to write out and explain the section. If the applicant was black, the explanation was almost invariably deemed faulty, although there were no guidelines for determining a passing answer. For example, one black minister with two degrees from Columbia University twice failed the voting test and was told that his membership in the NAACP was the reason. In 1960 most of the twenty-two thousand white residents were registered, while only twenty-five of about seventy-five hundred eligible blacks were.

Such enormous disparities attracted DOJ's attention early on. The department filed one of its first voting rights suits in Forrest County in January 1961. Its arguments were successful on appeal, but the practical result was minimal. By September 1962 only four of one hundred recent black applicants had been added to the rolls. This sham process demonstrated plainly to Washington that stronger measures were needed, and the eventual result was the Voting Rights Act of 1965.

At a march in front of the courthouse on a rainy January 21, 1964, while curious employees peered out the second-story windows, police first asked demonstrators to disperse. When that approach failed, yellow-slickered officers then invited marchers to register four at a time. It was the first time in Hattiesburg the police had allowed a line of marchers to remain without being harassed by them or by white bystanders. Fannie Lou Hamer, the activist from Ruleville, carried a sign that read WHICH SIDE ARE YOU ON?, and the marchers were sustained by little boxes of raisins and Crackerjack. Finally, in 1965, a federal court required Lynd to register 280 black voters who had been rejected. On January 15, 1966, throngs of mourners came to the same courthouse after the death of Vernon Dahmer, Sr., to pray and sing.

After the Voting Rights Act of 1965 took hold, more than five thousand blacks registered to vote. The courtroom, with globe lights and a huge Jim Crow balcony out of *To Kill a Mockingbird,* has been well preserved.

Mount Carmel Baptist Church
641 Mobile Street

Founded in 1886 by a breakaway black congregation from a white church, Mount Carmel under Rev. James Chandler provided the Movement a safe haven. In Movement times Mobile Street was flush with black businesses that stretched from Market Street to the Leaf River. There was no reason to go downtown, except to window-shop, because restaurants, a theater, drugstores, cleaners, filling stations, and professional offices all were within walking distance. The Masonic Temple housed the NAACP and hosted visiting ministers who marched down Mobile Street to City Hall in 1964. Mrs. Woods's boardinghouse at 503 Mobile took in people from out of town, and the Freedom Summer headquarters was right next door at No. 507 (both gone). Today only a few businesses remain from that era. The church continues to be active in voter registration and is currently supporting the effort to reopen the case against those allegedly involved in the killing of Vernon Dahmer, Sr.

St. John United Methodist Church
121 Sullivan Drive, Palmer's Crossing

Here in spring 1962 in this black railroad-crossing community, far from the county courthouse downtown, the Hattiesburg Movement's formative voter registration meeting took place under the aegis of the church's pastor, Rev. L. P. Ponder. Palmer's Crossing also was the neighborhood of Victoria Gray, who attended the early meetings, took over the Hattiesburg SNCC operation in late 1962, and later ran for Congress under the MFDP banner.

The Freedom School curriculum at Palmer's Crossing illustrates how Movement teachers sought to reshape their students' view of the world. The students fashioned their own Declaration of Inde-

St. John United Methodist Church at Palmer's Crossing, 1995. (Townsend Davis)

pendence, based on the supremacy of the U.S. Constitution over Mississippi law. In a map used in class all the familiar streets around the church were given new names: Martin Luther King, Jr., Freedom, and Medgar Evers. This exercise was one of many ways to get children to reimagine their surroundings with an eye toward civic equality. Decades later city councils throughout the South did in fact rename their streets after many of the same Movement figures.

Other Movement Churches in Hattiesburg

Morning Star Baptist Church
1406 Elizabeth Avenue

Freedom Schools were located here, as well as at St. John United Methodist Church at Palmer's Crossing.

Old St. James CME Methodist Church
408 East Seventh Street (now at 705 Country Club Road)

This was the second church to open its doors to the Movement and was the send-off point for a march to the courthouse the Sunday after Vernon Dahmer's death in 1966.

Mount Zion Baptist Church
901 Spencer Street

King spoke here a few months before his death. Mount Zion Baptist was a Movement church from its earliest days; the boycott of a white general store near the NAACP office on Mobile Street, for example, was announced here.

St. Paul United Methodist Church
209 East Fifth Street

The first church to open its doors to the Movement in Hattiesburg.

North Carolina

Greensboro, North Carolina

More Than a Cup of Coffee

Woolworth's

132 South Elm Street

Before malls most southern downtowns had several family-name department stores that offered one-stop shopping. Nearly every sizable town had a Woolworth's, and Greensboro's had been around since 1929. In the early 1960s the shelves were stocked with everything from combs to TV sets, and hot meals were served at a long L-shaped lunch counter.

On February 1, 1960, after a late-night discussion, four black freshmen from North Carolina A&T decided to try to get served in the sprawling store. A half hour before it closed, they bought a few small items, then sat down at the counter and waited. One asked for a cup of coffee. There was no violence, no arrests, no media—and no service. When the store closed, they got up and walked out.

Just as the somber-faced foursome left the building, *Greensboro News & Record* photographer Jack Moebes, lugging his clunky news camera, took the only surviving photo of the historic event. The first three had been members of the NAACP youth group in Greensboro,

Two of the original protesters, Joseph McNeil (left) and Franklin McCain (second from left), return with two classmates for a protest at Woolworth's on Feb. 2, 1960. (John G. ["Jack"] Moebes)

The Menu: "What Can I Get Y'All?"

The menu at Woolworth's during the 1960 sit-ins was typical of lunch counters all over the South:

Roast Turkey Dinner	65 cents
Ham and Cheese Club Sandwich	50 cents
Chicken Pot Pie	55 cents
Chicken Salad Club Sandwich	55 cents
Meat Loaf Dinner	55 cents
Country Steak Dinner	65 cents
Swiss Steak	65 cents
Vegetable Plate	50 cents
Pumpkin, Apple or Cherry Pie	15 cents
Home Style Coconut Layer Cake	15 cents
Banana Split	39 cents
"Shop Refilled" Coke	5 or 10 cents
Fresh Fruit Orangeade	10 cents
Hot Coffee	10 cents
Hot Chocolate with Whipped Topping	10 cents

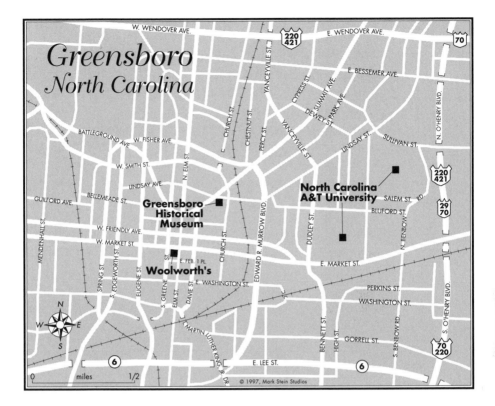

which had been active since the 1940s. On the left was David Richmond, wearing a beret. Next to him was Franklin McCain, the tallest of the group, wearing a soldier's cap. Ezell Blair, Jr., who carried a paper bag in one hand, was next. Joseph McNeil, from Wilmington, North Carolina, wore a white coat.

It was not the first sit-in. CORE had sponsored restaurant sit-ins in the North as far back as a 1942 campaign at Stoner's, a white-tablecloth restaurant on the Chicago Loop. CORE had started similar campaigns in St. Louis in 1949 and Baltimore in 1953. It also had tried to integrate an ice-cream stand at an Esso station in Marion, South Carolina, in 1959. Other individual efforts at desegregation in southern stores in the late 1950s had not made much headway.

But from the beginning the Greensboro sit-ins electrified those who were looking for a way to demonstrate discontent with segregation outside the courtroom. The following day, February 2, twenty-three men and four women visited the Woolworth's, with similar results. The next day the sit-in had filled sixty-three of the sixty-six seats at the counter. Dr. George Simkins, president of the Greensboro NAACP, called on CORE for advice about how to keep the campaign going.

With CORE's help and the media spotlight news of the sit-ins spread like concentric ripples on a still pond. Floyd McKissick, who later headed CORE, led a sit-in in Durham on February 8. "CORE has been on the front page of every newspaper in North Carolina for two days," exulted an organizer traveling to colleges and high schools in Greensboro, Raleigh, Chapel Hill, and High Point. Lincoln's Birthday brought the first demonstration in South Carolina, led by one hundred students in Rock Hill. The next day CORE led a sit-in in Tallahassee, Florida.

By the end of March the sit-ins had spread to sixty-nine southern cities. Woolworth's national sales showed a 9 percent drop from the previous March as a result of a CORE-led boycott and the commotion caused by the sit-ins. These efforts produced the first wave of agreements to integrate not just Woolworth's but all the major downtown stores. By July Greensboro and 27 other border state cities had adopted integration in some form. By spring 1961, 140 had come around.

Pledges to desegrate hardly brought calm to Greensboro. In spring 1963 more than a thousand protesters, led by North Carolina A&T student council president Jesse Jackson, marched each night, raising the arrest totals to more than nine hundred. On May 19 CORE president James Farmer led a march of two thousand to the Greensboro rehabilitation center (then serving as a makeshift jail). Swayed by these massive turnouts and a boycott of Greensboro's businesses, the city agreed to a biracial commission, and the marches were suspended. Greensboro was slow to implement changes, however, prompting five hundred exuberant students to occupy the area in front of City Hall. The following week, fifty Greensboro restaurants, motels, and theaters abolished the color line in exchange for an end to street demonstrations.

Woolworth's closed its doors here in 1993. The final meal at the counter was attended by all four original protesters, and the management reverted to 1960 menu prices as a tribute. Today plans are afoot for a three-floor museum created by a nonprofit group called Sit-In Movement, Inc. A portion of the counter, now shaped like four successive horseshoes, ringed with turquoise and pink vinyl seats, will remain on the street level in the back. Portions of the original counter are in the Greensboro Historical Museum (130 Summit Avenue) as part of an exhibit, but one section of the original remains in the store. Outside on the sidewalk are bronze footprints of the four original protesters.

Raleigh, North Carolina

The Rise and Fall of SNCC

Site of Greenleaf Hall, Shaw University

118 East South Street (between Wilmington and Blount Streets)

No organization existed in spring 1960 to harness the sit-in movement then moving through the Carolinas and the rest of the South. Ella Baker, a lifelong activist and executive director of SCLC, borrowed eight hundred dollars from SCLC and secured her alma mater, Shaw University, to set up the first forum for the protesters to sit down together. She felt strongly that the college students should have their own organization apart from the hierarchical, preacher-dominated SCLC. The Student Nonviolent Coordinating Committee (SNCC) was conceived as a nonorganization, a link between campuses in the North and South that nurtured local Movements.

The conference was held April 15–17, 1960, at this school, originally chartered by the state of North Carolina for former slave families and later a seminary for black women. "It was hot that night upstairs in the auditorium," recalled Jane Stembridge, one of SNCC's first staffers. "There was no SNCC, no ad hoc committees, no funds, just people who did not know what to expect. . . . It was inspiring because it was the beginning and because, in a sense, it was the purest moment." More than two hundred students showed up to hear King, James Lawson, and Ella Baker, who delivered a speech entitled "More Than a Hamburger" that sought to look beyond the heady sit-ins to a vision of structural change. In October 1960 SNCC moved to Atlanta and became a permanent organization.

In the early days SNCC was a conduit for sit-in news from sixteen states. As sit-ins accelerated, it set up shop in a corner of the SCLC office in Atlanta. "We could hardly put this newsletter together because so much was happening," declared the fourth issue of the SNCC newspaper, the *Student Voice*. "Suits us!" One of SNCC's visible acts during the first year was to send Marion Barry to the Democratic National Convention to urge federal enforcement of civil rights and to rebut former President Truman's charge that the sit-ins were Communist-inspired. SNCC workers also accosted President Eisen-

Conference at Shaw University, where SNCC was founded in March 1960: (Left to right) the Reverends Wyatt Tee Walker, Ralph Abernathy, King (sitting), Douglas Moore, Fred Shuttlesworth (sitting), and James Lawson.
(Don Uhrbrock/*Life* Magazine © Time, Inc.)

hower in the twilight of his term in December 1960 at the Bobby Jones Golf Course in Augusta, Georgia. In February 1961 a sit-in in Rock Hill, South Carolina, initiated the practice of "jail, no bail." An even more daring mission of mercy involved replacing the original Freedom Riders after violence in Birmingham in May of that same year.

Into this maelstrom walked James Forman, a teacher from Chicago with a mix of unique talents. A pipe-smoking, articulate man, Forman had a background in management, a flair for publicity, and a fervent devotion to the Movement. When he joined SNCC in Atlanta in fall 1961, he had to jimmy the door to get in because no one had given him the key to the office. The first few weeks involved cribbing office supplies, food, and lodging from sympathizers in an effort to build an organization without steady funding. "Organizationally we were infants," Forman noted later. Under his leadership SNCC became a more formal organization with the mission of serving as a much-needed spark to challenge segregation in southern communities.

In an effort to remain purely democratic and decentralized, SNCC meetings were renowned for being long on debate, short on resolution. As activist Joyce Ladner put it, "SNCC people would argue with a signpost." SNCC workers generally worked long hours for paltry and sporadic pay (forty dollars a week); endured beatings, intimidation, and twisted legal sanctions; and brought concrete programs to communities where other groups had not dared to venture. SNCC workers soon became known as the shock troops of the Movement.

James Forman and the SNCC staff singing in the SNCC headquarters on Raymond Street in Atlanta, 1964. (Danny Lyon/Magnum Photos)

In August 1961 SNCC began its first voting rights project, in McComb, Mississippi, under Bob Moses; that was followed by one in Albany, Georgia, under Charles Sherrod. The field reports from this period are full of insights into the depth of racism in the community as well as youthful exuberance, loneliness, and fear. "Sherrod is writing like a drunk Jack Kerouac," reported SNCC communications director Julian Bond in a note to Moses, "and O'Neal and Chatfield write like drunk Sherrods." In the cities SNCC combined a mixture of traditional voter registration work and direct action, which involved testing bus stations, restaurants, and movie theaters across the South. By spring 1963 SNCC staffers were running mass meetings and voting drives in rural regions where no activist had gone before: southwest Georgia, the Mississippi Delta, the Alabama Black Belt. The average age of the southwest Georgia staff, for example, was twenty-one. By 1964 SNCC had 150 people on its staff.

Its protean nature was both a blessing and a curse. "They met anywhere at any time," recalled an older Mississippi activist who guided many a SNCC worker around his community. "If eleven people who the power structure considered leaders went to jail this evening, tomorrow morning you have eleven more out there. And the next morning, eleven more." Harassment was backed by extreme legal sanctions. In 1962 three SNCC workers working in Baton Rouge, Louisiana, including chairman Chuck McDew, were charged with criminal anarchy for plotting to overthrow the state government, an offense carrying a sentence of ten years' hard labor and requiring bail that dwarfed SNCC's monthly operating budget. SNCC maintained its independence from SCLC and the NAACP but had only a fraction of their resources.

During Freedom Summer SNCC worked under the COFO umbrella in Mississippi and raised money. It published a pamphlet for seven cents that listed sixty-four acts of violence against SNCC workers in Mississippi. After the Voting Rights Act was passed in 1965, SNCC focused on assisting new black voters to understand the mechanics of local government.

By that time the organization's goals were splintering, and financial strain was showing. SNCC did not endorse the march in Selma known as Bloody Sunday, although SNCC chairman John Lewis helped lead it. That same year Cleveland Sellers, SNCC program director, was jailed for refusing military service in Vietnam. SNCC organized around the black panther logo in Lowndes County, Alabama, and raised the cry of "Black Power" during the Meredith March of 1966. The election of Stokely Carmichael as chairman that same year marked a shift toward Pan-Africanism, black self-sufficiency, and skepticism of white liberals. Many founding members disappeared to finish their degrees, try their hand at politics, or simply start new lives elsewhere.

Riven by personal disagreements, an ill-fated alliance with the Black Panther Party in California, heavy law enforcement pressure, lack of funds, and clashing agendas, SNCC could not last much longer. It held its last meeting in June 1969.

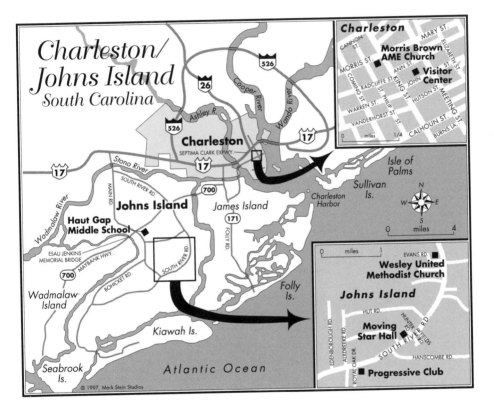

Charleston/
Johns Island
South Carolina

Charleston

MARY ST.
CANNON ST.
MORRIS ST.
**Morris Brown
AME Church**
ELIZABETH ST.
ANN ST.
**Visitor
Center**
COMING ST.
RADCLIFFE ST.
ST. PHILIP ST.
KING ST.
JOHN ST.
HUTSON ST.
MEETING ST.
WARREN ST.
VANDERHORST ST.
CALHOUN ST.
BURNS LA.

0 miles 1/4

526
26
Ashley R.
526
Cooper River
Wando River
17
Charleston
SEPTIMA CLARK EXPWY.
17
Stono River
SOUTH RIVER RD.
17
700
Johns Island
James Island
MAIN RD.
Wadmalaw River
**Haut Gap
Middle School**
171
FOLLY RD.
ESAU JENKINS
MEMORIAL BRIDGE
700
MAYBANK HWY.
SOUTH RIVER RD.
BOHICKET RD.
**Wadmalaw
Island**
Kiawah Is.
Folly
Is.
**Seabrook
Is.**
Atlantic Ocean
© 1997, Mark Stein Studios

*Charleston
Harbor*
*Sullivan
Is.*
**Isle of
Palms**

N
W   E
S
0 miles 4

0 miles
EVANS RD.
**Wesley United
Methodist Church**
Johns Island
HUT RD.
EDENBOROUGH RD.
AULDBROOKE RD.
**Moving
Star Hall**
HUNTER RD.
FIELDS
SOUTH RIVER RD.
HANSCOMBE RD.
ROYAL OAK DR.
Progressive Club

South Carolina

Charleston/Johns Island, South Carolina

The Citizenship Schools

The literacy tests South Carolina imposed on prospective black voters served an unintended function before they were swept away by the Civil Rights Act of 1965. In the process of mastering them some blacks came to see reading as the portal to first-class citizenship and community change. On Johns Island, a Sea Island off Charleston, citizenship classes in the 1950s designed to teach voter registration became the model for classes throughout the South. Their broader aims were to remedy the deficits of segregated education and to encourage local people to push for better conditions in their hometowns.

Before a bridge was built in 1929, getting to the isolated community on Johns Island required an eight-hour trip through creeks and swamps in a small rowboat or ferry. Most of the island's inhabitants were descendants of cotton plantation slaves who lived off peas, corn, and potatoes. Dirt roads wound through arcades of long-limbed, gnarled oaks draped in Spanish moss. Johns Island was the last repository of a rich, lively Gullah culture that grew from a combination of African, Caribbean, and European influences and carried its own English dialect, a wealth of folktales and medicines, and an old-style, praise house form of Christianity.

The island lacked modern facilities. Many residents ate the food that grew wild and in their fields and sold what they did not eat in Charleston. Sometimes the rivers and forests were bounteous; a hard season produced bouts of malnutrition. It was not uncommon to see wood houses wallpapered with newspaper and paste. Until the construction of Haut Gap High School (1861 Bohicket Road) in 1951 schools for blacks only went up to seventh grade with one teacher for all grades. Despite these difficult conditions, Johns Island was fertile ground for Movement organizing. Many people owned their own land, which gave them a measure of independence. Some had participated in successful strikes in the oyster and fish trades, and others had heard about blacks voting during Reconstruction.

South Carolina had been the site of several pioneering legal cases involving teacher salaries, segregated buses, and the exclusion of blacks from political primaries. Federal Judge Julius Waties Waring applied the Supreme Court decision requiring that primary elections be open to all races to Charleston in a ruling in 1947. The challenge to segregation in the Clarendon County schools by the Briggs family of Summerton became one of the cases consolidated into the U.S. Supreme Court's monumental ruling in *Brown* in May 1954. But in the 1950s Charleston itself still was hamstrung by segregation, and Johns Island was its majority-black outpost.

One institution that took an early interest in Johns Island was the Highlander Folk School in the mountains of Monteagle, Tennessee. Highlander had begun experimental schools in rural Alabama and Tennessee to train community leaders, but they had achieved mixed results. Highlander director Myles Horton and his wife, Zilphia, made several trips to the island starting in 1954. At preliminary meetings local people began to examine the reason why less than 30 percent of blacks were registered to vote.

That same year Highlander received its first visit from Septima Poinsette Clark, a Charleston schoolteacher. Her father, born a slave, was named for rice plantation owner Joel Poinsette, who as an emissary in Mexico had brought back the red-leafed flowering plant that became known as the poinsettia. Mrs. Clark first taught school in the patched log cabins of Johns Island for twenty-five dollars a month and wrote lessons out on dry cleaners' bags instead of a blackboard. In the 1920s she petitioned for the hiring of black teachers and principals in the Charleston public schools and was active in the Charleston YWCA and NAACP. When she revealed her NAACP membership in 1956, she was dismissed without a pension from her job in the Charleston school system after a long teaching career.

In 1955 her driver on a return visit to Highlander was Esau Jenkins, a Johns Island farmer who had made initial efforts to encourage voter registration in the 1940s and in 1956 ran for, and nearly won, a seat on a local school board. He and the other Johns Islanders who journeyed to Highlander believed that adult illiteracy was the primary obstacle to social and economic progress. In those days South Carolina was like other states that administered obscure civic questions for voting. After blacks made sporadic efforts to register, local officials relied even more heavily than before on literacy requirements and new technicalities to keep the rolls predominantly white.

Jenkins wanted to set up an adult reading class at night, and after permission to hold classes at the black school was denied for fear of white retaliation, he turned to Highlander for support. His request dovetailed with Highlander's interest in self-generating community education, and the school agreed to sponsor the first citizenship school, held in the back of a food co-op store on Johns Island called the Progressive Club.

Alice Wine (second from left), Septima Clark (center), and Bernice Robinson (standing) at a citizenship class on Johns Island during the 1950s. (Ida Berman)

View from the Front of the Classroom

Bernice Robinson, the first citizenship school teacher, described the first weeks of the class in this letter to her sponsors at Highlander:

"The school which we planned for three months is in progress and the people have shown great interest. They are so anxious to learn. I have fourteen adults, four men and ten women, and there are thirteen high school girls enrolled to learn sewing. There are three adults that have had to start from scratch because they could not read or write. I start out by having them spell their names. About eight of them can read a little, but very poorly. So far, I have been using that part of the South Carolina Constitution that they must know in order to register. From that, I take words that they find hard to pronounce and drill them in spelling and pronunciation and also the meaning of the words so they will know what they are saying. We have to give them some arithmetic. The men are particularly interested in figures.

"I have never before in my life seen such anxious people. They really want to learn and are so proud of the little gains they have made so far. When I get to the club each night, half of them are already there and have their homework ready for me to see. I tacked up the Declaration of Human Rights on the wall and told them that I wanted each of them to be able to read and understand the entire thing before the end of the school."[41]

The first citizenship class started in January 1957 during the laying-by season between harvesting and planting. Fourteen students learned the words and meaning of the South Carolina voting laws as well as how to order products from a catalog and how to fill out a money order. The next year more students came to a three-month course, and similar classes were set up on the nearby islands of Wadmalaw, Edisto, Daufuskie, and St. Helena. More than sixty people from the first two classes went into Charleston and registered to vote. Perhaps more important, residents urged others to do the same and began a series of community meetings on other issues, such as housing, taxes, and the need for a food cooperative, broadening the concept of citizenship from voting to full participation in public affairs. By the winter of 1959–60 the number of registered voters on Johns Island had tripled since the elections of 1956. Charleston newspapers discovered the existence of the Sea Islands citizenship schools a full three years after their semisecret creation.

In 1960 Highlander decided to replicate the Sea Island citizenship schools in other areas of the South, and they spread across a six-hundred-mile radius. Successful citizenship classes were organized in Huntsville, Alabama, and Savannah, Georgia. In 1961 Highlander sponsored four workshops to train eighty-eight teachers who led citizenship classes in Georgia, Alabama, and South Carolina, with a total enrollment of about fifteen hundred. The requirements for teaching were simple: some high school education, the ability to read well and write legibly on a blackboard, and knowledge of local government.

After the state of Tennessee temporarily shut down Highlander, the citizenship school training center moved to Dorchester Academy in Liberty County, Georgia, in July 1961 and was placed under the auspices of SCLC. From 1961 to 1965 sixteen hundred people of all ages were trained in citizenship teaching, passing their knowledge on to twenty-five thousand adult students from the East Coast to the Mississippi Delta.

In June 1963 Charleston itself was the subject of a broad ten-point NAACP campaign that demanded desegregation of everything from swimming pools to hospitals and the absorption of black workers into all levels of local government. Nine hundred demonstrators were arrested at desegregation targets such as the Fort Sumter Hotel, the Heart of Charleston Motel, the Chow Mein Inn, theaters, lunch

---

My Citizenship Booklet

By 1961 the curriculum developed by Bernice Robinson on Johns Island was incorporated into a booklet designed for use in other communities. In addition to explaining the voter registration requirements in a particular state, the booklet contained a civics minidictionary (under t: treasurer, trial, treason, and testimony), an explanation of the Social Security number, a sample "friendly" business letter, blank forms for mail orders and money orders, math problems ("Ten students were arrested in the sit-in movement and were fined $75.00 apiece. How much fine was paid?"), a lesson in manners, and sample stories to introduce new word groups. Here is a sample story designed to practice words that can be found within the word registration:

"Etta and Rita met ten students at the train station. For ten minutes the rain came down in torrents. It made great holes in the roads. It splashed off the tar roofs and flowed into drains on the side of the curb. It looked as if a ton of rotten leaves was being carried into strange openings made by the water.

"Suddenly the rain stopped, the sun came out and we went with the students to register. It was such a treat to look into the eyes of each stranger and see the satisfaction each had as the testing period ended. The great strain was over. Now they could wear a tag which reads, 'I have registered, have you?' "[42]

counters, city parks, and swimming pools. The cumulative total amount of bail rose to more than one million dollars. Demonstrations, picketing, and boycotts every day for thirteen weeks wore down the King Street merchants and the city, which in August agreed to operate on a desegregated basis.

Meanwhile the citizenship campaigns and parallel efforts by CORE were altering the makeup of state voter rolls, and fast. In 1960 there were 58,000 registered black voters in the state, and the registration offices were open only two days a month in Charleston County. Two years later there were 91,000 registered black voters statewide; by 1967 that number had climbed to 191,000, with registration offices in local communities open every day.

In April 1969 Charleston became the target of the last of SCLC's full-scale city campaigns. It began with local efforts to organize a hospital workers' association at South Carolina Medical College Hospital; twelve workers active in the drive were fired. Backed by a state law prohibiting negotiation with unions, the city declined to rehire them or to negotiate over wages, which averaged around $1.30 an hour for the kitchen and cleaning staff and nurses' aides. More than four hundred of the workers at the Medical College Hospital and Charleston County Hospital, most of them black, promptly walked off the job in protest. The campaign was masterminded by SCLC, hospital workers' Local 1199, which had won union recognition in the North, and Bill Saunders. Saunders was a Johns Island native and Korean War veteran who had attended a workshop at Highlander and coedited the radical *Low Country Newsletter*, which was printed on Johns Island. After a decline in the summer tourist trade and the prospect of a possible strike by unionized harbor workers, which would have tied up a five-hundred-million-dollar trading hub, the hospitals agreed to rehire the fired workers, allow a grievance procedure, and improve salaries and benefits, although the settlement did not include union recognition.

Today Johns Island is much changed since the 1960s. Federal grants have enabled the creation of low-cost housing, a nursing home, a health clinic, and a pharmacy. With the intervention of Esau Jenkins and Rev. Willis T. Goodwin, the pastor of five churches in the Sea Islands, including Wesley United Methodist Church, a group called Rural Mission began providing health assistance and Head Start education to the island in the late 1960s. Rural Mission was expanded to include health care and nursing under the Sea Island Comprehensive Health Care Corporation. Today literacy classes are among a wide range of community programs offered by

Striking hospital workers on a Charleston street, June 1969. (AP/Wide World Photos)

Our Lady of Mercy Community Outreach Services designed to improve the lives of the island's needy. Despite the improvements, Johns Island still stands in stark contrast with the luxury resorts developed on the adjacent islands of Seabrook and Kiawah. Luxury sedans zip along the paved roads of Johns Island to reach the security gates of the resorts.

Septima Clark, who had moved to Highlander to work full-time as director of education in 1957, returned to Charleston and was elected to the countywide school board in 1972. She remained

Septima Clark on Experiments

"**D**on't ever think that everything went right. It didn't. Many times there were failures. But we had to mull over those failures and work until we could get them ironed out. The only reason why I thought the Citizenship School program was right was because when people went down to register and vote, they were able to register and vote. They received their registration certificate. Then I knew that what I did must have been right. But I didn't know it before. It was an experiment that I was trying. . . . But I couldn't be sure that the experiment was going to work. I don't think anybody can be sure. You just try and see if it's coming."[43]

active in civil rights until her death in 1987. Today, as Route 17 enters Charleston, it becomes the Septima P. Clark Expressway. The Esau Jenkins Memorial Bridge over Church Creek links Johns Island with Wadmalaw Island.

Progressive Club

River Road at Royal Oak Drive, Johns Island

Esau Jenkins often worked at the co-op general store in this building, where the first citizenship classes in the nation took place. Proceeds from sales helped repay the fifteen hundred dollars given by the Highlander Folk School to revive the building, formerly a dilapidated schoolhouse. The goal was for all members of the club to become registered voters; they contributed about a dollar a month toward expenses. Classes were held for four years in two back rooms, which had no windows in order to avoid easy detection. Sleeping quarters for visitors were added in 1962, and a gym built the next year was used by students at Haut Gap High School.

From the start the citizenship classes were unlike traditional ones. Septima Clark's first qualification for a full-time teacher was someone who was not "highfalutin" and would not talk down to adults. She approached her cousin Bernice Robinson, a beautician

Bill Jenkins, son of Esau Jenkins, standing in 1995 outside the Progressive Club on Johns Island, where the first citizenship classes were held. (Townsend Davis)

who had worked on previous voter registration drives but had never taught before. Robinson agreed to try, and she opened the first class by discarding the elementary school materials she had brought and asking the fourteen people who attended what they wanted to learn.

They wanted to register to vote, but three of them could not read or write. Robinson asked them to trace their names over and over on a piece of poster board until they got them right. Some students used to handling a plow found it difficult to handle the delicate task of holding a pencil, but eventually they learned to write their names in cursive script without punching through the paper. They wrote out stories about farming from their daily lives and learned to read them aloud. She also introduced them to the South Carolina Constitution and the local election laws, which they learned word by word, syllable by syllable. A group of teenage girls also joined the class to learn to crochet. The classes met three times a week and ended with songs known on the island or freedom songs imported from Highlander. For many it was a revelation unlike any they had experienced. Robinson encouraged them to think critically and to speak up in class. She reported that those who successfully registered "came back to school fairly shouting."

Bernice Robinson taught classes in 1957 and 1958, then traveled several hundred miles a week in 1959 to supervise seven teachers at citizenship schools on the islands and to recruit students from around the state. Even as the citizenship teacher training moved to the Dorchester Center in Georgia, this club continued to host community education classes. It fell into disrepair in the 1980s and was nearly demolished by Hurricane Hugo in 1989. It is still standing but is not currently in use.

Moving Star Hall

River Road at Fields Road, Johns Island

In this wooden structure Johns Islanders kept alive the interdenominational praise house worship of plantation times through community effort and fervent singing. The Moving Star Young Association was first created to provide a gathering place and to collect money for health benefits and burials, in the tradition of the mutual aid societies of freed ex-slaves. Members banded together to tend to the sick and to perform as pallbearers and gravediggers. The hall itself was built in 1916 by the community, and at meetings one to three times a week members took turns praying and singing without the lead of a preacher. On special occasions, such as the Christmas

Eve and New Year's Eve watch celebrations, meetings went from midnight until daybreak.

These meetings were precursors of the most frequent Movement gatherings, the evening mass meetings. Led by strong singers, such as Johns Island native Janie Hunter, spirituals and hymns were sung in a shout style, unaccompanied by instruments other than stomping feet and clapping hands. The meetings served as reminders of the hardships of slavery and the perseverance of the participants' forebears. One of their songs, "Keep Your Eyes on the Prize," was heard by white folksinger Guy Carawan, who had first come to the island in 1959 to assist with the citizenship school and who later lived on the island for two years. He took the song back to Highlander and taught it to Highlander's many Movement visitors. It subsequently became a popular freedom song and the theme song for the 1986 television documentary about the Movement, "Eyes on the Prize." During a revival of interest in Gullah culture in the 1960s the Moving Star Hall Singers toured the country and cut three albums. Today the hall is owned by a Pentecostal church pastored by David Hunter.

Esau Jenkins Gravesite

Wesley United Methodist Church, 2726 River Road, Johns Island

In the late 1940s farmer Esau Jenkins supported his wife and seven children by trucking the vegetables he grew in his field on Legereville Road to market in Charleston. Along the way he gave rides to schoolchildren, tobacco farmers, longshoremen, and whoever else needed a lift into town. Eventually Jenkins bought himself a bus to make the trip. One morning he typed up the voting registration procedures, passed them out to the bus passengers, and began explaining. Even though she could not read, an elderly woman named Alice Wine memorized the required sections. When she later went to the registration office on Society Street in Charleston, she corrected the pronunciation of the woman in front of her in line who had stumbled over the word *miscegenation*. The registrar barked, "No coaching, please!" Wine had no problems registering herself and from then on was heard to say to her friends and neighbors, "I've got my card. Have you got yours?"

Jenkins saw the rolling classroom as the model for something larger. As a young man he had studied at night school to improve his formal education, which ended in the fourth grade. He realized that potential voters like Mrs. Wine could benefit from a broader introduction to the levers of government after they had overcome low literacy and years of viewing Charleston as a far-off mystery not worth studying. In summer 1955 Jenkins raised concern about illiteracy at a Highlander conference. Both he and the people at Highlander agreed Johns Island was an ideal place for the first citizenship schools because as early as the mid-fifties local people were already attending packed meetings to discuss their community problems. When Jenkins ran for the school board in 1956 and lost by a hundred votes, he spurred a number of black citizens to register for the first time.

From 1957 on Jenkins and others ran the Progressive Club store, where citizenship classes were held. He made frequent trips to Highlander to report on the program and to design new ones to move beyond the simple act of registration to full participation in voting, school boards, and local governance. The Citizens Committee of Charleston County advocated the hiring of the first black bus drivers and set up a voter information office, complete with a voting machine, in Charleston. Jenkins was persistent. When a minister once asked him to speak at a church on the condition that he refrain from mentioning a nascent credit union for the island's black residents, Jenkins began with a traditional prayer asking for God's blessings but couldn't resist praying for the credit union as well. The Community Organization Federal Credit Union became a reality in

Esau Jenkins (right), longtime activist from Johns Island. (Courtesy Highlander Research and Education Center)

1966 and extended credit to Johns Island and Charleston County residents previously unable to obtain it.

Jenkins was a family man, conducting a service at his home each Sunday and explaining to his children that being black was no barrier to achievement. They grew up with the usual conditions of a Movement household: surprise visits from well-traveled activists such as Martin Luther King, Jr., and Stokely Carmichael, police tagging behind them wherever they went, and phones that brought either vulgar threats of violence or the peculiar clicks, delays, and other oddities characteristic of a bugged line. Six of Jenkins's children were trained as teachers. Daughter Ethel Grimball started the citizenship school on Wadmalaw Island during the second year of the program, and another daughter, Elaine, was among the first black students at Charleston High School.

Esau Jenkins died in 1972 in a car accident while driving to Highlander. His headstone reads: "Love is Progress. Hate is Expensive," a saying that used to be lettered on the back of one of his buses. His wife, Janie, is still living.

The Philosophy of Esau Jenkins

"I have two question [sic] asked to me by other people. The question was, how was I able to educate five children and live, born and raised on Johns Island—have never taught a school in my life, have never work for the government—and they all have made good grades in school, and they have been very mannerable to everybody. The way you raise your children, you can make 'em be lovable in this world, or you make 'em be hated by people, so it's your responsibility. Since God is kind enough to give you a child, then you ought to raise 'em the way he should go.

"Then a man came to me and ask me, said, 'Look, I notice them buses you have look so nice, and I understand you have sent all your children to school and you have gotten some property you own and doing some business. Where do you buy your hoodoo root from?'

"Now you know that's silly. Hoodoo business. That's the thing that make people poor, because they believe in root. So I said to him. . . . 'Look friend, where I got my root from, it only takes obedience and a simple mind to go home and go into your closet and get on your knees and ask God for what you want.'

"And I tell you one thing: every progress that I have made in life, it came to me while I was doing some good for somebody."[44]

Morris Brown AME Church

13 Morris Avenue, Charleston

At this church Rev. Ralph Abernathy gave the first speech of SCLC's last citywide campaign, the Charleston hospital workers' strike of April 1969. Abernathy participated in numerous marches down King Street to the Medical College Hospital past lines of national guardsmen and submitted to his twenty-fifth arrest since his first in Montgomery with King thirteen years earlier. Although SCLC used its usual combination of nonviolent workshops and mass meetings, some of the marchers slipped into violence and burned one of Charleston's beloved historic homes. Ultimately the combined forces of the demonstrations, Abernathy's two-week jail term on charges of inciting a riot, and pressure from organized labor forced the city and county to rethink their prior refusal to negotiate with the hospital workers.

Orangeburg, South Carolina

The Other Kent State

The fatal shooting of three black students on the campus of South Carolina State College in 1968 was one of the Movement's darkest hours. Whites misunderstood the growing impatience of black students with traditional protests against inequality and overreacted to it. The impact of the shootings first was dulled by shoddy press accounts, then was eclipsed by the assassination of King two months later and the shootings at Kent State in Ohio two years later. Nonetheless it demonstrated that even after a dozen years of civil rights demonstrations, boycotts, lawsuits, and legislation all across the South, no city or town was immune from racial violence.

Orangeburg, about halfway between the state capital at Columbia and the coastal city of Charleston, had long been a center for black higher education in South Carolina. Claflin College was established in 1869 by northern philanthropist Lee Claflin and provided agricultural training to blacks under the auspices of the Methodist Episcopal Church. In 1896 the state legislature created a land-grant college

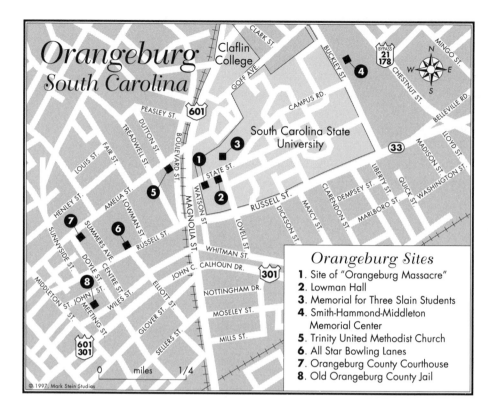

Orangeburg
South Carolina

Claflin College

South Carolina State University

Orangeburg Sites

1. Site of "Orangeburg Massacre"
2. Lowman Hall
3. Memorial for Three Slain Students
4. Smith-Hammond-Middleton Memorial Center
5. Trinity United Methodist Church
6. All Star Bowling Lanes
7. Orangeburg County Courthouse
8. Old Orangeburg County Jail

© 1997, Mark Stein Studios

nearby called the Colored Normal Industrial, Agricultural and Mechanical College of South Carolina, which in 1954 became South Carolina State College. About twenty miles southwest of Orangeburg was the small town of Denmark, home of another black college, Voorhees.

When news spread of the student sit-ins in Greensboro in February 1960, Orangeburg felt some of their earliest ripples. Organizers from CORE came to Claflin College and State College later that month in a statewide tour of South Carolina. Before SNCC even existed and the Nashville students had fully mobilized, CORE organizers held some of the first classes on nonviolent sit-in methods. Students were taught how to ball up and protect their eyes and heads from expected assaults and how to withstand showers of verbal and physical abuse. Several hundred Orangeburg students received such training.

Students carefully surveyed downtown Orangeburg and selected the Kress store as their first sit-in target. In late February a mass march proceeded downtown as shops hurriedly closed. No violence or arrests ensued. On March 14, in subfreezing weather, police responded to students by spraying them with tear gas and water blasts. They rounded up five hundred students, who jammed the local jail. The overflow arrestees were held in a chicken coop bounded by a seven-foot wire fence. State College's president next erected a fence with a barbed-wire fringe to separate the Claflin and State College campuses. Students called it the Berlin Wall. Charles McDew, a sociology major at State College who led the marching downtown, later became the second chairman of SNCC, serving from 1960 to 1963.

The academic enclaves and the town of Orangeburg could not have been more separate in those days. Most of the town's twenty thousand residents were white, and both the state headquarters of Truth about Civil Turmoil (TACT), an ultra-right-wing group, and segregationist Southern Methodist College were located there. George Wallace's state campaign manager in 1968 was the owner of a local radio station, WDIX. Although racial moderation had prevailed in some areas of the state since the admission of black architecture student Harvey Gantt to Clemson College in 1963, Orangeburg was still a world unto itself in 1968.

Entertainment for black students, who were not allowed at the drive-in theater and had to abide by college-imposed curfews, was limited. One prominent outlet explicitly closed to black students was the local bowling alley, near the campus on Russell Street. On February 5, 1968, State College senior John Stronman led a group of about three dozen students from Lowman Hall down to the bowling alley, which was closed on orders of the city police chief. The next day another group of students arrived, and this time the bowling alley was surrounded by police carrying nightsticks. The students were admitted to the bowling alley for about twenty-five minutes, then were arrested for trespassing.

When students on campus got word of the arrests, they went to the bowling alley to confront the officers, who had called for reinforcements. Despite Stronman's attempts to calm the crowd, which had grown to about four hundred students, jeers of "honky" and "burn, baby, burn" went up. After the city sent a fire truck to the scene, the crowd got even more restless, and a student broke a small window near the front door. Police then pushed out from the building, swinging clubs indiscriminately, felling both male and female students, and sending the remainder scampering back toward the campus. On the way back students broke the windows of several stores, including a Lincoln-Mercury dealer, and damaged a number of parked cars. More than a dozen students were treated at the college infirmary and at a local hospital, as were some of the officers. The governor put 250 national guardsmen on alert. Meanwhile patrons at the All Star Bowling Lanes continued to bowl the night away, apparently not aware of what had happened.

The next morning students presented a list of grievances to City Hall, requesting not only integration of the bowling alley but also action on police brutality and desegregation of the city work force, hospitals, and drive-in theaters. The city was noncommittal and looked to the federal government to take the initiative. That night armed national guardsmen set up roadblocks at U.S. 601 and Russell Street near the campus and in front of the bowling alley.

The next day, February 8, students attended classes as usual, and the college president, Maceo Nance, circulated a memo pledging support for the demands on City Hall but requesting that students stay on campus and remain calm. State officials pointed to nonstudent activist Cleveland Sellers as an "outside agitator" responsible for keeping tensions high. There were rumors of another student march. The National Guard was sent to protect public utilities on the theory that they would be the next targets, and the governor ordered their ranks boosted to more than four hundred by nightfall.

That night patrolmen first blocked off any marching route to the

South Carolina national guardsmen and highway patrolmen guarding the South Carolina State College campus after disturbances there, February 12, 1968. (UPI/Corbis-Bettmann)

Orangeburg

bowling alley and then encamped on the edge of the campus. A few students hurled debris at the officers, who opened fire on the students spread across the campus lawn. Three students were killed and twenty-seven injured in a hail of gunfire that caught most of the student victims in the rear or the side.

The aftermath was plagued by differences in perception that were exacerbated by conflicting press accounts and the conversion of Orangeburg into an occupied city. To politicians and many other whites, students had rushed the officers and even engaged them in gunfire, fulfilling the apocalyptic rhetoric of Black Power. Students remember brandishing no weapons at all, milling about in the dark at a time when tension was actually ebbing, and fleeing from officers who were either panicked or vengeful or both. Those espousing the latter view called it the Orangeburg Massacre.

Classes were suspended for two weeks at both Claflin and State College while DOJ filed briefs to desegregate the bowling alley and the local hospital. A federal judge ordered the alley desegregated, and on the first day of resumed classes, students John Stronman and James P. Davis bowled the first integrated frames at All Star Bowling Lanes. Martin Luther King, Jr., then in the midst of promoting the upcoming Poor People's Campaign, called for a trial of the officers who had shot the students, while SNCC chairman Rap Brown called for armed revenge, opining that the deaths and injuries were "too high a price to pay for a goddamn bowling alley." Students from the colleges staged vocal protests at the state Capitol in Columbia, prompting the governor to propose capital improvements for the college without admitting the officers had done anything wrong.

Cleveland Sellers, who had been injured in the shooting, was indicted for a staggering array of crimes related to the events of February 8, 1968. More than two years later he was tried on rioting charges in a barricaded Orangeburg County Courthouse in September 1970 and found guilty. He was sentenced to one year in prison, prompting his lawyer to label the event "the first one-man riot in history." Nine white officers involved in the shooting were tried under federal civil rights laws in Florence, South Carolina, in May 1969. They were found not guilty. Sellers, the only person convicted in the entire affair, served his sentence in 1974.

South Carolina State University
Watson and State Streets

Student life at State College (now University) in the mid-sixties was strict, still modeled on the dignified, industrious example of

Booker T. Washington's Tuskegee Institute. Students were required to wear coats and ties for the Sunday meal, attend chapel, and sit in assigned seats in class; only three absences were allowed per semester. Compared with its white counterparts, or even with its black counterparts in other states, State College was woefully underfunded.

By 1967 student discontent was brewing. Three white visiting professors were suspended for encouraging students to question the anachronistic nature of their education, which was largely devoid of civil rights discussions. Students responded by protesting in front of the college president's house. When three of them were suspended, the students, at the urging of senior class president Isaac Williams, boycotted classes for two weeks. The dispute was settled after students and NAACP representatives met with South Carolina Governor Robert McNair, who pledged to upgrade the quality of education at the college, and a federal court determined that the suspension of the protesters violated free speech. Students were given a voice in college affairs and were allowed to form an NAACP chapter. They

Cleveland Sellers in 1996, standing at the memorial for three slain students on the campus of South Carolina State University. (Jessica Allan)

also were granted permission to form a more militant group called the Black Awareness Coordinating Committee (BACC), modeled on SNCC and championed by young activist Cleveland Sellers, who lived near the campus but was not a student.

After a series of marches from campus to the bowling alley in town, the corner of Watson and State streets became the scene of the deadly standoff on February 8, 1968. Students made a bonfire of construction materials at the tip of the median dividing Watson Street and College Avenue near the entrance to the campus. Officers heard reports of a fizzled attempt to burn a warehouse, and sporadic gunfire was audible near the Claflin campus. After a bugle "charge" call from Lowman Hall, set back several hundred feet from the road, students from the State College campus added fuel to the bonfire, taunted the officers, and sang "We Shall Overcome" and "We Shall Not Be Moved." Four squads of highway patrolmen climbed up the embankment and occupied the corner periphery of the campus while a fire truck came and doused the fire in the street.

Most of the students then retreated toward the dorm, but stragglers remained in front of Lowman Hall. Some continued to insult the officers who were grouped on either side of the path with firearms pointed toward the hall. The highway patrol had been instructed to shoot only as a last resort. After an officer was felled by a flying wooden banister, one officer fired, apparently as a warning. Several other officers followed in a ten-second crossfire aimed at the students silhouetted on the lawn. Students who were not taken down by the shots either ran or crawled for cover.

Sophomore Henry Smith was hit with five shots in the chest, back, and neck; he spun around from their impact and fell to the ground. Smith had been active in BACC, had participated in the bowling alley protests, and had helped set the bonfire. He died that night in the emergency room of the still-segregated Orangeburg Hospital. Two other students who had nothing to do with the Movement also were killed: Samuel Hammond, a State College football player shot in the back, and Delano Middleton, a high school student whose mother worked as a maid at the college. Mrs. Middleton made it to the hospital in time to hold her son's hand and to recite the Twenty-third Psalm before he died. "You've been a good mama," he said just before he died, "but I'm gonna leave you now."

Today the lawn where the shootings took place is occupied by an administrative building. A stone memorial column for the three students stands in a small park across the street, where a memorial service is held each February. The Smith Hammond Middleton

The Odyssey of Cleveland Sellers

Cleveland Sellers was raised on hopes of equality in Denmark, South Carolina, population three thousand. His Movement journey led him through the most hazardous corridors of SNCC militancy, injury and prosecution in Orangeburg, and, finally, peace with his home state.

As a child Sellers took the segregated balconies of the Denmark movie theater and other strictures of segregation as givens. His father ran a taxi and motel business, and his mother was a dietitian. Sellers was an acolyte at the Episcopal church, a good and courteous student. But certain things began to gnaw at him. One was the 1955 killing in Mississippi of Emmett Till, a boy only three years older than he was. He found reports of the Greensboro sit-ins of 1960 exhilarating and helped orchestrate a copycat sit-in at a local drugstore. By the end of that year, at the age of fifteen, Sellers had already applied for an NAACP youth charter separate from the more conservative adult organization.

In 1964, after meeting activists Stokely Carmichael and Courtland Cox at Howard University, Sellers earned his first stripes on the SNCC front lines. In April he left college to join a protest against the appearance of George Wallace at a skating rink in Cambridge, Maryland. When a line of marchers met a line of troopers, Sellers struggled with a trooper, was buried by a protective pile-on of his peers, and retreated with them in a fog of noxious gas and gunfire. He was arrested and spent two days in jail.

That summer in Mississippi he joined secretive all-night searches for the three civil rights workers killed at the outset of Freedom Summer. "The tension that accompanied the coming of night centered in the abdomen," he later wrote. "It was precise and tended to heighten all the senses." The Movement search parties were so careful to avoid detection they shed their belt buckles to reduce light reflections and instead hitched up their pants with cord. Once the bodies were found, Sellers returned to his post at the SNCC office in Holly Springs, Mississippi, where he registered voters, taught children in Freedom Schools, and outfoxed, or outdrove, cops who questioned his right even to be in the state.

By 1966 SNCC was identifying with Third World liberation movements, denouncing U.S. involvement in Vietnam, and turning from integration to black nationalism. The election of Howard classmate Stokely Carmichael as chairman accelerated this trend. Sellers, who had become SNCC program secretary, joined Carmichael for the Meredith March through Mississippi. He also was arrested in Atlanta for refusing to heed his draft notice.

He first came back to Orangeburg in October 1967 to encourage the study of black history and culture at State College. He was more interested in structural changes at the college than in breaking the color line at the bowling alley. On the night of the shootings Sellers was not urging the students on but trying to lay low on campus. When the patrolmen started firing, Sellers, who was closer to Lowman Hall than to the line of troopers, saw bodies dropping in front of him until he felt the sting of a shot in the left shoulder. He dragged himself on his stomach through gutters, behind trees, and into a dormitory. From that point on the blame for the conflict fell on him. His criminal charges were patent overkill: arson, inciting to riot, assault and battery with intent to kill, and various property crimes, with bond of fifty thousand dollars. These charges hung over his head for the next two and a half years, and he was barred from appearing within five miles of Orangeburg.

Meanwhile Sellers was tried on his draft charge and attended the funeral of King in Atlanta by pushing his way into the memorial service along with other SNCC confreres. He was convicted on a concealed weapons charge in Louisiana. By this time, by his own account, "I didn't know if I was going or coming." He lived near the black universities in west Atlanta under constant surveillance, hustled for food, and encouraged students to take up arms in self-defense. On top of it all, SNCC was falling apart.

Through his attorney Sellers arranged to teach a course in black ideology at Cornell University in 1969, which led to his enrollment in a master's program at Harvard's School of Education. After his trial on the Orangeburg riot charges (the other charges were dismissed), he served eight months in prison, during which his first child was born. He then lived in Greensboro for twenty years, ran for city council, and got a Ph.D. in education administration from the University of North Carolina at Greensboro. But the Orangeburg conviction eliminated any chance of a university position. In 1993, twenty-five years after the Orangeburg shootings, South Carolina Educational Radio refused to broadcast a radio documentary on the subject, which prompted a public reexamination of the tragedy. On July 20, 1993, Sellers was granted a pardon for the riot conviction. That fall he began teaching in the African-American Studies Department at the University of South Carolina in Columbia. Today he is an assistant professor of history there.

Cleveland Sellers at the Orangeburg County Courthouse after his arraignment on riot charges connected with unrest on campus on February 8, 1968. (Dean Livingston/*Orangeburg Times & Democrat*)

Memorial Center, an auditorium, was dedicated in 1969.

Trinity United Methodist Church

185 Boulevard Street NE

Established in 1866 and now situated across the railroad tracks from the South Carolina State University campus, this church was a Movement meeting place and headquarters. The pastor during that period was Rev. Matthew D. McCollom.

All Star Bowling Lanes

559 East Russell Street NE

Orangeburg's only bowling alley, with its sign BOWL WHERE YOU SEE THE MAGIC TRIANGLE, became a focal point for black college students aspiring to equal treatment in Orangeburg. For years blacks had asked permission to bowl here, requesting one night a week for their own league. Owner Harry Floyd's answer was clear: He did not want to open the lanes to blacks. He first posted a whites-only sign and then changed it to one that said PRIVATELY OWNED. A dean of State College made several pleas to open the alley to all races, going so far as to consult the federal Community Relations Service, the local Chamber of Commerce, and the American Bowling Congress. But Floyd would not change his mind. Devoted black bowlers had to drive to Columbia, forty miles away, to satisfy their urge.

After the passage of the Civil Rights Act in 1964, Orangeburg's restaurants complied with its mandate to serve all customers regardless of race. But it was unclear whether this bowling alley, which had a snack bar, legally was bound by the act. Owner Floyd continued to assert that he could serve, and not serve, whomever he wanted. After the first march in February 1968 he asked members of the city council and the governor to protect his property.

On February 6 officers arrived here and repelled a crowd of students who had shown up to protest the arrest of their classmates. By the next day the students, the city, and the governor were wrestling with a list of ten long-standing racial grievances and facing an escalating armed occupation of the city that left the bowling alley in the background. Two nights later came two shootings on the State College campus, and the bowling alley was desegregated by court order shortly thereafter. By late February black students were admitted for the first time.

From that point on about a third of the bowling alley's customers have been black. "Never had a bit of trouble since that one time," owner Floyd later put it. One loyal customer in subsequent years was John Stronman, the black student leader, who bowled a 279 in February 1978, just after the shootings had receded ten years into history.

Orangeburg County Jail
229 Meeting Street

Dubbed the Pink Palace because of its turrets and lavender white-wash, this county jail was one of the first to hold large numbers of Movement protesters. Student marchers were arrested and held here beginning in 1960. In 1963 other marchers were taken out in front of the jail and hosed down with water during intensive protests. Although its bars are still visible, the jail is currently inactive.

The Pink Palace, formerly the Orangeburg County Jail, where protesters were held, photographed in 1996. (Jessica Allan)

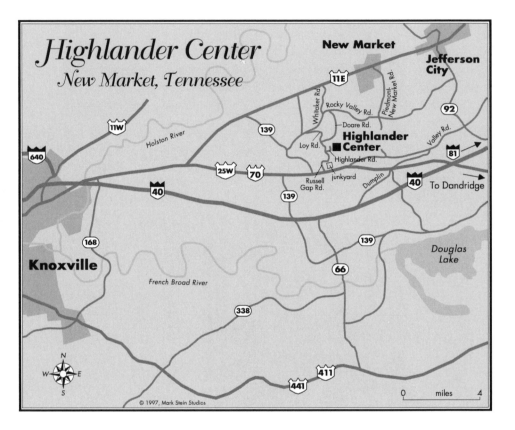

Highlander Center
New Market, Tennessee

New Market

Jefferson City

Knoxville

Tennessee

New Market, Tennessee

Movement Haven in the Mountains

Highlander Research and Education Center
1959 Highlander Way

Set apart from the world in the Cumberland Mountains, the Highlander Center has served as a Movement refuge and a place to put the torrent of events into perspective. Highlander was founded in 1932 by two white theology students, Myles Horton and Don West, as an incubator of social change in the South. The school deliberately avoided traditional models of education and vocational training. Instead it drew on the varied experiences of its students or, as one chronicler of Highlander put it, sought to "start their education where they are." Over the years Highlander has hosted miners and farmers, workers and union members, students and professors, community organizers and cultural activists, whose only common trait was a zeal for grass roots organizing.

It was an unlikely Movement haven. Rosa Parks, who attended a Highlander workshop on integration of the public schools in 1955, recalled taking a bus from her native Montgomery up into the Tennessee hills and seeing steadily fewer black faces. Few black families lived in Monteagle, northwest of Chattanooga in Grundy County, where the school was originally located. But since the 1940s the Highlander Folk School, as it was first known, was one of the few places in the South where blacks and whites could gather undisturbed. Visitors from Johns Island were so unaccustomed to eating with whites that they brought their own chickens to eat. Black visitors often returned home to report their experiences in the oasis of integration. As one young woman from Birmingham told her church upon returning, "We sang together, we talked together, and we washed dishes together."

Raised in Savannah, Tennessee, Horton got the idea for a mountain school after studying at Union Theological Seminary under theologian Reinhold Niebuhr. He refined the idea by visiting folk schools in Denmark that fostered agricultural traditions. Early programs at Highlander concentrated on training labor leaders, which drew Horton into a bitter strike of textile workers in North Lumberton, North Carolina, in 1937. The school's programs were racially

A meeting room at the Highlander Center in the mountains near New Market, 1995.
(Townsend Davis)

integrated from the beginning, and programs in the 1950s examined school integration in the wake of *Brown*. When Martin Luther King, Jr., came to Highlander to deliver a keynote speech in 1957, an undercover government agent shot a photo of him sitting in the audience. That photograph became one of the longest-lived pieces of racist propaganda he was to face. Georgia officials printed 250,000 copies with the headline MARTIN LUTHER KING AT COMMUNIST TRAINING SCHOOL, an image that kept popping up on billboards and in newspaper ads for the next decade.

Isolated and unorthodox, Highlander had always fired the imaginations of racists and Red-baiters. One newspaper reporter from Charleston, South Carolina, wrote that the flat-topped meetinghouse doubled as a landing pad for Russian helicopters. A hostile caller once asked, "How many mulattoes you got running around over there?" The Highlander staffer who answered the phone replied, "How many have you lost?" Sometimes the staff tried to win over its critics, as when Horton left an applesauce cake for an investigating FBI agent in 1941 along with a note inviting him to dinner. Highlander had loyal supporters in Monteagle, including a local schoolteacher named May Justus. But by 1959 Tennessee law enforcers had heard enough. They conducted a raid of the school grounds and brought a trumped-up charge of bootlegging. The Highlander property, including Horton's log cabin home, was forfeited and sold at public auction, and the school moved to a two-story house in Knoxville (1625 Riverside Drive, now demolished), across the street from a marble-cutting plant. Even then Tennessee lawmakers sought to excise "this cancerous growth from our state and cast it out to die in the richness of Americanism and loyalty," as one resolution put it. The Klan paraded by the school in full regalia.

Starting in 1957 with the establishment of the citizenship schools, which taught reading and civics to adults in the Sea Islands, Highlander played a crucial role in the Movement. It housed some of James Lawson's early recruits from the Nashville Movement. At one of its last workshops at Monteagle in August 1961 SNCC workers thrashed out whether to focus on voter registration (which attracted foundation money and the approval of the Kennedy administration) or direct action (prototypically sit-ins). After lengthy debate SNCC decided to form two wings to pursue both goals simultaneously. Through the mid-sixties Highlander sponsored civil rights workshops all across Mississippi, Georgia, and the Carolinas based on the citizenship school model.

After returning to the mountains and settling near New Market in 1972, Highlander also returned to its roots, sponsoring programs on poverty, mountain culture, and the environment. Today a workshop at Highlander is pretty much as it was in the 1930s. Meals are announced by a large bell, discussion of social change is mixed with music, and all participants are encouraged to put learning immediately into practice upon returning home. Although run from a meeting room filled with rocking chairs, Highlander workshops do not dwell on nostalgia or calm reflection but continually renew the school's mission of engagement with vigorous discussion and debate.

The Development of "We Shall Overcome" as Movement Anthem

The song originated with a traditional hymn called "I'll Be All Right," which carried a similar melody to the one we know today. The lyrics went: "If in my heart, I do not yield, I will be all right someday." In some areas the song was sung as "I'll Overcome" or "I Will Overcome," and this version was in widespread use by the end of the nineteenth century. In 1901 a black Methodist minister published a song "I'll Overcome Some Day," based on a different tune but with the same lyrics on the theme of spiritual perseverance.

During the 1940s the traditional church version was used by tobacco workers in the Charleston, South Carolina, area to open union meetings. In 1947 a group of white workers came to Highlander for a workshop and taught the song to Zilphia Horton, the music director and wife of the cofounder. She in turn rewrote the song based on the old melody and published it in Highlander songbooks under the title "We Will Overcome." Folksinger Pete Seeger, a frequent Highlander visitor, changed it to "We Shall Overcome" and added new verses. Another verse of the same song, "We Are Not Afraid," was composed by a Montgomery high school student named Mary Ethel Dozier during a police raid on Highlander in 1959.

When Movement students first came to Highlander in April 1960, they heard the song from Guy Carawan, who had taken over as music director. He introduced it at the founding of SNCC in Raleigh that same month. SNCC activists spread it to many towns and cities in the South in the coming years. The song was embellished and popularized during the Albany Movement of December 1961. In July 1963 one music critic called it "The Marseillaise" of the Movement, although no commercial recording or sheet music had yet become available. Eventually the song was copyrighted by the four folksingers who had a hand in its rearrangement and dissemination, and profits from it went to a special fund for the Food and Tobacco Workers and the Movement generally.[45]

Nashville, Tennessee

The University of Nonviolence

Nashville was the Movement's research laboratory. In most cities civil rights campaigns bubbled up like lava after an incident provided focus for long-standing racial injustices. Nashville had its share of these. But here the nonviolent sit-in was first methodically theorized, practiced, and tested months before four students in North Carolina publicized the method. The Nashville students also were the first to achieve concrete results, producing the first voluntary agreement to desegregate stores in a southern city.

With its high levels of education and exact replica of the Parthenon, Nashville viewed itself as the Athens of the South, a bastion of civilization. Blacks had long played a political role here, leading the

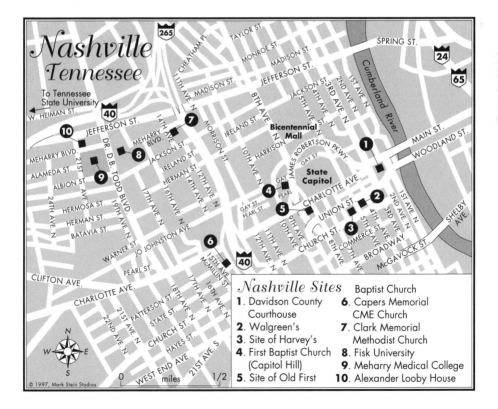

Nashville Tennessee

Nashville Sites

1. Davidson County Courthouse
2. Walgreen's
3. Site of Harvey's
4. First Baptist Church (Capitol Hill)
5. Site of Old First Baptist Church
6. Capers Memorial CME Church
7. Clark Memorial Methodist Church
8. Fisk University
9. Meharry Medical College
10. Alexander Looby House

© 1997, Mark Stein Studios

charge against the poll tax in the 1950s and constituting 43 percent of the city's population by 1960. They also were spending an estimated fifty million dollars locally, giving them clout that proved helpful when the Movement took hold. As was common in southern shopping districts, blacks in Nashville were welcome to buy merchandise but were not allowed to sit at a lunch counter, use the bathroom, or drink at a bar with whites. The auditorium, train station, and bus depot all were segregated, as were the public parks. Although barber Alfred Z. Kelley had filed one of the first lawsuits to integrate the schools in 1955, Nashville's grade-a-year integration plan became a model for resisting the *Brown* decision through delay and gradualism. The schools issue flared into violence in Clinton in 1957, which necessitated calling in the National Guard, and a revival of Klan activity in Nashville in 1957–58 resulted in the bombing of the integrated Hattie Cotton School and a Jewish Community Center that hosted biracial meetings.

Simultaneously a group of young black preachers was giving new meaning to the social gospel. On January 18, 1958, they met at Capers Memorial CME Church (315 Fifteenth Avenue North) to form the Nashville Christian Leadership Council (NCLC), an affiliate of SCLC, which had been formed the year before. The ministers were joined by James Lawson, who came to Nashville to study at the divinity school at Vanderbilt after studying abroad in India. Lawson ran workshops on nonviolence under the sponsorship of a Christian peace group called the Fellowship of Reconciliation. After practicing nonviolent protest techniques and discussing them in evening meetings through 1959, Lawson and a group of his students conducted their first test sit-ins in November and December. They went to two major downtown department stores, Harvey's and Cain-Sloan, bought small items, and sat at the lunch counters. When they were refused service, they simply left. Yet even this was considered an affront, as many whites viewed the breaking of bread as a societal sacrament to be shared only with their own kind.

Events in Greensboro the following February forced the Nashville group to accelerate its program. Douglas Moore, a North Carolina minister involved in the Greensboro sit-ins, called Lawson to request a sympathy demonstration. Although NCLC had a grand total of $87.50 in its treasury and the elders urged caution, the students convinced them that the time for half measures was past. Lawson started a crash course in nonviolence, which included instruction on how to minimize injuries and obey loitering laws. He

Rehearsing the Nonviolent Demonstration

Nonviolence workshops began at the First Baptist Church on March 26–28, 1958. At age twenty-nine Rev. James Lawson was already the professor emeritus of nonviolence. He had studied the teachings of Gandhi in India, been jailed as a conscientious objector to the Korean War, and studied the early Movement with great care.

Joining Lawson at the first workshops in the First Baptist basement were Glenn Smiley, a white colleague at the Fellowship of Reconciliation who had ridden beside Martin Luther King, Jr., during the first integrated bus trips in Montgomery, and Anna Holden, a white CORE organizer. By February 1959 the workshops were attracting students, other preachers, and members of the First Baptist congregation.

Usually the workshops began in the evening with a topic selected by Lawson. Then the participants simulated a lunch counter sit-in, rotating roles as heckler and protester. To toughen the protesters to likely harassment, the hecklers blew smoke in their faces, shouted insults, and jostled them. Afterward the participants described their feelings and assessed whether to take the next step, which was to go downtown to sit in at a public counter. Unlike previous efforts of the NAACP or CORE, the goal was publicity of injustice and moral suasion rather than creation of a legal test case.

The hallmark of Lawson's teaching was a disciplined application of the Christian notion of turning the other cheek. Students adhered closely to it while in jail, where they held regular prayer meetings, singing, and study periods. The jailer confessed he had never seen anything like it. As student leader Peggy Alexander reported, "Students went to the county workhouse and with every floor that was mopped, window that was washed, bar that was polished, or wall that was washed came the replenishment of faith, determination, love and hope. Love reigned supreme." In March 1960 Lawson himself was arrested for conspiracy to obstruct commerce and was hustled out of the First Baptist Church past the announcement for the Sunday sermon: "Father, Forgive Them."

Such euphoria made Nashville students eager to join the Freedom Rides in Alabama and attracted them to crises all across the South in the 1960s.

specified coats and ties for men and stockings and heels for women who wanted to venture into the fray.

Throughout February downtown Nashville saw increasing waves of student protesters sitting in. They were coordinated by a student advisory council whose members met daily, appointed leaders for each lunch counter, and phoned in their observations from watch

A march from north Nashville into downtown passes the state Capitol in September 1961. (*Nashville Tennessean*/Courtesy G. Rollie Adams and Ralph Jerry Christian)

posts at downtown phone booths. About three hundred students were arrested that month for disorderly conduct. More surprising still was the students' decision to serve out their jail terms, although the black community had hastily collected enough bail money for all of them. In a dramatic trial, at which the entire black bar of Nashville lined up to represent the protesters and spectators packed the Nashville courtroom, the students were sentenced to thirty-three days at the county workhouse. The more serious charge of conspiracy to obstruct trade was brought against students who sat in at bus terminals and at the Greyhound counter, where four students were severely beaten. Through their endurance the students convinced many skeptical whites that their cause was serious and not some springtime college prank.

James Lawson was seen as the mastermind of the operation, a "ramrod of strife," as the local paper put it. He was summarily expelled from Vanderbilt, prompting ten of the sixteen Divinity faculty to quit. Fisk economist Dr. Vivian Henderson and Rev. Kelly Miller Smith led the call for an Easter boycott of all downtown stores, which put a significant crimp in business. "The violence that preceded the boycott kept the white people out of town, and then none of the Negroes were coming to town," one merchant complained. "I sort of felt that the only customers we had left were the green people, and there aren't too many of them."

Then the bombing of black lawyer Alexander Looby's home brought the Movement out in numbers. Hours after the explosion on April 19, 1960, three thousand protesters from the black colleges and Pearl High School marched silently to the steps of City Hall. Mayor Ben West met the crowd at the top of the steps and, after a dialogue with the marchers, declared his support for integration of the lunch counters. On May 10 six leading stores, including Harvey's and Cain-

A firefighter examines damage to the house of Alexander Looby, Movement lawyer. The blast on April 19, 1960, blew out windows across the street. (UPI/Corbis-Bettmann)

Sloan, declared that blacks would be served on an equal basis. It took several more campaigns to make the pledge stick: sit-ins in November 1960 that resulted in the fumigation of students at Krystal Grill and the ejection of students at gunpoint from the Tic Toc Restaurant; protests at movie theaters in 1961; "sleep-ins" at hotels in 1962; and an all-out assault on discriminatory hiring and service in 1963–64. Ultimately the model the students created in 1960 erased most of Nashville's Jim Crow system before the implementation of the Civil Rights Act of 1964. With the notable exception of the schools, Nashville became an example for other southern cities.

First Baptist Church (Capitol Hill)
900 James Robertson Parkway

In most cities Movement activities were scattered among a few churches and civic groups, but in Nashville they were centered in this church. Like Dexter Avenue Baptist Church and the Capitol in Alabama, First Baptist stood in the shadow of the authority it opposed, the Tennessee legislature, perched on a nearby hill. First Baptist, formerly at 319 Eighth Avenue North and descended from the church of Nashville's first ordained black minister, was the ideal center for nonviolent experiments and workshops, which began here in 1958.

Rev. Kelly Miller Smith outside the old First Baptist Church at its Eighth Avenue location. (Photographic Archives/Vanderbilt University)

Nashville: Graduates of the University of Nonviolence

An extraordinary number of Movement leaders got their start in Nashville. Under the tutelage of James Lawson in 1959–60 these young people first wrestled with the implications of nonviolence in workshops and got their first taste of jail. Within a year they were active in SCLC, the fledgling SNCC, and programs at the Highlander Folk School. They served harrowing terms at the Parchman Penitentiary in the Mississippi Delta. The Nashville group responded to crises with bold five-alarm protests. They rushed to join jailed SNCC workers in Rock Hill, South Carolina, took over for adult Freedom Riders in Birmingham, and offered to continue the march of the slain postal worker William Moore through northern Alabama. Their organizational energy was felt throughout the South for the next decade.

Marion Barry: From Itta Bena, Mississippi, and Memphis. Fisk student who gave up a graduate school scholarship to work in the Movement. First chairman of SNCC and leader of a direct-action wing of SNCC that inspired the student sit-in at a bus station in McComb, Mississippi, and many other demonstrations. Later four-time mayor of Washington, D.C., who revived his political career after a narcotics conviction while in office.

James Bevel: Also from Itta Bena. Started as a student at American Baptist Theological Seminary, a visionary preacher and organizer with a knack for reaching young people. Freedom Rider. Wore a yarmulke for several years as a tribute to Hebrew prophets. Involved in every major SCLC campaign from Albany to Memphis. With his wife, Diane Nash, proposed the Alabama Project, a widespread nonviolent shutdown of Montgomery in 1963 that was never realized. Solidified his reputation for unpredictability in 1968 by claiming that suspected assassin James Earl Ray was not guilty of shooting King and offering to defend him.

Bernard Lafayette: From Tampa, Florida. Student at American Baptist Theological Seminary. First in his family to attend college, he first confronted segregation during a bus ride with John Lewis going home for Christmas in 1959. Freedom Rider. Sang with Bevel in a Movement doo-wop quartet and organized with him in Jackson, Mississippi, at the end of the Freedom Rides in 1961. Married a Movement coworker and honeymooned in Selma at the outset of a voting campaign there. Currently president of his alma mater, now called American Baptist College.

John Lewis: From Troy, Alabama. One of the first students from American Baptist Theological Seminary to attend the workshops, talked to King about integrating Troy State College but didn't because he was a minor and could not get his parents' consent. Arrested in the first Nashville sit-ins; his mother was informed by letter because his family did not have a phone. Missed giving his senior sermon because he was in jail. Injured in the Freedom Rides and Bloody Sunday, chairman of SNCC, speaker at the March on Washington in 1963.

(Continued on next page)

Devoted Movement soldier who was jailed more than forty times. Now a member of Congress from Atlanta.

Diane Nash: From Chicago. Fisk student and chair of the Nashville student Movement. Iron-willed and serious, with a beauty queen exterior. Was galvanized by the inability of black students to attend movie theaters in Nashville except under Jim Crow conditions. Considered nonviolent protest not just passive resistance but "active insistence" and expressed pride in the term *black* as early as 1961. Freedom Rider. Married Bevel; while pregnant, served ten days in a Mississippi jail for contempt and bore a child in Albany, Georgia, while awaiting a march of Movement wives.

C. T. Vivian: From Boonville, Missouri. Vice-president and head of direct action for NCLC, rose to become director of SCLC affiliates. Beaten during prison term of the Freedom Riders; confronted Dallas County Sheriff Jim Clark on courthouse steps in Selma in 1965. Later formed his own tutoring organization, Visions.

Eloquent, engaged, and handsome, Rev. Kelly Miller Smith gave the Movement forward momentum and helped explain it as the pastor here for thirty-four years. Born in the all-black Mississippi Delta town of Mound Bayou, Smith never lost his memory of a childhood lynch mob. He began preaching in the late 1940s in Vicksburg, where he shook up the black community and made an impression on a teenage Myrlie Evers, a church member there. Smith was a founding member of both SCLC and its Nashville affiliate, NCLC, and he pursued Movement projects with great energy. He volunteered his children for early desegregation suits, he bailed C. T. Vivian out of a Mississippi prison farm where he was held and beaten during the Freedom Rides, and he steadily spun learned sermons, drawing on his degrees from Morehouse and Howard. His collection of essays was entitled *Social Crisis Preaching.*

The church where he preached was razed along with five other black churches in the neighborhood during the conversion of Capitol Hill into a knot of modern parkways. A historical marker stands at the old site, and a spacious new church was built in 1972.

Walgreen's
226 Fifth Avenue North

In February 1960 this bustling shopping street became clogged with gawkers, ruffians, and wailing police cars as well-dressed black students from the Nashville Movement took to the stools of the city's lunch counters. On successive Saturdays, still intent on not missing class, the students led the first mass sit-ins in Nashville at downtown stores. Walgreen's is the last of these still in business.

On February 13, with the city under eight inches of snow, more than one hundred students marched downtown for the first time and held a rally in the Arcade (No. 228), the glass-enclosed shopping corridor with an entrance on Fifth Avenue. They then filtered into the five-and-dime stores on that block: Kress (No. 237), Woolworth's (No. 221), and McClellan's (No. 229). The stores were quickly closed, and the protest ended quietly. The students came again with two hundred protesters on February 18, with the same result.

The largest sit-in yet reached the counter of Walgreen's on February 20, when black and white protesters sat at the counter without service, and the owners put up a sign that read FOUNTAIN CLOSED IN INTEREST OF PUBLIC SAFETY. The staff placed rugs and flower pots on the counter to prevent the students from their usual posture of quietly poring over a textbook once service was denied. "This ain't no study hall room" was a familiar taunt from the hecklers.

The following Saturday, February 27, brought four hundred people and the first arrests. At the McClellan's counter across the street from here, hecklers singled out white protester Paul LaPrad, pulled him from his stool, and beat him until police came and arrested him for disorderly conduct. The other protesters were subjected to insults shouted at close range and cigarette butts on their backs or hair. Eighty other demonstrators went willingly to the police paddy wagon for arrest. They were the first group in Nashville to test the concept of "jail, no bail" to highlight injustice.

The Rules of Engagement

With paper "liberated" from a copy room at American Baptist Theological Seminary, where he studied and worked part-time as a janitor, John Lewis printed and distributed the first of the sit-in rules. This founding document encapsulated all that the students had learned in Lawson's many workshops:

"DON'T . . .

"1. Strike back nor curse if abused

"2. Laugh out

"3. Hold conversations with floor walker

"4. Leave your seat until your leader has given you permission to do so

"5. Block entrances to stores outside nor the aisles inside

"DO . . .

"1. Show yourself friendly and courteous at all times

"2. Sit straight; always face the counter

"3. Report all serious incidents to your leader

"4. Refer information seekers to your leader in a polite manner

"5. Remember the teaching of Jesus Christ, Mahatma Gandhi and Martin Luther King. Love and nonviolence is the way.

"MAY GOD BLESS EACH OF YOU."[47]

Today Walgreen's is part of a historic downtown walking tour designated by a bright paint stripe on the street. The lunch counter was formerly on the left as you enter the store.

Fisk Chapel, Fisk University

1000 Seventeenth Avenue North

Fisk joined three other historically black institutions—Meharry Medical College, American Baptist Theological Seminary, and Tennessee Agricultural and Industrial State College (later Tennessee State University)—to form the foundation of Nashville's student Movement. Fisk was founded by white abolitionists and graduated W. E. B. Du Bois and other academic luminaries. Since 1944, under sociologist Charles S. Johnson, Fisk hosted annual conferences known as the Race Relations Institute. Not surprisingly Fisk was fertile ground for integrationist programs in the 1950s. CORE established a chapter at Fisk in 1956 under the leadership of Anna Holden, who later helped found NCLC. The Fisk Chapel served as a meeting place and launchpad for marches.

A student central committee coordinated the activities of the various campuses. Sometimes the students worked with great speed and took administrators and the police by surprise. After the bombing of Alexander Looby's house, the committee assembled students from all four campuses in a matter of hours; in another instance it commandeered the college's public-address system to spread the word. Student activities in the past had taken place within the campus walls because of segregation downtown, and the sit-in Movement got the students to view themselves as citizens of a city, not just as occupants of an academic enclave.

Before venturing into Alabama to continue the Freedom Rides in May 1961, the Nashville group was warned by its Birmingham supporters not to come because of the prospects for more violence. Several students wrote wills or gave student leader Diane Nash letters to be mailed to relatives. But they were determined to continue the jail-ins they had started in downtown Nashville and tested in Rock Hill, South Carolina. When they arrived in Birmingham, they were

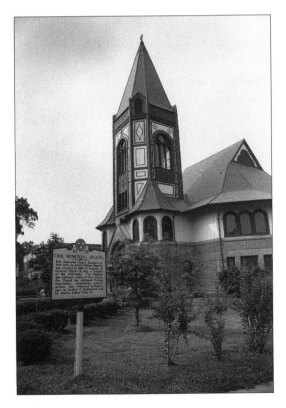

Fisk Memorial Chapel, where Movement meetings were held, photographed in 1995. (Townsend Davis)

escorted by Police Commissioner Bull Connor to the state line and dropped by the side of the road. Undeterred, they returned to Birmingham and carried out the last leg of the Freedom Rides under heavy guard, ending up in jail in Jackson, Mississippi.

In April 1967 addresses by Stokely Carmichael at Fisk and Tennessee A&I brought unrest to the campus. Carmichael had attracted the attention of the state legislature, which prompted calls to deport him to his native West Indies for his advocacy of Black Power. After police responded to a disturbance at a Jefferson Street tavern, students retreated to Fisk, where police faced off against students who pelted them with rocks and other debris. The disturbances caused minor property damage and tainted Nashville's reputation for peaceful protest.

Clark Memorial Methodist Church
1014 Fourteenth Avenue North

Along with First Baptist this was a frequent site of the NCLC workshops and early-morning meetings of student leaders.

Z. Alexander Looby House
2012 Meharry Boulevard

Attorney Alexander Looby was, as his wife puts it, "a heavy sleeper." So heavy that when sticks of dynamite were dropped outside his house at 5:30 A.M. on April 19, 1960, he didn't even stir. The blast knocked out 147 windows in a Meharry Medical College dorm across the street and damaged both Looby's house and the one next door. It was a turning point for the Nashville Movement, prompting a large and unified march to City Hall. The Loobys, meanwhile, spent the night in the janitor's quarters of an Episcopal church.

Looby came to the United States from Antigua, British West Indies, as a boy of fifteen, and he was not conditioned to the customary bowing and scraping expected of blacks in the U.S. South. He attended Howard University and Columbia Law School, taught economics at Fisk, and was first admitted to the Tennessee bar in 1929. As a lawyer for the NAACP during its early school challenges he walked into many a hostile courtroom and once was beaten in the hallway. When told, "Niggers sit in back," in a Memphis court-room, he refused to move and replied: "Let them sit there then."

After two unsuccessful runs at the city council, Looby and Robert Lillard became the first blacks to serve since 1914 when they were elected to the council in 1951. As a councilman Looby was respected for his independence and Buddha-like calm. When eighty-one Nashville students were first arrested in 1960 for sitting in, Looby was their lead counsel.

The day after his house was bombed Looby sat on the platform at a mass rally in the Fisk gymnasium, where King called the Nashville Movement "the best organized and the most disciplined in the Southland." The gym was evacuated after a bomb scare, but after the rally reconvened and the crowd gave Looby a standing ovation, his usually businesslike demeanor cracked. A photograph of him weeping from relief and gratitude ran in black newspapers nation-wide. Today a rebuilt version of the house is still inhabited by his widow, Grafta Looby Westbrook. No perpetrators of the bombing were ever found. Looby died in 1972. Today a library and commu-nity center in Nashville's Metro Center bear his name.

Grafta Looby Westbrook at home in 1995. The house was bombed and sparked a massive street demonstration in 1960. (Townsend Davis)

Davidson County Courthouse/City Hall

When a long line of protesters arrived unannounced at these steps on April 19, 1960, Mayor Ben West came out to greet them. To his left were C. T. Vivian, Diane Nash, and other student leaders, and in front of him stretched a seemingly interminable line snaking back toward north Nashville. Above him on massive bronze doors were six figures signifying Courage, Loyalty, Law, Justice, Security, and Wisdom.

Mayor West was in a tough spot. While serving as state senator from Davidson County, he had sponsored legislation to convert Nashville elections from at-large to single-district voting, allowing blacks to serve for the first time on the city council. Black support had given him the margin of victory in his 1951 run for mayor. But other than the appointment of a biracial committee, West had not made his position on the sit-ins clear.

He first expressed his sympathy for the protesters and a theoretical opposition to racial discrimination. Diane Nash then put the issue to him bluntly: "Do you recommend that the lunch counters be desegregated?" West said yes, and applause filled the plaza. The first desegregation agreement in a southern city soon followed. By midsummer twenty-two other cities had followed Nashville's lead. Today a plaque on the courthouse with a quote from the Book of Joshua commemorates the event.

Memphis, Tennessee

A Strike for Dignity—Assassination

That Martin Luther King, Jr., perished at the hands of a white assassin in Memphis is not only tragic but strange. The river city was known as the Place of Good Abode, and there had been no large-scale racial disturbances since skirmishes between blacks and the Irish in 1866. It lacked the kind of racial strife and plantation justice that caused the Movement to hold other cities up to the world as candidates for drastic social surgery. Black voters had been a part of Democratic politics here since the perennial mayoralties of Edward Hull ("Boss") Crump, who reigned from 1910 until his death in 1954. Blacks were known as the brown screws of his formidable political machine. By 1955 they made up fully a quarter of the voting population, with thirty-five thousand registered. The local NAACP chapter, founded in 1917, was strong and vocal. Memphians were proud of their cultural, business, and educational attainments, forming the foundation of an enlightened region known as the mid-South.

Nonetheless the engine of the Memphis Movement was a familiar one: stark racial inequity accumulated over a period of decades. In the late 1960s the incomes of black families in Shelby County were half that of whites, and about forty-seven thousand of them fell below the poverty line of three thousand dollars a year. More than half of black workers held service or manual labor jobs. Shops along Beale Street bustled with black customers but were mostly run by white owners. In the late 1960s a labor dispute involving the city sanitation workers was brewing, and it brought King to town for his last campaign.

By late 1967 economics was weighing heavily on his mind. As racial obstacles to voting and to customer service in public places began to fade, King spoke increasingly of the unequal burden of poverty and the inadequate resources aligned against it. When he first heard about the sanitation strike in Memphis, he was in the midst of planning the Poor People's Campaign. The most recent campaign, the Meredith March of 1966, had boosted voter registration but had ended without any new initiatives. What King found in Memphis was an opportunity to sound his bedrock themes of unity

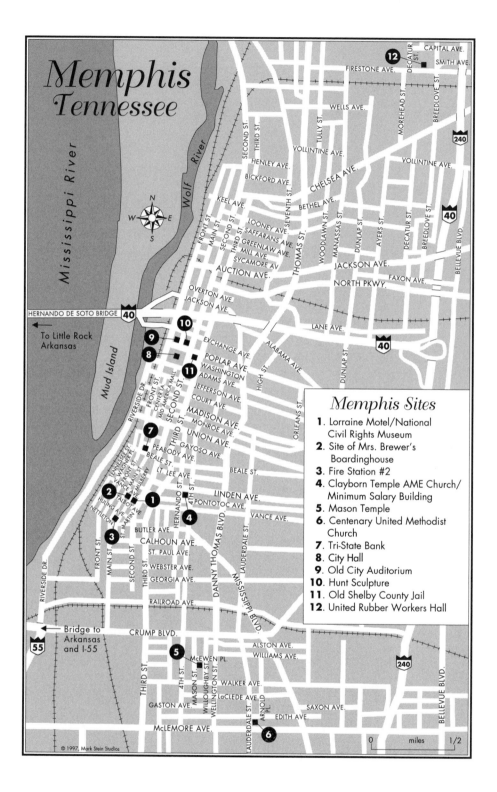

Memphis
Tennessee

Mississippi River

Wolf River

HERNANDO DE SOTO BRIDGE **40**

← To Little Rock
Arkansas

Mud Island

← Bridge to
Arkansas
and I-55

55

Memphis Sites

1. Lorraine Motel/National Civil Rights Museum
2. Site of Mrs. Brewer's Boardinghouse
3. Fire Station #2
4. Clayborn Temple AME Church/ Minimum Salary Building
5. Mason Temple
6. Centenary United Methodist Church
7. Tri-State Bank
8. City Hall
9. Old City Auditorium
10. Hunt Sculpture
11. Old Shelby County Jail
12. United Rubber Workers Hall

© 1997, Mark Stein Studios

0   miles   1/2

and nonviolence, which were increasingly under siege. Of all the city campaigns, the Memphis community's widespread, sustained response to the sanitation workers' strike resembled no effort so much as the bus boycott in Montgomery twelve years earlier. Although it was new territory for him, Memphis was for King a Movement homecoming.

Memphis had quietly dismantled legal segregation beginning in the late 1950s. Black students were first admitted to Memphis State University in 1958. At the urging of the NAACP nearly every aspect of city life followed suit within a few years: the buses, the parks, the boat docks. The NAACP applied equal pressure to private businesses, mounting an eighteen-month picketing and boycott operation against those restaurants, shops, and theaters that discriminated on the basis of race. Far ahead of other big cities in the South, Memphis schools began integrating in 1961, when thirteen black children attended an all-white school under heavy police protection and a news blackout designed to keep things calm.

As encouraging as these developments were, blacks still occupied the lower rungs of the economic ladder. Take the job of city sanitation worker, or tubtoter, which involved hauling heavy bins of garbage for eight hours a day or more for an average of about $1.60 an hour. In bad weather workers were sent home without pay. There was no workers' compensation for those afflicted with back problems, no written grievance procedure, no paid vacation. Fewer than half the tubtoters were part of a pension plan. Of the eleven hundred workers in the late 1960s, nearly all were black. They could be fired for any reason or no reason at all.

At the time municipal unions were a rarity in the South, although a dockworkers' strike in 1939 and a rubber workers' strike in 1942 had brought unionization to some of the city's major industries. Nonetheless thirty-two sanitation workers banded together in 1963 under the leadership of T. O. Jones and walked off the job. All were promptly fired and then rehired after they failed to secure any concessions from management. The following year the sanitation workers became affiliated with the American Federation of State, County, and Municipal Employees (AFSCME), a booming national union that was turning northern cities upside down with its campaigns on behalf of municipal workers. The Memphis sanitation workers' Local 1733 agreed to strike for better conditions in August 1966, but it was stopped in its tracks by a court injunction based on a law that banned all strikes by city workers.

In 1968 two incidents sharpened already existing grievances. After a morning shower on January 30 twenty-one black street repairmen were sent home with only two hours of "show-up" pay. White supervisors remained and collected a full day's pay. Two days later, in heavy rain, an outmoded garbage truck with a hydraulic compacting ram short-circuited and crushed two black sanitation workers inside. Echol Cole, thirty-five, and Robert Walker, twenty-nine, were killed. That neither had life insurance highlighted the lack of worker benefits and slipshod safety conditions.

Within days a list of union demands was drawn up, and at union meetings calls for a strike took on renewed urgency. The primary issue was city recognition of the union as the bargaining agent for the workers, but other demands included a pay raise, deduction of union dues from paychecks, overtime pay, and improved safety. Although some improvements already had been made, the city was as hostile to a strike as it had been two years earlier and refused to commit to major changes.

On February 12, Lincoln's Birthday, the sanitation workers struck en masse for the first time. The strike faced many obstacles, not the least of which was that it was a wildcat action taken without the approval of the national AFSCME office. Moreover, the fledgling local was in no position to support the workers' families for an extended period. The law banning strikes and a standing court order were also against them. But AFSCME quickly came to see Memphis as the first test of its mettle in the South, and members of the black communities provided crucial encouragement and support.

Negotiations began dismally. Mayor Henry Loeb, earnest and notoriously stubborn, took the position that he would hold for the entire strike: no negotiating with workers participating in an illegal strike. At a meeting at the City Auditorium with the workers, the mayor said the strike posed a "health menace" to the city and ordered them back to work. They responded with boos and laughter. Soon after that Loeb began the process of hiring replacement workers, who made the rounds of the city trailed by police cars for protection. Residents were asked to bring their garbage to the curb for pickup; many blacks refused to do so to show solidarity with the strikers. Whites bristled at the prospect of outside intervention. When union leader P. J. Ciampa arrived in Memphis, bumper stickers that barked "Ciampa Go Home" instantly materialized.

On February 22 the city council's committee on public works opened the floor to the union grievances. Chaired by Fred Davis,

Marchers file past national guardsmen, who have sealed off Beale Street, March 29, 1968. (UPI/Corbis-Bettmann)

one of the council's three black members, the meeting quickly devolved into a standoff, with seven hundred of the strikers and their supporters packing the hearing room. After the committee withdrew into private session, the strikers refused to move and staged an impromptu sit-in, complete with freedom songs and the making of hundreds of bologna sandwiches on the desk usually reserved for the city attorney. The committee then came back and endorsed recognition of the union, only to have the full council reverse that decision the next day. In order to vent the bitterness of the crowd at this decision, black leaders staged the first mass march in Memphis, from the City Auditorium to the Mason Temple. Seven blocks into the march on Main Street on February 23, police cars herded the crowd to one side, then disgorged swarms of white officers, who went after marchers with spray cans of Mace.

The incident escalated the local labor dispute into a national Movement involving the NAACP, local preachers, and students. One person who saw the workers' plight as inherently racial was Rev. James Lawson, the mentor of the Nashville student Movement who was then pastoring a Memphis church. "At the heart of racism is the idea that a man is not a man," he said early in the strike. An Easter boycott of shops was announced. Daily marches began downtown.

Blacks boycotted the local *Commercial Appeal* and *Press-Scimitar* and turned instead to two black papers, the *Memphis World* and the *Tri-State Defender.*

The police force was stretched to the limit, charged with guarding both the marchers and the replacement sanitation workers, monitoring mass meetings each night, and keeping a lid on a hurricane of rumors and petty vandalism. Although Memphis was crawling with civic groups, the level of substantive exchange on the strike issues remained low while support for the Movement grew.

Out of all the activity came the Community on the Move for Equality (COME), an umbrella organization headed by Lawson. In March 1968 Lawson, who had known King since the Montgomery bus boycott, convinced him to interrupt his planning for the Poor People's March to come to Memphis. "You are demonstrating that we are all tied in a single garment of destiny," King told a crowd at Mason Temple on March 18. Emboldened by his enthusiastic reception, he called for a citywide work stoppage the following Friday, March 22, and committed himself yet again to the fate of another southern city. When the day arrived, Memphis was blanketed with a freakish sixteen inches of snow, the second most in its history, which all but shut down the city anyway. King vowed to return on March 28 to lead a march.

That march was by all accounts a disaster. King's plane was delayed, and a restless crowd gathered in front of the Clayborn Temple. Earlier that morning a group of black students from Hamilton High School who had cut class lobbed bricks at a passing garbage truck, prompting police to charge them with nightsticks. Students from other area high schools—Carver, Northside, Southside, and Lester—soon converged on the Clayborn Temple, where daily marches originated. A sea of signs sprouted, including one that summed up the campaign with four short words: I AM A MAN. It was hot, and people were drinking and looking for an early start to the weekend.

When King finally arrived at about 11:00 A.M., he dispensed with the usual exhortation to nonviolence and stepped straight from his car into marching mode, linking arms with Rev. Ralph Abernathy and local ministers. They marched west on Beale Street past Handy Park, buffeted on all sides by bystanders. As Movement leaders crossed Second Street, they heard the first sounds of breaking glass behind them: Someone had punched through a store window. Despite frantic attempts to calm the crowd and get it to turn around, others took this sound as a green light and smashed several other storefronts. The march line further disintegrated both in front and behind King, and he boarded a passing car and took refuge at the Holiday Inn-Rivermont on the river. A line of police officers on Main Street waded into the march with gas masks on while several people hopped through broken windows to gather up display merchandise. By the time it was all over, seventy-four people had been wounded and marcher Larry Payne, a high school junior suspected of looting a Sears, had been shot dead by a police officer in the basement of a housing project. The National Guard was moved in that night in eight armored personnel carriers, and Chicago-bound trains from New Orleans skipped their usual Memphis stop.

CHICKEN A LA KING, taunted the next day's headline, but King had more serious problems. He had lost control of the march and had to contend with embittered supporters and a staff that had warned him to stay away from Memphis in the first place. The strikers' grievances had been overshadowed by photographs of an occupied city and mannequins strewn in the street. Now it became even more urgent to demonstrate the power of nonviolence. The following day, March 29, four hundred adults marched in perfect order to City Hall past rows of guardsmen with fixed bayonets and tanks that left ridges in the street. King met with the Invaders, a Black Power group youth named after a popular TV show that was blamed for the disruption. Union officials redoubled their support for the strike, and King pledged himself to march again on April 8.

When King returned to the city on April 3, he checked into room 306 at the Lorraine Motel in full view of the television cameras. The immediate issue was another court order issued against the Movement leaders. As he had several times before, King was pondering whether to defy or obey. A bomb threat had held up his flight from Atlanta, and although he had accepted police protection in the past, he declined it in Memphis. His staff found him moody and withdrawn. That night a storm brought thunder and lightning to the city and air-raid sirens warned of tornadoes in outlying areas. That night at Mason Temple he delivered his last speech, a messianic vision. The following evening, April 4, after a day of meetings, he was shot on the balcony of the Lorraine while waiting to go to a private dinner. He was pronounced dead an hour later at St. Joseph's Hospital.

In the aftermath the people of Memphis stumbled forward in a sad trance. Fires and sniper fire filled the night, and four thousand national guardsmen patrolled the streets. The next morning huge crowds of mourners showed up to view King's body at the R. S. Lewis & Sons Funeral Home on Vance Street, and a memorial service was held at LeMoyne College. A group of ministers of all faiths

In the courtyard of the Lorraine Motel, King receives a court order banning unauthorized marches the day before his death, April 3, 1968. He is surrounded by (from left to right) Abernathy, Rev. Andrew Young, James Orange, and Bernard Lee. (Barney Sellers/*Commercial Appeal*)

paraded behind a processional cross to City Hall, where they implored Mayor Loeb to act on the strikers' grievances in King's memory. "Let us not wrap ourselves up in slogans," said their spokesman, Rabbi James Wax. "Let us do the will of God for the good of this city." Palm Sunday, April 7, was a national day of mourning. The next day a massive memorial march moved into City Hall Plaza past lines of national guardsmen holding bayonets skyward "like the points of a listing picket fence." There King's widow, Coretta Scott King, spoke from a high platform in front of the city seal and encouraged the crowd to press onward.

Meanwhile, after nonstop negotiations at the Claridge Hotel, a settlement of the strike was ironed out. On April 16 the city council approved recognition of the union, a dues checkoff through a credit union, raises, new benefits, and a rehiring of the workers in exchange for a standard no-strike pledge. The union members approved the settlement by voice vote in a raucous meeting that left strike leader T. O. Jones crying in disbelief and relief. On April 17 the garbagemen went back to work.

In Search of James Earl Ray

James Earl Ray was a habitual crook who combined grand designs with clumsy execution. He appeared trim and neat, but he committed steadily more serious crimes until he was hauled in by the largest FBI manhunt in history after the shooting of King.

Born in Alton, Illinois, Ray was caught stealing a typewriter and then got two years for armed robbery in Chicago at age twenty-four. He got a three-year sentence for forging a money order in Hannibal, Missouri. He was sentenced to twenty years under a recidivist law for robbing a St. Louis supermarket in 1959.

On April 23, 1967, he escaped from the Missouri State Penitentiary in Jefferson City by hiding in a bread truck. From then on he careened around the continent like a pinball: St. Louis, Chicago, Montreal, Birmingham, Mexico. He stayed in Los Angeles long enough to complete a bartending course and take dancing lessons.

By mid-March 1968 he was stalking King. Exactly why is still unclear. The FBI later turned up copies of John Birch literature in his room, and a few people later said he used the word *nigger* when agitated. In spring 1968 Ray followed King to Selma and to his home in Atlanta. He drove to Birmingham, bought a Remington rifle at a shop near the airport, and drove to Memphis on April 3, the day of King's now-famous "Mountaintop" speech. On April 4 he checked into a boardinghouse across from the Lorraine Motel. That afternoon he shot King from a bathroom window and fled in his white Mustang, leaving behind a bewildering array of clues.

A manhunt of unparalleled intensity followed. The Memphis City Council and the local papers offered a combined reward of a hundred thousand dollars to catch the suspect. Agents combed parole records, tax rolls, and safe-deposit accounts under the names of Ray and his various aliases. They traced the laundry tag in his undershorts, left in an overnight bag, to a Los Angeles laundromat. FBI agents posed as hippies in Atlanta after they had discovered Ray had lived among them there. They began comparing his fingerprints manually with those of every white man under fifty wanted by the police, a number greater than fifty thousand. All in all, fifteen hundred agents worked on the case on any given day.

Ray continued to evade them, raising suspicion that he was part of a well-oiled conspiracy. The FBI found his car a week later abandoned in an Atlanta housing project. Ray had managed to get to Toronto and on a fake passport to London, where he robbed a bank when money ran low. He sought passage to Africa, where he intended to live as a mercenary. Finally, on June 8, he was arrested at Heathrow Airport in London just before boarding a flight to Brussels.

His return to Memphis for trial was cloaked in extraordinary caution, an

(Continued on next page)

attempt to avoid vigilantism of the sort that had resulted in the gunning down of Lee Harvey Oswald shortly after he had been apprehended. Ray was transported from Millington U.S. Naval Air Station to Memphis in the "Thompson Tank," an impregnable armored vehicle named for the mayor of Jackson and ordered for Mississippi's Freedom Summer of 1964. Air traffic over the Shelby County jail at 150 Washington Avenue (Ray was held in Block A on the third floor) was monitored, and the jail was covered with quarter-inch steel plating. Guided by a hundred-page manual of procedures, fourteen people at a time guarded Ray. His first interview with his lawyers was conducted lying on the concrete floor of his cell with the shower running to avoid his being overheard by microphones. Letters addressed to him were duplicated, and only the copies delivered, in case the originals carried poison.

In the end the many mysteries of the case were shuttered behind Ray's plea of guilty and sentence of ninety-nine years in prison. He was advised by his lawyers to plead guilty because his only defense was that the shooting was done by a phantom gunrunner he called Raoul. After an extensive recitation of his rights in court on March 10, 1969, he took the plea and thereby avoided a possible death sentence. In May 1971, after his legal appeals had run out, Ray pried loose two concrete wall blocks at the Brushy Mountain Penitentiary in Petros, Tennessee, and nearly escaped a second time by crawling through an air duct. Today he is held in the Riverbend Maximum Security Institution in Nashville. In 1996 both the King family and Ray, by then in poor health, began a campaign to withdraw the plea and press for a full trial.

Lorraine Motel/National Civil Rights Museum
450 Mulberry Street

Walter ("Bill") Bailey took over a two-story brick boardinghouse at 406 Mulberry Street in 1955. He added on to it a sleek fifty-unit motel in the fifties style, with a pool out front and home cooking delivered to guests. He named it for his wife, Lorraine. The motel served the many black musicians, preachers, and businessmen who came through Memphis.

On April 3 King and Abernathy checked into room 306 here, where they had stayed several times before. The cost: thirteen dollars a night. Below them in room 201 was Rev. A. D. King, Martin's younger brother. In surrounding rooms were a DOJ mediator, the press, a documentary photographer, and King's other aides. The next two days were filled with meetings. Visitors from his legal team and members of the Invaders shuttled in and out of the room, and

The Lorraine Motel in 1996, now the National Civil Rights Museum. A white wreath hangs on the balcony where King was shot. (Townsend Davis)

federal marshals served him in the motel courtyard with court papers relating to a proposed march.

April 4 was damp and cool, and the peripatetic King had a relatively light schedule. He and Abernathy shared catfish off a single platter after the waitress botched their lunch orders. King joked with his brother, A.D., and joined him in a rare phone call to their mother. At a staff meeting in the afternoon spirits were buoyed by the prospects of a court-approved march. Rev. Billy Kyles, pastor of the Monumental Baptist Church, arrived at about 5:30 P.M. to escort King to dinner at his house. One of the old guard chided a young Chicago organizer named Jesse Jackson for sporting the turtleneck and jeans favored by younger activists rather than a suit and tie.

When King walked out onto the balcony of the Lorraine at about 6:00 P.M, his group was getting ready for dinner. Abernathy was in a bathroom splashing aftershave on his face. Below him in the courtyard were driver Solomon Jones and Ben Branch, leader of the band for Jesse Jackson's Operation Breadbasket. King asked him to play "Precious Lord" at the mass meeting scheduled after dinner, and to "play it real pretty." His closest Movement cohorts were scattered around the courtyard: Andy Young, Hosea Williams, James Orange, and Jesse Jackson, along with his shadow and aide Bernard Lee and attorney Chauncey Eskridge. King was leaning on the railing with both hands, smoking a cigarette. Watching him on assignment from the Memphis Police Department was a black detective peering through binoculars from Fire Station No. 2 across the street.

A minute later King was reeling backward from the impact of a single shot that echoed through the courtyard like a firecracker. The bullet left a gaping wound in the right side of his face, and Abernathy rushed to the prone body. He held the head of his friend and repeated, "This is Ralph. This is Ralph." Within five minutes an ambulance came, and police had descended from Main Street into the Lorraine courtyard looking for the shooter. King was whisked to St. Joseph's Hospital by an ambulance driver who got the city to switch all the lights in his path to green. King's aides waited and prayed in the hospital anteroom. At 7:00 P.M a hospital administrator announced that despite efforts to revive him, King had died of injuries from a severed spinal cord.

At the motel after the shooting the SCLC leadership gathered in room 306 and endorsed what had been decided long before: that Abernathy would succeed King. Meanwhile it was discovered that upon hearing the news, Lorraine Bailey, co-owner of the motel, had

King lies fatally wounded on the balcony of the Lorraine Motel while Andrew Young (left) and others point toward the boardinghouse from which James Earl Ray fired the shot. (Joseph Louw/*Life* Magazine © Time, Inc.)

been stricken with a cerebral hemorrhage, from which she later died.

For years a wreath hung outside room 306. In the 1970s and 1980s, the motel deteriorated, as did many byways of the Jim Crow era. A week before the motel was scheduled for foreclosure, black radio station WDIA started a last-ditch fund-raising campaign to save it. A foundation collected funds patched together from local businesses, AFSCME, and the Tri-State Bank. The group scraped together enough money to buy the motel for ninety-two thousand dollars at an auction on the steps of the Shelby County Courthouse. State, county, and city funds helped convert it into a museum, maintained by admission fees and private donations. In panoramic splendor the museum covers everything from the streetcar boycotts against Jim Crow in the 1900s to the assassination of King. Room 306 has been meticulously preserved.

Site of Mrs. Brewer's Boardinghouse
418–22½ South Main Street

A series of coincidences allowed James Earl Ray to kill King quickly and escape in broad daylight from the crowded neighborhood of the Lorraine Motel.

At about 3:15 P.M on April 4 Ray checked into what was then a shabby rooming house. At the time it had ten rooms on the south side and six on the north, connected by a second-floor corridor. He took room 5B in the north wing, which had a staircase leading down to the street. He paid the weekly rate of $8.50 with a crisp $20 bill and had no luggage. He bought some binoculars at a shop on Beale Street and parked in front of Canipe's Amusement Company at 424 South Main, which sold used records for a quarter and was just below the boardinghouse. To the south was a billboard asking residents to be truthful, fair, and supportive of "a greater Memphis." To the north was Jim's Grill (No. 418), where the lunch special of sausages, eggs, toast, grits, and coffee cost sixty-two cents.

Ray watched King from the window of his room, then set up with his rifle in the bathroom at the end of the hallway. Although foliage framed his view, he had a clear shot at the balcony of the motel outside room 306. In his rifle was a single bullet. At about 6:00 P.M he fired from the window. He escaped down the stairs and dropped the gun in the doorway of Canipe's. Then he disappeared in his Mustang. A squad of police taking a break at Fire Station No. 2 down the street got the call about the shooting and missed Ray by seconds. The building today is the studio of an illustrator.

Clayborn Temple AME Church
294 Hernando Street

This church, first erected in 1891 of creamy stone and formerly the Second Presbyterian Church, became the send-off point for marches down Beale Street to City Hall starting on February 26, 1968. Two sets of marches, one in the early afternoon and one later, commenced like clockwork in front of the church each day. They formed a single-file line that bent west on Beale and then north to City Hall, a distance of about 1.3 miles. Even after King was killed, the marches kept on until April 16, when word came that the city council had endorsed a strike settlement. A jubilant rally then was held inside the church, which earlier had housed a gospel and soul concert to benefit the strikers. The church had also been the site of a memorial service for Larry Payne after he was killed in the rioting of March 28. Marchers took refuge here while police skirmished in the street with a group of brick throwers. The disorder was enough to keep ambulances away from the area and to allow tear gas to seep into the church sanctuary, causing some to flee out the back windows.

Next door was the Minimum Salary Building (280 Hernando), a headquarters for the secular concerns of the African Methodist Episcopal Church. Here the AME Church supplemented the incomes of its ministers nationwide when their congregations could not afford to pay them the "minimum" annual salary of three thousand dollars. Before the strike the building, which had opened with great

Clayborn Temple AME Church, 1995. (Townsend Davis)

fanfare and a clutch of dignitaries (including Mayor Loeb), was a quiet administrative building, headed by Rev. Ralph Jackson. Once the strike started, it was pressed into service as a Movement checkpoint and hospice, and Jackson, secure within the church hierarchy, lent his rousing voice to the strikers' cause. Here Mayor Loeb had his only face-to-face meeting with black ministers, which was fruitless.

Both buildings were bulwarks against the seediness of Beale Street. In the early 1900s Beale was a lively strip of bluesmen, conjurers, and flashy commerce fueled by a steady current of gambling and booze. Its transient character gave Memphis its unofficial title as the true capital of the Mississippi Delta and the "leader of evil doings in the world," as one musician called it. By the late 1960s Beale Street had given way to cut-rate shops and liquor stores. It was a prime candidate for urban "renewal," and police wisely kept their distance from the marchers who paraded down it every afternoon for nearly two months. Except for the unruly March 28, 1968, riots, the marches down Beale Street were a peaceful mix of preachers and pimps, students and scam artists. On March 28 the buildings on Hernando Street served as twin sanctuaries inside, while police skirmished with marchers and onlookers outside.

United Rubber Workers Hall (Firestone Hall)
1036 Firestone Avenue

Firestone Tire and Rubber was first lured to Memphis in 1937 by the prospect of cheap labor and a safe harbor from the labor agitation in its former home of Akron, Ohio. By fall 1940 it was the largest nonunion rubber factory in the country, employing three thousand workers, a third of them black. The CIO made it an organizing target, and by 1942 the union had established a local there after a long and bitter drive. Unlike the many segregated industries, the Firestone Workers' Local 186 was hospitable to city workers in their drive for recognition in 1968.

Initial gatherings of the sanitation union workers in February 1968 quickly outgrew the Labor Temple on South Second Street. From then on this hall became the scene of daily noontime meetings, where workers noisily discussed their plans. Labor leaders like AFSCME president Jerry Wurf, P. J. Ciampa, Bill Lucy, and T. O. Jones encouraged the workers to stick with an initially wobbly strike that was costing two thousand dollars a day for necessities alone. Wurf had weathered dozens of raucous municipal strikes in the North and roused the crowd with his finger-wagging oratory.

Centenary United Methodist Church

584 East McLemore Avenue

The shooting of James Meredith near Memphis at the outset of his March against Fear in 1966 brought together for the last time SCLC, CORE, and SNCC, which each vowed to continue the march from the spot on the highway where Meredith had been stopped. This church was used to coordinate that effort under Pastor James Lawson. When the first day of the Meredith March ended at the tiny town of Coldwater, Mississippi, the marchers gathered here to regroup.

Lawson had been a Movement preacher for more than a decade. He had arguably spent more time than anyone thinking through the prickly implications of using nonviolence as a sword of social change. Raised in a Methodist preacher's family in Massillon, Ohio, Lawson studied Gandhi and Niebuhr in college and heard about lunch counter sit-ins then being pioneered by CORE in the North. When he was drafted for the Korean War, he became a conscientious objector and served thirteen months in a federal prison. He next spent several years doing missionary work in India and returned to study theology.

From then on Lawson had a hand in seminal Movement events. He worked for the Fellowship of Reconciliation in Nashville and nurtured the Nashville student Movement in 1960, earning him expulsion from the Vanderbilt Divinity School. He addressed the founding conference of SNCC in Raleigh and rode the Freedom Rider buses in 1961. He was called to this church as pastor in 1962 and continued to work for the Movement as it caught fire from south Georgia to the Mississippi Delta.

During the Memphis strike of 1968 Lawson often put the bewildering blur of events into a larger moral framework and took a keen interest in strategy as the leader of COME. He invited King to speak in early March 1968, the nonviolent equivalent of declaring war. King held his last press conference here on April 3, when he declared, "We are not going to be stopped by Mace or injunctions."

Tri-State Bank

180 South Main Street

Movement meetings were held here in the midst of the sanitation workers' strike to mull over various proposals in March 1968. From the NAACP's heyday in the 1950s until the present this bank has been a vital Movement link.

After black businessmen were squeezed by local banks in retaliation for *Brown* and an NAACP revival, the NAACP created a
loan program of $280,000 for them. The program caused the banks
to restore credit for blacks in Mississippi after they realized that
their tactics were ineffective. When black teachers in Jackson, Mississippi, wanted to create a secret bank account to finance the first
equal-pay lawsuit, they surreptitiously raised $5,000 and deposited
it here.

Hunt Sculpture
Poplar Avenue and North Main Street

Created by Chicago sculptor Richard Hunt in 1977, "I Have Been
to the Mountaintop" is a sphinxlike steel tribute to King's last speech
on April 3, 1968. Thrusting heavenward, it represents his lofty
rhetoric. Today skateboarders use it for a stunt ramp.

City Hall
North Main Street

In 1966 the crowning achievement of civic reformers was the
establishment of the mayor and council form of city government to
replace the fiefdoms that had flourished during the era of Mayor
Crump. The council conducted the city's business inside a plush red-
carpeted chamber with thirteen members arrayed along an impressive dais.

Soon after the revamping of the council, its home became center
stage and the final destination of Memphis's most visible demonstrations. In February 1968, the NAACP staged an all-night vigil outside
it. A few days later on February 22 the city council's committee on
public works, chaired by Fred Davis, presided over a hearing that
was dominated by the presence of seven hundred sanitation workers who refused to budge and turned it into a spontaneous mass
meeting. Rev. Zeke Bell, a local black preacher, shocked the city
with talk of unequal prosperity and joked about tearing down the
city seal from the wall, which bore local symbols of industry (a
steamboat, a cotton stalk, an oak leaf, and a gear). When the council
announced in the City Auditorium the next day that no action
would be taken, council members hurriedly cut off the power to the
microphones and were escorted by police from the chamber. Their
recalcitrance triggered the first mass march in Memphis. Later a
group of students carried a plain wooden coffin to City Hall to give
freedom a mock burial. At the Movement meetings in the chamber,

one observer noted that the clerks sat "round-eyed, spellbound," giving the impression they had never heard blacks make such urgent demands on their elected officials.

In the mayor's office sat Henry Loeb, who did not waver in his insistence that the strike was simply illegal and nonnegotiable. Loeb's family ran several dry cleaners and barbecue spots in Memphis, and he sported a slick-haired look and jaunty, optimistic approach to problems that made him look more like a plainspoken big man on campus than a back room political operator. He had headed the department of public works, which included the sanitation workers, and had spoken out against integration in his term as a city commissioner. Loeb made a big show of conducting initial strike talks in front of the TV cameras, and he invited everyone to his office, from the strike leaders to a concerned group of white-gloved ladies. During the strike a shotgun was propped up under the desk while Loeb towered over it, trying to charm all visitors.

A block away was the City Auditorium (Ellis Auditorium, 225 North Main Street), where on February 13 the mayor faced a unified crowd of strikers for the first time. Loeb first tried to coax them back to work and insisted that his door was always open to them, but when the strikers laughed off his combination of threats and sweet talk, Loeb walked out of the meeting and began hiring replacement workers. Although he steadily increased the number of replacement garbage workers to nearly the normal level, he was slow to realize the exponential power of the strikers' message. Not until after the assassination of King did Loeb see that meaningful concessions were needed before the marches would be called off.

Mason Temple

930 Mason Street

Six days after the strike began the dimensions of the black community's vast and vital network began to show at a rally here. The committee of concerned citizens mounted a volunteer food and clothing drive while union officials hunkered down for the long haul. The vast temple was, and is, the headquarters of the Church of God in Christ, second only to Baptists in black membership, and is named for its founder, Charles Harrison Mason. It was perhaps the largest indoor space the Movement met in regularly, seating up to five thousand people. Fittingly King gave his last speech, one of his greatest, in this auditorium.

After police Mace attacks on February 23, 1968, marchers retreated to this temple to recover and resolved to raise the stakes with boycotts, daily marches, and the formation of a strategy committee. The next day an extraordinary meeting of 150 black ministers—Baptist, Pentecostal, AME, CME, Church of God in Christ—was held here to unify support. Although Rev. Billy Kyles and Rev. James Netters had dabbled in protest against segregation, this was the first time the stick-to-the-scripture preachers spoke on a social issue with one voice.

The campaign went national here on March 14, 1968, when Roy Wilkins of the NAACP and leading Movement strategist Bayard Rustin addressed the hall. Rustin said that the debate then raging in New York over the terms *colored, black,* and *Negro* was inconsequential compared with the workers' urgent work in Memphis. He heralded the Memphis Movement as a break with the past distance between blacks and unions. Shiny new garbage cans were used to take up a collection. On March 18 King spoke to a crowd that was packed in so tightly he had to be escorted to the stage in a flying wedge of handlers, and listeners sat in the rafters. "All labor has dignity," he said, "but you are doing another thing. You are reminding not only Memphis but the nation that it is a crime for people to live in this nation and receive starvation wages." Buoyed by his reception, he made a spontaneous call for a citywide work stoppage to show solidarity with the workers.

In his final speech King faced the unusual sight of canyons of empty seats. A spring storm on April 3, 1968, had reduced the crowd to about three thousand and knocked out power in some areas. Rev. Ralph Abernathy spoke first as a substitute, but he summoned King from the Lorraine Motel because he knew the crowd would be unsatisfied without a word from him. For some reason that night Abernathy introduced his friend with a lengthy life tribute that sounded something like an obituary. Two large vents in the temple banged in the wind.

When a tired King began his speech, it was clear that his theme was his own mortality. He imagined a conversation with his creator in which he would be given a choice of epochs to live in. After surveying the accomplishments of ancient Egypt through the Renaissance to the present day, he said he would pick "just a few years in the second half of the twentieth century." He mentioned his stabbing at a Harlem book signing ten years earlier, saying that if he had sneezed, he would have died and missed all the Movement's accomplishments from the sit-ins to the Memphis strike. He also mentioned the bomb threats on his latest flight from Atlanta. It was a dark vision, infused with the anxiety of death threats and challenges to his nonviolent credo. His final words were a prophetic and moving, if unintended, farewell. He ended it suddenly, then staggered back to his chair and collapsed amid frenzied applause.

"I May Not Get There with You . . ."

In the closing moments of his final speech on April 3, 1968, King told the world that he had crossed over. Gone were the everyday concerns about legal strategy, press coverage, funding, and personal squabbles. The crush of events since Montgomery twelve years earlier, the countless plunges into the unknown, were viewed in placid retrospect like a calmed sea. In an echo of his "I Have a Dream" speech, he sounded the call for an exodus from segregation for the last time:

"Well, I don't know what will happen now. We've got some difficult days ahead. But it really doesn't matter with me now because I've been to the mountaintop. And I don't mind. Like anybody I would like to live a long life. Longevity has its place. But I'm not concerned about that now. I just want to do God's will. And he's allowed me to go up to the mountain. And I've looked over, and I've seen the promised land. I may not get there with you. But I want you to know tonight that we as a people will get to the promised land. And so I'm happy tonight. I'm not worried about anything. I'm not fearing any man. Mine eyes have seen the glory of the coming of the Lord."[50]

The Mason Temple, where King gave his final speech on April 3, 1968, photographed in 1995. (Townsend Davis)

Chronology

May 17, 1954	U.S. Supreme Court announces *Brown v. Board of Education*, desegregating public schools.
July 1954	Citizens' Council is founded in Indianola, Mississippi.
September 1954	Martin Luther King, Jr., moves to Montgomery, Alabama, to become pastor of Dexter Avenue Baptist Church.
May 31, 1955	U.S. Supreme Court orders *Brown* implemented with "all deliberate speed."
August 28, 1955	Fourteen-year-old Emmett Till is killed in Money, Mississippi. The killers are acquitted in September at a trial in Sumner.
December 1, 1955	Rosa Parks is arrested on a Montgomery bus. A bus boycott begins four days later.
February 1, 1956	Autherine Lucy becomes the first black student to enroll at the University of Alabama in Tuscaloosa.
June 5, 1956	The Alabama Christian Movement for Human Rights is founded in Birmingham, Alabama.
December 1956	U.S. Supreme Court declares segregation on public buses unconstitutional. Montgomery bus boycott ends.

January 1957	First citizenship schools are conducted on Johns Island, South Carolina.
February 1957	SCLC is founded in New Orleans.
September 25, 1957	President Eisenhower sends federal troops to enforce desegregation at Central High School in Little Rock, Arkansas.
March 1958	Rev. James Lawson holds workshops on nonviolent protest in Nashville, Tennessee.
February 1, 1960	Sit-ins begin in Greensboro, North Carolina, and spread throughout the South.
April 1960	SNCC is founded in Raleigh, North Carolina.
January 1961	Hamilton Holmes and Charlayne Hunter are admitted to the University of Georgia in Athens.
May 4, 1961	The Freedom Riders leave Washington, D.C., intent on desegregating bus stations in the Deep South. Despite attacks in Anniston, Birmingham, and Montgomery, two buses make it to Jackson, Mississippi, by the end of May.
August 1961	Bob Moses and other SNCC staff launch a voting campaign in McComb, Mississippi. Herbert Lee is killed in September.
August 28, 1961	Highlander Folk School is forced by Tennessee authorities to close and move from Monteagle to Knoxville.
October 1961	Local Movement in Savannah, Georgia, ends its yearlong boycott.
February 1962	COFO is founded in Clarksdale, Mississippi, to coordinate Movement efforts in that state.
September 30, 1962	Rioting at Ole Miss in Oxford precedes the enrollment of James Meredith.
December 1962	Dr. King supports a local Movement in Albany, Georgia.
April 3, 1963	SCLC launches Project C in Birmingham during which Dr. King writes the "Letter from a Birmingham Jail."
April 21, 1963	William Moore begins the Postman's March in Chattanooga, Tennessee, and is shot on the road near Attalla, Alabama.
June 12, 1963	Medgar Evers is assassinated in Jackson, Mississippi.

August 28, 1963	The March on Washington, where Dr. King delivers his "I Have a Dream" speech.
September 15, 1963	Bombing at the Sixteenth Street Baptist Church in Birmingham kills four black girls.
Fall 1963	In Mississippi eighty thousand voters not allowed to vote hold their own Freedom Vote for political offices.
June 1964	Training for Freedom Summer begins in Oxford, Ohio. Freedom Schools conduct classes all over Mississippi, along with other volunteer programs, during the summer.
June 21, 1964	Chaney, Goodman, and Schwerner (three civil rights workers) disappear outside Philadelphia, Mississippi. They are found dead later that summer.
July 2, 1964	Civil Rights Act of 1964 signed.
August 1964	MFDP challenges the all-white Mississippi delegation at the Democratic National Convention in Atlantic City, New Jersey.
December 10, 1964	Dr. King is awarded the Nobel Peace Prize.
March 1965	Selma voting rights campaign, Bloody Sunday, and the Selma to Montgomery March.
August 6, 1965	Voting Rights Act signed.
May 1966	Stokely Carmichael is elected chairman of SNCC.
January 10, 1966	Murder of black businessman Vernon Dahmer, Sr., in Hattiesburg, Mississippi.
April 1966	Lowndes County Freedom Movement, with its black panther logo, mobilizes black voters in the Alabama Black Belt.
June 1966	Meredith March in Mississippi, and the first use of the Black Power slogan in Greenwood.
April 1967	King announces his opposition to the Vietnam War.
February 8, 1968	Three students are killed at South Carolina State College in Orangeburg, South Carolina.
March 1968	Sanitation workers' strike in Memphis, Tennessee.
April 4, 1968	Dr. King is assassinated in Memphis. He is later buried in Atlanta.
Spring 1968	Poor People's March to Washington is led by Abernathy.

April 1969	Charleston, South Carolina, hospital workers' strike.
May 13, 1970	Two students are shot and killed at Jackson State University in Jackson.
November 1972	Barbara Jordan (Texas) and Andrew Young (Georgia) are the first two blacks elected to Congress from the South since Reconstruction.

Civil Rights Laws

Fifteenth Amendment to the U.S. Constitution (1870)

Declared "the right of citizens of the United States to vote shall not be abridged . . . on account of race, color, or previous condition of servitude." Empowered Congress to pass enforcement legislation.

Civil Rights Act of 1957

Established the Civil Rights Division of the Department of Justice and an investigative body, the U.S. Commission on Civil Rights. Allowed DOJ to file suits to stop violations of the Fifteenth Amendment. In forty-six counties in which suits were filed, less than 10 percent of more than half a million eligible blacks had registered. Enforcement was hampered by the difficulty of getting records from locally controlled clerks' offices and dependence on local juries.

Civil Rights Act of 1960

The Department of Justice was given the right to examine local voting records on demand. Provided for lawsuits against pattern or practice of discrimination in voting and, upon such a finding, gave federal courts the right to enroll rejected applicants. Covered economic, not just physical, retaliation for exercising right to vote. DOJ brought sixty-six lawsuits by 1964 at the direction of attorney John Doar and

Kennedy aide Burke Marshall, but proving violations remained difficult.

Civil Rights Act of 1964

Signed July 2, 1964. Banned racial discrimination in places of public accommodation, such as restaurants and hotels. Expedited handling of voting rights cases in a three-judge federal court. Created the Community Relations Service to mediate local civil rights disputes. Specified that only written literacy tests were allowed and that standards must be applied uniformly. Allowed private suits against segregated intrastate transit for first time.

Twenty-fourth Amendment to the U.S. Constitution (1964)

Ratified August 1964. Banned use of poll taxes in national elections. Most of the debate on this issue occurred in the 1940s, forming one of the first interracial coalitions on civil rights. Amendment still allowed use of poll taxes for state and local elections.

Civil Rights Act of 1965 (the Voting Rights Act)

Signed August 6, 1965. Reauthorized in 1970, amended several times. Made proof of age and residency the sole requirements for voting. Banned traditional devices used to restrict black voting: poll taxes, literacy tests, knowledge-of-government tests. Provided for federal registrars to carry out registration. Shifted enforcement from the executive branch to the judiciary. Required "preclearance" by the Department of Justice or a special court for any alterations in voting procedure, including redistricting, in districts that historically excluded blacks. Within two months of enactment more than fifty-six thousand blacks registered to vote in twenty counties in which federal examiners were installed.

Twenty-sixth Amendment to the U.S. Constitution (1971)

Lowered the legal voting age from twenty-one to eighteen.

Appendix

Map Index

Appendix

The Historical Sites

ALABAMA

Anniston

Route 202

Birmingham

Armstrong's Barbershop
Bethel Baptist Church (Collegeville)
Birmingham City Hall
Birmingham City Jail (Southside)
Birmingham Civil Rights Institute
Birmingham Realty Office
John Drew House
Dynamite Hill
First Baptist Church (Ensley)
A. G. Gaston Motel
Graymont School
Greenwood Cemetery
Greyhound Bus Station
Jefferson County Courthouse
Kelly Ingram Park

A. D. King House
Kress
Loveman's
Masonic Temple
Miles College
New Pilgrim Baptist Church
Ollie's Barbecue
Parker High School
Phillips High School
Pizitz
Sardis Baptist Church
Shadow Lawn Cemetery
Arthur Shores House
Sixteenth Street Baptist Church
Sixth Avenue Baptist Church

Birmingham (continued)

St. James Baptist Church
St. John AME Church
St. Luke AME Church
St. Paul United Methodist Church

Thirgood Memorial CME Church
Trailways Bus Station
Woolworth's

Fort Payne

De Kalb County Jail

Lowndes County

First Baptist Church, Hayneville
Frank ("Bud") Haralson's Store,
    White Hall
Lowndes County Courthouse,
    Haynesville
Lowndes County Jail, Hayneville

Mount Gillard Baptist Church, Trickem
United States Post Office, Fort Deposit
Varner's Cash Store, Hayneville
Viola Liuzzo Memorial,
    U.S. Highway 80

Montgomery

Alabama State Capitol
Alabama State University
Alabama Supreme Court
Bell Street Baptist Church
Ben Moore Hotel
City of St. Jude
Civil Rights Memorial
Cleveland Courts
Court Square
Dean's Drug Store
Dexter Avenue King Memorial
    Baptist Church
Dexter Avenue Baptist Church
    Parsonage/King House
Eastwood Memorial Gardens
Empire Theater Bus Stop
First Baptist Church ("Brick-a-Day")

Georgia Gilmore House
Greyhound Bus Station
Richard Harris House
Holt Street Baptist Church
Hutchinson Street Baptist Church
Jackson Street Baptist Church
Rufus Lewis House
Montgomery City Hall
Montgomery City Jail
Montgomery County Courthouse
Montgomery Fair
Mount Olive Baptist Church
Mount Zion AME Zion Church
E. D. Nixon House
Oak Park
E. L. Posey Parking Lot
Trailways Bus Station

Trinity Lutheran Church
Trinity Lutheran Church Parsonage
United States Courthouse

Perry County

Jimmie Lee Jackson Gravesite
Lee's Funeral Home
Mack's Cafe
Mount Tabor Baptist Church

Perry County Jail
Obadiah Scott House
Zion United Methodist Church

Selma

Boynton House
Boynton Real Estate and Insurance
    Office
Brown Chapel AME Church
Burwell Infirmary
Cecil C. Jackson Public Safety Building
Concordia College
Craig Air Base
Dallas County Courthouse
Dunn Rest Home
Edmundite Missions Office
Edmund Pettus Bridge
Elks Lodge
First Baptist Church
George D. Wilson Community Center
George Washington Carver Homes/
    Civil Rights Walking Tour

Good Samaritan Hospital
Green Street Baptist Church
Sullivan Jackson House
Lannie's Bar-B-Q Spot
National Voting Rights Museum and
    Institute
Old Depot Museum
Reformed Presbyterian Church (Knox)
Selma City Hall
Selma University
Silver Moon Cafe
Tabernacle Baptist Church
Torch Motel
United States Courthouse
United States Highway 80
Walker's Cafe

Tuscaloosa

Foster Auditorium, University of Alabama
Smith Hall, University of Alabama

ARKANSAS

Little Rock

Daisy Bates House
Central High School

GEORGIA

Albany

Albany City Hall
Albany City Jail
Albany Civil Rights Movement Museum
Albany Movement Monument
Albany State College
William Anderson House
Carnegie Library
Dougherty County Courthouse

King Family Plot, Oakview Cemetery
C. B. King Law Office
Slater King House
Monroe High School
Mount Zion Baptist Church
Shiloh Baptist Church
Trailways Bus Station

Americus

Sumter County Jail

Athens

University of Georgia

Atlanta

APEX Museum
Atlanta University
Atlanta University Center
Auburn Avenue
B. B. Beamon's Restaurant
Big Bethel AME Church
Butler Street YMCA
Clark Atlanta University
Ebenezer Baptist Church
Frasier's Cafe
Fulton County Jail
Mount Moriah Baptist Church
Park Service Visitor Center
Paschal's Restaurant
The Pickrick
Providence Baptist Church
Rich's
Rush Memorial Congregational Church
Georgia State Capitol

Heart of Atlanta Motel
Interdenominational Theological
   Center
Lincoln Cemetery
Martin Luther King, Jr., Birth Home/
   Williams House
Martin Luther King, Jr., Center for
   Nonviolent Social Change
Marx Building
Morehouse College
Morris Brown College
SCLC Headquarters
Southview Cemetery
Spelman College
Warren Memorial United Methodist
   Church
West Hunter Street Baptist Church
Wheat Street Baptist Church

Camilla

Mitchell County Jail

Lee County

Shady Grove Baptist Church

Midway

Dorchester Academy Boys Dormitory

Reidsville

Georgia State Penitentiary

Savannah

Bolton Street Baptist Church
Daffin Park
First African Baptist Church
Johnson Square
Levy's Department Store
Manger Hotel
Morrison's Cafeteria
Mount Zion Baptist Church

Ralph Mark Gilbert Civil Rights
    Museum
Savannah High School
St. Philip AME Church
Tomo-chi-chi Rock
Tybee Island Beach
West Broad Street YMCA
Wright Square

Terrell County

I Hope Baptist Church
Mount Mary Baptist Church
Mount Olive Baptist Church

MISSISSIPPI

Biloxi

Public Beach

Canton

Asbury Methodist Church
McNeal Elementary School

The Delta

Delta Health Center, Mound Bayou
Fannie Lou Hamer House/Gravesite,
    Ruleville

Aaron Henry Drugstore, Clarksdale
Freedom Farm, Sunflower County
Greenville Air Force Base, Greenville

Indianola Public Library, Indianola
Knights and Daughters of Tabor Hospital,
    Mound Bayou
George Lee Gravesite, Belzoni
Joe McDonald House, Ruleville
Mileston Community Center, Mileston
Amzie Moore House, Cleveland
Parchman Penitentiary, Sunflower
    County
Ruleville High School, Ruleville
Herman and Hattie Sisson House,
    Ruleville
Sunflower County Courthouse,
    Indianola
Tallahatchie County Courthouse,
    Sumner
Tucker House, Ruleville
Hartman Turnbow House, Mileston
Westlawn Memorial Gardens,
    Cleveland
William Chapel Missionary Baptist
    Church, Ruleville
Young's Gro and Market, Money

Edwards

Mount Beulah Center (Bonner-Campbell College)

Greenwood

Booker's Cafe
Broad Street Park
Century Funeral Home
COFO/SNCC Offices
East Percy Street Christian Church
    (First Christian Church)
Elks Hall
Friendship Missionary Baptist Church
Dewey Greene House
Greenwood City Hall
Leflore County Courthouse
Leflore Theater
Plaza Hotel and Liquor Store
St. Francis of Assisi Catholic Center
Turner Chapel
Union Grove MB Church
Wesley United Methodist Church

Hattiesburg

Forrest County Courthouse
Kelly Settlement
Masonic Temple
Morning Star Baptist Church
Mount Carmel Baptist Church
Mount Zion Baptist Church
St. James CME Methodist Church
St. John United Methodist Church
    (Palmer's Crossing)
St. Paul United Methodist Church
University of Southern Mississippi
Vernon Dahmer Gravesite
Mrs. Woods's Boardinghouse

Jackson

Gladys Noel Bates House
COFO Office
College Hill Baptist Church
Collins Funeral Home
Medgar Evers House
Farish Street
Farish Street Baptist Church
Greyhound Bus Station
Hinds County Detention Center
Jackson Public Library
Jackson State University
Masonic Temple/NAACP Office
A. H. McCoy Federal Building
Millsaps College

Mississippi State Fairgrounds
Morning Star Baptist Church
Mount Olive Cemetery
New Jerusalem Baptist Church
Old Capitol/State Historical Museum
Pearl Street AME Church
Smith Robertson Museum
Steven's Kitchen
Tougaloo College
Trailways Bus Station
United States Courthouse
    (James O. Eastland Building)
Woodworth Chapel, Tougaloo College
Woolworth's

Magnolia

Pike County Courthouse/Jail

McComb

Burglund High School
Burglund Super Market
C. C. Bryant House
Continental Hotel
Freedom House
Greyhound Bus Station
Heffner House
Holiday Inn

Martin Luther King, Jr.,
    Community Center
Masonic Hall
McComb City Hall
Palace Theater
Alyene Quin House
Society Hill MB Church
St. Paul United Methodist Church
Woolworth's

Meridian

James Chaney Gravesite
COFO/CORE Office
First Union Baptist Church
Fitkins Memorial Chapel of the Nazarene

Meridian Baptist Seminary
Schwerner House
United States Post Office Building

Oxford (University of Mississippi)

Baxter Hall
The Lyceum

Peabody Building
Shoemaker Hall

Philadelphia

Benwalt Hotel
Kate Black House
COFO/MFDP Office
Lillie Jones House
Mount Nebo Missionary Baptist Church

Mount Zion Methodist Church
Neshoba County Courthouse
Neshoba County Fairgrounds
Neshoba County Jail
Old Jolly Farm

Winona

Montgomery County Jail

NORTH CAROLINA

Greensboro

Greensboro City Hall
Greensboro Historical Museum

North Carolina A&T
Woolworth's

Raleigh

Greenleaf Hall, Shaw University

SOUTH CAROLINA

Charleston

Charleston County Hospital
Chow Mein Inn
Fort Sumter Hotel
Heart of Charleston Motel

Morris Brown AME Church
South Carolina Medical College
   Hospital

Johns Island

Esau Jenkins Gravesite
Haut Gap High School
Moving Star Hall

Progressive Club
Wesley United Methodist Church

Orangeburg

All Star Bowling Lanes
Claflin College
Kress
Lowman Hall, South Carolina
   State University

Orangeburg City Hall
Orangeburg County Courthouse
Orangeburg County Jail
South Carolina State University
Trinity United Methodist Church

TENNESSEE

New Market

Highlander Research and Education Center

Nashville

American Baptist College
The Arcade
Cain-Sloan Department Store
Capers Memorial CME Church
Clark Memorial Methodist Church
Davidson County Courthouse/City Hall
First Baptist Church (Capitol Hill)
Fisk Chapel, Fisk University
Hattie Cotton School
Harvey's Department Store

Jewish Community Center
Kress
Krystal Grill
Z. Alexander Looby House
McClellan's
Meharry Medical College
Tennessee State University
Tic Toc Restaurant
Walgreen's
Woolworth's

Memphis

Mrs. Brewer's Boardinghouse
Centenary United Methodist Church
Claridge Hotel
Clayborn Temple AME Church
Fire Station No. 2
Hamilton High School
Holiday Inn-Rivermont
Hunt Sculpture
LeMoyne College
Lorraine Motel/National Civil Rights
    Museum
Mason Temple

Memphis City Auditorium
Memphis City Hall
Minimum Salary Building
R. S. Lewis & Sons Funeral Home
Shelby County Courthouse
Shelby County Jail
St. Joseph's Hospital
Tri-State Bank
United Rubber Workers Hall
    (Firestone Hall)
William F. Bowld Hospital

Endnotes

1. Steven M. Millner, "The Emergence and Career of a Social Movement," in Garrow, *Walking City*, p. 524.
2. Garrow, *Bearing the Cross*, p. 16–17.
3. Highlander Center Records, record group 2, box 2, series I, folder 38, transcript pp. 6–9.
4. King Speeches and Sermons, "Address to the Initial Meeting of the Montgomery Improvement Association," December 5, 1955.
5. Graetz, *White Preacher*, p. 57.
6. Lesher, *Wallace*, p. 174.
7. King Speeches and Sermons, "How Long? Not Long," March 25, 1965.
8. General Code of the City of Birminghan (effective Dec. 8, 1944).
9. Alabama Christian Movement for Human Rights, "Four Years of Progress of the Alabama Christian Movement for Human Rights 1956–60," ACMHR program, 1960 (courtesy of Lola Hendricks).
10. King, *Why We Can't Wait*, pp. 82–84.
11. Connor Papers, folder 13.4
12. Clarke, "Goals and Techniques," pp. 34–74.
13. Connor Papers, transcript of April 12, 1963, folder 13.2.
14. Petition prepared by the Dallas County Citizens' Council, Sept. 1, 1955, copy in author's possession (courtesy of the Old Depot Museum, Selma, Alabama).
15. John Lewis, speech in front of Brown Chapel, Selma, Alabama, March 6, 1994.
16. Mendelsohn, *The Martyrs*, pp. 169–71.
17. Transcript of the Malcolm X Press Conference, February 4, 1965, on file at the Birmingham Public Library.

18. Dallas County voting test, copy in author's possession (courtesy of Marie Foster).
19. Reddick, *Crusader without Violence,* p. 95.
20. Long, "Black Power in the Black Belt," p. 23.
21. Lowndes County Freedom Organization pamphlet, p. 2, Highlander Center Records, folder "Bolivar-Sunflower 1967 Materials Used."
22. King Papers, vol. I, pp. 103–04.
23. King Speeches and Sermons, March 3, 1963, Ebenezer Baptist Church.
24. King Speeches and Sermons, January 16, 1966, Ebenezer Baptist Church.
25. King Speeches and Sermons, March 3, 1963, Ebenezer Baptist Church.
26. King Speeches and Sermons, April 30, 1967, Ebenezer Baptist Church.
27. King Papers, vol. I, p. 121.
28. Watters, *Down to Now,* pp. 7–9.
29. Reagon, "Songs of the Civil Rights Movement," at 136 (quoting Guy and Candie Carawan. *We Shall Overcome: Songs of the Southern Freedom Movement.* New York: Oak Publications, 1963, p. 62).
30. *Jet,* August 23, 1962, pp. 14–18, copy in King Speeches and Sermons.
31. Douglas Kiker, "Old Savannah Battered by Racial Tidal Wave," *Atlanta Journal,* April 23, 1960, p. 3.
32. McAdam, *Freedom Summer,* p. 257.
33. Ibid., pp. 78–79.
34. Grant, *Black Protest,* p. 303.
35. Silver, *The Closed Society,* p. 119.
36. Scheips, *Role of the Army,* pp. 99–100.
37. Charles McLaurin, "Notes on Organizing," in Mark Levy Materials.
38. Mississippi Oral History Project (Hamer), transcript p. 45.
39. Meredith, "Big Changes Are Coming," pp. 23–27.
40. Mississippi Oral History Project (E. Dahmer), transcript p. 30.
41. Horton, *Highlander Folk School,* p. 224.
42. Highlander Center Records, record group 1, box 2, series II, folder 25.
43. Clark, *Ready from Within,* p. 126.
44. Carawan and Carawan, *Ain't You Got,* p. 141.
45. Reagon, "Songs of the Civil Rights Movement," pp. 65–82.
46. Smith, *Social Crisis Preaching,* p. 79.
47. Smith, unfinished manuscript "Pursuit of a Dream," ch. 6, p. 12, in Kelly Miller Smith Papers, box 28, files 7 and 8.
48. "Sit-In: NBC White Paper."
49. Nash, in Ahmann, *New Negro,* pp. 47–48.
50. King, "Mountaintop," April 3, 1968, "Martin Luther King Speaks" SCLC audiotape series.

Selected Sources

Interviews

Alexander, Robert. June 1, 1995, Nashville, TN

Anderson, Dr. James. April 28, 1995, Jackson, MS

Anderson, Rev. L. L. March 7, 1994, March 7, 1995, Selma, AL

Armstrong, James. March 20, 1995, Birmingham, AL

Bailey, Sam. April, 19, 1995, Jackson, MS

Balton, Kirkwood. March 23, 1995, Birmingham, AL

Bates, Gladys Noel. February 27, 1996, Denver, CO

Bevel, James. March 6 and 7, 1995, Selma, AL

Black, Kate. May 2, 1995, Philadelphia, MS

Bowie, Rev. Harry John. May 9, 1995, Greenville, MS

Boyd, Rev. Horace C. December 11, 1995, Albany, GA

Boynton, Bruce. March 7, 1995, Selma, AL

Bridges, Edgar. April 18, 1995, Jackson, MS

Brooks, Owen. May 10, 1995, Greenville, MS

Brown, Helen. February 12, 1995, New York, NY

Bryant, C. C. April 24, 1995, McComb, MS

Bullins, Willie. May 23, 1995, Greenwood, MS

Carr, Johnnie. March 28, 1995, Montgomery, AL

Chestnut, J. L., Jr. March 6, 1994, August 5, 1995, Selma, AL

Clark, Obie. May 4, 1995, Meridian, MS

Cochran, Eddie. May 22, 1995, Greenwood, MS

Cooper, Annie. March 21, 1994, Selma, AL

Crosby, Fred. May 4, 1995, Meridian, MS

Dahmer, Vernon, Jr. May 5, 1995, Hattiesburg, MS

Davis, Reuben. March 30, 1995, Birmingham, AL

Drew, Addine. March 25, 1995, Birmingham, AL

Elliot, Dorothy. May 4, 1995, Meridian, MS

Fairley, Rev. Kenneth. May 5, 1995, Hattiesburg, MS

Fairley, J. C. May 5, 1995, Hattiesburg, MS

Gadsden, Eugene H. December 14, 1995, Savannah, GA

Gardner, Rev. Edward. August 23, 1996, Birmingham, AL

Garrett, Simon. May 21, 1995, Greenwood, MS

Gillard, Lillie W. August 18, 1996, Midway, GA

Gilmore, Rev. Thomas. March 29, 1995, Ensley, AL

Goodson, Dr. J. S. March 30, 1995, Birmingham, AL

Gray, Fred. August 31, 1995, Montgomery, AL

Grimball, Ethel. December 15, 1995, Johns Island, SC

Harrington, Evans. April 27, 1995, Oxford, MS

Harris, Rev. Jerome. April 9, 1995, Selma, AL

Harris, Vera. August 31, 1995, Montgomery, AL

Harrison, Alferdteen. April 18, 1995, Jackson, MS

Hatcher, Lula. March 7, 1995, Selma, AL

Hebert, Gerald. March 3, 1995, Selma, AL

Hendricks, Lola. March 20, 1995, Birmingham, AL

Hillegas, Jan. April 30, 1995, Jackson, MS

Holmes, Alvin. August 31, 1995, Montgomery, AL

Horton, Aimee. June 4, 1995, New Market, TN

Hulett, John. August 7, 1995, Hayneville, AL

Jackson, Eugene. December 6, 1995, Atlanta, GA

James, Harry. December 13, 1995, Savannah, GA

Jefferson, Jacquelyne. February 2, 1996, Johns Island, SC

Jenkins, William. December 15, 1995, February 8, 1996, Johns Island, SC

Johnson, Rev. Aaron. May 11, 1995, Greenwood, MS

Johnson, Rev. Charles. May 3, 1995, Meridian, MS

Johnson, June. April 20, 1995, Washington, DC

Johnson, Colonel Stone. March 18, 1995, Birmingham, AL

Jordan, David. May 22, 1995, Greenwood, MS

Joseph, Wilhelm. February 16, 1995, New York, NY

King, Carol and Clennon. December 10, 1995, Albany, GA

King, Rev. Ed. April 21 and 29, 1995, Jackson, MS

Lacy, Jimmy. May 11, 1995, Ruleville, MS

Lafayette, Bernard. June 1 and 6, 1995, August 20 and 22, 1995, Nashville, TN

Law, W. W. December 12, 1995, February 2, 1996, Savannah, GA

Lewis, John. December 1, 1994, Washington, DC

Logan, Tom. August 14, 1995, Montgomery, AL

Lowery, Rev. Joseph. March 7, 1995, Selma, AL

Mars, Florence. April 15, 1996, Philadelphia, MS

Martin, Barbara. March 27, 1995, Birmingham, AL

Martin, Jean. July 26, 1995, Selma, AL

Martin, Joe. April 24, 1995, McComb, MS

McGrue, Joseph. March 8, 1994, Selma, AL

McKinstry, Carolyn. March 31, 1995, Birmingham, AL

McLaurin, Charles. May 20, 1995, August 25, 1996, Indianola and Ruleville, MS

McLaurin, Lillie. March 15, 1996, Hattiesburg, MS

Miller, Bernice. July 26, 1995, Selma, AL

Miller, Lorene. May 22, 1995, Greenwood, MS

Moebes, Jack. June 3, 1995, Greensboro, NC

Moore, James. May 22, 1995, Greenwood, MS

Morgan, Carl. March 4, 1995, Selma, AL

Moss, Otelia. March 7, 1994, Selma, AL

Neeley, Mary Ann. March 10, 1995, Montgomery, AL

Pickett, Marie. April 1, 1995, Birmingham, AL

Porter, Rev. John. March 29, 1995, Birmingham, AL

Quin, Alyene. April 24, 1995, McComb, MS

Rand, Debbie. February 10, 1995, New York, NY

Roberts, Rev. Joseph. December 8, 1995, Atlanta, GA

Robinson, Amelia Boynton. March 13, 1995, Tuskegee, AL

Robinson, Estella. March 7, 1994, Marion, AL

Sanders, Hank. August 7, 1995, Selma, AL

Saunders, Bill. September 12, 1996, Johns Island, SC

Sellers, Cleveland. August 17, 1996, Orangeburg, SC

Smith, Rev. N. H. March 31, 1995, Birmingham, AL

Smitherman, Joe T. March 3, 1995, Selma, AL

Summerlin, M. E. March 8, 1994, Selma, AL

Swift, George ("Cap"). April 11, 1995, Selma, AL

Tisdale, Eva. May 2, 1995, Philadelphia, MS

Turner, Albert. March 7, 1994, April 12, 1995, Marion, AL

Vann, David. March 30, 1995, Birmingham, AL

Wax, Helen. May 17, 1995, Memphis, TN

Wells, Rev. Samuel B. December 9, 1995, Albany, GA

Westbrook, Grafta Looby. May 29, 1995, Nashville, TN

Williams, Fred and Mary Ellen. April 10, 1995, Selma, AL

Williamson, Arance. May 10, 1995, Greenwood, MS

Willie, Louis J. March 20, 1995, Birmingham, AL

Wimberly, Louretta. April 10, 1995, Selma, AL

Woods, Rev. Abraham. March 26, 1995, Birmingham, AL

Woods, Rev. Calvin. March 22, 1995, Birmingham, AL

Young, Gene. April 18, 1995, Jackson, MS

Books and Dissertations

Abernathy, Ralph David. *And the Walls Came Tumbling Down: An Autobiography.*
New York: Harper & Row, 1989.

Adams, Frank, with Myles Horton. *Unearthing Seeds of Fire: The Idea of Highlander.*
Winston-Salem: John F. Blair, 1975.

Adams, George Rollie, and Ralph Jerry Christian. *Nashville: A Pictorial History.* Norfolk, VA: Donning Co., 1981.

Agronsky, Jonathan. *Marion Barry: The Politics of Race.* Latham, NY: British American Publishing, 1991.

Ahmann, Mathew H., ed. *The New Negro.* Notre Dame: Fides Publishers, 1961.

Allen, Ivan, Jr., with Paul Hemphill. *Mayor: Notes on the Sixties.* New York: Simon & Schuster, 1971.

American Automobile Association. *Go Guide to Pleasant Motoring.* Washington, D.C.: Andrew F. Jackson Associates, Inc., 1957 and 1964.

Bailey, D'Army. *Mine Eyes Have Seen: Dr. Martin Luther King, Jr.'s Final Journey.* Memphis: Towery Publishing, 1993.

Baldwin, Frederick. *". . . We Ain't What We Used to Be."* Savannah: Telfair Academy of Arts and Sciences, 1983.

Baldwin, Lewis V., and Aprille V. Woodson. *Freedom Is Never Free: A Biographical Portrait of Edgar Daniel Nixon, Sr.* Nashville: Office of Minority Affairs, Tennessee General Assembly, 1992.

Barnes, Catherine A. *Journey from Jim Crow: The Desegregation of Southern Transit.* New York: Columbia University Press, 1983.

Barrett, Russell H. *Integration at Ole Miss.* Chicago: Quadrangle Books, 1965.

Bass, Jack. *Taming the Storm: The Life and Times of Judge Frank M. Johnson, Jr., and the South's Fight over Civil Rights.* New York: Doubleday, 1993.

———. *Unlikely Heroes.* Tuscaloosa: University of Alabama Press, 1991.

———, and Jack Nelson. *The Orangeburg Massacre.* Macon, GA: Mercer University Press, 1984.

Bates, Daisy. *The Long Shadow of Little Rock: A Memoir.* New York: David McKay Co., 1962.

Beals, Melba Pattillo. *Warriors Don't Cry: A Searing Memoir of the Battle to Integrate Little Rock's Central High.* New York: Washington Square/Pocket Books, 1994.

Beifuss, Joan Turner. *At the River I Stand.* Memphis: St. Luke's Press, 1990.

———, foreword. *I Am a Man: Photographs of the 1968 Memphis Sanitation Strike and Dr. Martin Luther King, Jr.* Memphis: Memphis Publishing Co., 1993.

Belfrage, Sally. *Freedom Summer.* Charlottesville: University Press of Virginia, 1965.

Bishop, Jim. *The Days of Martin Luther King, Jr.* New York: G. P. Putnam's Sons, 1971.

Boddie, Charles Emerson. *God's "Bad Boys."* Valley Forge, PA: Judson Press, 1972.

Bolster, Paul Douglas. "Civil Rights Movements in Twentieth Century Georgia." Ph.D. dissertation, University of Georgia, 1972.

Booker, Simeon. *Black Man's America.* Englewood Cliffs, NJ: Prentice-Hall, 1964.

Borders, William Holmes. *Seven Minutes at the "Mike" in the Deep South.* Atlanta: Arnold's Printing Service, 1980.

Branch, Taylor. *Parting the Waters: America in the King Years 1954–63.* New York: Simon & Schuster, 1988.

Bullard, Sara, ed. *Free at Last: A History of the Civil Rights Movement and Those Who Died in the Struggle.* Montgomery: Teaching Tolerance, the Southern Poverty Law Center, 1989.

Burner, Eric R. *And Gently He Shall Lead Them: Robert Parris Moses and Civil Rights in Mississippi.* New York: New York University Press, 1994.

Cagin, Seth, and Philip Dray. *We Are Not Afraid: The Story of Goodman, Schwerner, and Chaney and the Civil Rights Campaign for Mississippi.* New York: Macmillan, 1988.

Campbell, Clarice T. *Civil Rights Chronicle: Letters from the South.* Jackson, MS: University Press of Mississippi, 1997.

Carawan, Guy and Candie. *Ain't You Got a Right to the Tree of Life? The People of Johns Island, South Carolina—Their Faces, Their Words, and Their Songs.* Athens: University of Georgia Press, 1989.

Carmichael, Stokely, and Charles V. Hamilton, *Black Power: The Politics of Liberation in America.* New York: Random House, 1967.

Carson, Clayborne. *In Struggle: SNCC and the Black Awakening of the 1960s.* Cambridge, MA: Harvard University Press, 1981.

————, et al., eds. *The Eyes on the Prize Civil Rights Reader: Documents, Speeches, and Firsthand Accounts from the Black Freedom Struggle 1954–90.* New York: Penguin Books, 1991.

————, et al., eds. *The Papers of Martin Luther King, Jr.,* vols. 1, 2, and 3. Berkeley: University of California Press, 1992, 1994, 1996.

Carter, Hodding. *So the Heffners Left McComb.* Garden City, NY: Doubleday, 1965.

Chafe, William H. *Civilities and Civil Rights: Greensboro, North Carolina, and the Black Struggle for Equality.* Oxford: Oxford University Press, 1980.

Chestnut, J. L., Jr., and Julia Cass. *Black in Selma: The Uncommon Life of J. L. Chestnut, Jr.* New York: Farrar, Straus and Giroux, 1990.

Clark, E. Culpepper. *The Schoolhouse Door: Segregation's Last Stand at the University of Alabama.* New York: Oxford University Press, 1993.

Clark, Septima P. *Ready from Within: Septima Clark and the Civil Rights Movement.* Navarro, CA: Wild Trees Press, 1986.

Clarke, Jacquelyne, M. J. "Goals and Techniques in Three Negro Civil Rights Organizations in Alabama." Ph.D. dissertation, Ohio State University, 1960.

Clayton, Edward T., ed. *The SCLC Story in Words and Pictures.* Atlanta: Southern Christian Leadership Conference, 1964.

Cobb, James. *The Most Southern Place on Earth: The Mississippi Delta and the Roots of Regional Identity.* New York: Oxford University Press, 1992.

Cobbs, Elizabeth H./Petric J. Smith. *Long Time Coming: An Insider's Story of the Birmingham Church Bombing That Rocked the World.* Birmingham: Crane Hill Publishers, 1994.

Cochran, Lynda Dempsey. "Arthur Davis Shores: Advocate for Freedom." M.A. history thesis, Georgia Southern College, 1977.

Coffin, William Sloane, Jr. *Once to Every Man: A Memoir.* New York: Atheneum, 1977.

Coffman, Mary Ruth. *Build Me a City: The Life of Reverend Harold Purcell.* Montgomery: Pioneer Press, 1984.

Cohn, David L. *Where I Was Born and Raised.* Boston: Houghton Mifflin, 1948.

Cohodas, Nadine. *Strom Thurmond and the Politics of Southern Change.* New York: Simon & Schuster, 1993.

Davidson, Chandler, and Bernard Grofman, eds. *Quiet Revolution in the South: The*

Impact of the Voting Rights Act 1965–90. Princeton: Princeton University Press, 1994.

Dent, Thomas C. *Southern Journey: A Return to the Civil Rights Movement.* New York: William Morrow, 1997.

———, Richard Schechner, and Gilbert Moses, eds. *The Free Southern Theater by the Free Southern Theater.* Indianapolis: Bobbs-Merrill, 1969.

Dittmer, John. *Local People: The Struggle for Civil Rights in Mississippi.* Urbana: University of Illinois, 1994.

Doar, John, and Dorothy Landsberg. "The Performance of the FBI in Investigating Violations of Federal Laws Protecting the Right to Vote—1960–67," Hearings Before the Senate Select Committee to Study Governmental Operations with Respect to Intelligence Activities, U.S. Senate, 94th Congress, First Session, Vol. 6, Attachment 4, pp. 888–991.

Douglas, Ellen. *A Long Night.* Nouveau Press/Mississippi Civil Liberties Union, 1986.

Doyle, Don. H. *Nashville since the 1920s.* Knoxville: University of Tennessee Press, 1985.

Dunbar, Tony. *Delta Time: A Journey through Mississippi.* New York: Pantheon, 1990.

Dunson, Josh. *Freedom in the Air: Song Movements of the Sixties.* New York: International Publishers, 1965.

Durr, Virginia Foster, and Hollinger F. Barnard, ed. *Outside the Magic Circle: The Autobiography of Virginia Foster Durr.* New York: Simon & Schuster, 1985.

Eagles, Charles W. *Outside Agitator: Jon Daniels and the Civil Rights Movement in Alabama.* Chapel Hill: University of North Carolina, 1993.

Edds, Margaret. *Free at Last: What Really Happened When Civil Rights Came to Southern Politics.* Bethesda, MD: Adler & Adler, 1987.

Egerton, John. *Nashville: The Faces of Two Centuries.* Nashville: Plus Media, 1979.

———. *Speak Now against the Day: The Generation before the Civil Rights Movement in the South.* Chapel Hill: University of North Carolina Press, 1995.

Eskew, Glenn T. "The Alabama Christian Movement and the Birmingham Struggle for Civil Rights, 1956–63." M.A. history thesis, Auburn University, 1987.

Evans, Zelia S., and J. T. Alexander, eds. *Dexter Avenue Baptist Church, 1877–1977.* Montgomery: Dexter Avenue Baptist Church, 1977.

Evers, Charles. *Evers.* New York: World Publishing, 1971.

———, and Andrew Szanton. *Have No Fear: The Charles Evers Story.* New York: John Wiley & Sons, 1997.

Evers, Myrlie B., with William Peters. *For Us, the Living.* Jackson: University Press of Mississippi, 1996.

Fager, Charles E. *Selma 1965.* New York: Scribners, 1974.

———. *Uncertain Resurrection: The Poor People's Washington Campaign.* Grand Rapids: William B. Eerdmans Publishing Co., 1969.

Fairclough, Adam. *To Redeem the Soul of America: The Southern Christian Leadership Conference and Martin Luther King, Jr.* Athens: University of Georgia Press, 1987.

Farmer, James. *Lay Bare the Heart: An Autobiography of the Civil Rights Movement.* New York: Arbor House, 1985.

Fitts, Alston. *Selma: Queen City of the Black Belt.* Selma: Clairmont Press, 1989.

Selected Sources

Forman, James. *The Making of Black Revolutionaries*. Washington, DC: Open Hand Publishing, Inc., 1985.

———. *Sammy Younge, Jr.: The First Black College Student to Die in the Black Liberation Movement*. New York: Grove Press, 1968.

Frady, Marshall. *Jesse: The Life and Pilgrimage of Jesse Jackson*. New York: Random House, 1996.

Frank, Gerold. *An American Death: The True Story of the Assassination of Dr. Martin Luther King, Jr., and the Greatest Manhunt of Our Time*. Garden City, NY: Doubleday, 1972.

Franklin, Jimmie Lewis. *Back to Birmingham: Richard Arrington, Jr., and His Times*. Tuscaloosa: University of Alabama Press, 1989.

Garrett, Franklin M. *Atlanta and Environs: A Chronicle of Its People and Events*, vol. 2. Athens: University of Georgia Press, 1969.

Garrow, David J., ed., *Atlanta, Georgia, 1960–1961: Sit-Ins and Student Activism*. Brooklyn, NY: Carlson Publishing, Inc., 1989.

———. *Bearing the Cross: Martin Luther King, Jr., and the Southern Christian Leadership Conference*. New York: Vintage, 1988.

———, ed. *Birmingham, Alabama, 1956–1963: The Black Struggle for Civil Rights*. Brooklyn, NY: Carlson Publishing, Inc., 1989.

———. *The FBI and Martin Luther King, Jr.: From "Solo" to Memphis*. New York: W. W. Norton, 1981.

———. *Protest at Selma: Martin Luther King, Jr., and the Voting Rights Act of 1965*. New Haven: Yale University Press, 1978.

———, ed. *The Walking City: The Montgomery Bus Boycott, 1955–56*. Brooklyn, NY: Carlson Publishing, Inc., 1989.

———. *We Shall Overcome: The Civil Rights Movement in the United States in the 1950's and 1960's*. Brooklyn, NY: Carlson Publishing, Inc., 1989. 3 vols.

Gaston, A. G. *Green Power: The Successful Way of A. G. Gaston*. Troy, AL: Troy State University Press, 1968.

Good, Paul. *The Trouble I've Seen: White Journalist/Black Movement*. Washington, DC: Howard University Press, 1975.

Graetz, Robert S. *Montgomery: A White Preacher's Memoir*. Minneapolis: Fortress Press, 1991.

Grant, Joanne, ed. *Black Protest: History, Documents, and Analyses 1619 to the Present*. Greenwich, CT: Fawcett Publications, 1968.

Gray, Fred D. *Bus Ride to Justice: Changing the System by the System: The Life and Works of Fred D. Gray*. Montgomery: Black Belt Press, 1995.

Greenberg, Jack. *Crusaders in the Courts: How a Dedicated Band of Lawyers Fought for the Civil Rights Revolution*. New York: Basic Books, 1994.

Greenberg, Polly. *The Devil Has Slippery Shoes: A Biased Biography of the Child Development Group of Mississippi*. London: Macmillan, 1969.

Gregory, Dick, with Robert Lipsyte. *Nigger*. New York: E. P. Dutton & Co, 1964.

Hampton, Henry, and Steve Fayer, eds. *Voices of Freedom: An Oral History of the Civil Rights Movement from the 1950s through the 1980s*. New York: Bantam Books, 1990.

Holt, Len. *The Summer That Didn't End*. London: Heinemann, 1966.

Honey, Michael K. *Southern Labor and Black Civil Rights: Organizing Memphis Workers*. Urbana: University of Illinois Press, 1993.

Horton, Aimee Isgrig. *The Highlander Folk School: A History of Its Major Programs, 1932–1961*. Brooklyn, NY: Carlson Publishing, Inc., 1989.

Huie, William Bradford. *He Slew the Dreamer: My Search for the Truth and James Earl Ray and the Murder of Martin Luther King*. New York: Delacorte Press, 1968.

———. *Three Lives for Mississippi*. London: Heinemann, 1965.

Jacoway, Elizabeth, and David R. Colburn, eds. *Southern Businessmen and Desegregation*. Baton Rouge: Louisiana State University Press, 1982.

Jenkins, Herbert. *Keeping the Peace: A Police Chief Looks at His Job*. New York: Harper & Row, 1970.

Johnston, Erle. *Mississippi's Defiant Years 1953–1973*. Forest, MS: Lake Harbor Publishers, 1990.

Kasher, Steven. *The Civil Rights Movement: A Photographic History, 1954–68*. New York: Abbeville Press Publishers, 1996.

Kennedy, Stetson. *Jim Crow Guide to the USA*. London: Lawrence & Wishart, 1959.

King, Coretta Scott. *My Life with Martin Luther King, Jr.* New York: Penguin Books, 1993.

King, Martin Luther, Jr. *Stride toward Freedom*. New York: Harper & Bros., 1958.

———. *Where Do We Go from Here: Chaos or Community?* New York: Harper & Row, 1967.

———. *Why We Can't Wait*. New York: Harper & Row, 1963.

King, Martin Luther, Sr., with Clayton Riley. *Daddy King: An Autobiography*. New York: William Morrow, 1980.

King, Mary. *Freedom Song: A Personal Story of the 1960s Civil Rights Movement*. New York: William Morrow, 1987.

Kluger, Richard. *Simple Justice: The History of Brown v. Board of Education and Black America's Struggle for Equality*. New York: Alfred A. Knopf, 1976.

Lane, Mark, and Dick Gregory. *Code Name "Zorro": The Murder of Martin Luther King, Jr.* Englewood Cliffs, NJ: Prentice Hall, 1977.

Lawson, Steven F. *Black Ballots: Voting Rights in the South 1944–1969*. New York: Columbia University Press, 1976.

Lemann, Nicholas. *The Promised Land: the Great Black Migration and How It Changed America*. New York: Alfred A. Knopf, 1991.

Lesher, Stephan. *George Wallace: American Populist*. Reading, MA: Addison-Wesley, 1993.

Levine, Ellen. *Freedom's Children: Young Civil Rights Activists Tell Their Own Stories*. New York: Avon/Flare, 1993.

Levy, Peter B. *Let Freedom Ring: A Documentary History of the Modern Civil Rights Movement*. New York: Praeger, 1992.

Lewis, Anthony. *Make No Law: The Sullivan Case and the First Amendment*. New York: Random House, 1991.

Lewis, David Levering. *King: A Critical Biography*. New York: Praeger, 1970.

Lewis, Selma S. "Social Religion and the Memphis Sanitation Strike." Ph.D. dissertation, Memphis State University, 1976.

Lincoln, C. Eric. *The Black Church since Frazier*. New York: Schocken Books, 1974.

Loewen, James W., and Charles Sallis, eds. *Mississippi: Conflict and Change*. New York: Pantheon, 1974.

Longenecker, Stephen L. *Selma's Peacemaker: Ralph Smeltzer and Civil Rights Mediation*. Philadelphia: Temple University Press, 1987.

Lord, Walter. *The Past That Would Not Die*. New York: Harper & Row, 1965.

Lowery, Charles D., and John F. Marszalek. *Encyclopedia of African-American Civil Rights from Emancipation to the Present*. New York: Greenwood Press, 1992.

Lynd, Staughton, ed. *Nonviolence in America: A Documentary History*. Indianapolis: Bobbs-Merrill, 1966.

Lyon, Danny. *Memories of the Southern Civil Rights Movement*. Chapel Hill: University of North Carolina Press, 1992.

Marable, Manning. *Race, Reform and Rebellion: The Second Reconstruction in Black America 1945–1982*. Jackson: University Press of Mississippi, 1984.

Mars, Florence. *Witness in Philadelphia*. Baton Rouge: Louisiana State University Press, 1977.

Martin, Harold H. *Atlanta and Environs: A Chronicle of Its People and Events*, vol. 3, *Years of Change and Challenge 1940–1976*. Athens: University of Georgia Press, 1987.

Mason, Herman ("Skip"), Jr. *Going against the Wind: A Pictorial History of African-Americans in Atlanta*. Atlanta: Longstreet Press, 1992.

Mays, Benjamin E. *Born to Rebel: An Autobiography*. New York: Scribners, 1971.

McAdam, Doug. *Freedom Summer*. New York: Oxford University Press, 1988.

McLemore, Leslie Burl. "The Mississippi Freedom Democratic Party: A Case Study of Grass-Roots Politics." Ph.D. dissertation, University of Massachusetts, 1971.

McMillen, Neil R. *The Citizens' Council: Organized Resistance to the Second Reconstruction, 1954–64*. Urbana: University of Illinois Press, 1971.

Meier, August, and Elliott Rudwick. *CORE: A Study in the Civil Rights Movement, 1942–1968*. New York: Oxford University Press, 1973.

————, ————, and John Bracey, Jr. *Black Protest in the '60s: Articles from the New York Times*. New York: Markus Weiner Publishing, 1991.

Mendelsohn, Jack. *The Martyrs: Sixteen Who Gave Their Lives for Racial Justice*. New York: Harper & Row, 1966.

Meredith, James. *Three Years in Mississippi*. Bloomington: Indiana University Press, 1966.

Mills, Kay. *This Little Light of Mine: The Life of Fannie Lou Hamer*. New York: Plume, 1994.

Mills, Nicolaus. *Like a Holy Crusade: Mississippi 1964—The Turning of the Civil Rights Movement*. Chicago: Ivan R. Dee, 1992.

Moody, Anne. *Coming of Age in Mississippi*. New York: Dell, 1968.

Moore, Charles (text by Michael S. Durham). *Powerful Days: The Civil Rights Photography of Charles Moore*. New York: Stewart, Tabori & Chang, 1991.

Morgan, Charles, Jr. *A Time to Speak*. New York: Harper & Row, 1964.

Morris, Aldon D. *The Origins of the Civil Rights Movement: Black Communities Organizing for Change*. New York: Free Press, 1984.

Myrdal, Gunnar. *An American Dilemma: The Negro Problem and Modern Democracy*. New York: Harper & Bros., 1944.

Neary, John. *Julian Bond: Black Rebel*. New York: William Morrow, 1971.

Nelson, Jack. *Terror in the Night: The Klan's Campaign Against the Jews*. New York: Simon & Schuster, 1993.

Norrell, Robert J. *Reaping the Whirlwind: The Civil Rights Movement in Tuskegee.* New York: Random House, 1985.

Nossiter, Adam. *Of Long Memory: Mississippi and the Murder of Medgar Evers.* Reading, MA: Addison-Wesley, 1994.

Nunnelly, William A. *Bull Connor.* Tuscaloosa: University of Alabama Press, 1991.

Oates, Stephen B. *Let the Trumpet Sound: The Life of Martin Luther King, Jr.* New York: Harper & Row, 1982.

Olendorf, Sandra Brenneman. "Highlander Folk School and the South Carolina Sea Island Citizenship Schools: Implications for the Social Studies." Ph.D. dissertation, University of Kentucky, 1987.

Oppenheimer, Martin. *The Sit-In Movement of 1960.* Brooklyn, NY: Carlson Publishing, Inc., 1989.

O'Reilly, Kenneth. *"Racial Matters": The FBI's Secret File on Black America 1960–72.* New York: Free Press, 1989.

Oshinsky, David M. *"Worse than Slavery": Parchman Farm and the Ordeal of Jim Crow Justice.* New York: Free Press, 1996.

Parker, Frank R. *Black Votes Count: Political Empowerment in Mississippi after 1965.* Chapel Hill: University of North Carolina Press, 1990.

Payne, Charles M. *I've Got the Light of Freedom: The Organizing Tradition and the Mississippi Freedom Struggle.* Berkeley: University of California Press, 1995.

Peck, James. *Freedom Ride.* New York: Simon & Schuster, 1962.

Pomerantz, Gary M. *Where Peachtree Meets Sweet Auburn: The Saga of Two Families and the Making of Atlanta.* New York: Scribners, 1996.

Powdermaker, Hortense. *After Freedom: A Cultural Study in the Deep South.* Madison: University of Wisconsin Press, 1993.

Powledge, Fred. *Free at Last? The Civil Rights Movement and the People Who Made It.* Boston: Little, Brown, 1991.

Raines, Howell. *My Soul Is Rested: Movement Days in the Deep South Remembered.* New York: Putnam, 1977.

Reagon, Bernice Johnson. "Songs of the Civil Rights Movement 1955–1965: A Study in Culture History." Ph.D. dissertation, Howard University, 1975.

Reddick, Lawrence D. *Crusader without Violence: A Biography of Martin Luther King, Jr.* New York: Harper & Bros., 1959.

Robinson, Amelia Boynton. *Bridge across Jordan.* Washington, DC: Schiller Institute, 1991.

Robinson, Jo Ann. *The Montgomery Bus Boycott and the Women Who Started It: The Memoir of Jo Ann Gibson Robinson.* Knoxville: University of Tennessee Press, 1987.

Salter, John R., Jr. *Jackson, Mississippi: An American Chronicle of Struggle and Schism.* Malabar, FL: Robert E. Krieger Publishing, 1987.

Savage, Beth L., ed. *African American Historic Places.* Washington, DC: Preservation Press/National Register of Historic Places, 1994.

Scheips, Paul J. *The Role of the Army in the Oxford, Mississippi, Incident 1962–1963.* Histories Division, Office of the Chief of Military History, Department of the Army, June 24, 1965 (OCMH Monograph No. 73M).

Schulke, Flip. *He Had a Dream: Martin Luther King, Jr., and the Civil Rights Movement.* New York: W. W. Norton, 1995.

———, ed. *Martin Luther King, Jr.: A Documentary—Montgomery to Memphis*. New York: W. W. Norton, 1976.

———, and Penelope Ortner McPhee. *King Remembered*. New York: W. W. Norton, 1986.

Seay, Solomon S., Sr. *I Was There by the Grace of God*. Montgomery: S. S. Seay, Sr., Educational Foundation, 1990.

Seeger, Pete, and Bob Reiser. *Everybody Says Freedom: A History of the Civil Rights Movement in Songs and Pictures*. New York: W. W. Norton, 1989.

Sellers, Cleveland, with Robert Terrell. *The River of No Return: The Autobiography of a Black Militant and the Life and Death of SNCC*. Jackson: University Press of Mississippi, 1990.

Sikora, Frank. *The Judge: The Life and Opinions of Alabama's Frank M. Johnson, Jr.* Montgomery: Black Belt Press, 1992.

———. *Until Justice Rolls Down: The Birmingham Church Bombing Case*. Tuscaloosa: University of Alabama Press, 1991.

Silver, James W. *Mississippi: The Closed Society*. New York: Harcourt, Brace & World, 1966.

Sitkoff, Harvard. *The Struggle for Black Equality 1954–1980*. New York: Hill & Wang, 1981.

Smith, Kelly Miller. *Social Crisis Preaching: The Lyman Beecher Lectures 1983*. Macon, GA: Mercer University Press, 1984.

Spofford, Tim. *Lynch Street: The May 1970 Slayings at Jackson State College*. Kent, OH: Kent State University Press, 1988.

Stone, Clarence N. *Regime Politics: Governing Atlanta, 1946–88*. Lawrence: University Press of Kansas, 1989.

Sugarman, Tracy. *Stranger at the Gates: A Summer in Mississippi*. New York: Hill & Wang, 1966.

Sutherland, Elizabeth, ed. *Letters from Mississippi*. New York: McGraw-Hill, 1965.

Tjerandsen, Carl. *Education for Citizenship: A Foundation's Experience*. Santa Cruz, CA: Emil Schwarzhaupt Foundation, 1980.

Tucker, Shirley, ed. *Mississippi from Within*. New York: Arco Publishing, 1965.

Van Hoffman, Nicholas. *Mississippi Notebook*. New York: David White Co., 1964.

Viorst, Milton. *Fire in the Streets: America in the 1960s*. New York: Simon & Schuster, 1979.

Vivian, C. T. *Black Power and the American Myth*. Philadelphia: Fortress Press, 1970.

Vollers, Maryanne. *Ghosts of Mississippi: The Murder of Medgar Evers, the Trials of Byron de la Beckwith, and the Haunting of the New South*. Boston: Little, Brown & Co., 1995.

Walker, Lydia. *Challenge and Change: The Story of Civil Rights Activist C. T. Vivian*. Alpharetta, GA: W. H. Wolfe Associates, 1993.

Walker, Wyatt Tee. *"Somebody's Calling My Name": Black Sacred Music and Social Change*. Valley Forge, PA: Judson Press, 1979.

Watters, Pat. *Down to Now: Reflections on the Southern Civil Rights Movement*. New York: Pantheon, 1971.

———, and Reese Cleghorn, *Climbing Jacob's Ladder: The Arrival of Negroes in Southern Politics*. New York: Harcourt, Brace & World, 1967.

Webb, Sheyann, and Rachel West Nelson (as told to Frank Sikora). *Selma, Lord, Selma: Childhood Memories of the Civil Rights Days*. Tuscaloosa: University of Alabama Press, 1980.

West, Thomas R., and James W. Mooney, eds. *To Redeem a Nation: A History and Anthology of the Civil Rights Movement*. St. James, NY: Brandywine Press, 1993.

Westin, Alan F., and Barry Mahoney. *The Trial of Martin Luther King*. New York: Thomas Y. Crowell, 1974.

Whitehead, Don. *Attack on Terror: The FBI against the Ku Klux Klan in Mississippi*. New York: Funk & Wagnalls, 1970.

Whitfield, Stephen J. *A Death in the Delta: The Story of Emmett Till*. Baltimore: Johns Hopkins University Press, 1988.

Williams, Juan. *Eyes on the Prize: America's Civil Rights Years 1954–65*. New York: Penguin Books, 1988.

Williams, Roger M. *The Bonds: An American Family*. New York: Atheneum, 1971.

Wilson, Charles Reagan, and William Ferris, eds. *Encyclopedia of Southern Culture*. New York: Doubleday, 1989. 4 vols.

Withers, Ernest C. *Let Us March On!: Selected Civil Rights Photographs of Ernest C. Withers 1955–1968*. Boston: Massachusetts College of Art and Northeastern University, 1992.

Wolff, Miles. *Lunch at the 5 & 10*. Chicago: I. R. Dee, 1990.

Woodward, C. Vann. *The Strange Career of Jim Crow*. New York: Oxford University Press, 1955.

Yeakey, Lamont H. "The Montgomery, Alabama Bus Boycott, 1955–56." Ph.D. dissertation, Columbia University, 1979.

Young, Andrew. *An Easy Burden: The Civil Rights Movement and the Transformation of America*. New York: HarperCollins, 1996.

———. *A Way Out of No Way: The Spiritual Memoir of Andrew Young*. Nashville: T. Nelson Publishers, 1994.

Youth of the Rural Organizing and Cultural Center (introduction by Jay MacLeod). *Minds Stayed on Freedom: The Civil Rights Struggle in the Rural South*. Boulder, CO: Westview Press, 1991.

Zinn, Howard. *SNCC: The New Abolitionists*. Boston: Beacon Press, 1964.

———. *The Southern Mystique*. New York: Alfred A. Knopf, 1964.

Articles, Periodicals, Pamphlets, and Reports

Analavage, Robert. "Jackson: Death of a Movement Soldier." *Southern Patriot,* vol. 25 (June 1967), p. 1.

———. "What They're Saying in Lowndes County." *Southern Patriot,* vol. 24 (Oct. 1966), p. 3.

———. "Lowndes Party Girds for Future." *Southern Patriot,* vol. 24 (Dec. 1966), p. 1.

Anderson, William G. "Reflections on the Origins of the Albany Movement." *Journal of Southwest Georgia History,* vol. IX (Fall 1994), pp. 1–14.

ASU Today. Civil Rights Special Issue, vol. 7, no. 1 (Jan.–Feb. 1990).

Bailey, Ronald. "Remembering Medgar . . . For a New Generation." Civil Rights Research and Documentation Project (1988).

Barker, George. "Man behind the Move," *Nashville Tennessean*, April 16, 1961, pp. 12–13; "No Place to Hide," *Nashville Tennessean*, April 23, 1961, pp. 14–15.

Birmingham News (April 1 to May 30, 1963).

Braden, Ann. "Montgomery, Where Now?" *Southern Patriot*, vol. 23 (Jan. 1965), p. 1.

Braden, Carl. "How Poor People Built Political Power." *Southern Patriot*, vol. 29 (Feb. 1971), p. 1.

Brown, Joe David. "Birmingham, Alabama: A City in Fear." *Saturday Evening Post*, vol. 236 (March 2, 1963), pp. 12–18.

Carson, Clayborne. "SNCC and the Albany Movement." *Journal of Southwest Georgia History*, vol. II (Fall 1984), pp. 15–25.

Cass, Julia. "Selma: The Struggle Continues." *Philadelphia Inquirer*, August 11, 1985.

Chafe, William. "The Greensboro Sit-Ins." *Southern Exposure*, vol. 6 (Fall 1978), pp. 78–87.

Chalfen, Michael. "Rev. Samuel B. Wells and Black Protest in Albany 1945–65." *Journal of Southwest Georgia History*, vol. IX (Fall 1994), pp. 37–64.

———. "'The Way Out May Lead In': The Albany Movement beyond Martin Luther King, Jr." *Georgia Historical Quarterly*, vol. LXXXIX (Fall 1995), pp. 560–98.

Chevigny, Bell Gale. "Mississippi Stories I—The Fruits of Freedom Summer." *Nation*, vol. 259 (August 8–15, 1994), pp. 154–57.

———. "Mississippi Stories II—Still It's a Fight for Power." *Nation*, vol. 259 (August 22–29, 1994), pp. 196–200.

Clark, Septima P. "Literacy and Liberation." *Freedomways*, vol. 4 (Winter 1964), pp. 113–24.

Cohodas, Nadine. "Remembering the Voting Rights Revolution." *Legal Times* (August 7, 1995), p. 1.

Davis, Jingle. "Laying Down the Law." *Atlanta Journal-Constitution*, February 26, 1995, p. M1.

Dean, Andrea Oppenheimer. "Savannah's Law." *Historic Preservation* (Jan.–Feb. 1995), pp. 29–35, 92–93.

Fallin, Wilson, Jr. "The African-American Church and the Civil Rights Movement in Birmingham," 1993. Unpublished paper in author's possession.

Forman, James. "What Is the Student Nonviolent Coordinating Committee?" Unpublished manuscript prepared for November 1964 SNCC meeting, in Highlander Collection, record group 1, series I–V.

Freedomways (Second Quarter 1965), pp. 231–342. (Special Issue on Mississippi)

Fuller, Helen. "We Are All So Very Happy." *New Republic*, vol. 142 (April 25, 1960), pp. 13–16.

Good, Paul. "Birmingham Two Years Later." *Reporter*, vol. 33 (December 2, 1965), pp. 21–27.

Halberstam, David. "A Good City Gone Ugly." *Reporter*, vol. 22 (March 31, 1960), pp. 17–19.

———. "The Kids Take Over." *Reporter,* vol. 24 (June 22, 1961), pp. 22–23.

———. "People in Mississippi: A County Divided against Itself." *Reporter,* vol. 13 (December 15, 1955), pp. 30–32.

Harding, Vincent. "A Beginning in Birmingham." *Reporter,* vol. 28 (June 6, 1963), pp. 13–19.

Heinz, W. C., and Bard Lindeman. "Great Day at Trickem Fork." *Saturday Evening Post,* vol. 238 (May 22, 1965), pp. 30–31.

Hinkle, Warren, and David Welsh. "Five Battles of Selma." *Ramparts,* vol. 4 (June 1965), pp. 19–52.

Holt, Len. "Freedom Schools." *Southern Exposure,* vol. IX (Spring 1981), pp. 42–45.

Kempton, Murray. "Pilgrimage to Jackson." *New Republic,* vol. 148 (May 11, 1963), pp. 14–16.

King, Slater. "The Bloody Battleground of Albany." *Freedomways,* vol. 4 (Winter 1964), pp. 93–101.

———. "Our Main Battle in Albany." *Freedomways,* vol. 5 (Summer 1965), pp. 417–23.

Kopkind, Andrew. "The Lair of the Black Panther." *New Republic,* vol. 155 (Aug. 13, 1966), pp. 10–13.

Leonard, George B., Jr. "The Second Battle of Atlanta." *Look,* vol. 25 (April 25, 1961), pp. 31–48.

Long, Margaret. "Black Power in the Black Belt." *Progressive,* vol. 30 (Oct. 1966), pp. 20–24.

Lyon, Danny. "Through the Camera's Eye: Memories of the Southwest Georgia Movement." *Journal of Southwest Georgia History,* vol. IX (Fall 1994), pp. 26–36.

McComb Enterprise-Journal, "Racial Stories" scrapbook.

Meredith, James. "Big Changes Are Coming." *Saturday Evening Post,* vol. 239 (August 13, 1966), pp. 23–27.

Mitchell, Jerry. "Legacy of Caring with Roots in Pain." *Jackson Clarion Ledger,* Dec. 18, 1994, p. 1G.

Montgomery Advertiser, March 1965.

Moore, Julia. "From Jubilee Bell Tower." *Fisk News* (Spring and Summer 1960), pp. 16–18 (Spring), 8–9 (Summer).

Nashville Banner/Tennessean (select dates 1960–63).

"The New Fighting South: Militant Negroes Refuse to Leave Dixie or Be Silenced." *Ebony,* vol. 10 (August 1955), p. 69.

Oates, Stephen B. "The Albany Movement: A Chapter in the Life of Martin Luther King, Jr." *Journal of Southwest Georgia History,* vol. II (Fall 1984), pp. 26–39.

The Ole Miss Magazine: The Meredith Crisis in Retrospective, vol. 2, no. 1 (Sept. 30, 1982).

Ottenad, Thomas W. "Desperate Struggle: In Albany, Georgia, Negroes Wage Massive Attack on Discrimination." *St. Louis Post-Dispatch,* Aug. 5, 1962, pp. 10–15.

Poston, Ted. "The Negroes of Montgomery." *New York Post,* June 11–24, 1956.

Reddick, L. D. "The State vs. the Student." *Dissent,* vol. VII (Summer 1960), pp. 219–28.

Ricks, John A. " 'De Lawd' Descends and Is Crucified: Martin Luther King, Jr., in Albany, Georgia." *Journal of Southwest Georgia History,* vol. 2 (Fall 1984), pp. 3–14.

Savannah State College Library, civil rights scrapbooks, vols. 1–6.

Selma Times-Journal, March 1965.

Shuttlesworth, Fred. "Birmingham Revisited." *Ebony,* vol. 26 (August 1971), pp. 114–18.

Sikora, Frank. "Different Days, New People: Wallace Welcomes Selma Marchers." *Birmingham News/Post-Herald,* March 11, 1995, p. 1.

Smothers, Ronald. "25 Years Later, Racial Tensions Revive in Selma." *New York Times,* Aug. 11, 1990.

Stanfield, J. Edwin. "In Memphis: More Than a Garbage Strike." Atlanta: Southern Regional Council, March 22, 1968.

———. "In Memphis: Mirror to America?" Atlanta: Southern Regional Council, April 28, 1968.

———. "In Memphis: Tragedy Unaverted." Atlanta: Southern Regional Council, April 3, 1968.

Student Nonviolent Coordinating Committee, *The Student Voice,* vols. 1–6 (June 1960–Sept. 1965).

Thornton, J. Mills, III. "Challenge and Response in the Montgomery Bus Boycott of 1955–1956." *Alabama Review,* vol. 33 (July 1980), pp. 163–235.

Trilling, Calvin. "State Secrets." *The New Yorker,* vol. 71 (May 29, 1995), pp. 54–64.

Tuck, Stephen. "A City Too Dignified to Hate: Civic Pride, Civil Rights, and Savannah in Comparative Perspective." *Georgia Historical Quarterly,* vol. LXXIX (Fall 1995), pp. 539–59.

"25 Years Later: Opening the Closed Society?" *Jackson Clarion Ledger,* June 18, 1989.

U.S. Department of the Interior, National Park Service. Historic American Buildings Survey, Sixteenth Street Baptist Church, Birmingham, AL, HABS No. AL-898, 40 pp. (draft, n.d.).

———, southeast regional office. "Martin Luther King, Jr. National Historic Site Resource Study," August 1994.

Van Clark, Benjamin. "Siege at Savannah." *Freedomways,* vol. 4 (First Quarter 1964), pp. 131–36.

Vivian, Octavia, ed. *Selma to Montgomery: The 30th Anniversary of the Right to Vote.* Selma, AL: The National Voting Rights Museum and Institute, 1995.

Wills, Garry. "Martin Luther King Is Still on the Case!" *Esquire,* vol. 70 (August 1968), pp. 98–104, 124–29.

Wynn, Linda T. "The Dawning of a New Day: The Nashville Sit-Ins Feb. 13–May 10, 1960." *Tennessee Historical Quarterly,* vol. 50 (Spring 1991), pp. 42–54.

Zinn, Howard. *Albany: A Study in National Responsibility.* Atlanta: Southern Regional Council, 1962.

———. "The Limits of Nonviolence." *Freedomways,* vol. 4 (First Quarter 1964), pp. 143–48.

Audio and Video Recordings

At the River I Stand, California Newsreel, documentary film directed by David Appleby, Allison Graham, and Steven Ross, 1993.

Been in the Storm So Long: Spirituals, Folk Tales and Children's Games from John's Island, South Carolina, Smithsonian/Folkways SF 40031 (compact disk), 1990.

Birmingham, Alabama, 1963 Mass Meeting, New York: Folkways Records FD 5847, 1980.

"Black Radio: Telling It Like It Was," Program No. 8 ("In Control"), Radio Smithsonian, 1996.

"Black Radio: Telling It Like It Was," Program No. 9 ("Civil Rights"), Radio Smithsonian, 1996.

"Children of McComb," Pacifica Radio Archive, #BB0225, recorded in Durham, NC, Oct. 27, 1961.

Dr. Martin Luther King, Jr.—An Amazing Grace, Del Mar, CA: McGraw-Hill Films, 1978, produced by WABC-TV.

"Eyes on the Prize," Henry Hampton, exec. producer, Blackside, Inc., 1986 (Part I) and 1990 (Part II).

Freedom on My Mind, documentary film directed by Connie Fields and Marilyn Mulford, 1994.

Freedom Songs: Selma, Alabama, Smithsonian/Folkways Cassette No. 05594, 1992.

Fundi: The Ella Baker Story, Wayne, NJ: New Day Films, produced and directed by Joanne Grant, 1985.

Highlander Oral History Collection (twenty-one audiotape cassettes of Birmingham mass meetings and related interviews by Guy Carawan), Highlander Center, New Market, TN.

King, Martin Luther, Jr., "Martin Luther King Speaks," a series of forty-eight radio addresses and speeches, Atlanta, GA: SCLC, various dates.

Lest We Forget 2: Birmingham, Alabama, 1963, Smithsonian/Folkways Cassette No. 05487, 1991.

Mississippi Oral History Project, University of Southern Mississippi, vols. 281 (Ellie Dahmer, July 2, 1974), 375 (J. C. Fairley, Jan. 31, 1977, and Feb. 4, 1977), 31 (Fannie Lou Hamer, April 14, 1972, and Jan. 25, 1973), and 184 (Amzie Moore, March 29, 1977, and April 13, 1977).

Sit-In: Nashville, Tennessee, Folkways Records, Album No. FH 5590, 1960.

Sit-In: NBC White Paper, McGraw-Hill Films, narrated by Chet Huntley, 1960.

The Sit-In Story, Friendly World Broadcasting, Folkways Records, Album No. FH 5502, narrated by Edwin Randall, 1961.

The Story of Greenwood, Smithsonian/Folkways Album No. FD 5593, 1965.

The Streets of Greenwood, New Time Films, by Jack Willis, John Reavis, Jr., and Fred Wardenburg, 1964.

"Testament of Nonviolence," audio recordings by Radio Riverside, March 1963, WRVR-FM Radio Series (parts 1–6), Birmingham Public Library.

"Where Do We Go from Here?," Pacifica Radio Archive, #BB 4817a & #BB 4817b, recorded in Jackson, MS, June 28, 1963.

"Who Speaks for Birmingham?," New York: CBS-TV, narrated by Howard K. Smith, 1961.

"Will the Circle be Unbroken?," twenty-six-part radio series produced by the Southern Regional Council, 1997.

You Got to Move: Stories of Change in the South, documentary film, produced by Lucy Massie Phenix and Veronica Selver, 1985.

Collections

Materials of the Alabama Christian Movement for Human Rights (courtesy of Lola Hendricks, Birmingham, AL).

Bull Connor Papers, Birmingham Public Library, Linn-Henley Research Library, Department of Archives and Manuscripts, Birmingham, AL.

Delta Health Center Records, Southern Historical Collection, University of North Carolina, Chapel Hill, NC.

Records of the Highlander Research and Education Center, New Market, TN.

Martin Luther King, Jr., Papers, Series III, Speeches, Sermons, Articles, Statements, 1954–1968, Martin Luther King, Jr., Center for Nonviolent Social Change, Atlanta, GA.

Mark Levy Materials on Freedom Summer, copy in author's possession (courtesy of Bob Bailey).

Alexander Looby Papers, Fisk University, Special Collections, Nashville, TN.

Jimmie Morgan Papers, Birmingham Public Library, Linn-Henley Research Library, Department of Archives and Manuscripts, Birmingham, AL.

SCLC Papers, Martin Luther King, Jr., Center for Nonviolent Social Change, Atlanta, GA.

Kelly Miller Smith Papers, Vanderbilt University, Jean and Alexander Heard Library, Nashville, TN.

SNCC Papers, Martin Luther King, Jr., Center for Nonviolent Social Change, Atlanta, GA.

Southern Educational Reporting Service, Facts on Film (microform), 1954–65, Bobst Library, New York University, New York, NY.

Tougaloo Nine Collection, Tougaloo College, Jackson, MS.

Legal Cases

Boynton v. Virginia, 364 U.S. 454 (1960).

Embry v. City of Montgomery, 140 So.2d 291 (Ct. App. Ala. 1962).

Hanson v. Alabama, 166 So.2d 886 (Ct. App. Ala. 1964).

Katzenbach v. McClung, 379 U.S. 294 (1964).

King v. City of Montgomery, 140 So.2d 292 (Ct. App. Ala. 1962).

McLaurin v. City of Greenville, 187 So.2d 854 (S. Ct. Miss. 1966).

NAACP v. Alabama ex rel. Flowers, 377 U.S. 288 (1964).

New York Times v. Sullivan, 376 U.S. 254 (1964).

Parks v. City of Montgomery, 92 So.2d 683 (Ct. App. Ala. 1957).

Walker v. City of Birmingham, 388 U.S. 307 (1967).

Williams v. Wallace, 240 F. Supp. 100 (M.D. Ala. 1965).

Wright v. Georgia, 373 U.S. 284 (1963).

Index

Page numbers in *italics* refer to maps and illustrations.

Date Due

MAY 5 1998			
NOV 1 2 1999			
APR 2 8 2000			
NOV 1 2000			
DEC 1 8 2001			

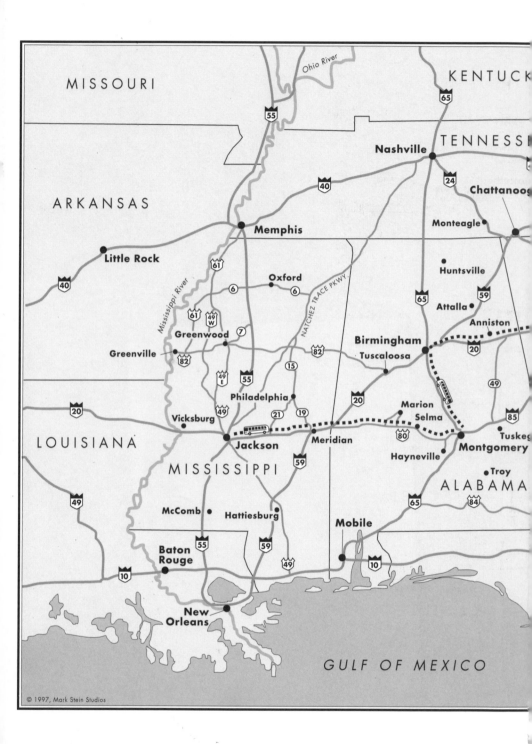